Human Activity and Behavior Analysis

Human Activity and Behavior Analysis relates to the field of vision and sensor-based human action or activity and behavior analysis and recognition. The book includes a series of methodologies, surveys, relevant datasets, challenging applications, ideas, and future prospects.

The book discusses topics such as action recognition, action understanding, gait analysis, gesture recognition, behavior analysis, emotion and affective computing, and related areas. This volume focuses on two relevant activities in three main subject areas: Healthcare and Emotion, Mental Health, and Nurse Care Records.

The editors are experts in these arenas and the contributing authors are drawn from high-impact research groups around the world. This book will be of great interest to academics, students, and professionals working and researching in the field of human activity and behavior analysis.

Ubiquitous Computing, Healthcare and Well-being

Human Activity Recognition has been researched in thousands of papers, with mobile/environmental sensors in ubiquitous/pervasive domains, and with cameras in vision domains. Human Behavior Analysis is also explored for long-term health care, rehabilitation, emotion recognition, human interaction, and so on. However, many research challenges remain for realistic settings, such as complex and ambiguous activities/behavior, optimal sensor combinations, (deep) machine learning, data collection, platform systems, and applications.

The *Ubiquitous Computing, Healthcare and Well-being* Series provides a forum for capturing the latest advances and setting the course for future research in these areas. Books in the series will typically be presented by leading researchers globally and will cover, among other things: original methods; exploration of new applications; excellent survey papers; presentations on relevant datasets; challenging applications; ideas and future scopes; guidelines.

Series Editors:

***Sozo Inoue**, Professor and Director of the Care XDX Center, Kyushu Institute of Technology, Japan*

***Md Atiqur Rahman Ahad**, Associate Professor of Artificial Intelligence and Machine Learning, Department of Computer Science and Digital Technology, University of East London, UK*

Human Activity and Behavior Analysis: Advances in Computer Vision and Sensors: Volume 1
Edited by Md Atiqur Rahman Ahad, Sozo Inoue, Guillaume Lopez, Tahera Hossain

Human Activity and Behavior Analysis: Advances in Computer Vision and Sensors: Volume 2
Edited by Md Atiqur Rahman Ahad, Sozo Inoue, Guillaume Lopez, Tahera Hossain

For more information about this series please visit:
https://www.routledge.com/UbiquitousComputingHealthcareandWell-being/book-series/UCHAWB

Human Activity and Behavior Analysis

Advances in Computer Vision and Sensors: Volume 1

Edited by
Md Atiqur Rahman Ahad, Sozo Inoue,
Guillaume Lopez, and Tahera Hossain

CRC Press
Taylor & Francis Group
Boca Raton London New York

CRC Press is an imprint of the
Taylor & Francis Group, an **informa** business

Designed cover image: Shutterstock

First edition published 2024
by CRC Press
6000 Broken Sound Parkway NW, Suite 300, Boca Raton, FL 33487-2742

and by CRC Press
4 Park Square, Milton Park, Abingdon, Oxon, OX14 4RN

CRC Press is an imprint of Taylor & Francis Group, LLC

ISBN: 9781032443119 (hbk)
ISBN: 9781032430812 (pbk)
ISBN: 9781003371540 (ebk)

DOI: 10.1201/9781003371540

Typeset in Minion
by codeMantra

Contents

Preface

Sensors and cameras are exploited for the analysis and recognition of human activity and behavior. In the book *Human Activity and Behavior Analysis: Advances in Computer Vision and Sensors*, we have divided across two volumes, 40 wonderful chapters under five parts: Part 1: Healthcare and Emotion (Chapters 1–7), Part 2: Mental Health (Chapters 8–14), Part 3: Nurse Care Records (Chapters 15–26), Part 4: Movement and Sensors (Chapters 27–36), and Part 5: Sports Activity Analysis (Chapters 37–40). These chapters were developed from the *Fourth International Conference on Activity and Behavior Computing* (ABC 2022, https://abc-research.github.io/), held at University of East London, UK. These chapters were selected after a rigorous review process by related top experts, and strict review rebuttal process. We believe the chapters will enrich the research community in the field of *Activity and Behavior Computing (ABC)*. We hope that this book will ignite several exciting research directions. We cordially thank all authors, reviewers, and chairs for their great efforts.

Best regards,
Md Atiqur Rahman Ahad, *University of East London, UK*
Sozo Inoue, *Kyushu Institute of Technology, Japan*
Guillaume Lopez, *Aoyama Gakuin University, Japan*
Tahera Hossain, *Aoyama Gakuin University, Japan*

Editors

Md Atiqur Rahman Ahad, PhD, is Associate Professor of AI and M at the University of East London, UK.

Sozo Inoue, PhD, is Professor at the Kyushu Institute of Technology, Japan.

Guillaume Lopez, PhD, is Professor at Aoyama Gakuin University, Japan.

Tahera Hossain, PhD, is Assistant Professor (Project) at Aoyama Gakuin University, Japan.

Contributors

Nouran Abdalazim
Faculty of Informatics
Università della Svizzera Italiana (USI)
Lugano, Switzerland

Md. Akhtaruzzaman Adnan
Department of Computer Science and
    Engineering
University of Asia Pacific
Dhaka, Bangladesh

Md Atiqur Rahman Ahad
Department of Computer Science & Digital
    Technology
University of East London
London, UK

Wasim Akram
Department of Computer Sicence and
    Engineering
East West University
Dhaka, Bangladesh

Sumya Akter
Department of Computer Science and
    Engineering
University of Asia Pacific
Dhaka, Bangladesh

Leonardo Alchieri
Faculty of Informatics
Università della Svizzera Italiana (USI)
Lugano, Switzerland

Lidia Alecci
Faculty of Informatics
Università della Svizzera Italiana (USI)
Lugano, Switzerland

Sayeda Shamma Alia
Department of Life Science and System
    Engineering
Kyushu Institute of Technology
Kitakyushu, Japan

R. Askari
Department of Chemical and Biological
    Engineering
Illinois Institute of Technology
Chicago, Illinois

A. Cinar
Department of Chemical and Biological
    Engineering
Department of Biomedical Engineering
Illinois Institute of Technology
Chicago, Illinois

Ian Cleland
School of Computing
Ulster University
Northern Ireland, United Kingdom

Zachary Dair
Department of Computer Science
Munster Technological University
Cork, Ireland

Pritom Debnath
American International
    University-Bangladesh
Dhaka, Bangladesh

Samantha Dockray
Department of Applied Psychology
University College Cork
Cork, Ireland

Gulustan Dogan
Department of Computer Science
University of North Carolina
Wilmington, USA

Muhammad Fikry
Department of Life Science and System
  Engineering
Graduate School of Life Science and
  Systems Engineering
Kyushu Institute of Technology
Kitakyushu, Japan
and
Universitas Malikussaleh
Lhokseumawe, Indonesia

Björn Friedrich
Department of Health Services Research
Carl von Ossietzky University
Oldenburg, Germany

Kensi Fujiwara
Department of Computer Science and
  Engineering
Toyohashi University of Technology
Toyohashi, Japan

Christina Garcia
Department of Life Science and Systems
  Engineering
Kyushu Institute of Technology
Kitakyushu, Japan

Shkurta Gashi
Faculty of Informatics
Università della Svizzera Italiana (USI)
Lugano, Switzerland

Cappon Giacomo
Department of Information Engineering
University of Padova
Padova, Italy

Nuno Gomes
The Instituto Superior de Engenharia de
  Lisboa
Instituto Politécnico de Lisboa
Lisboa, Portugal

Defry Hamdhana
Department of Life Science and System
  Engineering
Kyushu Institute of Technology
Kitakyushu, Japan

Andreas Hein
OFFIS R+D Division Health, Escherweg
Oldenburg, Germany

John Hendricks
Department of Computer Science
University of North Carolina
Wilmington, USA

Kazuki Honda
Graduate School of Science and Engineering
Aoyama Gakuin University
Tokyo, Japan

Shahera Hossain
Department of Computer Science and
  Engineering
University of Asia Pacific
Dhaka, Bangladesh

Tahera Hossain
Graduate School of Science and Engineering
Aoyama Gakuin University
Tokyo, Japan

Yoshinori Ideno
Nagoya University
Nagoya, Japan
and
Global Business Division
Carecom Co., Ltd
Tokyo, Japan

Sozo Inoue
Department of Life Science and Systems
  Engineering
Kyushu Institute of Technology
Kitakyushu, Japan

Mohammad Sabik Irbaz
Department of Computer Science and
  Engineering
Islamic University of Technology
Gazipur City, Bangladesh

Naoko Ishibashi
Department of Child Development
Sugiyama Jogakuen University
Nagoya, Japan

Naoya Isoyama
Department of Information Science
Nara Institute of Science and Technology
Ikoma, Japan

Miyuki Iwamoto
Department of Advanced Fibro-Science
Kyoto Institute of Technology
Kyoto, Japan

Md. Kabiruzzaman
Department of Electrical and Electronic
    Engineering
American International
    University-Bangladesh
Dhaka, Bangladesh

Rashid Kamal
School of Computing
Ulster University
Northern Ireland, United Kingdom

Haru Kaneko
Department of Life Science and Systems
    Engineering
Kyushu Institute of Technology
Kitakyushu, Japan

Yusuke Kawasaki
Graduate School of Science and Engineering
Aoyama Gakuin University
Tokyo, Japan

Maryam Khalid
Department of Electrical Computer
    Engineering
Rice University
Houston, Texas

Kiyoshi Kiyokawa
Department of Information Science
Nara Institute of Science and Technology
Ikoma, Japan

Huakun Liu
Department of Information Science
Nara Institute of Science and Technology
Ikoma, Japan

Guillaume Lopez
College of Science and Engineering
Department of Integrated Information
    Technology
Aoyama Gakuin University
Tokyo, Japan

Lutfun Nahar Lota
Department of Computer Science and
    Engineering
Islamic University of Technology
Gazipur City, Bangladesh

Andrè Lourenço
Instituto Superior de Engenharia de Lisboa
Instituto Politécnico de Lisboa
Lisboa, Portugal
and
CardioID Technologies
Lisboa, Portugal

Cossu Luca
Department of Information Engineering
University of Padova
Padova, Italy

Vettoretti Martina
Department of Information Engineering
University of Padova
Padova, Italy

Paul McCullagh
School of Computing
Ulster University
Northern Ireland, United Kingdom

Atzeni Michele
Department of Information Engineering
University of Padova
Padova, Italy

Nazmun Nahid
Department of Life Science and System
    Engineering
Kyushu Institute of Technology
Kitakyushu, Japan

Atsushi Nakazawa
Graduate School of Interdisciplinary Science
    and Engineering in Health Systems
Okayama University
Kyoto, Japan

Kizito Nkurikiyeyezu
Graduate School of Science and Engineering
Aoyama Gakuin University
Tokyo, Japan

Chris Nugent
School of Computing
Ulster University
Northern Ireland, United Kingdom

Ruairi O'Reilly
Department of computer science
Munster Technological University
Cork, Ireland

Ren Ohmura
Department of Computer Science and
    Engineering
Toyohashi University of Technology
Toyohashi, Japan

Akira Omi
Department of Computer Science and
    Engineering
Toyohashi University of Technology
Toyohashi, Japan

Shintaro Oyama
Department of Hand Surgery
Hospital Medical IT Center
Nagoya University
Nagoya, Japan

Matilde Pato
Instituto Superior de Engenharia de Lisboa
Instituto Politécnico de Lisboa and
    LASIGE, FCUL
Universidade de Lisboa
Lisboa, Portugal

Urja Pawar
Department of Computer Science
Munster Technological University
Cork, Ireland

Monica Perusquía-Hernández
Department of Information Science
Nara Institute of Science and Technology
Ikoma, Japan

Tanmoy Sarkar Pias
Department of Computer Science
Virginia Tech
Blacksburg, Virginia

Yeasin Arafat Pritom
Department of Electrical and Electronic
    Engineering
University of Dhaka
Dhaka, Bangladesh

Rumman Ahmed Prodhan
Department of Computer Science and
    Engineering
University of Asia Pacific
Dhaka, Bangladesh

L. Quinn
Department of Biobehavioral Nursing
    Science
University of Illinois
Chicago, Illinois

Vu Nguyen Phuong Quynh
Department of Life Science and System
    Engineering
Graduate School of Life Science and
    Systems Engineering
Kyushu Institute of Technology
Kitakyushu, Japan

Hasib Ryan Rahman
Department of Electrical and Electronic
    Engineering
University of Dhaka
Dhaka, Bangladesh

Md. Sohanur Rahman
Department of Electrical and Electronic
    Engineering
University of Dhaka
Dhaka, Bangladesh

M. Rashid

Department of Chemical and Biological
    Engineering
Illinois Institute of Technology
Chicago, Illinois

Md. Golam Rasul

Department of Data Science
Universitat Potsdam
Potsdam, Germany

Lourenço Rodrigues

Instituto Superior de Engenharia de Lisboa
Instituto Politécnico de Lisboa
Lisboa, Portugal
and
CardioID Technologies
Lisboa, Portugal

Muhammad Saad

Department of Computer Science
Munster Technological University
Cork, Ireland

Yuji Sakamoto

Global Business Division
Carecom Co., Ltd
Tokyo, Japan

Fardin Ahsan Sakib

Department of Computer Science and
    Engineering
George Mason University
George Mason, Virginia

Akane Sano

Department of Electrical Computer
    Engineering, Computer Science, and
    Bioengineering
Rice University
Houston, Texas

Silvia Santini

Faculty of Informatics
Università della Svizzera Italiana (USI)
Lugano, Switzerland

Pedro Santos

The Instituto Superior de Engenharia de
    Lisboa
Instituto Politécnico de Lisboa
Lisboa, Portugal

Tanjila Alam Sathi

Department of Computer Science and
    Engineering
Islamic University of Technology
Gazipur City, Bangladesh

Alicia Choto Segovia

Department of Electrical Computer
    Engineering
Rice University
Houston, Texas

M. Sevil

Department of Biomedical Engineering
Illinois Institute of Technology
Chicago, Illinois

L. Sharp

Department of Pharmacy Systems
    Outcomes and Policy
University of Illinois Chicago
Chicago, Illinois

Md. Mamun Sheikh

Department of Electrical and Electronic
    Engineering
University of Dhaka
Dhaka, Bangladesh

Tomohiro Shibata

Department of Life Science and System
    Engineering, Graduate School of Life
    Science and Systems Engineering
Kyushu Institute of Technology
Kitakyushu, Japan

Yuko Shibata

Department of Life Science and System
    Engineering, Graduate School of Life
    Science and Systems Engineering
Kyushu Institute of Technology
Kitakyushu, Japan

Mohammad Shidujaman
Department of Computer Science and
    Engineering
Independent University
Dhaka, Bangladesh

Shadril Hassan Shifat
Department of Computer Science and
    Engineering
American International
    University-Bangladesh
Dhaka, Bangladesh

Riku Shinohara
Department of Information Science
Nara Institute of Science and Technology
Ikoma, Japan

Jonathan Sturdivant
Department of Computer Science
University of North Carolina
Wilmington, USA

Tomoya Suzuki
Department of Integrated Information
    Technology
Aoyama Gakuin University
Tokyo, Japan

Akihito Taya
Department of Integrated Information
    Technology
Aoyama Gakuin University
Tokyo, Japan

Tahia Tazin
Department of Human Intelligence Systems
Kyushu Institute of Technology
Kitakyushu, Japan

Yoshito Tobe
Department of Integrated Information
    Technology
Aoyama Gakuin University
Tokyo, Japan

Masato Uchimura
Department of Life Science and Systems
    Engineering
Kyushu Institute of Technology
Kitakyushu, Japan

Hideaki Uchiyama
Department of Information Science
Nara Institute of Science and Technology
Ikoma, Japan

Thomas Vaessen
Faculty of Behavioural, Management and
    Social Sciences (BMS), Psychology,
    Health and Technology (PGT)
University of Twente
Drienerlolaan, Netherlands

John Noel Victorino
Department of Life Science and System
    Engineering, Graduate School of Life
    Science and Systems Engineering
Kyushu Institute of Technology
Kitakyushu, Japan

Keiko Yamashita
Innovative Research Center for Preventive
    Medical Engineering
Institute of Innovation for Future Society
Nagoya University
Nagoya, Japan

Huiyuan Yang
Department of Electrical Computer
    Engineering
Rice University
Houston, Texas

Han Yu
Department of Electrical Computer
    Engineering
Rice University
Houston, Texas

Abrar Zarif
Department of Electrical and Electronic
    Engineering
University of Dhaka
Dhaka, Bangladesh

Sayeda Fatema Tuj Zohura
Department of Computer Sicence and
    Engineering
East West University
Dhaka, Bangladesh

I

Healthcare and Emotion

Forecasting Parkinson's Disease Patients' Wearing-Off Using Wrist-Worn Fitness Tracker and Smartphone Dataset

John Noel Victorino, Yuko Shibata, Sozo Inoue, and Tomohiro Shibata

Kyushu Institute of Technology

1.1 INTRODUCTION

Parkinson's disease (PD) is a neurogenerative disorder affecting patients' motor and non-motor functions. Due to the lack of dopamine-producing cells in the patient's brain [15,36], their motor abilities start to deteriorate with tremors, slowness of movement (bradykinesia), muscle stiffness (rigidity), and postural instability as PD's cardinal symptoms. Over time, non-motor symptoms manifest, such as mood changes, sleep, speech, and mental difficulties. These motor and non-motor symptoms negatively influence PD patients' daily life and quality of life (QoL) [32].

One of the difficulties experienced by PD patients is called the "wearing-off phenomenon". This phenomenon happens when symptoms reappear earlier than their scheduled Levodopa (L-dopa) treatment intake. L-dopa treatment is one of the best treatments doctors and clinicians prescribe to PD patients to manage their symptoms. Taking an L-dopa dose increases the dopamine production inside the brain, temporarily relieving the patient's symptoms [7]. However, the prolonged use of L-dopa treatment shortens the treatment's effective time. During the wearing-off period, the symptoms re-emerge, causing discomfort to the patients. Thus, PD patients' clinicians must monitor and discuss the wearing-off phenomenon.

DOI: 10.1201/9781003371540-2

Upon assessment by their doctors, they can properly adjust their patients' L-dopa treatment plan or entirely change their treatment [3,8,28,31].

As a contribution to PD management, we forecast future wearing-off in the next hour using the fitness tracker datasets from earlier periods, e.g., data from one day before. Then, existing deep learning architectures were compared to examine the wearing-off forecasting with the fitness tracker features. This chapter's contributions can be summarized by answering these research questions.

1. Can wrist-worn fitness tracker datasets be used to forecast wearing-off in the next hour?

2. Which among the six deep learning architectures performed well in forecasting wearing-off in the next hour?

We used existing and simple deep learning architectures to answer the research questions. Our results showed that a CNN model could forecast the next hour's wearing-off with an average balanced accuracy of 80.64% ± 10.36% across ten participants. Furthermore, the current period's and the previous day's data were necessary for forecasting wearing-off, as both models had high AUC and balanced accuracy scores, respectively. PD patients and clinicians can use the results of this study to monitor and manage PD symptoms during wearing-off periods. PD patients can get early warnings before a wearing-off period. Thus, the PD patient can adapt using such future information. Furthermore, clinicians can deploy personalized forecasting models to collect and monitor wearing-off periods in PD patients.

This chapter is divided into different sections. Section 1.2 provides existing wearing-off prediction models using different datasets from various devices. Section 1.3 describes this chapter's approach to developing wearing-off forecasting models from data collection (Section 1.3.1), data processing (Section 1.3.2), and model development (Section 1.3.3). Then, Sections 24.4 and 1.5 present and discuss the result of the developed forecasting models for wearing-off. Finally, Section 24.5 summarizes the goals of this chapter, along with the future directions of this research.

1.2 RELATED STUDIES

This section summarizes existing approaches to detect and predict wearing-off periods among PD patients. In practice, clinicians use their experience and clinical rating scales to regularly assess each patient's PD situation [3,10]. Then, clinicians adjust the PD patients' treatment plan based on their assessment. The latest approaches in monitoring PD patients' symptoms have utilized wearable devices like Parkinson's Kinetigraph (PKG). PKG collects accelerometer data to detect tremors, bradykinesia, and dyskinesia among PD patients. The collected motion data from the PD patients assist clinicians' evaluation of wearing-off [14]. In other studies, various motor-related datasets from accelerometer, gyroscope, and electromyography (EMG) have been used to detect or predict any PD symptoms or wearing-off events. Aside from motor-related datasets, non-motor features from wearable devices have been introduced to predict wearing-off to understand and match wearing-off periods in terms of non-motor symptoms.

In a literature review conducted on wearable technologies to detect or predict wearing-off, the utilization of wearable devices showed promise in improving the management of PD symptoms. For example, models estimated "on" and "off" states [2] using machine learning algorithms with accelerometer data. In this study, PKG was deployed to collect accelerometer data. Then, different statistical and gait parameters were used to train Random Forest, Support Vector Machine (SVM), k-Nearest Neighbor, and Naive Bayes classifiers to detect "on" and "off" states. Based on its results, the Random Forest classifier produced the best accuracy of 96.72% among the other classifiers, which shows that wearing-off could be detected using accelerometer data [2]. Similarly, other studies have used motion-based datasets, particularly accelerometer data, to detect wearing-off states utilizing different machine learning techniques. Other models have also detected specific PD symptoms. These models produced an accuracy of at least 81% [1,5,16,18,20,26,29]. Given these studies, it was suggested to extend the use of machine learning models to non-motor symptoms in detecting wearing-off [5].

Commercially available fitness trackers' datasets were utilized to predict wearing-off. Two PD participants wore the fitness tracker for 30 days while reporting wearing-off using the Wearing-Off Questionnaire (WoQ-9) [3,11] on their smartphone application [21]. Correlation analysis showed the relationship between PD participants' sleep features and wearing-off symptoms. Intuitively, the time elapsed from the last drug intake strongly predicted wearing-off [35]. Then, each PD participant's prediction model resulted in a balanced accuracy ranging from 70.0% to 76.9% using Gradient Boosting or Logistic Regression learning algorithms. Although the balanced accuracy was lower than those models using motor features from an accelerometer or gyroscope, detecting wearing-off using mainly the non-motor datasets from fitness trackers was feasible [34].

Within the current landscape, detection or prediction models classify whether a PD patient currently suffers wearing-off or not, given the present input features. In the studies mentioned, detection and prediction have been interchangeably used for the classification task. As such, this chapter aims to forecast future wearing-off periods like in the next 30 minutes or 1 hour. Forecasting wearing-off periods drew inspiration from other studies in different domains. Forecasting results provided action points before the event or insights ahead of the anticipated event [23]. For instance, a forecasting model predicted COVID-19 symptoms and signs of viral infection three days before the onset of the symptoms. This study utilized a smart ring's physiological outputs such as heart rate (HR), body temperature, and sleep with the self-reported symptoms from a mobile application [9]. Another similar example used smartwatch data to detect pre-symptomatic COVID-19 cases 4–7 days before the onset of the symptoms [4,22]. In these examples, the insight by the forecasting model provides action points like taking a COVID-19 test. Similarly, this chapter aims to provide similar insights by forecasting future wearing-off events (Table 1.1).

TABLE 1.1 Comparison of Previous Studies on Detecting Specific PD Symptoms or Detecting Eearing-off

Study	Aim	Data Used	Method	Result
Keijsers [20]	Determine between "on" and "off" based on daily activities using wearable data	Accelerometer	Unsupervised method using frequency-based method	Sensitivity: 97% Specificity: 97%
Jeon [18]	Classify severity of tremors from wearable data	Accelerometer, gyroscope	Decision Tree (DT), k-Nearest Neighbor (kNN), Random Forest (RF), Support Vector Machine (SVM), Discriminant Analysis	DT: 85.55% accuracy
Sama [26]	Detect gait-related disorders using wearable data	Accelerometer	SVM	Accuracy: 91.81% across 12 patients
Aich [1]	Detect freezing of gait (FoG) using wearable data	Accelerometer	SVM, kNN, DT, Naïve Bayes (NB)	SVM: 88% accuracy
Steinmetzer [29]	Detect motor dysfunctions using wearable data	Accelerometer, gyroscope, magnetometer	Convolutional Neural Network (CNN)	Accuracy: 93.40%

(*Continued*)

TABLE 1.1 (*Continued*) Comparison of Previous Studies on Detecting Specific PD Symptoms or Detecting Eearing-off

Study	Aim	Data Used	Method	Result
Hssayeni [16]	Detect "on" and "off" states	Gyroscope	SVM with fuzzy labeling	Accuracy: 90.5% Sensitivity: 94.2% Specificity: 85.4%
Aich [2]	Detect "on" and "off" using gait signals	Accelerometer	RF, SVM, kNN, NB	Accuracy: 96.72% Sensitivity: 97.35%
Victorino [34]	Predict "wearing-off" on individual-level	Heart rate, Stress score, Sleep features, Step count	RF, GB, DT, Logistic Regression (LR), Linear SVM	Balanced accuracy Participant 1: 70.00%–71.70% Participant 2: 76.10%–76.90%
Current study	Forecasting next hour "wearing-off" on individual-level	Heart rate, stress score, sleep features, step count	Multilayer perceptron (MLP), Long short-term memory (LSTM), CNN	Balanced accuracy 80.64% ± 10.36% across ten patients

1.3 METHODOLOGY

This section describes (1) how the datasets were collected from the PD patients, (2) how the data was processed for model development, and (3) how each deep learning architecture was developed to forecast wearing-off. This chapter introduces the feasibility of forecasting wearing-off from fitness tracker datasets in previous periods. As such, the target wearing-off forecast is 1-hour into the future. The following subsections detail the data collection, processing, and model development.

1.3.1 Data Collection

The data collection process was similar to the previous work on understanding and predicting wearing-off among the two PD patients [34,35]. The Garmin vivosmart4 fitness trackers were distributed to PD participants to collect the heart rate, stress score, sleep data, and step count. In addition, Android smartphones were provided to the PD participants with the needed applications. These two tools mainly collected fitness tracker datasets and wearing-off periods among PD participants.

Both tools collect and send data from PD participants to their respective servers. On the one hand, vivosmart4 sends data to the Garmin Connect smartphone application through Bluetooth. Then, Garmin Connect uploads the received data to Garmin servers. Finally, collected datasets were accessed using Garmin Health API.[1] On the other hand, PD patients answered different questionnaires through a customized smartphone application. The wearing-off questionnaire asked what symptoms were experienced, and when the symptoms started and ended. The data collected from PD participants were received by different servers, as illustrated in Figure 1.1 [34,35].

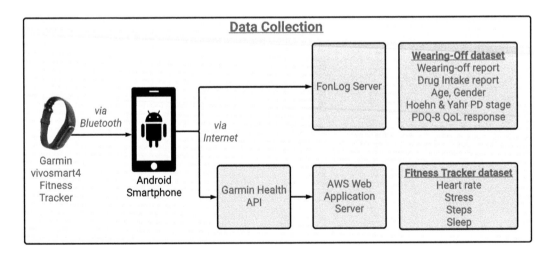

Figure 1.1 The data collection process from the tools to the servers where each dataset can be accessed [34].

TABLE 1.2   Garmin Vivosmart4 Collected Datasets via Garmin Health API

Dataset	Interval	Description
Heart rate	15-second	Beats per minute
steps	15-minute	Cumulative step count per interval, with 0 as the lowest value
Stress score	3-minute	Estimated stress score [13] • 0–25: resting state, • 26–50: low stress, • 51–75: medium stress, • 76–100: high stress, • −1: not enough data to detect stress, • −2: too much motion
Sleep stages with each sleep duration	Varying interval for each date	Start and end time for each sleep stage [12] • Light sleep • Rapid eye movement (REM) sleep • Deep sleep • Awake

Various datasets collected and provided by each tool were also presented in Figure 1.1. For the vivosmart4 fitness tracker, Garmin Health API provides access to the heart rate, stress score, number of steps, and sleep duration for each sleep stage. Each dataset from Garmin Health API comes in different time intervals. The heart rate (HR) in beats per minute (bpm) is reported every 15 seconds. Meanwhile, the number of steps is accumulated every 15 minutes. Then, the stress score is estimated by Garmin's algorithm. Stress scores are estimated every 3 minutes, ranging from 0 to 100, where 100 is the most stressful. Stress scores can also be reported with "-1" and "-2" for insufficient data and too much motion, respectively [24,30]. Finally, the sleep duration is grouped by date and by sleep stages [12] (Table 1.2).

For the smartphone application, the wearing-off periods, drug intake time and its effect on each wearing-off symptom, and other basic information were collected from PD participants. PD participants manually answered each questionnaire. The wearing-off periods, the drug intake time, and the drug effects were recorded using the Japanese version of the Wearing-Off Questionnaire (WoQ-9). The first part of the WoQ-9 asked PD participants whether they experienced these nine wearing-off symptoms or not [3,11]. In addition, the PD participants had to specify when the symptoms started and ended.

1. Tremors,

2. Slowing down of movement,

3. Change in mood or depression,

4. Rigidity of muscles,

5. Sharp pain or prolonged dull pain,

6. Impairment of complex movements of the hand & fingers,

7. Difficulty integrating thoughts or slowing down of thoughts,

8. Anxiety or panic attacks, and

9. Muscle spasm.

Then, the second part of the WoQ-9 asked about the drug intake time and its effects. The PD participant had to indicate whether each symptom subsided or not. Other pieces of information were asked using the smartphone application, such as age, sex, Hoehn and Yahr (H&Y) scale, the Japan Ministry of Health, Labor, and Welfare's classification of living dysfunction (JCLD) for the PD stage [6,19], and the Parkinson's Disease Questionnaire (PDQ-8) for the PD patient's self-assessed quality of life [17]. These datasets are summarized in Table 1.3.

This research study has received the University's ethical review. Meanwhile, the two tools were distributed to PD participants. PD participants can participate in this research if (1) they experience wearing-off, (2) they can use the tools, and (3) they do not have any severe illnesses or symptoms that could affect them during the data collection period. PD participants are referred to either by their doctor or by other PD patients. Before starting the data collection period, PD patients were informed of the research goals. Then, we asked for their written consent. Afterward, the tools were distributed to begin the data collection period. PD participants were asked to contribute seven (7) days' worth of data. However, they can freely discontinue or opt out of the research study if they cannot proceed with the data collection.

During the data collection period, participants were asked to wear the Garmin vivosmart4 every time, even when taking a bath or sleeping. Meanwhile, it is important to wear it during the night to capture the sleep duration data. On the other hand, recording the participant's wearing-off at their own convenient time

TABLE 1.3 The Smartphone Application Collected Datasets

Data Type	Description
WoQ-9	Symptoms onset and drug intake time
Basic Information	Age and gender
Hoehn and Yahr Scale (H&Y), Japan Ministry of Health, Labor, and Welfare's classification of living dysfunction (JCLD)	Participant's PD stage
PDQ-8	Participant's QoL measurement specific to PD: 0%–100%, with 100% showing the worst QoL

was emphasized to the participants. Using the smartphone application was suggested during their "on" state or when their wearing-off symptoms are less severe. In addition, PD participants were instructed to correct and review their responses with the correct time in the application. Aside from the previously stated constraints and suggestions, there were no strict limitations during the data collection period.

1.3.2 Data Processing

The Garmin vivosmart4 and smartphone application wearing-off datasets were processed and combined to develop the wearing-off forecasting model. This section describes the data processing for each dataset and the combined dataset.

On the one hand, the raw Garmin vivosmart4 datasets were cleaned, processed, and re-sampled to the chosen time interval. First, missing values were supplied with "−1," like how Garmin supplied missing values [12]. A value of "−1" also indicated that the fitness tracker was not worn. Next, each fitness tracker dataset was re-sampled due to different intervals provided by Garmin Health API, as shown in Table 1.2. The combined dataset was re-sampled into 15-minute intervals to match the highest interval provided by Garmin. The last available data was used to fill the missing values caused by the re-sampling. Finally, the sleep duration for each sleep phase was distributed in each record by its calendar date. Additional sleep features were extracted from the sleep dataset as shown in Equations 1.1– 1.4 [25,27].

$$\text{Total non-REM duration} = \text{Deep sleep duration} + \text{Light sleep duration}, \quad (1.1)$$

$$\text{Total sleep duration} = \text{Total non-REM duration} + \text{REM sleep duration} \quad (1.2)$$

$$\text{Total non-REM percentage} = \frac{\text{Total non-REM duration}}{\text{Total sleep duration}} \quad (1.3)$$

$$\text{Sleep efficiency} = \frac{\text{Total sleep duration}}{\text{Total sleep duration} + \text{Total awake duration}} \quad (1.4)$$

On the other hand, the raw smartphone application dataset was also transformed like with raw Garmin vivosmart4 datasets. First, overlapping wearing-off periods were combined into one wearing-off period. Then, each wearing-off report was matched with the re-sampled 15-minute timestamp. If wearing-off falls within the interval, a value of "1" was assigned for the wearing-off symptom. Otherwise, the wearing-off symptom was given a value of "0". Likewise, the drug intake reports and their effect on the symptom were processed to match each timestamp. If the symptom subsided after taking medicine, the symptom was marked with "0". However, if the symptom was still experienced, the value of "1" was kept.

Finally, the two datasets were combined by matching the 15-minute timestamp. The hour of the day and the day of the week were also included. The day of the week was encoded with "0" to "6", matching "Monday" to "Sunday." Meanwhile, the hour of the day was encoded using sine and cosine functions. Finally, the following features were used to develop the wearing-off forecasting model.

x_1: Heart rate (HR)

x_2: Step count (Steps)

x_3: Stress score (Stress)

x_4: Awake duration during the estimated sleep period (Awake)

x_5: Deep sleep duration (Deep)

x_6: Light sleep duration (Light)

x_7: REM sleep duration (REM)

x_8: Total non-REM sleep duration (NonREMTotal)

x_9: Total sleep duration (Total)

x_{10}: Total non-REM sleep percentage (NonREMPercentage)

x_{11}: Sleep efficiency (SleepEfficiency)

x_{12}: Day of the week (TimestampDayOfWeek)

x_{13}: Sine value of Hour of the day (TimestampHourSin)

x_{14}: Cosine value of Hour of the day (TimestampHourCos)

y: Wearing-off

1.3.3   Model Development

This section presents the development of the wearing-off forecasting model. This section includes the data split specification among training, validation, and test sets, the metrics used to evaluate the forecasting model, and the architectures considered in developing the wearing-off forecasting model. The wearing-off forecast models were built individually per PD participant because it was assumed that each PD participant experienced PD differently. The data processing and model development used different Python libraries such as Pandas, Tensorflow, and Keras.

The wearing-off forecasting models were built for each PD participant. Individualized forecasting models were built instead of a general forecasting model because this chapter assumes that each patient experiences PD differently. Then, each PD participant's dataset was divided sequentially into training, validation, and test sets. The first 60% of the PD participant's dataset was used for training, while the next 20% was used for validation. The final 20% of the PD patient's dataset was held out to test and evaluate the forecasting model on different metrics. The balanced accuracy (*Bal.Acc.*) was the main metrics to evaluate the developed wearing-off forecast models because of the imbalance in the dataset. *Bal.Acc.* took into consideration the distribution of wearing-off within the PD participants' datasets, as shown in

Equation 1.5. Other than *Bal.Acc.*, *Accuracy*, *F1Score*, *Precision*, *Recall*, and *AUC* were also reported and calculated as follows:

$$\text{Bal. Acc.} = \frac{\frac{\text{TP}}{P} + \frac{\text{TN}}{N}}{2}, \tag{1.5}$$

$$\text{Accuracy} = \frac{\text{TP} + \text{TN}}{\text{TP} + \text{FP} + \text{TN} + \text{FN}}, \tag{1.6}$$

$$\text{F1 Score} = \frac{2 \cdot \text{TP}}{2 \cdot \text{TP} + \text{FP} + \text{FN}}, \tag{1.7}$$

$$\text{Precision} = \frac{\text{TP}}{\text{TP} + \text{FP}}, \tag{1.8}$$

$$\text{Recall} = \frac{\text{TP}}{\text{TP} + \text{FN}}, \tag{1.9}$$

TP is the number of true positives where the predicted wearing-off is equal to the actual wearing-off ("1"), while TN is the number of true negatives where the predicted normal state is equal to the actual normal state ("0"). Then, P is the total number of wearing-offs, and N is the total number of a normal state. Finally, FP is the number of false positives or where the predicted value is wearing-off, but the actual value is a normal state, and FN is the number of false negatives or where the predicted value is a normal state, but the actual value is wearing-off.

1.3.3.1 Experiments

In terms of deep learning architectures, there were six architectures considered in this chapter. Equation 1.10 defines the general model of the six architectures.

$$y_{t+1} = f(X_t, y_t), X_t = \{x_1, x_2, \ldots, x_{14}\} \tag{1.10}$$

In finding the wearing-off in the next hour y_{t+1}, the models accept the 14 features $X_t = \{x_1, x_2, \ldots, x_{14}\}$ at the current time t explained in Section 1.3.2. The models also accept the wearing-off at the current time y_t. Equation 1.10 summarizes the first three architectures, *Baseline*, *Linear*, and *Single time-step Dense*.

The *Baseline* architecture copied the wearing-off label into the next hour t_1. Next, the *Linear* architecture or a multi-layer perceptron model applied a linear transformation in the form of a single *Dense* layer. Another version of the *Linear* architecture contained more *Dense* layers to compare how adding more layers differed from a single *Dense* layer. As specified in Equation 1.10, these first three architectures only used the features at the current time to forecast the next hour. Hence, no historical context has been incorporated into these architectures [33].

The following three architectures used multiple time steps to forecast wearing-off in the next hour. Equation 1.11 accepts a matrix M of 14 features and wearing-off in previous time steps from the current time until w time step before the current time. This chapter used the last day's data ($w = 23$).

$$y_{t+1} = f(M(X, y, w)), M = \begin{bmatrix} X_t & y_t \\ X_{t-1} & y_{t-1} \\ \vdots & \vdots \\ X_{t-w} & y_{t-w} \end{bmatrix} \quad (1.11)$$

The *Multi time-step Dense* architecture extended the *Single time-step Dense* architecture by accepting 1-day's worth of input data $t_0 \ldots t_{24}$. Each time step was flattened as another set of features before passing onto the two *Dense* layers. Like the *Multi time-step Dense* architecture, the *CNN* architecture incorporated multiple time steps as its input. However, the *CNN* architecture step had an initial *Conv1D* layer that could accept an input of any length. On the other hand, the *Multi time-step Dense* architecture could only accept a fixed input length. Finally, the *LSTM* architecture has been considered well-suited for time-series data since it keeps an internal state from one time step to the subsequent step [33]. Table 1.4 provides the specification of each architecture.

Finally, the models were implemented in a computer with an Intel i7-6700 CPU @ 3.40 GHz with four cores and 16 GB RAM. The architectures were trained with the following set of hyperparameters. The maximum number of epochs was fixed at 200, with an early stopping mechanism based on the validation's loss until ten epochs. A binary cross-entropy loss function was used for training the models. Then, the Adam algorithm was used for optimization with a learning rate of 0.001. Eight mini-batches were also produced for training each model.

TABLE 1.4   Architectures Considered for Wearing-off Forecast Model [33]

Architecture	Input	Output	Layers
Baseline	t_0	t_1	N/A
Linear	t_0	t_1	Dense(1, sigmoid)
Single time-step dense	t_0	t_1	Dense(64, ReLu)
			Dense(64, ReLu)
			Dense(1, sigmoid)
Multi time-step dense	$t_0 \ldots t_{23}$	t_{24}	Flatten
			Dense(64, ReLu)
			Dense(64, ReLu)
			Dense(1, sigmoid)
CNN	$t_0 \ldots t_{23}$	t_{24}	Conv1D((64, 24), ReLu)
			Dense(64, ReLu),
			Dense(1, sigmoid)
LSTM	$t_0 \ldots t_{23}$	t_{24}	LSTM(16, return_sequence=True)
			Dense(1, sigmoid)

Each architecture forecasts the wearing-off in the next hour (t_1 or t_{24}), given previous fitness tracker features and wearing-off (t_0 or $t_0 \ldots t_{23}$).

1.4 RESULTS

In this chapter, we have built wearing-off forecasting models for each of the 10 PD participants who joined the research study. The 7-day data collection started upon their written consent. Some PD participants have contributed more than others. In contrast, two participants lacked the number of days needed due to the discomfort caused by their symptoms or for other reasons. This variation in the data collection duration resulted in an average of 9 days $\pm$ 1.826. In general, PD participants have met the prescribed 7-day data collection since the average PD stage of the participants was 2.8 $\pm$ 0.632 on Hoehn & Yahr Scale, while 1.7 $\pm$ 0.483 for Japan's Ministry of Health, Labor, and Welfare's Classification of Impairment of Life Function. The average PD stage was characterized by shaking of either or both limbs, muscle stiffness on either or both sides, no to mild physical disability, and some inconvenience with daily life [6,19]. Furthermore, PD participants' self-reported quality of life according to their PDQ-8 response was 42.50% $\pm$ 0.192, which indicated a low to middle quality of life for a PD patient (Table 1.5).

1.4.1 Can Wrist-worn Fitness Tracker Datasets Be Used to Forecast Wearing-off in the Next Hour?

Each PD participant's model was able to forecast 1-hour future wearing-off. With the current time's fitness tracker datasets and the current wearing-off status. The single time-step dense forecasting model provided the highest *Bal.Acc.* and *AUC* scores of 79.05% $\pm$ 7.09% and 69.14% $\pm$ 10.60%. Meanwhile, with 1-day's worth of fitness tracker datasets and wearing-off periods, the CNN model showed the highest *Bal.Acc.* and *AUC* scores of 80.64% *pm* 10.36% and 60.52% *pm* 30.26%, respectively. These results showed that we could forecast wearing-off in the next hour, either with the current period or with the previous day's fitness tracker datasets and wearing-off periods.

TABLE 1.5 The Participants Demographics

Participant	Age	Gender	H&Y	JCLD	PDQ-8	Number of Collection Days
1	43	Female	2	1	37.50%	9
2	38	Female	3	2	65.63%	6
3	49	Female	3	2	34.38%	10
4	69	Female	3	1	78.13%	10
5	49	Female	2	2	37.50%	8
6	56	Female	2	2	37.50%	9
7	48	Male	3	1	15.63%	6
8	77	Male	3	2	34.38%	11
9	84	Male	4	2	59.38%	11
10	58	Male	3	2	25.00%	10
Average	57.1		2.8	1.7	42.50%	9
Std. Dev.	15.059		0.632	0.483	0.192	1.826

TABLE 1.6 Wearing-Off Forecast Model Performance

Architectures	Bal. Acc. (%)	AUC (%)	Accuracy (%)
Baseline	79.05 ± 7.09	50.20 ± 5.68	86.97 ± 7.19
Linear	79.05 ± 7.09	64.71 ± 16.25	70.33 ± 28.13
Single time-step dense	79.05 ± 7.09	69.14 ± 10.60	92.49 ± 3.62
Multi time-step dense	80.64 ± 10.36	60.23 ± 28.33	81.73 ± 26.99
CNN	80.64 ± 10.36	60.52 ± 30.26	85.09 ± 12.41
LSTM	50.00 ± 0.00	57.83 ± 17.13	85.67 ± 10.73
Architectures	**Precision (%)**	**Recall (%)**	**F1 Score (%)**
Baseline	7.81 ± 10.16	7.59 ± 9.66	7.69 ± 9.90
Linear	5.08 ± 6.34	28.73 ± 33.58	8.09 ± 9.68
Single time-step dense	6.25 ± 13.50	6.15 ± 15.83	5.10 ± 11.37
Multi time-step dense	18.55 ± 32.29	36.17 ± 42.24	20.40 ± 29.72
CNN	18.61 ± 31.98	25.06 ± 39.10	15.58 ± 21.31
LSTM	3.20 ± 5.17	8.10 ± 14.78	3.83 ± 6.24

The reported metric scores were averaged across the individual metric scores for each participant. While some participants had extremely low precision, recall, and F1 scores.

1.4.2 Which among the Six Deep Learning Architectures Performed Well in Forecasting Wearing-off in the Next Hour?

Among the six architectures considered in this chapter, single time-step Dense, multi time-step dense, and CNN models produced the best metric scores. Both multi time-step Dense model and the CNN model had the best *Bal.Acc.* across all 10 PD participants. However, the CNN model produced the highest precision and recall scores of 18.61% ± 31.98% and 36.17% ± 42.24%. Our results have shown that despite being used prominently in time-series datasets, the LSTM model performed the worst among the architectures and just a little above the Baseline model. However, this chapter did not optimize the hyperparameters or customize each architecture. Table 1.6 presents how each architecture performed in each metric.

1.5 DISCUSSIONS

The multi time-step dense and CNN models produced similar results across all metrics. These two architectures were the same, except that the CNN model can accept varying input lengths. The CNN model's first layer handled the sliding window to accommodate the variation in input data. Despite having a similar architecture, the multi time-step dense model provided the highest recall score among all architectures. However, the recall score was lower than 50%. We wanted a higher recall score because we did not want the forecasting model to miss a wearing-off event. For example, the wearing-off forecasting model was deployed to notify the PD participant whether a wearing-off could happen in the next hour. With the current highest recall score, the forecasting model missed informing the actual wearing-off events. These missed events were illustrated in the confusion matrix (Figure 1.2),

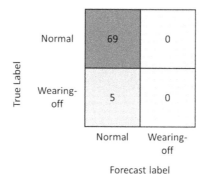

Figure 1.2 Confusion matrix produced by the CNN model using participant 1's combined data. The CNN model for participant 1 failed to forecast the wearing-off label (TP = 0). A similar confusion matrix with TP = 0 was evident among the other five participants.

where the forecasting model had missed all the actual wearing-off events. Five participants had zero recall scores with multi time-step dense model. In comparison, six participants had zero recall with the CNN model. These cases caused the average recall, precision, and F1 scores to have low scores.

Within the context of a notification application for PD patients, we wanted a higher recall score because we did not want to miss actual wearing-off. However, we also wanted to minimize false positives because we did not want to overwhelm the PD patients with the notifications, only to end up as false alarms. The AUC metric balances the true positive rate or recall and the false positive rate. That was why the single time-step dense model had also been considered due to having the highest AUC score.

Finally, Figures 1.3 and 1.4 present the sample forecast made by the model. For participant 10's sample forecast (Figure 1.3), the forecast at t_{25} and t_{26} matched the ground truth labels. However, for participant 6's sample forecast (Figure 1.4), the forecast at t_{25} did not exceed the 0.5 default threshold, despite having increased forecast probability. These results and observations happened with other participants' forecasts, affecting the metric scores. Thus, optimizing the threshold value for each PD patient's forecasting model should be considered in future work.

1.6 CONCLUSION

This chapter demonstrates that deep learning models can forecast wearing-off in the next hour using wrist-worn fitness tracker datasets. The PD patients used the wrist-worn fitness tracker for nine days on average to collect their heart rate, stress score, sleep duration in each sleep stage, and the number of steps. The trained deep learning models have forecasted wearing-off in the next hour, given either the current time or the previous day's dataset as input to the model. The deep learning

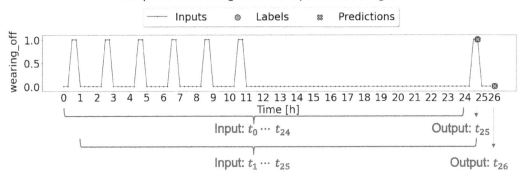

Figure 1.3 Sample wearing-off forecasting using the CNN model with participant 10's combined data. The CNN model used the last day's data (Input: $t_0 \ldots t_{24}$) to forecast the next hour's wearing off (Output: t_{25}). The forecast was marked with "X" while the ground truth was labeled with "O". The y-axis represented the forecast probabilities with "0" as no wearing-off and "1" as wearing-off.

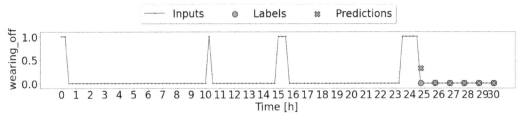

Figure 1.4 Sample wearing-off forecasting using the CNN model with participant 6's combined data. At the time t_{25}, the forecast had a slightly higher forecast probability but was not considered with a wearing-off label of 1.

models have performed well compared to the baseline model, which only copied the last period's wearing-off state. However, the models can still be improved to minimize false positives and negatives in their forecast.

As shown in the sample wearing-off forecasts, the best architecture in this paper (CNN model) showed increased probability scores during actual wearing-off periods. However, it was lower than the default 50% threshold for wearing-off. The threshold level can be optimized for each PD participant's model in future work to reduce the false negative and provide a better future forecast. These can be achieved by fine-tuning the architecture's hyperparameters, modifying the loss function, or giving hidden states that consider prior information about wearing-off.

This chapter has shown that the wearing-off forecasting model can use either the previous day's data or only the current period's data. The Single time-step Dense model used only the current period's data and produced the highest AUC score. Meanwhile, the CNN model had the highest *Bal.Acc.* given the previous day's data. These results lead to future work balancing the historical context of the wearing-off and the current wearing-off state. The historical data taught the forecasting model patterns on when wearing-off could occur, e.g., what hour of the day or at which heart rate or stress score wearing-off occurs. Meanwhile, the current wearing-off provides immediate state of the patient, like when a wearing-off period has begun, and PD patient has shown an extended period of wearing-off. Thus, future forecasting models should be able to balance the historical and the current information while identifying the best-suited forecasting period 15, 30 minutes, or 1 hour into the future.

Finally, in real-life applications, wearing-off reports were not immediately accessible. For example, this scenario happens when forecasting models are trained to accept the current wearing-off state. PD patients report wearing-off after the event occurs; as such, the current wearing-off state is unknown. The forecasting model should provide probability distribution for the missing current wearing-off in future work. Then, the model will use that current period's probability distribution to forecast wearing-off in the next hour. The model should dynamically update the probabilities given the new information when the PD patient reports the actual wearing-off periods. This last suggestion will benefit PD patients in real-life applications where patients and their clinicians can be asked to label only specific periods. The targetted labeling should produce the optimal changes in the forecasting model. This system allows monitoring and reporting of wearing-off and PD patients' symptoms while the models yield actionable insights.

Note

1. https://developer.garmin.com/gc-developer-program/health-api/

BIBLIOGRAPHY

[1] Satyabrata Aich, Pyari Mohan Pradhan, Jinse Park, Nitin Sethi, Vemula Sai Sri Vathsa, and Hee-Cheol Kim. A validation study of freezing of gait (FoG) detection and machine-learning-based FoG prediction using estimated gait characteristics with a wearable accelerometer. *Sensors*, 18(10):3287, 2018.

[2] Satyabrata Aich, Jinyoung Youn, Sabyasachi Chakraborty, Pyari Mohan Pradhan, Jinhan Park, Seongho Park, and Jinse Park. A supervised machine learning approach to detect the on/off state in Parkinson's disease using wearable based gait signals. *Diagnostics*, 10(6):421, 2020.

[3] Angelo Antonini, Pablo Martinez-Martin, Ray K. Chaudhuri, Marcelo Merello, Robert Hauser, Regina Katzenschlager, Per Odin, Mark Stacy, Fabrizio Stocchi, Werner Poewe, Oliver Rascol, Cristina Sampaio, Anette Schrag, Glenn T. Stebbins, and Christopher G. Goetz. Wearing-off scales in Parkinson's disease: Critique and recommendations: Scales to assess wearing-off in PD. *Movement Disorders*, 26(12):2169–2175, 2011.

[4] H. Ceren Ates, Ali K. Yetisen, Firat Güder, and Can Dincer. Wearable devices for the detection of COVID-19. *Nature Electronics*, 4(1):13–14, 2021.

[5] Mercedes Barrachina-Fernández, Ana María Maitín, Carmen Sánchez-Ávila, and Juan Pablo Romero. Wearable technology to detect motor fluctuations in Parkinson's disease patients: Current state and challenges. *Sensors*, 21(12):4188, 2021.

[6] Roongroj Bhidayasiri and Daniel Tarsy. Parkinson's disease: Hoehn and Yahr Scale. In Roongroj Bhidayasiri and Daniel Tarsy, editors, *Movement Disorders: A Video Atlas (Current Clinical Neurology)*, pp. 4–5. Humana Press: Totowa, NJ, 2012.

[7] Cleveland Clinic. Parkinson's disease: Causes, symptoms, stages, treatment, support, 2022.

[8] Delia Colombo, Giovanni Abbruzzese, Angelo Antonini, Paolo Barone, Gilberto Bellia, Flavia Franconi, Lucia Simoni, Mahmood Attar, Emanuela Zagni, Shalom Haggiag, and Fabrizio Stocchi. The "gender factor" in wearing-off among patients with Parkinson's disease: A Post Hoc Analysis of DEEP study, 2015.

[9] Pierre-François D'Haese, Victor Finomore, Dmitry Lesnik, Laura Kornhauser, Tobias Schaefer, Peter E. Konrad, Sally Hodder, Clay Marsh, and Ali R. Rezai. Prediction of viral symptoms using wearable technology and artificial intelligence: A pilot study in healthcare workers. *PLoS One*, 16(10):e0257997, 2021.

[10] Parisa Farzanehfar, Holly Woodrow, and Malcolm Horne. Assessment of wearing off in Parkinson's disease using objective measurement. *Journal of Neurology*, 268(3):914–922, 2021.

[11] Jiro Fukae, Masa-aki Higuchi, Shosaburo Yanamoto, Kosuke Fukuhara, Jun Tsugawa, Shinji Ouma, Taku Hatano, Asako Yoritaka, Yasuyuki Okuma, Kenichi Kashihara, Nobutaka Hattori, and Yoshio Tsuboi. Utility of the Japanese version of the 9-item wearing-off questionnaire. *Clinical Neurology and Neurosurgery*, 134:110–115, 2015.

[12] Garmin. Garmin vivosmart 4, 2020.

[13] Garmin. Vívosmart 4 - heart rate variability and stress level, 2020.

[14] Robert I. Griffiths, Katya Kotschet, Sian Arfon, Zheng Ming Xu, William Johnson, John Drago, Andrew Evans, Peter Kempster, Sanjay Raghav, and Malcolm K. Horne. Automated assessment of Bradykinesia and Dyskinesia in Parkinson's disease. *Journal of Parkinson's Disease*, 2(1):47–55, 2012.

[15] Sietske Heyn and Charles Patrick Davis. Parkinson's disease early and later symptoms, 5 stages, and prognosis, 2020.

[16] Murtadha D. Hssayeni, Michelle A. Burack, Joohi Jimenez-Shahed, and Behnaz Ghoraani. Assessment of response to medication in individuals with Parkinson's disease. *Medical Engineering & Physics*, 67:33–43, 2019.

[17] Crispin Jenkinson, Ray Fitzpatrick, Viv Peto, Richard Greenhall, and Nigel Hyman. The PDQ-8: Development and validation of a short-form Parkinson's disease questionnaire. *Psychology & Health*, 12(6):805–814, 1997.

[18] Hyoseon Jeon, Woongwoo Lee, Hyeyoung Park, Hong Ji Lee, Sang Kyong Kim, Han Byul Kim, Beomseok Jeon, and Kwang Suk Park. Automatic classification of tremor severity in Parkinson's disease using a wearable device. *Sensors*, 17(9):2067, 2017.

[19] K. Kashiwara, A. Takeda, and T. Maeda. みんなで学ぶパーキンソン病：患者さんとともに歩む診療をめざして QA付き *(Learning Parkinson's disease together with patients: Toward a medical practice that works with patients, with Q&A)*. Nankodo, Tokyo, Japan, 2013.

[20] Noël L. W. Keijsers, Martin W. I. M. Horstink, and Stan C. A. M. Gielen. Ambulatory motor assessment in Parkinson's disease. *Movement Disorders*, 21(1):34–44, 2006.

[21] Nattaya Mairittha, Tittaya Mairittha, and Sozo Inoue. A mobile app for nursing activity recognition. In *Proceedings of the 2018 ACM International Joint Conference and 2018 International Symposium on Pervasive and Ubiquitous Computing and Wearable Computers*, Singapore, pp. 400–403, 2018.

[22] Tejaswini Mishra, Meng Wang, Ahmed A. Metwally, Gireesh K. Bogu, Andrew W. Brooks, Amir Bahmani, Arash Alavi, Alessandra Celli, Emily Higgs, Orit Dagan-Rosenfeld, Bethany Fay, Susan Kirkpatrick, Ryan Kellogg, Michelle Gibson, Tao Wang, Erika M. Hunting, Petra Mamic, Ariel B. Ganz, Benjamin Rolnik, Xiao Li, and Michael P. Snyder. Pre-symptomatic detection of COVID-19 from smartwatch data. *Nature Biomedical Engineering*, 4(12):1208–1220, 2020.

[23] Senthilkumar Mohan, A. John, Ahed Abugabah, M. Adimoolam, Shubham Kumar Singh, Ali Kashif Bashir, and Louis Sanzogni. An approach to forecast impact of Covid-19 using supervised machine learning model. *Software: Practice and Experience*, 52(4):824–840, 2022.

[24] Nanna J. Mouritzen, Lisbeth H. Larsen, Maja H. Lauritzen, and Troels W. Kjær. Assessing the performance of a commercial multisensory sleep tracker. *PLoS One*, 15(12):e0243214, 2020.

[25] David L. Reed and William P. Sacco. Measuring sleep efficiency: What should the denominator be? *Journal of Clinical Sleep Medicine : JCSM : Official Publication of the American Academy of Sleep Medicine*, 12(2):263–266, 2016.

[26] A. Samà, C. Pérez-López, D. Rodríguez-Martín, A. Català, J. M. Moreno-Aróstegui, J. Cabestany, E. de Mingo, and A. Rodríguez-Molinero. Estimating bradykinesia severity in Parkinson's disease by analysing gait through a waist-worn sensor. *Computers in Biology and Medicine*, 84:114–123, 2017.

[27] Lynn A. Schroeder, Olivier Rufra, Nicolas Sauvageot, François Fays, Vannina Pieri, and Nico J. Diederich. Reduced rapid eye movement density in Parkinson disease: A polysomnography-based case-control study. *Sleep*, 39(12):2133–2139, 2016.

[28] Mark Stacy, Robert Hauser, Wolfgang Oertel, Anthony Schapira, Kapil Sethi, Fabrizio Stocchi, and Eduardo Tolosa. End-of-dose wearing off in Parkinson disease: A 9-question survey assessment. *Clinical Neuropharmacology*, 29(6):312–321, 2006.

[29] Tobias Steinmetzer, Michele Maasch, Ingrid Bonninger, and Carlos M. Travieso. Analysis and classification of motor dysfunctions in arm swing in Parkinson's disease. *Electronics*, 8(12):1471, 2019.

[30] Suzanne Stevens and Catherine Siengsukon. Commercially-available wearable provides valid estimate of sleep stages. *Neurology*, 92(15 Supplement): P3.6-042, 2019.

[31] F. Stocchi, A. Antonini, P. Barone, M. Tinazzi, M. Zappia, M. Onofrj, S. Ruggieri, L. Morgante, U. Bonuccelli, L. Lopiano, P. Pramstaller, A. Albanese, M. Attar, V. Posocco, D. Colombo, and G. Abbruzzese. Early detection of wearing off in Parkinson disease: The deep study. *Parkinsonism & Related Disorders*, 20(2):204–211, 2014.

[32] Sigurlaug Sveinbjornsdottir. The clinical symptoms of Parkinson's disease. *Journal of Neurochemistry*, 139(S1):318–324, 2016.

[33] Tensorflow. Time series forecasting. https://www.tensorflow.org/tutorials/structured_data/time_series, June 2022.

[34] John Noel Victorino, Yuko Shibata, Sozo Inoue, and Tomohiro Shibata. Predicting wearing-off of Parkinson's disease patients using a wrist-worn fitness tracker and a smartphone: A case study. *Applied Sciences*, 11(16):7354, 2021.

[35] John Noel Victorino, Yuko Shibata, Sozo Inoue, and Tomohiro Shibata. Understanding wearing-off symptoms in Parkinson's disease patients using wrist-worn fitness tracker and a smartphone. *Procedia Computer Science*, 196:684–691, 2022.

[36] K. Yamabe, H. Kuwabara, R. Liebert, and I. Umareddy. The burden of Parkinson's disease(Pd) in Japan. *Value in Health*, 19(7):A435, 2016.

CHAPTER 2

Toward Human Thermal Comfort Sensing: New Dataset and Analysis of Heart Rate Variability (HRV) Under Different Activities

Tahera Hossain, Yusuke Kawasaki, Kazuki Honda, Kizito Nkurikiyeyezu, and Guillaume Lopez

Aoyama Gakuin University

2.1 INTRODUCTION

Thermal comfort is a mental state characterized by satisfaction with one's thermal environment, which is critical for everyday productivity [5,25], safety [33], and human well-being [24,34]. Existing research [6,30] indicates that thermal discomfort has an impact on occupiers' productivity as well as their long-term health. Long-term exposure to high temperatures can result in cardiac issues or heart failure (heat stroke), whereas prolonged exposure to cold temperatures lowers the core temperature, which can cause drowsiness, lethargy, and even death. On a broad scale, the relationship between heat stress, health, and performance is well recognized. However, the physiological elements that affect a worker's vulnerability are still up for debate. Therefore, increasing a person's or a group's level of comfort is a worthwhile goal.

As specified in thermal comfort standards such as ASHRAE Standard 55 [2,7], EN 15251 [1], and ISO 7730 [3], the indoor thermal environment design and thermostat settings in the vast majority of buildings with mechanical systems rely on air temperature control values derived from the existing predicted mean value (PMV) model. PMV is the most commonly used metric for assessing thermal comfort levels in a mechanically controlled environment. PMV is an indicator that predicts the mean value of a set of occupants' thermal sensation votes. The PMV model takes into account two human-related elements, the user's clothing insulation and metabolic rate, as well as environmental parameters such as temperature, air velocity, mean radiant temperature, and relative humidity.

Recent research have revealed various shortcomings of the PMV model when used in real-world scenarios. Firstly, because the model was created to estimate the average level of comfort for a large group of users, it has a low predictive accuracy when applied to a small sample of users. As well as, for the PMV model it is sometimes difficult to determine the exact value of the input variables in real-world circumstances. For example, throughout the day, the metabolic rate can fluctuate. Additionally, in a real-world setting, clothing insulation may not be constant over time, resulting in inconsistencies in PMV measurement. In general, these models, however, don't account for the complexity of human thermoregulation or the sufficiency of the thermal comfort offered; instead, they just show how the environment affects a person's thermal comfort. Furthermore, they disregard factors such as psychophysics, gender, age, and other physiological, psychological, cultural, and social settings that are known to influence how comfortable people feel in their surroundings [9,23]. As a result, they fail to provide optimal thermal comfort in practice [11,19].

Furthermore, different occupants may have distinct subjective responses when all other factors are equivalent. The scientific community has examined thermal comfort from the perspective of the individual and his or her perception of the environment, as thermal comfort is intimately tied to behavioral, physiological, and psychological aspects and hence varies between individuals [19].

In our previous research [20], we proposed a thermal comfort provision method based on environmental thermal sensation in four hot thermal environments. Since thermal comfort is a subjective psychological sensation and thermoregulation results in observable physiological changes [29], it would be more effective to provide thermal comfort based on a person's physiological signals and subjective responses. In this research, we focus on predicting personalized thermal comfort from empirically collected data in various work conditions: i.e., reading, typewriting, and gymnastics, focusing on hot thermal conditions in accordance with the ASHRAE scale: normal, slightly warm, warm, and hot thermal environments and evaluated subjective thermal responses on very hot, hot, warm, slightly warm, neutral, fresh, and cool scale. We present a thermal comfort providing approach using heart rate variability (HRV) data from simple wristwatch-like device equipped with various sensors to collect autonomic nervous system activity data. In this study, we collected data from 33 participants' 10 days data to evaluate the individuals' thermal comfort focusing on hot environment. During the experiment, participants reported their subjective thermal sensation states every five minutes using a thermal assessment logging application that we designed and placed on a smart tablet. We compared the environmental PMV thermal comfort prediction with subjective thermal assessment and found that almost 74% personal assessment did not match with PMV environmental thermal prediction.

As well, in this chapter, we compared machine learning algorithms KNN, ET, LightGBM prediction performance with CNN prediction performance based on the person's HRV indices to predict the subjective thermal sensation sates. We checked the models' performance with low-granularity easily accessible data (e.g., only heart rate, accelerometers, skin temperature) but our investigation shows that only heart rate data with other low-granularity signal data cannot perform well for predicting thermal comfort labels hence the accuracy is only 56% in CNN model. On the other hand, the model performs good while several HRV indices were used as input to machine learning models as well as for the CNN model with HRV signals to anticipate users' personalized thermal sensation, providing an accuracy of 97.6%.

The rest of this chapter proceeds as follows: first, Section 2.2 begins by reviewing the related literature on estimating thermal sensation, comfort, and preference. Section 2.3 explains the methodology of this research, which includes data collection process, collected data overview, difference in PMV and individual thermal assessment, feature extraction process, and model development details. Section 2.4 presents the results of the prediction of different thermal sensations and classification methods with discussions. The conclusions drawn are presented with some future work points in Section 2.5.

2.2 BACKGROUND: THERMAL SENSATION, COMFORT AND PREFERENCE

It is challenging to provide a single definition for the concept of 'thermal comfort' since it is a phrase that can refer to a variety of subjective sensations and is influenced by all aspects that affect the thermal condition that an occupant experiences. All conditions under which a person would not choose a different environment are frequently referred to as human thermal comfort [40]. An additional definition of thermal comfort is given by American standard ASHRAE 55 [7], which characterizes it as a subjective term related to physical and psychological well-being with the environment. Because each person is unique, this word is typically used to describe a set of ideal conditions, for which the majority of a group of people can feel comfortable in their surroundings [13].

The term thermal comfort refers to every element that affects how heat is exchanged between the human body and its surroundings. This allows us to distinguish between factors related to the human body, such as age, gender, weight, metabolic rate, type of activity, etc.; factors related to clothing, such as thermal resistance, material structure, and number of layers; and factors related to the environment, such as air temperature, velocity, humidity, and pressure [12,13]. A personal thermal comfort model's main benefit is its ability to self-learn and update to suit a person with a data-driven approach, leading to improved prediction power.

By inputting various inputs into machine learning algorithms, numerous recent studies have built personal thermal comfort models. (1) Environmental information, (2) occupant behavior, and (3) physiological signals are the three main kinds of variables. The classification of occupants' personal thermal comfort using temperature and humidity sensors was done using a data-driven approach with the indoor environment [17]. The second method is to observe how occupants behave, such as modifying thermostats [22] or personal heating/cooling device settings [35], in order to infer their level of comfort and preference with regard to the temperature. In addition to behavior-tracking, physiological markers including skin temperature [10,44], heart rate variability [32], electroencephalogram (EEG) [45], skin conductance [16], and accelerometry [39] also demonstrate a substantial link with human thermal feeling and comfort. Personal thermal sensation models were created by Sim et al. [43] based on wrist skin temperature readings from wearable sensors. By combining environmental, physiological, and behavioral data from the occupants, a "personalized" model can be created [26]. Other recent attempts [4,21] combined ambient sensors (such as temperature and air speed) with commercial wearable sensors to anticipate each individual occupant's comfort.

Although all of the research discussed above asserted improved prediction accuracy compared to traditional PMV and adaptive models, we highlight a few significant flaws or restrictions in those studies. In steady-state short-term lab testing, the dynamics of thermal comfort among many daily activities and their interactions cannot be properly recorded. Studies conducted under steady-state circumstances were unable to record human activity or mobility. Personal thermal comfort models created under realistic settings may be technically possible, but they may also be inaccurate.

Previous studies using wearable sensors frequently used readily available, inexpensive commercial sensors. Although the manufacturers claimed that the built-in sensors were accurate and reliable, it is unknown how well these sensors operated when worn. The manufacture specification was typically based on laboratory validation in a static setting, which could be very different when end users employed the sensors. For instance, a wristband like the Empatica E4 (Empatica Inc., USA) wristband [27] be reliable when there are less motions, like when sleeping and sitting at a table.

In this study, we developed personal thermal comfort models using lab-grade, wearable sensors that continuously analyze physiological inputs. We propose using heart rate variability (HRV) to discretely characterize individuals' thermal comfort state. HRV represents the time difference between two consecutive heartbeats. Heartbeat intervals (also known as the R–R intervals) are not periodic. Instead, the time between two successive R–R intervals changes from heartbeat to heartbeat. This variance, however, is not random; rather, it varies according to complicated extrinsic protocols placed on the heart [36]. HRV is also associated with homeostasis, which is the human body's ability to maintain optimal circumstances despite changing environmental stressors [37]. The hypothalamus in the human brain controls several mechanisms to enhance or decrease energy production in order to restore the body's core temperature. The parasympathetic nervous system (PNS) and the sympathetic nervous system (SNS) work together to keep the body in balance (SNS). The two systems have opposite effects on the heart rate: the SNS makes the heart beat faster, while the PNS slows it down [38].

Since thermal comfort is a personal subjective assessment of the satisfaction of the mind with the thermal environment and that thermal changes in the environment affect homeostasis, which in turn affects HRV [8], we consider that thermal comfort state could be predicted more accurately using HRV. Thus, in this study, we evaluated subjective HRV indices under different work conditions and different hot thermal environments in order to classify the thermal comfort state of individuals in hot environment by using a simple wristband E4 empatica, which is a medical-grade wearable device that offers real-time physiological data.

2.3 METHODS

In this section, we describe the data collection procedure, data overview, differences between PMV and individual thermal assessment, physiological metrics used in this research, feature extraction, and model building process elaborately.

2.3.1 Data Collection

This section provides an overview of the data collection protocol, wearable sensors, participants, data collection process, and tools used for the experiment. Each participant gave informed consent to the processing of their data, which was obtained with the approval of the local ethics committee.

2.3.1.1 Data Collection Protocol

The data collection protocol designed for this experiment focuses on collecting data on hot thermal environments (neutral to hot environmental thermal states) under different activities (Figure 2.1). In a single data collection experiment, each participant experienced eight different experimental session conditions. Table 2.1, presents each experiment session condition elaborately. The experiment session conditions are focused on different work environments, such as reading, typing, and gymnastics with a focus on hot environments and settings in accordance with the ASHRAE scale. We have set these activities in real-world circumstances. For example, elderly people reading/watching television at home will be associated with reading activities, office work classroom study will be aligned with reading and typing activities, and factory/outdoor labor requiring higher effort will be aligned with heavy work activities like radio gymnastics (Figure 2.1).

Each session was planned with a specific activity and various humidity and temperature levels. For instance, gymnastics activities were recorded in both a hot condition (temperature 32°C and humidity 80%) and a warm state (temperature was 25°C and humidity 60%). In addition, reading and type writing activities were also recorded in varied temperature and humidity states. The duration of gymnastics activities was 10 minutes whereas other activities were 15 minutes. Participants took

TABLE 2.1 Data Collection States for a Single Experiment

Experiment Session Conditions	Task	Temperature (°C)	Humidity (%)	Duration (minutes)
1	Radio gymnastics	32	80	10
2	Radio gymnastics	25	60	10
3	Reading	25	60	15
4	Reading	32	80	15
5	Reading	27	60	15
6	Reading	32	80	15
7	Typewriting	32	80	15
8	Typewriting	27	60	15

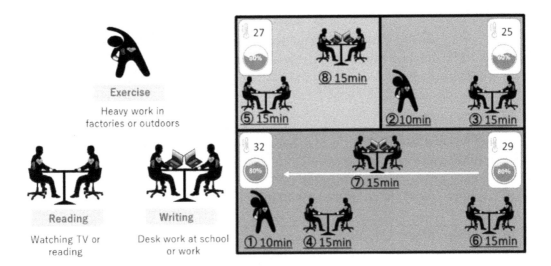

Figure 2.1 Experiment outline; data collection under different activities in different temperatures.

a 5-minute break after completing the gymnastics activities, which were recorded in hot temperatures (32°C/humidity 80%) and (temperature was 25°C/humidity 60%), so that the heavy activity in hot temperatures and humidity conditions did not affect the following experiment.

2.3.1.2 Wearable Sensors

Participants were requested to wear Empatica E4 wristbands[1], it is a wristband that looks like a watch and contains numerous sensors, including an Electrodermal activity (EDA) monitor sensor, a photoplethysmography (PPG) sensor (which measures the Blood Volume Pulse (BVP), which is a metric that may be used to determine heart rate variability to assess sympathetic nervous system activity and heart rate simultaneously at the same time), and a three-axis accelerometer (ACC), and an optical thermometer. At a sampling rate of 4 Hz, EDA shows how the skin's electrical properties are constantly changing. Increased skin conductivity is caused by an increase in the level of sweating. The PPG sensor, which measures the BVP at a frequency of 64 Hz, can be used to determine the IBI and HRV. Under seated rest, paced breathing, and recovery conditions, the Empatica E4 wrist band [28] accurately measures HRV. Thus, the E4 is outfitted with sensors that are designed to collect high-quality data [27].

2.3.1.3 Participants and Procedure

Data was collected from a total of 33 participants, whose ages ranged from 22 to 50 years old (10 women, 23 men). The individuals who participated were given specific instructions on how to do a specified task while they were inside in a temperature-controlled environment. For this experiment, data were collected for 10 days. We made adjustments to the temperature and humidity at the time of data collection for each activity. The continuous pulse intervals of 33 adult males and females were measured in three different work situations involving reading, typing, and radio gymnastics under varying environmental conditions of temperature and humidity. During the experiment, participants wore the E4 Empatica wristband, which was connected with an android smartphone application named E4 real time via Bluetooth signal (Figure 2.2). Participants uploaded the data to the cloud server of E4 connect after each session ended.

For subjective evaluation, we developed a separate subjective thermal assessment logging application which was installed in a smart tablet and participants recorded their personal thermal sensation states in each 5 minutes during the experiment (Figure 2.3). The date and thermal comfort are recorded each time the user touches an icon. In the application, there is a timer sets which gives reminder to participants to record their personal assessment in every 5 minutes.

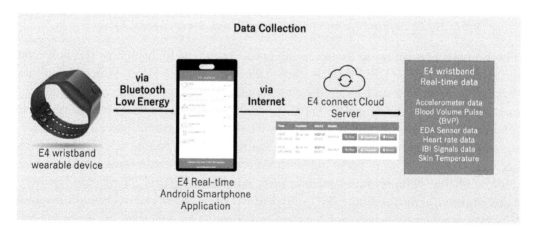

Figure 2.2 Overview of the data collection process.

Figure 2.3 Subjective thermal assessment logging application.

2.3.2   Data Overview

The physiological data measured in this study includes heart rate, skin potential, body surface temperature, and body movement data. Participants wear a Empatica E4 wristbands and measure physiological information in either of the following states:

- Reading activity (equivalent to rest in a chair including reading and listening to music).

- Typewriting (equivalent to office work and studying).

- Exercise (equivalent to heavy household work or work at outside).

- Continuous work time in different thermal states for reading activity.

- Set temperature/humidity environmental conditions of the living room during work fluctuate between "comfortable" (25°C/60%) and "very hot" (32°C/80%) defined by the international standard (ASHRAE).

The number of reading activities is disproportionately high among the collected data because this activity's data were collected as continuous work time under varying temperature and humidity conditions. For the typing activity, we considered not typing at random. Participants suggested reading an article and typing it afterward to induce the stress associated with this task. Figure 2.4, depicts the activity information and activity counts. The reading activity counts are relatively high because these data were collected with considering the continuous working state under different temperature and humidity situation. Figure 2.5 reflects the data collection temperature where 32° temperature situation is relatively high because this experiment target is to collect the data considering hot thermal environment. Because of the high stress level of the activity, the HRV standard deviation for these two experiments was much higher than the HRV standard deviation for the other studies, reading and typing (Figure 2.6)

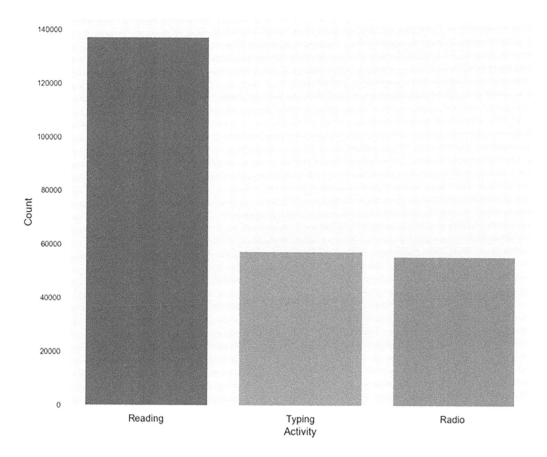

Figure 2.4 Activity counts; the relatively high 'reading' activity counts can be attributed to the fact that this activity data was collected while considering continuous working states under varying temperature and humidity conditions.

2.3.3 PMV Thermal States and Individual Thermal Assessment

The PMV thermal comfort model was developed based on results from extensive laboratory work done on people over an extended period of time in a variety of temperature states. [14]. To predict the average thermal experience of a large group of individuals, this model takes into account the ambient air temperature, the mean radiant temperature, the air velocity, the relative humidity, people's metabolic rate, and their clothing insulation level [14]. Since its conception, the PMV model has been utilized to predict the average thermal perception of building occupants. It has been adopted into worldwide thermal comfort standards for its fair performance [18] (e.g., ISO 7730, ASHRAE 55).

The thermal sensation experienced by a person might change based on the temperature of the surrounding air. The ASHRAE seven-point scale was used to evaluate the individuals' temperature feelings in the PMV model (Figure 2.7). The ASHRAE scale is used to determine how warm or cool an individual feels in a specific indoor environment. The seven stages that make up the projected PMV

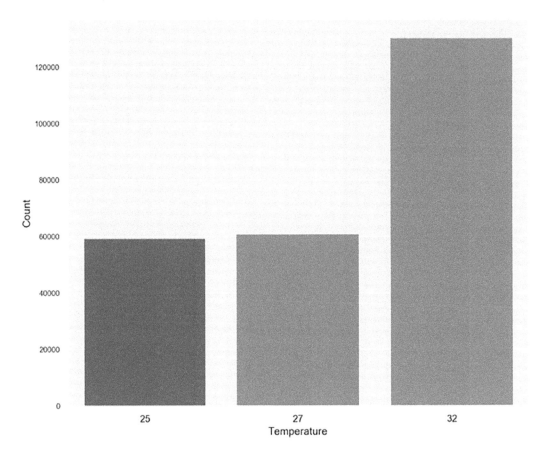

Figure 2.5 The temperature during data collection, where the 32° temperature is relatively high because of the hot thermal environment.

are as follows: cold, cool, slightly cool, neutral, slightly warm, warm, and hot. Because we want to be able to forecast how comfortable a person will be in a hot environment, we conducted this research in an experimental setting that replicated all four stages of circumstances ranging from normal to extremely hot.

Figure 2.8 illustrates the four different PMV thermal states that may be found in the dataset, with warm conditions having a disproportionately high number of recordings in comparison to the other thermal states. Figure 2.9 depicts the personal thermal sensation feedback states, where during subjective evaluation time neutral state having high number of records. When we compared PMV thermal states with subjective evaluation, we found that 74% of the thermal states label were not matched with subjective assessment (Figure 2.10). Because each person's feelings are completely unique, we cannot generalize about how people are feeling. PMV model was developed to predict the general thermal comfort of a population as a whole, rather than the comfort of an individual person. This is the primary cause of the significant mismatch between the predicted thermal comfort states of the PMV models and individual thermal states.

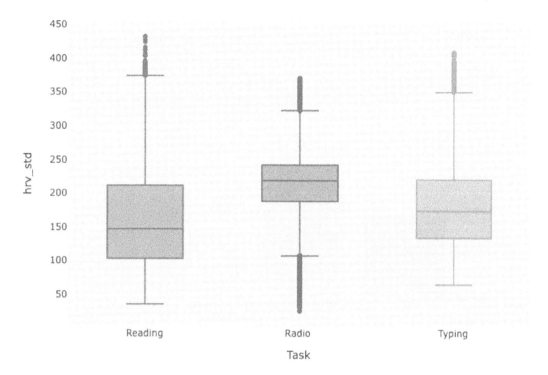

Figure 2.6 Activity basis HRV standard deviation.

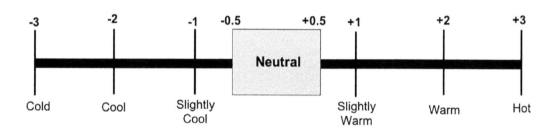

Figure 2.7 The thermal feeling scale according to ASHRAE standard 55.

Figure 2.11 is the brief comparison graph for four PMV thermal states (hot, warm, slightly warm, and neutral) with subjective assessment data during that specific temperature. Majority of participants recorded that they were feeling neutral in all four PMV thermal states.

2.3.4 Physiological Metrics

Throughout the experiment, the PPG signal was gathered by means of an Empatica E4 wristband at a range of temperatures while the subject was engaged in a variety of activities. We assessed the subjects' IBI signals, which were derived from a PPG signal that was collected using an Empatica E4 wristband. IBI stands for "interbeat interval" and refers to the amount of time that passes between each individual

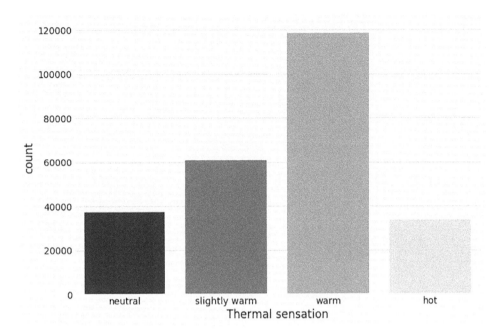

Figure 2.8 PMV thermal sensation; 'warm' conditions having a disproportionately high number of recordings in comparison to the other PMV thermal states.

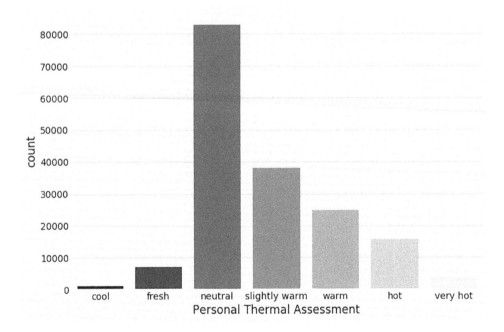

Figure 2.9 Records of individuals' personal thermal sensations that were collected using thermal assessment logging application.

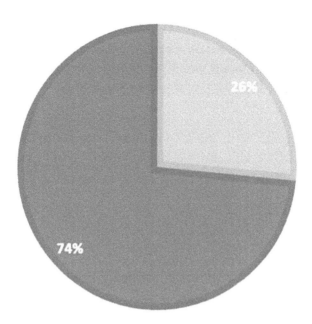

Figure 2.10 Label comparison.

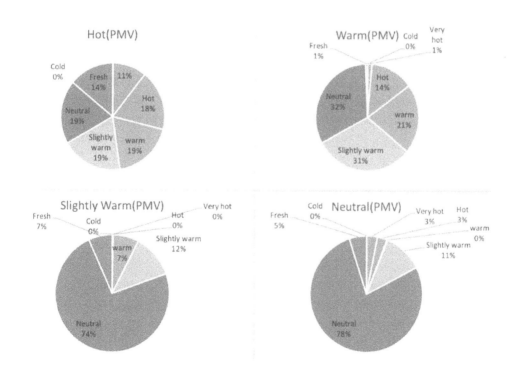

Figure 2.11 Label comparison of PMV models' predicted thermal comfort states and individual thermal states.

beat of the heart. Using a sliding window technique, we estimated heart rate, inter beat intervals in milliseconds, and heart rate variability from physiological data gathered such as blood volume pulse. We computed each HRV feature on a moving window as follows: For the first HRV index, we used an array of IBI measurements taken every five minutes. Then, a new IBI sample is added to the IBI array, and the oldest IBI sample at the beginning of the IBI array is removed. The next HRV index is calculated using the new IBI array that was created. Thus, the newly derived IBI array is utilized to compute the next HRV index. We kept doing this until the end of the IBI array. With the help of these IBI data, we are able to generate HRV measurements that indicate the change that occurs between two successive heartbeats.

2.3.5 Feature Extraction

Afterward, we chose time-domain and frequency-domain analyses of HRV indices for this study. Calculating and comprehending HRV Indices in the time domain is not complicated. Time domain HRV features characterize the beat-to-beat variability. This group's variability from beat to beat can be characterized using statistical methods. The RMSSD index, which measures the root mean square of successive differences between normal heartbeats, and the pNNx index, which measures the proportion of absolute deviations between successive normal sinus intervals that exceed a certain threshold value, are two examples of the many time-domain features that can be examined. The statistic obtained is referred to as pNN50, and the most widely used threshold is 50 ms. The members of the HRV research community regard these characteristics to be key features [41]. The root mean squared standard deviation, or RMSSD, is the square root of the mean of the sum of changes between consecutive R-R intervals, also known as beat-to-beat intervals. The notation pNNx is used to indicate the proportion of R-R consecutive pairings that differ from one another by x ms. It is also necessary to use an epoch of 2 minutes when calculating the percentage of neighboring NN periods that differ by more than 50 ms (pNN50).

Spectral HRV analysis methods are used to split pulse variability into its underlying frequency components for the purpose of frequency-domain feature analysis. This enables a better understanding of heartbeat variation. There are several different approaches to take when determining the HRV spectrum components. In particular, the techniques known as the Fast Fourier Transform (FFT) and the autoregressive (AR) modeling are utilized rather frequently [42]. Using FFT or AR modeling [31,42], we are able to separate HRV into its constituent ULF, VLF, LF, and HF rhythms, all of which operate within unique frequency ranges.

On a window segment utilizing a window size of 300 samples, each and every HRV index was determined (something close to 3 minutes and with a step size of 30 seconds). The features are computed using the flirt library [15]. Tables 2.2 and 2.3, summarize the time-domain and frequency-domain selected HRV indices that were utilized in this research. In addition to HRV features, our feature matrix also included accelerometer data, age, gender, and skin temperature information.

TABLE 2.2   Description of the Selected Time-Domain HR and HRV Features

HRV Index	Short D'escription
NUM_IBIS	The total amount of NNI intervals
HRV_MEAN_NNI	The average of all of the NNI intervals
HRV_MEDIAN_NNI	Median of all of the NNI intervals
SDSD	The standard deviation of all of the interval differences that exist between neighboring RR intervals
RMSSD	Square root of the mean of the sum of the squares of the difference between adjacent RR intervals
HRV_NNI_50	The percentage of consecutive NN intervals that are separated by more than 50 ms
HRV_NNI_20	The percentage of consecutive NN intervals that are separated by more than 20 ms
HRV_pNNI_50	The percentage of R-R consecutive pairs that are separated by a time gap of 50 ms
SDNN	The standard deviation for each and every NN interval
HRV_SD1	The short-term heart rate variability is measured in milliseconds using SD1
HRV_SD2	Long-term heart rate variability is measured in milliseconds using SD2
HR_MEAN	Average heart rate, measured in beats per minute
HR_MIN	The lowest heart rate, measured in beats per minute
HR_MAX	Maximum Heart Rate, measured in terms of the number of heartbeats per minute
HR_STD	Standard deviation of Heart Rate
HRV_MEAN	Mean of IBIs
HRV_STD	Standard deviation of IBIs
HRV_MIN	Lowest of IBIs
HRV_MAX	Maximum value of IBIs
HRV_SKEWNESS	Skewness of all IBIs
HRV_KURTOSIS	Kurtosis of all IBIs
HRV_PEAKS	Peak value of IBIs
HRV_Energy	The energization provided by the IBIs
HRV_CVSD	Variation coefficient of successive differences equal to RMSSD divided by average NN interval
HRV_n_Above_Mean	Number of IBIs above the mean
HRV_n_Below_Mean	Number of IBIs below the mean
HRV_IQR	Interquartile range of the IBIs between the 25th and 75th percentiles
HRV_Entropy	Entropy of the IBIs
HRV_RMS	Square root of the mean of the sum of the squares of differences between adjacent NN intervals

TABLE 2.3   Description of the Selected Frequency-Domain HRV Features

HRV Index	Short Description
HRV_VLF	Power spectral in the extremely low range of frequencies (0.003–0.04 Hz)
HRV_LF	Spectral power in frequencies in the low range (0.04–0.15 Hz)
HRV_HF	Spectral power in high range frequencies (0.15 Hz)
HRV_LF_HF_RATIO	Power in comparison between the LF and HF bands
TP	The overall power of the spectrum (0–0.4 Hz)
HRV_LFnu	A low-frequency band HRV in normalized unit
HRV_HFnu	A high-frequency band HRV in normalized unit

2.3.6   Model Building to Predict Different Thermal states

To understand the environmental thermal states using PMV model [20], we extracted data from the E4 wristbands worn by participants while they performed light work (metabolic rate 1.1) and heavy work (metabolic rate 3.0) in four thermal chambers with temperature settings that corresponded to those of a normal, slightly warm, warm, and hot thermal sensation on a PMV index scale (Table 2.4). After extracted HRV indices, the HRV indices of all participants in all temperature settings were combined after they were retrieved. Thus, we calculated the PMV (environmental thermal sensation) for each states. Afterward, we compared the subjective assessment data with the time obtained from the subjective assessment with the time obtained from the E4 wristband. In the corresponding matched time (smartwatch vs assessment), we recorded the label written in assessment with the combined HRV indices file. Thus, we merger the subjective assessment in the same interval settings for all participantsWe utilized the subject's self-assessment to develop machine models that estimate each subject's thermal comfort level. For this, we use KNN, ET, lightgbm machine learning models and 1D Convolutional Neural Network (CNN) model to predict the comfort status of a person through participants' HRV indices and subjective assessment. For CNN model, it consists of two convolutional layers, two max pooling layer and two fully connected layers. Each of first and second convolutional layers has 64 filters and kernel size is 1×3. Both machine learning and CNN model trained to predict thermal states based on the subject's HRV indices and their seven stages of assessment cold, cool, slightly cool,

TABLE 2.4   Thermal Environment Settings

	Hot	Warm	Slightly Warm	Neutral
Activity level	3.0	1.1	1.0	1.0
clothing level	1	1	1	1
Air temperature	32.0	32.0	27	25
Humidity	80	80	60	60
PMV	2.85	1.87	0.66	0.06

neutral, slightly warm, warm and hot. Then, we utilized a 10-folds cross-validation method to assess the performance of each model.

2.4 RESULTS ANALYSIS AND DISCUSSION

To evaluate the prediction performance, we used accuracy as evaluation metric. The accuracy of the model is obtained using Equation 2.1, in the equation, the meanings of TP, TN, FP and FN are stated as: TP = True Positive, TN = True Negative, FP = False Positive, and FN = False Negative.

$$\text{Accuracy} = \frac{\text{TP} + \text{TN}}{\text{TP} + \text{FP} + \text{FN} + \text{TN}} \tag{2.1}$$

Among the machine learning models, ET performs the best with an accuracy of 99%, while Lightgbm obtained 98% accuracy and KNN obtained 70% accuracy (Figure 2.12) compares the accuracy of these four models. On the other hand, CNN model achieved 96.6% while using all HRV signal data. In contrast, the model's performance decreases to 61.3% when only HR and other low granularity signals

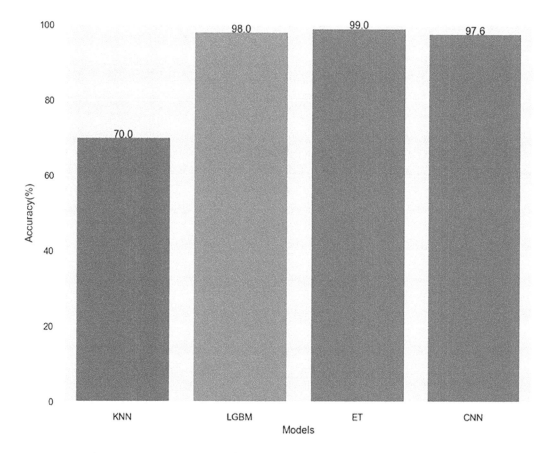

Figure 2.12 Accuracy comparison of different models.

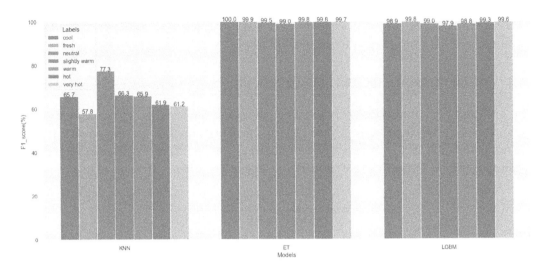

Figure 2.13   F1 score comparison of ML models.

data are utilized. Figure 2.13 compare the F1-score values for all machine learning models for each thermal comfort labels.

The confusion matrix (Figures 2.14 and 2.15) presents for CNN model both HRV and HR data. It has been observed that while using low granularity signals data in CNN model then slightly warm mostly miss-classified with warm state also warm and hot state miss-classified mostly. We calculated the precision, recall, and F1-score of the CNN model HRV data for each class. In the dataset, the proportion of samples that were incorrectly classified as false, also known as false negatives (FN), is represented by the recall (Equation 2.3), while the proportion of samples that were correctly classified as true positives (TP) versus false negatives (FP) is expressed by the precision (Equation 2.2). The F1 score is calculated by taking the harmonic mean of the metrics for precision and recall (Equation 2.4). According to Figure 2.16 of the CNN HRV model classification report, the lowest precision score is 92.0% for the warm state, while the greatest F1-scores are for the hot and fresh states.

$$\text{Precision} = \frac{\text{TP}}{\text{TP} + \text{FP}} \tag{2.2}$$

$$\text{Recall} = \frac{\text{TP}}{\text{TP} + \text{FN}} \tag{2.3}$$

$$F1 = \frac{2 * \text{Precision} * \text{Recall}}{\text{Precision} + \text{Recall}} = \frac{2 * \text{TP}}{2 * \text{TP} + \text{FP} + \text{FN}} \tag{2.4}$$

Thermal comfort is a subjective concept impacted by a variety of factors, including a person's psychometrics and biological composition. In this preliminary study, we investigate the ability of a newly collected dataset to predict a subjective thermal comfort in a hot setting. With HRV features data, the trained classifier has a very

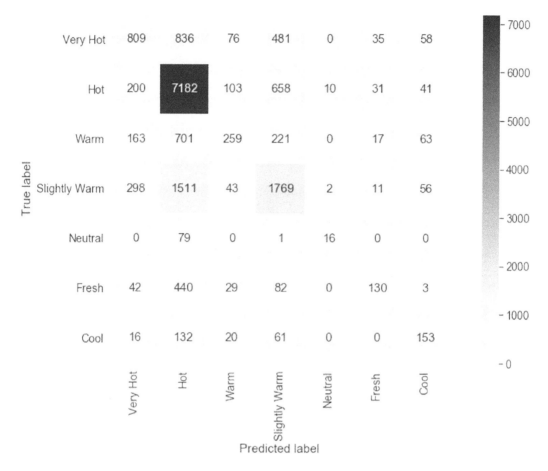

Figure 2.14 Confusion matrix for CNN model HR data.

good classification accuracy. This demonstrates that only a small percentage of a person's IBI signal can be used to estimate the personal thermal comfort. The scope of this research is limited to pulse fluctuation data from where we extracted heart rate variability. The performance of low granularity signals data is low because of not able to recognize the specific pattern of data which can be improved through high level extracted features from data. It reduces the quantity of duplicated data in the data collection through feature extraction hence improve the performance. In the future, we will examine domain adaptation and transfer learning models to enhance performance with low granularity.

This experiment is, however, not limited in nature (33 users and in four thermal comfort environmental settings) in various work conditions. In future, we will evaluate the person dependent and independent model's performance with a variety of age range and gender variance. Because, the individual differences in responses to thermal comfort are well known, but generally the differences between male and female subjects are not well evaluated. We will also focus on the effect of other biological signals other than pulse fluctuation.

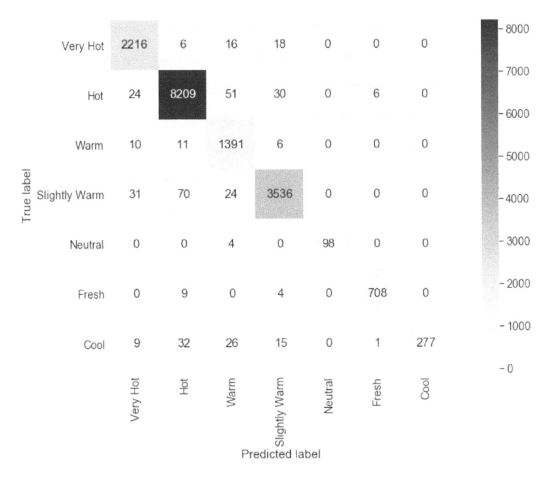

Figure 2.15 Confusion matrix CNN model HRV data.

However, to predict human thermal comfort under different work activities is important. Compared to the previous year, heat stroke deaths are increasing and becoming a significant risk factor, especially for the people working in the outdoor. People who work outside or in factories, as well as those who are elderly, are at a particularly high risk of suffering from heat stroke. Taking regular readings of a worker's temperature, weight, and heart rate while they are on the job is essential for minimizing the potential for injury and avoiding unnecessary stress. In this regard, it is necessary to investigate the thermoregulatory response that results from heat exposure, as well as the associated work burden and the mechanism that causes heat stroke. On the basis of this preliminary evaluation, we plan to conduct additional research on this dataset in the near future in order to forecast subjective thermal comfort and sensation to the prediction of the risk of individual heatstroke as a result of variations in the level of thermal stress felt by different people.

	Precision	Recall	F1-score	Support
Neutral	1.00	0.96	0.98	102
Fresh	0.99	0.98	0.99	721
Warm	0.92	0.98	0.95	1418
Hot	0.98	0.99	0.99	8320
Slightly Warm	0.98	0.97	0.97	3661
Cool	1.00	0.77	0.87	360
Very Hot	0.97	0.98	0.97	2256

Figure 2.16 CNN model classification report with HRV data.

2.5 CONCLUSIONS AND FUTURE WORKS

In this research, we focus on collecting participants' data in a variety of work environments in various work conditions, i.e., reading, typewriting, and gymnastics, focusing on hot conditions with settings in accordance with the ASHRAE scale in hot thermal environment. Our goal is to gain a better understanding of how individuals respond to high temperatures while performing different tasks. We set these activities in the context of real-life scenarios and place an emphasis on hot thermal conditions (the risk of heatstroke, higher levels of dissatisfaction, and greater difficulty to cope than cold). Initially, we collected 33 participants' data and evaluated subjective HRV indices under different work conditions in order to classify the thermal comfort state of individuals in hot environment by using a simple wristband E4 empatica which is a medical-grade wearable device that offers real-time physiological data.

In our study, we compared the prediction performance of machine learning algorithms KNN, ET, and LightGBM with that of a 1-D CNN (convolutional neural network) based on an individual's HRV indices to predict the subjective thermal sensation state. Our study revealed that ET was the best-performing machine learning model, achieving an accuracy rate of 99%. Meanwhile, the CNN model achieved an accuracy of 96.6% when utilizing all HRV signal data. Our future research will center on examining the performance of both person-dependent and person-independent models. Furthermore, we will evaluate the separate model for different age and gender groups. Because older people are more susceptible to the adverse effects of prolonged exposure to high temperatures than those of younger ages. In addition to age, research has also shown that different gender groups respond differently to temperature changes. Therefore, it is essential to consider both age and gender when evaluating the impact of temperature on individuals. Also, we need to focus on the methodological part to see how we can improve the models' performance with low granularity signals, which are easily available data through any smartwatch. In the future, we will therefore focus on individual levels, comfort, and differences in order to examine a model that can comprehend/prevent the risk of individual heatstroke under varying work conditions.

ACKNOWLEDGMENT

This work was supported by SECOM Science and Technology Foundation research grant. The experiments were carried out with the cooperation of Fujitsu General Limited, providing the experimental environment. Entire experimental protocols were approved by the ethics committee of Aoyama Gakuin University (H21-009).

Note

1. https://www.empatica.com/research/e4/.

BIBLIOGRAPHY

[1] EN 15251:2007. Criteria for the indoor environment including thermal, indoor air quality, light and noise, european committee for standardization, brussels, belgium, 2007.

[2] ASHRAE Standard 55. Thermal environmental conditions for human occupancy, vol. 55. American Society of Heating, Refrigerating and Air-Conditioning Engineers, 2004.

[3] ISO 7730. Ergonomics of the thermal environment: Analytical determination and interpretation of thermal comfort using calculation of the PMV and PPD indices and local thermal comfort criteria, Geneva, Switzerland, 2005.

[4] Moatassem Abdallah, Caroline Clevenger, Tam Vu, and Anh Nguyen. Sensing occupant comfort using wearable technologies. In *Construction Research Congress 2016*, pp. 940–950, San Juan, Puerto Rico, 2016.

[5] Takashi Akimoto, Shin-ichi Tanabe, Takashi Yanai, and Masato Sasaki. Thermal comfort and productivity: Evaluation of workplace environment in a task conditioned office. *Building and Environment*, 45(1):45–50, 2010. *International Symposium on the Interaction between Human and Building Environment Special Issue Section.*

[6] Takashi Akimoto, Shin-ichi Tanabe, Takashi Yanai, and Masato Sasaki. Thermal comfort and productivity: Evaluation of workplace environment in a task conditioned office. *Building and Environment*, 45(1):45–50, 2010.

[7] ASHRAE. ASHRAE thermal environmental conditions for human occupancy; Addendum d to ANSI/ASHRAE standard 55-2004, proposed Addendum d to standard 55-2004. American Society of Heating, Refrigerating and Air Conditioning Engineers, Inc.: Atlanta, GA, 2008.

[8] Gary Berntson, John Thomas Bigger, Dwain Eckberg, Paul Grossman, Peter Kaufmann, Marek Malik, Haikady Nagaraja, Stephen Porges, Pearl Saul, Peter Stone, and Maurits van der Molen. Heart rate variability: Origins, methods, and interpretive caveats. *Psychophysiology*, 34:623–48, 1997.

[9] Cristiana Croitoru, Ilinca Nastase, Florin Bode, Amina Meslem, and Angel Dogeanu. Thermal comfort models for indoor spaces and vehicles: Current capabilities and future perspectives. *Renewable and Sustainable Energy Reviews*, 44:304–318, 2015.

[10] Changzhi Dai, Hui Zhang, Edward Arens, and Zhiwei Lian. Machine learning approaches to predict thermal demands using skin temperatures: Steady-state conditions. *Building and Environment*, 114:1–10, 2017.

[11] Richard de Dear. Revisiting an old hypothesis of human thermal perception: Alliesthesia. *Building Research and Information*, 39:108–117, 2011.

[12] Noel Djongyang, René Tchinda, and Donatien Njomo. Thermal comfort: A review paper. *Renewable and Sustainable Energy Reviews*, 14(9):2626–2640, 2010.

[13] Poul O. Fanger et al. *Thermal Comfort: Analysis and Applications in Environmental Engineering*. R.E. Krieger Publishing Company: Malabar, FL, 1970.

[14] Povl Ole Fanger. Assessment of man's thermal comfort in practice. *British Journal of Industrial Medicine*, 30:313 – 324, 1973.

[15] Simon Foll, Martin Maritsch, Frederica Spinola, Varun Mishra, Filipe Barata, Tobias Kowatsch, Elgar Fleisch, and Felix Wortmann. FLIRT: A feature generation toolkit for wearable data. *Computer Methods and Programs in Biomedicine*, 212:106461, 2021.

[16] Adolf Pharo Gagge, Jan A. J. Stolwijk, and James Daniel Hardy. Comfort and thermal sensations and associated physiological responses at various ambient temperatures. *Environmental Research*, 1(1):1–20, 1967.

[17] Ali Ghahramani, Chao Tang, and Burcin Becerik-Gerber. An online learning approach for quantifying personalized thermal comfort via adaptive stochastic modeling. *Building and Environment*, 92:86–96, 2015.

[18] Edward Halawa and Joost van Hoof. The adaptive approach to thermal comfort: A critical overview. *Energy and Buildings*, 51:101–110, 2012.

[19] Joost van Hoof. Forty years of fanger's model of thermal comfort: Comfort for all? *Indoor Air*, 18:182–201, 2008.

[20] Tahera Hossain, Yusuke Kawasaki, Kizito Nkurikiyeyezu, and Guillaume Lopez. *Toward the Prediction of Environmental Thermal Comfort Sensation using Wearables*. IOS Press: Amsterdam, 2022.

[21] Chuan-Che (Jeff) Huang, Rayoung Yang, and Mark W. Newman. The potential and challenges of inferring thermal comfort at home using commodity sensors. In *Proceedings of the 2015 ACM International Joint Conference on Pervasive and Ubiquitous Computing, UbiComp '15*, New York, pp. 1089–1100, 2015. Association for Computing Machinery.

[22] Brent Huchuk, William O'Brien, and Scott Sanner. A longitudinal study of thermostat behaviors based on climate, seasonal, and energy price considerations using connected thermostat data. *Building and Environment*, 139:199–210, 2018.

[23] Sami Karjalainen. Gender differences in thermal comfort and use of thermostats in everyday thermal environments. *Building and Environment*, 42(4):1594–1603, 2007.

[24] Li Lan, Zhiwei Lian, and Li Pan. The effects of air temperature on office workers' well-being, workload and productivity-evaluated with subjective ratings. *Applied Ergonomics*, 42(1):29–36, 2010.

[25] Li Lan, Pawel Wargocki, and Zhiwei Lian. Quantitative measurement of productivity loss due to thermal discomfort. *Energy and Buildings*, 43(5):1057–1062, 2011. Tackling building energy consumption challenges: Special issue of ISHVAC 2009, Nanjing, China.

[26] Da Li, Carol C. Menassa, and Vineet R. Kamat. Personalized human comfort in indoor building environments under diverse conditioning modes. *Building and Environment*, 126:304–317, 2017.

[27] Cameron McCarthy, Nikhilesh Pradhan, Calum Redpath, and Andy Adler. Validation of the Empatica e4 wristband. In *2016 IEEE EMBS International Student Conference (ISC)*, pp. 1–4, Ottawa, Ontario, Canada, 2016.

[28] Luca Menghini, Evelyn Gianfranchi, Nicola Cellini, Elisabetta Patron, Mariaelena Tagliabue, and Michela Sarlo. Stressing the accuracy: Wrist-worn wearable sensor validation over different conditions. *Psychophysiology*, Journal, Online, 56:e13441, 2019.

[29] Shaun Morrison and Kazuhiro Nakamura. Central neural pathways for thermoregulation. *Frontiers in Bioscience : A Journal and Virtual Library*, 16:74–104, 2011.

[30] Jonn Myhren and Sture Holmberg. Flow patterns and thermal comfort in a room with panel, floor and wall heating. *Energy and Buildings*, 40:524–536, 2008.

[31] Kizito Nkurikiyeyezu, Anna Yokokubo, and Guillaume Lopez. Affect-aware thermal comfort provision in intelligent buildings. *International Conference on Affective Computing and Intelligent Interaction Workshops and Demos (ACIIW)*, Cambridge, September 2019.

[32] Kizito N. Nkurikiyeyezu, Yuta Suzuki, Yoshito Tobe, Guillaume F. Lopez, and Kiyoshi Itao. Heart rate variability as an indicator of thermal comfort state. In *2017 56th Annual Conference of the Society of Instrument and Control Engineers of Japan (SICE)*, Kanazawa, pp. 1510–1512, 2017.

[33] David Ormandy and Véronique Ezratty. Health and thermal comfort: From who guidance to housing strategies. *Energy Policy*, 49:116–121, 2012. Special Section: Fuel Poverty Comes of Age: Commemorating 21 Years of Research and Policy.

[34] Katerina Pantavou, George Theoharatos, Anastasios Mavrakis, and Mat Santamouris. Evaluating thermal comfort conditions and health responses during an extremely hot summer in athens. *Building and Environment*, 46(2):339–344, 2011.

[35] Wilmer Pasut, Hui Zhang, Ed Arens, and Yongchao Zhai. Energy-efficient comfort with a heated/cooled chair: Results from human subject tests. *Building and Environment*, 84:10–21, 2015.

[36] U. Rajendra Acharya, Paul K. Joseph, Natarajan Kannathal, Choo Min Lim, and Jasjit S. Suri. Heart rate variability: A review. *Medical and Biological Engineering and Computing*, 44(12):1031–1051, 2006.

[37] Francesco Riganello, Sergio Garbarino, and Walter G. Sannita. Heart rate variability, homeostasis, and brain function. *Journal of Psychophysiology*, 26(4):178–203, 2012.

[38] Brian F. Robinson, Stephen E. Epstein, David G. Beiser, and Eugene Braunwald. Control of heart rate by the autonomic nervous system. *Circulation Research*, 19(2):400–411, 1966.

[39] Megan P. Rothney, Emily V. Schaefer, Megan M. Neumann, Leena Choi, and Kong Y. Chen. Validity of physical activity intensity predictions by actigraph, actical, and RT3 accelerometers. *Obesity*, 16(8):1946–1952, 2008.

[40] Matheos Santamouris and Dimosthénis Asimakopoulos. *Passive Cooling of Buildings*. Earthscan: Oxford, 1996.

[41] Roberto Sassi, Sergio Cerutti, Federico Lombardi, Marek Malik, Heikki Huikuri, Chung-Kang Peng, Georg Schmidt, Yoshiharu Yamamoto, Bulent Gorenek, Gregory Lip, Guido Grassi, Gulmira Kudaiberdieva, James Fisher, Markus Zabel, and Robert John MacFadyen. Advances in heart rate variability signal analysis: Joint position statement by the e-cardiology ESC working group and the European heart Rhythm association co-endorsed by the ASIA pacific heart Rhythm society. *Europace*, 17:1341–1353, 2015.

[42] Fred Shaffer and Jack Ginsberg. An overview of heart rate variability metrics and norms. *Frontiers in Public Health*, 5:258, 2017.

[43] Soo Young Sim, Myung Jun Koh, Kwang Min Joo, Seungwoo Noh, Sangyun Park, Youn Ho Kim, and Kwang Suk Park. Estimation of thermal sensation based on wrist skin temperatures. *Sensors*, 16(4):420, 2016.

[44] Danni Wang, Hui Zhang, Edward Arens, and Charlie Huizenga. Observations of upper-extremity skin temperature and corresponding overall-body thermal sensations and comfort. *Building and Environment*, 42(12):3933–3943, 2007. *Indoor Air 2005 Conference*.

[45] Fan Zhang, Shamila Haddad, Bahareh Nakisa, Mohammad Naim Rastgoo, Christhina Candido, Dian Tjondronegoro, and Richard de Dear. The effects of higher temperature setpoints during summer on office workers' cognitive load and thermal comfort. *Building and Environment*, 123:176–188, 2017.

CHAPTER 3

Reducing the Number of Wearable Sensors and Placement Optimization by Missing Data Imputation on Nursery Teacher Activity Recognition

Akira Omi, Kensi Fujiwara, and Ren Ohmura

Toyohashi University of Technology

Naoko Ishibashi

Sugiyama Jogakuen University

3.1 INTRODUCTION

Recently, the shortage of nursery teachers has increased the workload of nursery teachers in Japan [1]. In addition, while childcare scholars are studying the quality of nursery care, there are still a few studies that quantitatively analyze the activity of nursery teachers [2,3]. Against this background, there is a need to record and analyze the work of nursery teachers. Therefore, an activity recognition technique is expected to record the activity of nursery teachers efficiently, and their recorded daily work will facilitate its analysis and lead to the development of high-quality childcare. In this study, we tried to recognize the activity of nursery teachers using the activity recognition technique with wearable sensors, which does not limit the location of the subject [4,5], because nursery teachers may take care of children in a variety of locations, both indoors and outdoors.

DOI: 10.1201/9781003371540-4

To recognize various and complicated nursery activities, a nursery teacher needs to wear many sensors. However, wearing many sensors is a time-consuming task and can interfere with the work. Also, it is necessary to consider the positions of sensors that enables to obtain highly accuracy of recognition with limited sensors.

Some studies have been conducted to examine the number of sensors and their position and method of feature extraction that achieve high recognition accuracy with a limited number of using sensors [6–8]. These studies are basically aimed at finding situations in which the loss of accuracy is minimized when the number of sensors is reduced. This approach has been used in many previous studies to reduce the number of sensors. We thought we could achieve high accuracy even with a small number of sensors by recovering the reduced sensor data by using sensor data imputation technology.

A study on imputation processing of missing sensor data, for example [9], proposed a method to fill in missing sensor data such as acceleration and angular velocity collected by smartphones, using time series information and correlation information of features with other sensor data. This study used only data collected on a single smartphone. Therefore, there is no consideration of using correlation information with another sensor at a different wearing position when multiple wearable sensors are used.In the case of permanent loss of sensor data, it is impossible to use time series information for imputation, and this technique is difficult to use in this research to reduce the number of sensors.

Meanwhile, the data imputation technique for the permanent loss of sensor data using deep learning has been investigated. Reference [10] proposed a technique to fill in missing wearable sensor data for a walking activity recognition system using the Denoising AutoEncoder (DAE) [11]. Reference [12] proposed a data impute method with generative adversarial networks (GAN) [13] for robust human activity recognition using smartphones. These studies show that sensor data imputation is effective in restoring recognition accuracy when sensor data is missing.

Therefore, we exploited the data imputation technique to reduce the number of wearable sensors for the recognition of nursery activity. Using data imputation technique, we can expect to minimize the degradation of recognition accuracy even when the number of wearable sensors is reduced. As a basic idea of this study, we initially collected activity data from nursery teachers using six wearable sensors and then created a classifier that can recognize with high accuracy using the entire data. Next, in the classification phase, we deal with some of the sensors as "missing sensors", and the missing sensor data is recovered from the available sensor data using an imputation technique. Recognition is performed using these imputed data that are virtually collected from a large number of sensors. This makes it possible to achieve high accuracy even with a small number of sensors. In this chapter, we report the recognition results both using the missing data and using the imputed data with several settings and clarify the effectiveness of the proposed imputation technique, as well as the appropriate number of wearable sensors and their positions when the imputation technique is used.

This chapter is organized as follows. In Section 3.2, we discuss related research on the number of sensors and positions, as well as imputation technique for the sensors. Section 3.3 describes the purpose of this study and the experimental procedure, and Section 3.4 describes the detailed method of the experiments carried out in this study. Section 3.5 presents the results of the experiments, and Section 3.6 discusses the results. Finally, Section 3.7 concludes the chapter.

3.2 RELATED WORK

This chapter describes existing research. First, the existing research about "Consideration of the number of sensors and their position" and then about "Imputation of missing sensor data" are illustrated. Finally, the existing study about "Imputation of permanently missing data in activity recognition" is described.

3.2.1 Consideration of the Number of Sensors and Their Position

There are some studies on the number of sensors and positions [6,7], and studies on feature values for high accuracy recognition with the smaller number of sensors [8]. In Ref. [6], sensors were mounted at 17 positions, and 10 types of human activity data, such as standing and sitting, were collected. The activities were then recognized by a Support Vector Machine (SVM). Based on the recognition accuracy, the appropriate position of the wearable accelerometer was investigated for each number of wearable accelerometers. In Ref. [7], a convolutional neural network (CNN) was constructed using the public dataset "Daily and Sports Activities" [14] to examine the appropriate position of the wearable sensor based on the recognition accuracy and to compare it with machine learning methods. Reference [8] investigated some feature values for accurate recognition even with a smaller number of sensors with a "PAMAP2" [15] public dataset.

These studies have compared the recognition accuracy with each number and position of sensors to reduce the number of sensors and find the optimum position of sensors by investigating recognition methods and feature values. However, few studies have applied imputation techniques to suppress the degradation of recognition accuracy, thereby reducing the number of sensors and placing them in optimum position.

3.2.2 Imputation of Missing Sensor Data

An imputation technique to retrieve missing accelerometer and angular velocity data on a smartphone, using time series information and correlation information between the feature values of the sensor data is proposed [9]. This study uses a DAE based on Long Short-Term Memory (LSTM) [16] to recover missing sensor data. The imputed data are classified into four positions of a smartphone and four types of activities (lying, sitting, walking, and other), 16 labels in total.

This study uses sensor data collected from a single smartphone only and did not consider using correlation information with sensors at different positions of multiple wearable sensors. Also, if sensor data are permanently missing, it does not work correctly because the method uses time series information for imputation. Therefore, the method is difficult to adopt for this study.

3.2.3 Imputation of Permanently Missing Data in Activity Recognition

Studies that apply imputation techniques to permanent missing sensor data in activity recognition include a proposed imputation technique for missing wearable sensors in a walking activity recognition system [10], an imputation method for missing smartphone sensor data using GAN [12]. Reference [10] proposed a Multi-Source Denoising AutoEncoder (MSDA) to impute missing data by building a DAE-based neural network (NN). This study classifies four types of walking activities (walking, Nordic walking, and climbing stairs up and down) and other activities from the "PAMAP2" dataset from sensors worn on the subject's arm, waist, and ankle. Then, missing each sensor data and input to the MSDA, recover sensor data to prevent degradation of recognition accuracy. Reference [12] compares the recognition accuracy of sensor data from the WISDM dataset [17] and Shoaib et al. [18] between missing data and data imputed by GAN and an average value depending on the size of the missing part.

As shown in Section 3.2.1, there are some studies to reduce the number of wearing sensors and consider the wearing position in the field of activity recognition. In addition, as mentioned above, there are some studies in the field of activity recognition that perform imputation technique for missing data. By combining these studies and treating sensors that are not used in classification phase as sensors that are missing permanently, it is expected that the degradation of recognition accuracy can be minimized and the number of using sensors can be reduced further.

GAN is expected to have higher performance to recover the missing data. However, it is known that it has very high computational complexity. DAE is already used as an imputation technique of missing sensor data in some activity recognition studies [9,10]. In this study, we use DAE as the method of missing data imputation.

3.3 PURPOSE OF THIS STUDY AND EXPERIMENTAL PROCEDURE

In this study, we aim to achieve accurate recognition with a smaller sensor using the sensor data imputation technique. Then, we clarify the appropriate number and positions of wearable sensors for activity recognition of nursery work.

First, we collected nursery activity data from a teacher who worked in a real nursery school using six wearable sensors. Then, we perform activity recognition using all the data and confirm the accuracy of the recognition. Next, we create missing data that artificially drop arbitrary numbers and positions of sensor data. Applying the imputation technique, we create imputed data that recreate the missing data using the imputation technique. Using these data, we compared the recognition accuracy.

With each number and position of missing sensor conditions, we compared the recognition accuracy when the classifier is trained with no missing data and recognized the missing data (baseline condition), when the classifier is trained with missing data and recognized the missing data (missing data condition), when the classifier is trained with imputation data and recognized the imputation data (imputation data condition). This will clarify the effectiveness of the imputation technique for nursery teacher activities and the appropriate number of sensors and wearing positions for activity recognition of nursery teacher activities.

Figure 3.1 shows the training and classification methods of the classifier in the case where the collected data has no missing data (baseline condition). Figure 3.2 shows the training and classification methods for the case where the collected data are missing (missing data condition). Figure 3.3 shows the training and classification methods of the classifier in the case where the collected data are missing and imputation to missing data (imputation data condition).

Each condition is the same from the collection of sensor data to the feature extractions, but the process after that is different. The box written as "Data Missing" in Figures 3.1–3.3 is the process of missing sensor data, and the box written as

Training and Classifying of baseline Cond.

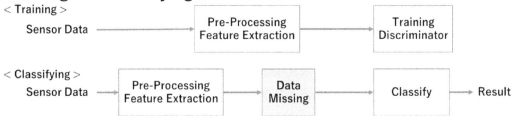

Figure 3.1 How to train classifiers and classify when there is no missing data in the collected data (baseline condition).

Training and Classifying of missing data Cond.

Figure 3.2 How to train classifiers and classify when there is missing data in the collected data (missing data condition).

Training and Classifying of imputation data Cond.

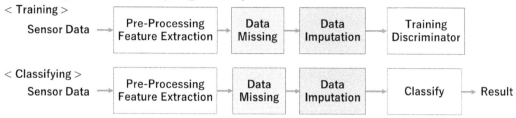

Figure 3.3 How to train classifiers and classify when collected data has missing and impute missing data (imputation data condition).

"Data Imputation" in Figure 3.3 is the process of imputation of the missing sensor data. Condition of the baseline (Figure 3.1), the classifier trains and classifies the feature data without missing data.

In the condition of missing data (Figure 3.2), the feature data that is assumed to be missing are filled with zeros. The average recognition accuracy of each missing sensor is calculated by creating a classifier for each number of missing sensors and each missing sensor position. The pattern of missing sensors is described in Section 4.4.

In the condition of the imputation data (Figure 3.3), the missing data are first created as described in Figure 3.2. The missing data are inputted into the DAE and data to impute the missing parts. Then, the imputation data is trained to the classifier and classifies the imputation data. The average recognition accuracy of each missing sensor is calculated by creating a classifier for each number of missing sensors and each missing sensor position.

For training a classifier, we can take: (1) one classifier is trained for all missing patterns, (2) multiple classifiers are trained for each missing pattern, and (3) multiple classifiers are trained for each missing number of sensors. Because the amount of training data can be used equally for each classifier, the classifiers are created for each missing pattern (the second type) for all conditions.

As described, for each number of missing sensors and wearing position, we compare the recognition accuracy when using the data with no missing sensors (baseline condition), the accuracy when using the missing data (missing data condition), and the recognition accuracy when applying the imputation technique (imputation data condition).

3.4 METHOD OF EXPERIMENT

This chapter describes the method of experiment. At first, we explain how to collect nursery teacher's activity data. Next, we discuss data pre-processing and feature extraction. Then, we describe how to missing data and impute data. Finally, we describe the condition of classification and evaluation.

3.4.1 Collection of Nursery Teacher Activity Data

In this experiment, a nursery work in a nursery school was fitted with six wearable sensors to collect data on their work both indoors and outdoors. The child was 5 years old, and activity was recorded for a total of 4 hours from 9:00 to 11:00 and from 13:00 to 15:00. Figures 3.4 and 3.5 show the appearance of the experiment.

TSND121/151 (ATR-Promotions [19]) was used to collect activity data. This sensor can collect three axis acceleration and angular velocity data at a sampling frequency of up to 1 kHz, with an acceleration range of ±16 G and an angular velocity range of ±2000 dps. In this experiment, data were collected at a sampling frequency of 100 Hz. Figure 3.6 shows the sensors used.

Figure 3.7 shows the wearing positions of the wearable sensors on the nursery teacher who participated to our experiment. After considering the wearing positions

Figure 3.4 Indoor experiment.

Figure 3.5 Outdoor experiment.

Figure 3.6 Sensors used in the experiment.

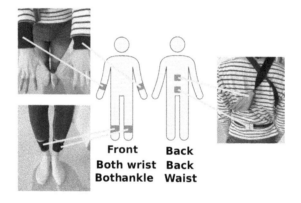

Figure 3.7 Wearing positions of the wearable sensors.

that would not interfere with the movements of the nursery teacher, the sensor was attached to six locations: the right and left wrists, ankles, waist, and back (in a tightly attached pouch).

3.4.2 Labeling

During the experiment, we shot a video, and the collected sensor data were labeled while watching the appearance of the experiment. For the activity labels, we asked an expert in nursery care to determine candidates, and we selected from that. The activities whose total length was less than 20 seconds were considered insufficient for recognition, so we were not included in the list of activities to be recognized. As a result, the activities shown in Table 3.1 were selected for recognition.

TABLE 3.1   List of Activities to Be Recognized

Label Number	Label Name	Number of Instance
0	Talking while sitting	3386
1	Moving something in/out	1114
2	Walking	1549
3	Handing something	386
4	Talking while bending forward	1167
5	Reading a comm. notebook	113
6	Talking while standing	7882
7	Talking on a phone	168
8	Looking around	178
9	Counting something	288
10	Carrying something	1864
11	Tidying something up	289
12	Toughing a child	321
13	Standing	679
14	Talking while walking	288
15	Talking while crouching down	331
16	Writing	293
17	Opening/closing a door	113
18	Picking up something	52
19	Counting children	168
20	Drawing a line by foot	215
21	Clapping their hand	317
22	Opening/closing the shelf	72
23	Sitting	349
24	Holding something	814
25	Folding a paper	360
26	Cutting a paper	219

3.4.3   Pre-Processing and Feature Extraction

We used the sliding window technique to divide the sensor data into subseries, and the feature values were calculated from the subseries. In this experiment, feature extraction was performed with a window size of $W = 640$ ms and a sliding width of $S = 50\%$. Nine features were extracted for each axis of both acceleration and angular velocity: maximum value, minimum value, mean value, median value, variance, number of zero crossings, axis correlation coefficient within sensor, energy, and peak frequency. (This data is referred to "no-missing data" in this paper.)

3.4.4   Data Missing

In this experiment, we artificially created a situation in which the number of sensors was reduced by losing the sensor data corresponding to each wearing position. The data missing in Figures 3.2 and 3.3 were performed at the feature level as follows. From the collected data (wearing six sensors), we assumed a state in which

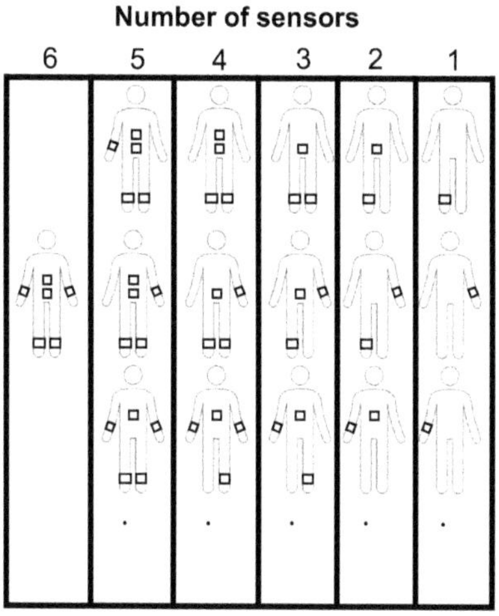

Number of sensors

Figure 3.8 The pattern of missing positions for each number of sensors.

each sensor was missing from 1 to 5 sensors, and we are missing the feature data corresponding to the missing sensor. Figure 3.8 shows the pattern of missing sensors. The number in the upper part of Figure 3.8 shows the number of sensors in operation. That is, "6" indicates that the sensor is working without missing, and "5" indicates that one of the sensors is missing. The squares on the human body diagram indicate active sensors. For example, if one sensor is missing, one of the sensors on the right wrist, left wrist, back, waist, right ankle, and left ankle can be assumed to be missing. When the right wrist sensor is missing, the feature values calculated from the sensor at the right wrist (9 types of feature values for acceleration and angular velocity, 18 in total) are missing. Missing data were defined as missing data by replacing the corresponding feature values with 0. (This data is referred to "missing data" in this paper.)

When m is the number of sensors and n is the number of missing sensors, the number of missing patterns for each missing sensor is:

$$_mC_n \tag{3.1}$$

The sensor missing pattern when n sensors are missing is:

$$_6C_n \tag{3.2}$$

due to $m = 6$ in this study. The total number of missing patterns is:

$$\sum_{n=1}^{6} {}_6C_n = 63 \tag{3.3}$$

as a result, we create the missing data corresponding to all 63 patterns.

3.4.5 Data Imputation

In this study, the state in which all sensors were worn and working was recovered using an imputation technique. Here, we impute missing data in feature values. From the preliminary experiment, we found that the raw sensor data was quite complicated to impute, and data imputation technique couldn't perform well. Thus, we apply the data imputation technique on feature values in this study.

The data imputation in Figure 3.3 was performed as follows. The missing feature data was input to DAE for imputation, and the data output from DAE will be imputed missing data that were replaced by zero, and the part of the data that was not missing is also corrected. In this study, the DAE output was used for the missing data by the method described in Section 3.4.4, and the features calculated from the sensor data before applying DAE were used for the part of the not-missing data.

The input data to the DAE was created by arranging the feature data in two dimensions. As described in Section 3.4.1, six sensors were used in this study. From each sensor, six-axis data (three acceleration axes and three angular velocity axes) can be obtained. As described in Section 3.4.3, nine feature values are calculated for each axis. As shown in Figure 3.9, the data were arranged in a 6 (sensor) × 6 (axis) in two dimensions on 9 feature channels. The DAE is trained with no missing data. The data filled with zeros for the missing features were inputted for DAE, and the imputed output was obtained. (This data is referred to "imputation data" in this paper.)

As shown in Figure 3.10, the DAE consists of three encoder layers and three decoder layers, for a total of six layers. The DAE learned with 30 epochs and 10 batch sizes and imputed missed data.

3.4.6 Classification and Evaluation

As a classification algorithm, Random Forest in Python's sklearn library was used with 100 trees and other parameters set by default. In the baseline condition

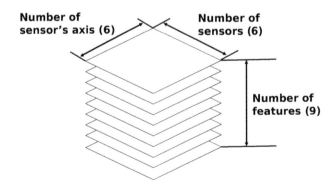

Figure 3.9 Input data structure for DAE.

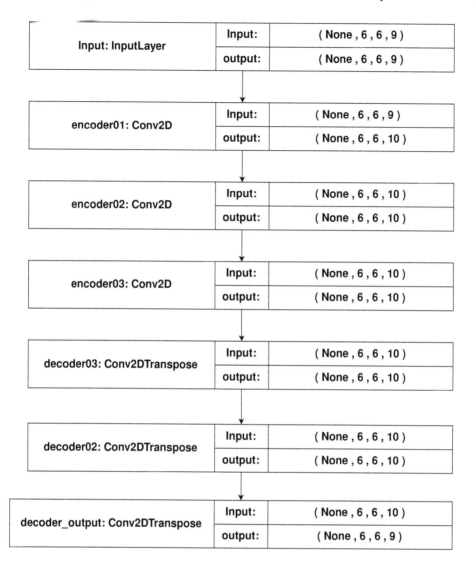

Figure 3.10 DAE models.

(Figure 3.1), no missing feature values were used to train the classifier. In the missing data condition (Figure 3.2), the classifier is trained with missing data in which the missing part was filled with zeros. In the data imputation condition (Figure 3.3), the classifier is trained with imputed data in which the missing part of the data was imputed by DAE.

As described in Chapter 3.3, classifiers were created for each missing pattern. In the missing data condition and the imputation data condition, classifiers corresponding to each missing pattern (63 patterns) were created.

We evaluated each classifier with Stratified K-Fold Cross Validation (SKFCV) at $K = 5$, which is implemented in sklearn library, with their accuracy.

3.5   RESULT OF EXPERIMENT

As a result of feature extraction, the total number of instances was 22,975. In each activity, the maximum number of instances was 7882, the minimum was 52, and the median was 317. Table 3.1 shows the number of instances for each activity.

3.5.1   Appropriate Number of Sensors When Using Imputation Techniques

Figure 3.11 shows the average recognition accuracy of the "baseline condition", "missing data condition", and "imputed data condition", for each number of missing sensors from 1 to 5, with each missing pattern as shown in Figure 3.8.

In the case of the "baseline condition", the recognition accuracy significantly decreases (from 0.05 to 0.20 per sensor) as the number of missing sensors increases. The "missing data condition" shows that the recognition accuracy decreases much less than the "baseline condition". Moreover, the "imputation data condition" significantly suppressed the decrease compared to the "baseline condition", and is also less than the "missing data condition". Comparing the "missing data condition" and the "imputation data condition", the recognition accuracy of imputed data is higher than the missing data condition, regardless of the number of missing sensors. These results indicate that the number of sensors can be reduced by using the classifier trained with missing data and/or trained with imputed data, maintaining higher recognition accuracy.

In Figure 3.11, the recognition accuracy for the "baseline condition" on 0 missing sensors is 0.877. The "missing data condition" gives the recognition accuracy as 0.869, with one missing sensor, 0.856 with two missing sensors, and 0.835 for three

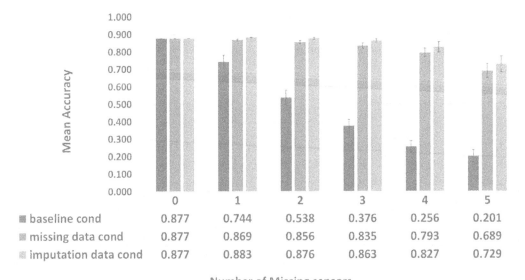

	0	1	2	3	4	5
■ baseline cond	0.877	0.744	0.538	0.376	0.256	0.201
▨ missing data cond	0.877	0.869	0.856	0.835	0.793	0.689
▨ imputation data cond	0.877	0.883	0.876	0.863	0.827	0.729

Number of Missing sensors

Figure 3.11   Average recognition accuracy (error bars: standard deviation) at baseline, missing data, and imputed data condition.

missing sensors. The "imputation data condition" rather increases the recognition accuracy to 0.883 when one sensor is missing, and gives almost the same 0.876 when two sensors are missing. Also, 0.863 even when three sensors are missing. The difference between the "baseline" of 0 missing and the "imputation" of three missing is about 0.014. This indicates that the imputation technique achieves almost the same recognition accuracy as with all six sensors, even when three sensors are missing.

3.5.2 Appropriate Position of Sensors with Imputation Techniques

We examine the effective positions of wearable sensors when three sensors of six sensors are missing, i.e., three sensors are wearing, and the imputation technique is used. Figure 3.12 shows the top five patterns of sensor positions with high recognition accuracy. The leftmost pattern in Figure 3.12 is the pattern with the highest recognition accuracy, and the rightmost pattern is the pattern with the fifth highest accuracy.

The top four patterns in Figure 3.12 are the left or right wrist, ankle, and back. The maximum recognition accuracy of the four patterns is 0.883, while the minimum is 0.871. The difference of recognition accuracy is 0.012, which is not a large difference. The fifth pattern also shows almost no differences in recognition accuracy, and is the waist instead of the back, while the top four patterns do not include the back. Therefore, the appropriate positions of three wearable sensors to recognize nursery activities are considered to be on the left or right wrist, ankle, and back.

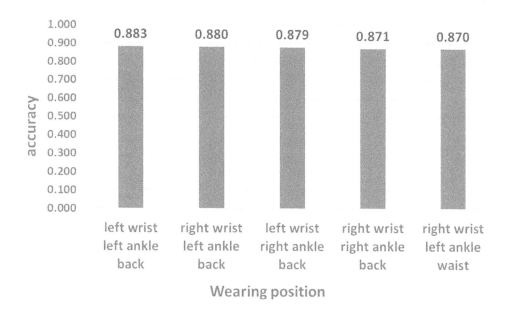

Figure 3.12 Sensor position with high recognition accuracy with three sensors using the imputation technique.

3.6 DISCUSSION

The evaluation described above has been conducted on 27 activities (Table 3.1). Here, we consider to limit the analyzing situations and the recognizing activities and to further reduce the number of sensors necessary.

Here, assuming that the purpose of nursing work analysis would be limited to "the situation of nursery teacher's direct guiding of children", we limited the activities to be subject to recognition. As same with the activities in Table 3.1, we asked an expert in nursery care to choose the activities required for the purpose. Table 3.2 shows the activities chosen. In Table 3.2, the activities marked with a "○" indicate those that must (are necessary to) be captured for the purpose. The activities marked with "△" represent the activities that are recommended to be captured. The number of sensors and the positions were examined by comparing

TABLE 3.2 List of Activities Necessary for an Analysis of Direct Guiding of Children by a Nursery Teacher (○: Necessary △: Recommended)

Label Number	Label Name	Necessary?
0	Talking while sitting	○
1	Moving something in/out	
2	Walking	△
3	Handing something	○
4	Talking while bending forward	○
5	Reading a comm. notebook	
6	Talking while standing	○
7	Talking on a phone	
8	Looking around	○
9	Counting something	
10	Carrying something	
11	Tidying something up	
12	Toughing a child	○
13	Standing	○
14	Talking while walking	○
15	Talking while crouching down	○
16	Writing	
17	Opening/closing a door	
18	Picking up something	
19	Counting children	○
20	Drawing a line by foot	
21	Clapping their hand	○
22	Opening/closing the shelf	
23	Sitting	△
24	Holding something	△
25	Folding a paper	○
26	Cutting a paper	○

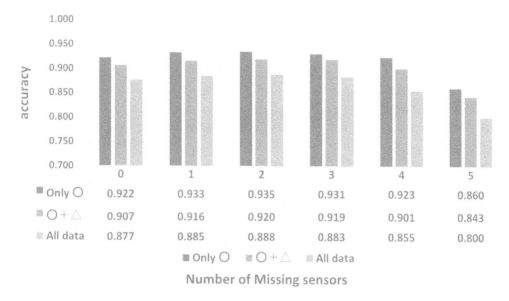

accuracy	0	1	2	3	4	5
■ Only ◯	0.922	0.933	0.935	0.931	0.923	0.860
■ ◯ + △	0.907	0.916	0.920	0.919	0.901	0.843
■ All data	0.877	0.885	0.888	0.883	0.855	0.800

■ Only ◯   ■ ◯ + △   ■ All data

Number of Missing sensors

Figure 3.13 Highest recognition accuracy for each number of missing sensors in the set of activities necessary for the analysis of "direct guiding of children."

the recognition accuracy for the ◯ activities and the ◯ + △ activities shown in Table 3.2, and all activities in Table 3.1.

In the experiment, activities are recognized in the same way as in Section 3.4. Figure 3.13 shows the maximum accuracy for each number of missing sensors in the three cases. In Figure 3.13, for any number of missing sensors, both limiting the activity set achieve higher recognition accuracy than all activity sets. In the case of ◯ activities, the recognition accuracy is 0.860 even with one sensor alone and 0.923 with two sensors. In the case of ◯+△ activities, the recognition accuracy gets 0.843 with one sensor and 0.901 with two sensors. When there are three to six sensors, the recognition accuracy is around 0.88–0.89 for all activities. This indicates that if limiting recognizing activities with the purpose of analyzing "direct guiding of children", only one or two sensors can achieve enough high accuracy, which is higher than for all activities with all sensors (0 missing).

For both the activity set of ◯ and the activity set of ◯ + △, the sensor on the left ankle gives the maximum recognition accuracy when using only one sensor. Also, when two sensors were used, the left ankle and back obtained the maximum accuracy. The results are different from the case of all activities described in Section 3.5.2. That shows that the effective sensor position is different depending on the recognizing activities, even if the imputation is performed and the activity set has inclusion relation. This needs to be verified more carefully because here we conduct only with the assumed purpose of analyzing "direct guiding of children by nursery teacher". However, they suggest that limiting the set of recognizing activities according to the purpose of an analysis can further reduce the number of required wearable sensors.

3.7   CONCLUSION

In this study, we investigated the optimum number of sensors and positions using a sensor data imputation technique to reduce the number of sensors necessary for the activity recognition of nursery work. In the experiment, we collected data on working nursery teachers and artificially created missing data in which several sensors were virtually dropped. The data were imputed using DAE.

The experimental results showed that the recognition accuracy with the imputation technique was 0.863 when the number of sensors was limited to three. Which is equivalent to the accuracy of 0.877 when all sensors (six sensors) were used. It is also found that the optimum positions of sensors are either the left or right wrist, an ankle, and back.

Furthermore, we recognized activity dataset that was limited to necessary activity in the analysis of "direct guiding of children". It was found that the accuracy was about 0.85 only with one sensor, and more than 0.90 when wearing two sensors using the imputation technique. This suggests that it is possible to further reduce the number of sensors required by limiting the set of activities to be recognized according to the content to be analyzed.

Although this study focused on the activity of nursery work, we believe that the method using imputation is effective for many sets of activities. The results of this study can be expected to ease the problems of wearing the number of sensors in activity recognition and contribute to improving its practicality.

ACKNOWLEDGEMENT

We thank all the staff of Sugiyama preschool for their cooperation in our experiments. We also thank Moena Tajiri, a student of Sugiyama Jogakuen University, for her support in experiments and help to annotate activity data. This work was partly supported by JSPS KAKENHI Grant Number 20H04175.

BIBLIOGRAPHY

[1] Ministry of Health, Labour and Welfare. "Summary of Related Situations such as Nursery Schools (April 1, 2nd Year of Reiwa)(in Japan)", https://www.mhlw.go.jp/content/11922000/000678692.pdf, Cited 19 May 2022.

[2] M. Shiomi, N. Hagita. "Social Acceptance of a Childcare Support Robot System", *24th IEEE International Symposium on Robot and Human Interactive Communication (RO-MAN)*, pp. 13–18, 2015, doi:10.1109/ROMAN.2015.7333658.

[3] B. Zhang, T. Nakamura, T. Nagai, T. Omori, M. Kaneko, H. Xia, R. Ushiogi, N. Oka, H. Lim. "Multiple Children Identification and Tracking for the Childcare Assisting System", *IEEE 2nd International Conference on Electronic Information and Communication Technology (ICEICT)*, pp. 268–273, 2019, doi: 10.1109/ICEICT.2019.8846332.

[4] A. Gupta, K. Gupta, K. Gupta, K. Gupta. "A Survey on Human Activity Recognition and Classification", *International Conference on Communication and Signal Processing*, India, pp. 0915–0919, 2020.

[5] A. D. Antar, M. Ahmed, M. A. R. Ahad. "Challenges in Sensor-Based Human Activity Recognition and a Comparative Analysis of Benchmark Datasets: A Review", *International Conference on Communication and Signal Processing*, India, pp. 134–139, 2020.

[6] C. Xia, Y. Sugiura. "Wearable Accelerometer Optimal Positions for Human Motion Recognition", *IEEE 2nd Global Conference on Life Sciences and Technologies (LifeTech)*, Kyoto, Japan, pp. 19–20, 2020.

[7] L. Tong, Q. Lin, C. Qin, L. Peng. "A Comparison of Wearable Sensor Configuration Methods for Human Activity Recognition Using CNN", *IEEE International Conference on Progress in Informatics and Computing (PIC)*, Shanghai, China, pp. 288–292, 2021.

[8] D. Wang, E. Candinegara, J. Hou, A. H. Tan, C. Miao. "Robust Human Activity Recognition Using Lesser Number of Wearable Sensors", *International Conference on Security, Pattern Analysis, and Cybernetics (SPAC)*, Shenzhen, China, pp. 290–295, 2017.

[9] Z. Huo, T. Ji, Y. Liang, S. Huang, Z. Wang, X. Qian, B. Mortazavi. "Dynimp: Dynamic Imputation for Wearable Sensing Data through Sensory and Temporal Relatedness", *IEEE International Conference on Acoustics, Speech and Signal Processing (ICASSP)*, Singapore, pp. 3988–3992, 2022.

[10] C. Xie, S. Bi, M. Dong, Y. Li. "Recovery method for missing sensor data in multi-sensor based walking recognition system", *IEEE 8th Annual International Conference on CYBER Technology in Automation, Control, and Intelligent Systems (CYBER)*, Tianjin, China, pp. 558–563, 2018.

[11] P. Vincent, H. Larochelle, Y. Bengio, P. A. Manzagol. "Extracting and Composing Robust Features with Denoising Autoencoders", *Machine Learning, Proceedings of the Twenty-Fifth International Conference (ICML)*, Helsinki, Finland, pp. 1096–1103, 2008.

[12] D. Hussein, A. Jain , G. Bhat. "Robust Human Activity Recognition Using Generative Adversarial Imputation Networks", *Design, Automation & Test in Europe Conference & Exhibition (DATE)*, pp. 84–87, 2022, doi: 10.23919/DATE54114.2022.9774548.

[13] J. Gui, Z. Sun, Y. Wen, D. Tao, J. Ye. "A Review on Generative Adversarial Networks: Algorithms, Theory, and Applications", *IEEE Transactions on Knowledge and Data Engineering*, 2021, doi:10.1109/TKDE.2021.3130191.

[14] UCI Machine Learning Repository. "Daily and Sports Activities Data Set", https://archive.ics.uci.edu/ml/datasets/daily+and+sports+activities, Cited 19 May 2022.

[15] UCI Machine Learning Repository. "PAMAP2 Physical Activity Monitoring Data Set", https://archive.ics.uci.edu/ml/datasets/pamap2+physical+activity+monitoring, Cited 19 May 2022.

[16] S. Hochreiter, J. Schmidhuber. "Long Short-Term Memory," *Neural Computation*, vol. 9, pp. 1735–1780, Nov. 1997.

[17] J. R. Kwapisz, G. M. Weiss, S. A. Moore. "Activity Recognition Using Cell Phone Accelerometers," *ACM SIGKDD Explorations Newsletter*, vol. 12, no. 2, pp. 74--82, 2011, doi: 10.1145/1964897.1964918.

[18] M. Shoaib, S. Bosch, O. D. Incel, H. Scholten, P. J. M. Havinga, "Fusion of Smartphone Motion Sensors for Physical Activity Recognition," *Sensors*, vol. 14, no. 6, pp. 10146–10176, 2014, doi: 10.3390/s140610146.

[19] ATR-Promotions. "Small Wireless Multifunction Sensor "TSND121/151" ", http://www.atr-p.com/products/TSND121_151.html, Cited 18 May 2022.

CHAPTER 4

Optimal EEG Electrode Set for Emotion Recognition from Brain Signals: An Empirical Quest

Rumman Ahmed Prodhan, Sumya Akter, and Md. Akhtaruzzaman Adnan

University of Asia Pacific

Tanmoy Sarkar Pias

Virginia Tech

4.1   INTRODUCTION

On any given day, we experience a wide range of emotions. Some are happy, some are sad, and some are in between. In other words, our emotions result from the biological stimuli triggered by certain events. For example, one might feel happy if they see someone they love. So, emotion is the mental state that arises spontaneously due to certain stimuli. It is a feeling accompanied by specific physiological changes in the body. Emotion can be positive or negative [1] and can affect our thoughts, feelings, and behavior. Emotion recognition is the only interdisciplinary field that can combine psychology, computer science, neuroscience, and cognitive science.

The ability to read and understand the emotions of others is crucial for effective communication. Interestingly, most emotions are expressed by facial expressions, which are interpreted subconsciously by the other person. According to Paul Ekman and Friesen's [2] theory of emotion, there are six basic emotions: happiness, sadness, anger, fear, surprise, and disgust. While these expressions are universal, the intensity of each emotion can vary from culture to culture. The ability to identify and understand the emotions of others is a critical social skill. It enables us to

DOI: 10.1201/9781003371540-5

navigate relationships, respond effectively to emotional cues, and empathize with others. Despite its importance, emotion recognition remains a challenging task. To better understand and recognize emotion, it is important to first have a general understanding of what emotion is. Emotion has been characterized as a complicated state of feeling that is related to thoughts, behaviors, and physiological [3] changes. It is important to note that emotion is not just one feeling but a spectrum of feelings that can range from happiness and excitement to sadness and anger. There are various techniques to perceive emotions, such as brain waves, facial expressions, body language, and tone of voice.

In this research, we have explored the effective ways to identify emotions from brain waves. EEG [4] denotes an electroencephalogram through which we can identify brain activity. We have used EEG to monitor the brain waves. It is a process by which we may examine a brain's electrical activity by putting tiny metal electrodes on the scalp. EEG has many uses [5–7]. Even some researchers are trying to decode imagined speech from EEG signals [8]. This is why we need to know how electrodes monitor brain activity [9] and provide us output as a person's mental state. So, it is necessary to know where to position the electrodes on the scalp that provide the correct emotion. Researchers have provided varied viewpoints on this and have designed several sets of electrodes to get optimal electrodes that can give a precise result. Decreasing the number of electrodes can correspondingly affect the accuracy of recognizing a pattern [10]. However, there is not any particular set of electrodes that delivers the best results. That is why it produces ambiguity among the researchers because we do not have any suitable answer concerning these electrode sets.

In this study, we experimented with different types of electrode sets found in the literature and analyzed the results based on their performance. There are many EEG datasets are available like DEAP [11], SEED [12], AMIGOS [13], MAHNOB-HCI [14], and THINGS-EEG [15]. Among these, we have used the DEAP dataset for its popularity. DEAP dataset is constructed using an EEG cap containing 32 electrodes. We have conducted our experiment according to the sequence of DEAP dataset electrode rank. The cerebrum, cerebellum, and brainstem are the three primary areas of the brain. The cerebrum is the brain's biggest part. It is split into two halves (left and right) and four lobes within each hemisphere (frontal, parietal, temporal, and occipital). The cerebrum regulates voluntary muscle movement, speech, thought, perception, reasoning, and emotion. We have also experimented with the most significant lobes to get accurate emotion.

Zhang and Chen [16] considered the brain regions for emotion creation and showed the use of just a modest number of electrodes positioned on the frontal area of the scalp.

Most of the previous research [17] utilized all 32 electrodes from the DEEP dataset. However, it is unlikely that all regions of the human brain would contribute to emotions. So, in this chapter, we quest to find the brain regions associated with emotion by identifying an optimal set of electrodes. Some recent studies have proposed different strategies to acquire optimal electrodes for emotion recognition.

They examined by applying their feature extraction approach together with chosen algorithms to acquire the best result. To the best of our knowledge, there is no comparative analysis on effective feature extraction and machine learning algorithm for getting optimal electrode set for correct identification of emotion. So, we work to fill up this research gap by proposing a comparative analysis of different electrode sets and an optimal electrode set.

The contribution in this work is to use our feature extraction approach, which is a fast Fourier transform [18] to compare the electrode set we have found from literature to acquire the optimum electrode set along with the region of the electrode on the scalp.

The rest of this chapter is organized as follows: Section 4.2 shows the previous related studies and their limitations; Section 4.3 is dedicated to the DEAP dataset; Section 4.4 demonstrates our methodology, including preprocessing, feature extraction, and CNN modeling technique; Section 4.5 demonstrates the experiment and result, and finally the study is concluded in Section 4.6.

4.2 LITERATURE REVIEW

Different types of sensors can be used for human activity recognition [19–26] as well as vehicle recognition [27]. Nowadays, smartwatches have heart rate sensors that can be used to detect human emotions [28]. However, the brain wave can be used for most appropriate mental state recognition, such as attention level [29] and emotion recognition [30]. The brain wave captured as a form of EEG data can be utilized to recognize mental diseases [31] as well as emotional states [30].

Numerous investigations for finding optimal electrode sets for detecting emotion have been conducted in recent years. Most researchers used the DEAP dataset, which is publicly available. In the DEAP dataset, emotions are classified into five labels: valence, arousal, dominance, liking, and familiarity. In this study, we have used FFT for feature extraction. Many other feature extraction techniques are used in this literature. Choosing an optimal electrode set is essential for effectively classifying emotions [32]. Table 4.1 shows the optimal electrode set according to the previous publications.

Zhang and Chen [16] found 12 electrodes as an optimal electrode set. They used Wavelet entropy and Wavelet energy as feature extraction methods. Moreover, KNN, NB, SVM, and RF are used as different modeling techniques. They ranked the optimal electrode set using mRMR, and ReliefF techniques [33]. Also, they worked on two labels of the DEAP dataset and got an average of 90% accuracy.

Joshi and Ghongade [34] got 73.37% of accuracy by using linear formulation of differential entropy, DE, and Hjorth parameters as feature extraction. Also, they used biLSTM as a modeling technique. Then They found four electrodes as an optimal electrode set. Moreover, they classified the emotion as Happy, Angry, Sad, and Clam.

Wang et al. [17] found eight electrodes for valence and ten electrodes for arousal as an optimal electrode set by using short-time Fourier transform (STFT) as a

TABLE 4.1 Literature Overview of Optimal EEG Channels Used in DEAP Dataset to Recognize Emotion

Research	Year	Feature Extraction	Modeling Technique	Number of Electrodes	Labels	Accuracy (%)
Zhang and Chen [16]	2020	Wavelet entropy, wavelet energy	KNN, NB, SVM, RF	12	Valence, arousal	90
Joshi and Ghongade [34]	2020	Linear formulation of differential entropy, DE, hjorth parmeter	biLSTM	04	Happy, angry, sad, clam	73.37
Wang et al. [17]	2019	STFT	SVM	08, 10	Valence, arousal	74.41, 73.64
Topic et al. [35]	2022	CGH	CNN, SVM	10, 10	Valence, arousal, dominance	90.76, 92.92, 92.97
Msonda et al. [36]	2021	Wavelet decomposition	AdaBoost, second order polynomial, LR, SVC, RF	08	Valence	90

feature extrusion method. Moreover, they used SVM as a modeling technique. After that, they ranked the optimal electrode set using the Normalized mutual information (NMI) connection matrix technique. Finally, they got an accuracy of 74.41% for valence and 73.64% for arousal from this optimal electrode set.

Topic et al. [35] got an accuracy of 90.76% for valence, 92.92% for arousal, and 92.97% for dominance by using computer-generated holography (CGH) [37] as a feature extraction method. Also, they used CNN and SVM as a classifier. After that, they ranked the electrode by using Relief and Neighborhood Component Analysis (NCA) method and found ten electrodes for ReliefF and ten electrodes for Neighborhood Component Analysis (NCA) as an optimal electrode set.

Lastly, using the Mean Squared Error(MSE) method, Msonda et al. [36] found eight electrodes as an optimal electrode set. They achieved 67% of accuracy by using Wavelet Decomposition as a feature extraction technique. Also, they used different modeling techniques like AdaBoost, Logistic Regression, Linear Support Vector Classifier (SVC), second-order polynomial, and Random Forest (RF).

4.3 DATASET

The DEAP dataset is multi-modal and used to assess humans' emotional states. A group consisting of 32 participants is shown 120 music videos with a one-minute length. Each participant has a .bdf file in the DEAP dataset, and they are all recorded with 48 channels at 512 Hz. Two distinct locations have been used to record this dataset. Participants 1-22's data are logged in Twente, whereas participants 23-32's are logged in Geneva. The summary of the DEAP dataset is provided in Figure 4.1.

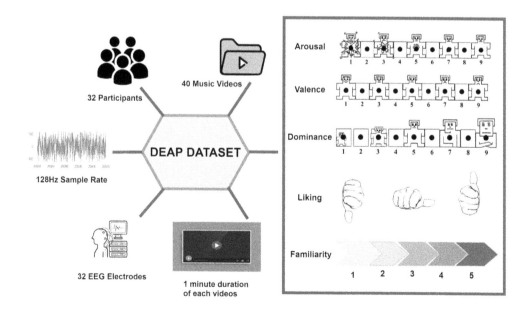

Figure 4.1 Overview of the DEAP dataset.

In the DEAP dataset, additional preprocessed files have been provided, which are down-scaled to 128 Hz. The DEAP dataset offers two down-sampled zip files. The preprocessed Python zip file, which contains 32 files in .dat format, is used for this study. A single .dat file represents a single participant. There are two arrays in each file. The data array contains 8064 data over 40 channels across 40 trials. Every trial lasts for 63 seconds. As a result, the data is $128 \times 63 = 8064$. The label array consists of four labels—valence, arousal, dominance, and liking—and 40 trials. Among the 40 channels, there are 32 EEG channels. Also, there are eight other channels.

4.4 METHODOLOGY

Figure 4.2 illustrates the workflow of finding the optimal EEG electrodes for emotion recognition. At first, the DEAP dataset is selected as the source of raw EEG data. Then different types of preprocessing were applied to remove noise and artifacts. After that, using FFT, the feature extraction is performed on the specific electrode set mentioned in the literature. All of the tests are performed on a 1D CNN to maintain the consistency of the evaluation.

Algorithm 4.1 Select optimal electrode set

Input: electrode_sets, CNN, DEAP_Preprocessed
Output: max_accuracy, best_set, electrode_accuracy
Begin
    electrode_sets = [set1, set2, set3, set4, set5, set6, set7, set8]
    electrode_accuracy = []
    max_accuracy = 0
    best_set = None
    For set in electrode_sets
        train_data_segment = DEAP_Preprocessed[set].train()
        test_data_segment = DEAP_Preprocessed[set].test()
        classifier = CNN()
        classifier.train(train_data_segment)
        accuracy = classifier.get_accuracy(test_data_segment)
        electrode_accuracy.append(accuracy)
        If accuracy >max_accuracy
            max_accuracy = accuracy
            best_set = set
        End If
    End For
    Return max_accuracy, best_set, electrode_accuracy
End

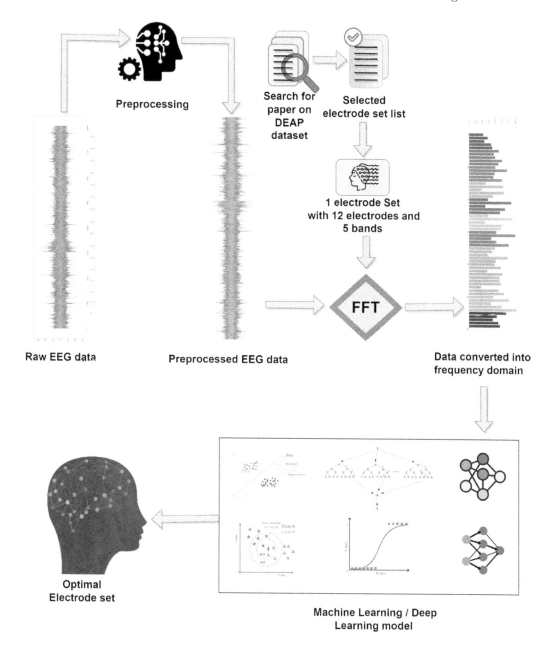

Figure 4.2 Workflow diagram for searching for optimal electrode set to recognize emotions using 1D-CNN.

4.4.1 Preprocessing

The 512 Hz EEG data has been downsized into 128 Hz. Eye artifacts are eliminated using a blind source separation technique [38]. A bandpass frequency filter with 4.0–45.0 Hz is implemented. The data is averaged following the commonly used reference. The EEG channels are rearranged following the Geneva order because the EEG data was recorded in two distinct places. Each trial's data is divided into 60 seconds and a baseline of 3 seconds. The pre-trial phase is then trimmed out. Additionally, the trials are rearranged to experiment video order instead of the presentation order.

4.4.2 Feature Extraction

Feature extraction is critical for effective learning, minimizing signal loss, overfitting, and computational overhead. In general, designing an effective feature extraction method can produce better classification performance than raw data. Frequency-domain features are used to break down signal data into the subbands represented in Figure 4.3. We have used 256 as a window size and 16 as a step size in this experiment.

Wavelet transform (WT), fast Fourier transform (FFT), equivocator methods (EM), etc., are frequently used for EEG feature extraction. Among these techniques, fast Fourier transform has proven to be the most effective according to recent publications [39]; thus, this technique is used in this study. The discrete Fourier transform or inverse discrete Fourier transform (DFT) of a sequence can be determined using the FFT technique. Most of the actual signal is composed of several frequencies. The Fourier transformation is an effective method to extract those fundamental frequencies. After decomposing the raw EEG data with a fast Fourier transform, we have found five sub-bands of brain waves. These are the theta ranges from 4 to 8 Hz, alpha ranges from 8 to 12 Hz, low beta ranges from 12 to 16 Hz, high beta ranges from 16 to 25 Hz, and gamma ranges from 25 to 45 Hz shown. An actual signal can be long, so to make it faster and more accurate, FFT is used where the whole signal is divided into multiple segments on which FT is applied to extract frequencies. The DFT can be expressed as follows:

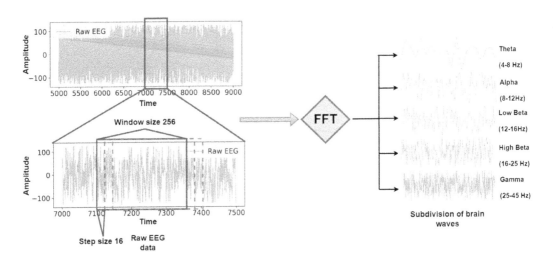

Figure 4.3 Feature extraction: FFT using sliding window and decomposing into five sub-bands.

$$x[k] = \sum_{n=0}^{N-1} x[n]e^{\frac{-j2\pi kn}{N}} \tag{4.1}$$

In this case, the domain size is n. Each value of a discrete signal $x[n]$ should be multiplied by an e-power to some function of n to determine the DFT for that signal. The results obtained for a given n should then be added together. Calculating a signal's DFT is $O(N^2)$ in complexity. As its name suggests, fast Fourier Transform (FFT) is much quicker than discrete Fourier Transform (DFT). The complexity is reduced using FFT from $O(N^2)$ to O (NlogN).

4.4.3   EEG Electrodes Set

The DEAP dataset team used an international 10–20 electrode placement system [40] to collect the EEG signals. The majority of the EEG electrodes associated with emotions are the frontal lobe denoted by the color blue; the parietal lobe is yellow; the occipital lobe is red; the temporal lobe is green; and the central areas in squares shown on the left of Figure 4.4. The letters FP, AF, F, FC, T, P, and O stand for the front polar, anterior frontal, frontal, front central, temporal, parietal, and occipital regions of the brain. An odd-number suffix represents the left hemisphere, whereas an even-number suffix represents the right hemisphere. These regions perfectly mirror how emotions are created physiologically. By changing the electrode distribution, it is possible to decrease the extracted feature dimension. The experiment can be made simpler and carried out more efficiently by reducing the complexity of the calculations. The position of the 32 EEG electrodes on the scalp is shown on the right of Figure 4.4.

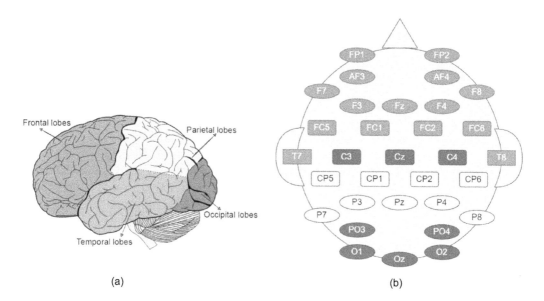

(a)   (b)

Figure 4.4   Illustration of the four main lobes of cerebral hemisphere [41] (a) and position of the 32 electrodes used in DEAP dataset on the scalp [42] (b).

TABLE 4.2   Electrode Mapping According to the Lobes of Cerebral Hemisphere

Brain Area	Number of Electrodes	Electrodes
Frontal	13	Fp1, Fp2, AF3, AF4, F7, F8, F3, Fz, F4, FC5, FC1, FC2, FC6
Parietal	9	CP5, CP1, CP2, CP6, P7, P3, Pz, P4, P8
Occipital	5	PO3, PO4, O1, Oz, O2
Temporal	2	T7, T8
Central	11	FC5, FC1, FC2, FC6, C3, Cz, C4, CP5, CP1, CP2, CP6

First, identifying the parts of the brain that are responsible for emotion recognition is essential. Table 4.2 shows the group of electrodes according to the brain areas. Those are mainly frontal, parietal, occipital, temporal, and central.

After identifying the parts of the brain that are responsible for emotion, it is important to find out the specific set of EEG electrodes. From the literature, the best work on emotion recognition, along with their optimal EEG electrode set, are extracted. All the electrodes are selected according to the valence label on the DEAP dataset to maintain consistency. The selected EEG electrode sets are shown in Table 4.3.

TABLE 4.3   Electrode Sets Proposed in Different Publications

Set No.	Research	Ranking Method	Electrodes
01	Zhang and Chen [16]	mRMR	F7, P8, O1, F8, C4, T7, PO3, Fp1, Fp2, O2, P3, Fz
02	Zhang and Chen [16]	ReliefF	PO3, F8, Fp1, P3, Fp2, F3, O2, P8, Oz, F7, T8, Cz
03	Joshi and Ghongade [34]	Prefrontal	FP1, AF3, FP2, AF4
04	Wang et al. [17]	NMI	FC1, P3, Pz, Oz, CP2, C4, F4, Fz
05	Topic et al. [35]	ReliefF	FP1, AF3, F3, F7, T7, O1, OZ, FP2, F8, P8
06	Topic et al. [35]	NCA	FP1, AF3, F7, T7, CP5, P7, FP2, AF4, FC6, T8
07	Msonda et al. [36]	Mean squared error	CP6, F3, F8, Fp1, O2, P7, T7, T8
08	-	-	Fp1, AF3, F3, F7, FC5, FC1, C3, T7, CP5, CP1, P3, P7, PO3, O1, Oz, Pz, Fp2, AF4, Fz, F4, F8, FC6, FC2, Cz, C4, T8, CP6, CP2, P4, P8, PO4, O2

4.4.4 CNN Model Structure

Numerous signal processing tasks, such as early arrhythmia identification in electrocardiogram (ECG) beats [43], emotion recognition from EEG, activity recognition job from accelerometer data, etc., have made 1D CNN increasingly popular. Thus in this study, a 1D CNN with hidden layers shown in Figure 4.5 is used to accurately recognize emotions from brain signals. The proposed model uses the residual connection, a kind of skip connection [44]. Initially, the model is changed from sequential to functional to construct the residual connection.

In Table 4.4, the proposed CNN model's summary is given. The input size of the model depends on the number of electrodes multiplied by the number of bands. Thus, the input size must be changed for each EEG electrode set. There are four convolution (Conv) layers. Each Conv layer is followed by a batch normalization and a max pooling layer. There are three dense layers followed, each followed by a dropout of 0.2 to prevent the model from overfitting the training data.

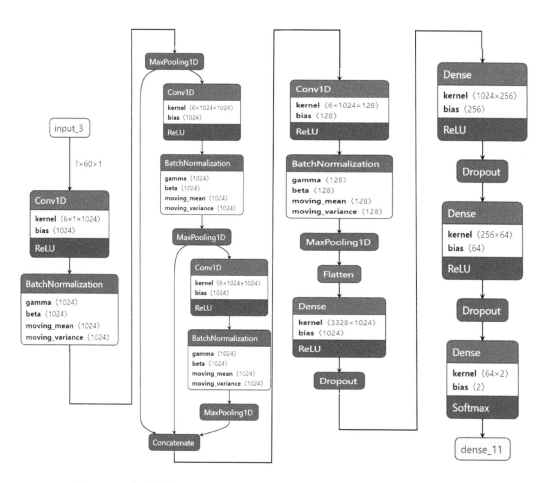

Figure 4.5　Proposed 1D-CNN model architecture with residual connection.

TABLE 4.4 Proposed CNN Model Summary

Layer (Type)	Output Shape	Param #
conv1d (Conv1D)	(None, 60, 1024)	7168
batch_normalization (BatchNormalization)	(None, 60, 1024)	4096
conv1d_1 (Conv1D)	(None, 30, 1024)	6,292,480
batch_normalization_1 (BatchNormalization)	(None, 30, 1024)	4096
conv1d_2 (Conv1D)	(None, 15, 1024)	6,292,480
batch_normalization_2 (BatchNormalization)	(None, 15, 1024)	4096
conv1d_3 (Conv1D)	(None, 52, 128)	786,560
batch_normalization_3 (BatchNormalization)	(None, 52, 128)	512
dense (Dense)	(None, 1024)	3,408,896
dense_1 (Dense)	(None, 256)	262,400
dense_2 (Dense)	(None, 64)	16,448
dense_3 (Dense)	(None, 2)	130
Total params:		17,079,362
Trainable params:		17,072,962
Non-trainable params:		6,400

4.5 EXPERIMENT AND RESULT ANALYSIS

For this study, CNN and LSTM are selected as the deep learning model, and SVM, Logistic regression, Decision Tree, Naive Bayes, and XGBoost are selected for the machine learning model. Binary class classification on valence label is used for all the EEG sets to maintain the consistency of experiments. The result of these models according to the brain area is shown in Table 4.5. Here, the 1D CNN model with residual connections clearly got the best testing accuracy than other deep learning and machine learning models.

Thus Figure 4.6 illustrates the testing accuracy of the 1D CNN model for the individual electrode sets according to the brain area. The same 1D CNN is used for all the sets. Residual connections are used to improve performance. The frontal lobe's electrode sets perform best for emotion recognition. Following that, the central lobe is the second best. The frontal lobe is more critical for recognizing emotions than other brain areas.

TABLE 4.5 Test Accuracy of Different Modeling Techniques on Electrode Sets According to the Lobes of the Cerebral Hemisphere

Brain Area	CNN (%)	LSTM (%)	SVM (%)	Logistic Regression (%)	Decision Tree (%)	Naive Bayes (%)	XGBoost (%)
Frontal	**95.81**	75.38	70.38	59.34	82.03	56.65	63.41
Parietal	**94.92**	75.28	68.81	57.75	80.26	55.03	62.6
Occipital	**90.99**	73.70	66.39	58.9	74.86	55.61	62.15
Temporal	**80.22**	67.10	58.80	56.57	68.80	54.79	58.34
Central	**95.76**	74.67	69.82	58.62	81.97	54.76	63.61

Note: The bold values indicate the best results of the proposed method.

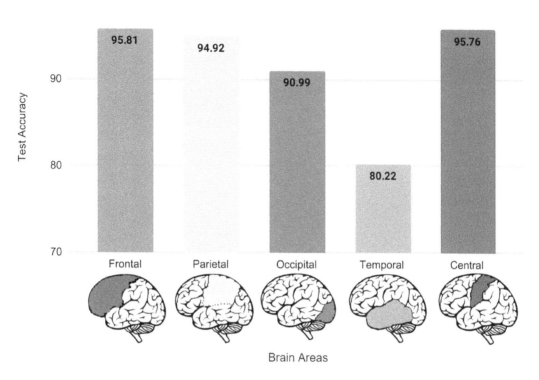

Figure 4.6 Test accuracy with CNN model of electrode sets according to the lobes of cerebral hemisphere.

In Table 4.6, different modeling techniques, including deep and machine learning models, are tested on the electrode found from Table 4.3. As before, the CNN model outperforms other deep learning and machine learning models greatly while maintaining similar leads between electrode sets. Thus, the rest of the comparison is shown using the proposed 1D CNN model.

Figure 4.7 plots the training accuracy and loss of every epoch for all the eight electrode sets in Table 4.3. For the first 20 epochs, a massive increase in accuracy and decrease in loss is observed. The improvement is moderate from 20 to 30 epochs, and the progress is meager from 30 to 50 epochs.

The table 4.7 shows the train and test accuracy for each electrode sets by the 1D CNN model. As the difference between the training and testing set is small, it indicates that the model does not face any overfitting or underfitting issue. The model achieved moderate training accuracy as the experiment was done with only 50 epochs. It is good enough for comparing the optimal EEG electrode set, but with more epochs, higher accuracy could be achieved with this proposed CNN model.

Table 4.8 shows the previous accuracy of each electrode set proposed by different publications and the accuracy achieved by the proposed 1D CNN model. All the electrode sets are run with the CNN model shown in Figure 4.5 for 50 epochs.

TABLE 4.6 Comparing Results of Different Modeling Techniques with Different Electrode Sets

Set No.	Electrodes	CNN (%)	LSTM (%)	SVM (%)	Logistic Regression (%)	Decision Tree (%)	Naive Bayes (%)	XGBoost (%)
01	F7, P8, O1, F8, C4, T7, PO3, Fp1, Fp2, O2, P3, Fz	**95.69**	75.11	71.36	59.88	81.31	55.24	63.95
02	PO3, F8, Fp1, P3, Fp2, F3, O2, P8, Oz, F7, T8, Cz	**95.6**	75.42	70.93	59.56	81.41	56.23	64.10
03	FP1, AF3, FP2, AF4	**90.21**	73.76	64.85	57.08	76.70	55.98	61.28
04	FC1, P3, Pz, Oz, CP2, C4, F4, Fz	**95.01**	75.08	69.03	58.60	81.27	55.84	63.03
05	FP1, AF3, F3, F7, T7, O1, OZ, FP2, F8, P8	**95.67**	75.08	69.96	58.86	81.79	56.32	63.25
06	FP1, AF3, F7, T7, CP5, P7, FP2, AF4, FC6, T8	**95.51**	72.37	69.64	58.21	81.29	55.65	63.03
07	CP6, F3, F8, Fp1, O2, P7, T7, T8	**93.02**	74.41	69.18	58.90	79.43	55.69	63.84
08	Fp1, AF3, F3, F7, FC5, FC1, C3, T7, CP5, CP1, P3, P7, PO3, O1, Oz, Pz, Fp2, AF4, Fz, F4, F8, FC6, FC2, Cz, C4, T8, CP6, CP2, P4, P8, PO4, O2	**97.34**	76.58	73.62	62.84	83.63	56.55	65.12

Note: The bold values indicate the best results of the proposed method.

Figure 4.7 Training accuracy and loss of 1D CNN model for two label classification on eight electrode sets.

The proposed CNN model outperforms all the previous work's accuracy. All 32 electrode set eight got the best accuracy of 97.34%, but it is not optimal. The electrode set one by Zhang et al. using mRMR is the most optimal electrode set. With only 12 electrodes, it achieved 95.69% testing accuracy with the proposed 1D CNN. Following that, the second most optimal electrode set is number five, found using ReliefF by Topic et al., which achieved 95.67% testing accuracy with the proposed model. Zhang et al.'s ReliefF and Topic et al.'s NCA are the third and fourth most optimal electrode sets with 95.60% and 95.51% testing accuracy, respectively, with the 1D CNN model.

The proposed CNN model's high gain in accuracy is based on two main technical adaptations. The first one is the use of fast Fourier transformation, which can extract frequency domain features [39]. Second, the use of residual connections to make the CNN model more robust. The residual connections are organized in a

TABLE 4.7   Train and Test Results of Electrode Sets with the Proposed CNN Model

Set No.	Electrodes	Train acc. (%)	Test acc. (%)
01	F7, P8, O1, F8, C4, T7, PO3, Fp1, Fp2, O2, P3, Fz	98.95	95.69
02	PO3, F8, Fp1, P3, Fp2, F3, O2, P8, Oz, F7, T8, Cz	98.91	95.60
03	FP1, AF3, FP2, AF4	95.56	90.21
04	FC1, P3, Pz, Oz, CP2, C4, F4, Fz	98.67	95.01
05	FP1, AF3, F3, F7, T7, O1, OZ, FP2, F8, P8	98.77	95.67
06	FP1, AF3, F7, T7, CP5, P7, FP2, AF4, FC6, T8	98.87	95.51
07	CP6, F3, F8, Fp1, O2, P7, T7, T8	96.86	93.02
08	Fp1, AF3, F3, F7, FC5, FC1, C3, T7, CP5, CP1, P3, P7, PO3, O1, Oz, Pz, Fp2, AF4, Fz, F4, F8, FC6, FC2, Cz, C4, T8, CP6, CP2, P4, P8, PO4, O2	99.36	97.34

TABLE 4.8   Comparing Previous Results of Electrode Sets with the Proposed CNN Model

Set No.	Electrodes	Previous Accuracy (%)	Our Accuracy (%)
01	F7, P8, O1, F8, C4, T7, PO3, Fp1, Fp2, O2, P3, Fz	90 [16]	**95.69**
02	PO3, F8, Fp1, P3, Fp2, F3, O2, P8, Oz, F7, T8, Cz	90 [16]	**95.60**
03	FP1, AF3, FP2, AF4	73.37 [34]	**90.21**
04	FC1, P3, Pz, Oz, CP2, C4, F4, Fz	74.41 [17]	**95.01**
05	FP1, AF3, F3, F7, T7, O1, OZ, FP2, F8, P8	90.76 [35]	**95.67**
06	FP1, AF3, F7, T7, CP5, P7, FP2, AF4, FC6, T8	90.76 [35]	**95.51**
07	CP6, F3, F8, Fp1, O2, P7, T7, T8	90 [36]	**93.02**
08	Fp1, AF3, F3, F7, FC5, FC1, C3, T7, CP5, CP1, P3, P7, PO3, O1, Oz, Pz, Fp2, AF4, Fz, F4, F8, FC6, FC2, Cz, C4, T8, CP6, CP2, P4, P8, PO4, O2	75.16 [17]	**97.34**

Note: The bold values indicate the best results of the proposed method.

way so that the dense layer (mainly responsible for classification with given deep features) can have direct access to all convolutional layers' output for decision-making.

This study also tries to determine the correlation between the number of electrodes and testing accuracy. Here, electrode set 2, 6, and 7 are not considered for this correlation experiment as with the same number of electrodes, there are better sets that got better accuracy. It is observed that there is a clear correlation between the number of electrodes and testing accuracy. Increasing the number of electrodes from 4 to 10 greatly increases the testing accuracy. However, from the above ten electrodes, the improvement of testing accuracy is not so much. So, it can be stated that the optimal number of electrodes for emotion recognition is 10.

While aiming to find the optimal EEG electrode sets, the proposed model achieved a notable gain in accuracy compared to previous works shown in Table 4.8. This gain in accuracy is mainly caused by using FFT as preprocessing technique, 1D CNN for deep feature extraction, and dense net for classification. Also, using the residual connection is designed to enable the model to directly access all the previous layer's extracted deep features for better classification by the dense net. In Figure 4.8 the proposed CNN model's train and validation accuracy is plotted on the optimal electrode set to prove further that the model does not have any overfitting or underfitting issues.

Topic et al. [35] use a similar strategy to list the electrode sets from the literature. However, our process of selecting the most effective electrode set from the list is very different from their approach. Their method of comparison among different electrode sets is questionable as their approach is not method-agnostic. They compared their electrode sets with others' accuracy, where others have used different approaches for recognition which is not fair as the accuracy difference might be the outcome of the difference in recognition method. For example, Topic et al. [35] used CNN + SVM on N-HOLO-FM of ten electrodes and got accuracy (%) Valance: 81.88, Arousal: 82.45, and Dominance: 88.35, and one of other study used kNN on Entropy and energy of ten other electrodes and got accuracy Valance: 86.75 and Arousal: 84.05. So, getting different performances might be the result of using different preprocessing techniques and utilizing different machine learning models. So, this method of selecting an optimal electrode set is not practical as there are different factors in play.

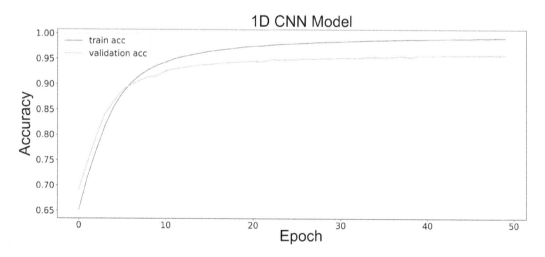

Figure 4.8 Proposed CNN model train vs validation accuracy graph on the optimal electrode set.

Our study is completely free from this kind of limitation and is method-agnostic. We tested all of the reported performances from previous publications on the same ground (FFT + CNN) to make a fair comparison, and we believe it is a justified approach for selecting optimal electrodes. So, the main difference from their study is that our method is method-agnostic, and theirs is not.

4.6 CONCLUSION

This study demonstrates that the frontal lobe is the most important brain-region for emotions. Then the evaluation of different electrode sets created by other researchers is conducted. Deep learning models like CNN, LSTM, and machine learning models like SVM, Logistic regression, Decision tree, Naive Bayes, and XGboot are used on each electrode set to evaluate their performance.

This study mainly focuses on finding the optimal electrode set using the same testing environment (preprocessing technique, ML model, and performance metrics). Moreover, from a variety of preprocessing techniques from the literature and ML models from experiment Tables 4.5 and 4.6, the most promising one based on performance is selected. So, FFT is selected as a preprocessing technique, 1D CNN for deep feature extraction, and dense net for classification. Based on the experiments, this combination demonstrates the state-of-the-art performance and the reason behind our adaptation. One of the technical contributions of this study is the effective design of residual connections. The residual connection is designed to enable the model to directly access all the previous layer's extracted deep features for better classification by the dense net. After that, the experiments are conducted based on this selected test environment (preprocessing and recognition model) which is the sole purpose of this study. In summary, the main reason for the proposed CNN model's accuracy gain over all other studies is the effective EEG recognition framework.

As there is only one dataset, the DEAP dataset is selected, a well-recognized benchmark dataset, because this is the most adapted dataset (based on the citation on Google scholar). After studying the data collection method of the DEAP dataset, it was found to be unquestionably good. So, it could be stated that the selected optimal electrode set would perform similarly to other benchmark datasets. Though using multiple datasets would make the claim stronger, however, finding the same set of electrodes is very difficult over multiple datasets as the different datasets use different kinds of EEG devices to collect brain signals, which would lead to additional complexity. As this study aims to search and find an optimal electrode set, using only one dataset would make this study simple and easily understandable.

The valence label of the DEAP dataset is selected for all the experiments to maintain consistency. The 32 electrode set got the best testing accuracy of 97.34%. However, the most optimal EEG electrode set is the one proposed by Zhang et al. with 12 electrodes using mRMR, which achieved 95.69%. Those 12 electrodes are F7, P8, O1, F8, C4, T7, PO3, Fp1, Fp2, O2, P3, Fz. Also, the optimal number of electrodes is 10. Nevertheless, there could be other electrode sets that have not yet been experimented with by any authors, thus not included in this study. Also, different electrodes are responsible for different labels of emotions like happy, sad, and angry. In the future, we want to find the correlation between different labels of emotion with single electrode.

BIBLIOGRAPHY

[1] Prete, G., Croce, P., Zappasodi, F., Tommasi, L., & Capotosto, P. (2022). Exploring brain activity for positive and negative emotions by means of EEG microstates. *Scientific Reports*, 12(1). https://doi.org/10.1038/s41598-022-07403-0.

[2] Ekman, P. & Friesen, W. V. (1971). Constants Across Cultures in the Face and Emotion. *Journal of Personality and Social Psychology*, 17(2) , 124-129.

[3] Dod, J. (1999). Effective substances. In S. Gangolli (ed.), *The Dictionary of Substances and Their Effects*. Royal Society of Chemistry, Cambridge. Available via DIALOG, http://www.rsc.org/dose/title.

[4] Kumar, J. S., & Bhuvaneswari, P. (2012). Analysis of Electroencephalography (EEG) Signals and Its Categorization–A Study. *Procedia Engineering*, 38, 2525–2536. https://doi.org/10.1016/j.proeng.2012.06.298.

[5] Krugliak, A., & Clarke, A. (2022). Towards real-world neuroscience using mobile EEG and augmented reality. *Scientific Reports*, 12(1). https://doi.org/10.1038/s41598-022-06296-3.

[6] Hassan, R., Hasan, S., Hasan, M. J., Jamader, M. R., Eisenberg, D., & Pias, T. (2020). Human Attention Recognition with Machine Learning from Brain-EEG Signals. *2020 IEEE 2nd Eurasia Conference on Biomedical Engineering, Healthcare and Sustainability (ECBIOS)*. https://doi.org/10.1109/ecbios50299.2020.9203672.

[7] Pirrone, D., Weitschek, E., di Paolo, P., de Salvo, S., & de Cola, M. C. (2022). EEG Signal Processing and Supervised Machine Learning to Early Diagnose Alzheimer's Disease. *Applied Sciences*, 12(11), 5413. https://doi.org/10.3390/app12115413.

[8] Proix, T., Delgado Saa, J., Christen, A., Martin, S., Pasley, B. N., Knight, R. T., Tian, X., Poeppel, D., Doyle, W. K., Devinsky, O., Arnal, L. H., Mégevand, P., & Giraud, A. L. (2022). Imagined speech can be decoded from low- and cross-frequency intracranial EEG features. *Nature Communications*, 13(1). https://doi.org/10.1038/s41467-021-27725-3.

[9] Pascual-Marqui, R. D. (2002). Standardized low-resolution brain electromagnetic tomography (sLORETA): technical details. *Methods Find Exp Clin Pharmacol*, 24(Suppl D), 5-12.

[10] Tacke, M., Janson, K., Vill, K., Heinen, F., Gerstl, L., Reiter, K., & Borggraefe, I. (2022). Effects of a reduction of the number of electrodes in the EEG montage on the number of identified seizure patterns. *Scientific Reports*, 12(1). https://doi.org/10.1038/s41598-022-08628-9.

[11] Koelstra, S., Muhl, C., Soleymani, M., Jong-Seok Lee, Yazdani, A., Ebrahimi, T., Pun, T., Nijholt, A., & Patras, I. (2012). DEAP: A Database for Emotion Analysis; Using Physiological Signals. *IEEE Transactions on Affective Computing*, 3(1), 18–31. https://doi.org/10.1109/t-affc.2011.15.

[12] Lu, B.-L. (n.d.). SEED Dataset. Https://Bcmi.Sjtu.Edu.Cn/. Retrieved July 31, 2022, from https://bcmi.sjtu.edu.cn/home/seed/index.html

[13] Miranda-Correa, J. A., Abadi, M. K., Sebe, N., & Patras, I. (2021). AMIGOS: A Dataset for Affect, Personality and Mood Research on Individuals and Groups. *IEEE Transactions on Affective Computing*, 12(2), 479–493. https://doi.org/10.1109/taffc. 2018.2884461.

[14] Soleymani, M., Lichtenauer, J., Pun, T., & Pantic, M. (2012). A Multimodal Database for Affect Recognition and Implicit Tagging. *IEEE Transactions on Affective Computing*, 3(1), 42–55. https://doi.org/10.1109/t-affc.2011.25.

[15] Grootswagers, T., Zhou, I., Robinson, A. K., Hebart, M. N., & Carlson, T. A. (2022). Human EEG recordings for 1,854 concepts presented in rapid serial visual presentation streams. *Scientific Data*, 9(1). https://doi.org/10.1038/s41597-021-01102-7.

[16] Zhang, J., & Chen, P. (2020). Selection of Optimal EEG Electrodes for Human Emotion Recognition. *IFAC-Papers on Line*, 53(2), 10229–10235. https://doi.org/10.1016/j.ifacol.2020.12.2753.

[17] Wang, Z. M., Hu, S. Y., & Song, H. (2019). Channel Selection Method for EEG Emotion Recognition Using Normalized Mutual Information. *IEEE Access*, 7, 143303–143311. https://doi.org/10.1109/access.2019.2944273.

[18] Franchetti, F., & Puschel, M. (2011). FFT (Fast Fourier Transform). *Encyclopedia of Parallel Computing*, 658–671. https://doi.org/10.1007/978-0-387-09766-4_243.

[19] Ahmed, M., Das Antar, A., & Ahad, M. A. R. (2019, May). An Approach to Classify Human Activities in Real-time from Smartphone Sensor Data. *2019 Joint 8th International Conference on Informatics, Electronics & Vision (ICIEV) and 2019 3rd International Conference on Imaging, Vision & Pattern Recognition (IcIVPR)*. https://doi.org/10.1109/iciev.2019.8858582.

[20] Hossain, T., & Inoue, S. (2019, May). A Comparative Study on Missing Data Handling Using Machine Learning for Human Activity Recognition. *2019 Joint 8th International Conference on Informatics, Electronics & Vision (ICIEV) and 2019 3rd International Conference on Imaging, Vision & Pattern Recognition (IcIVPR)*. https://doi.org/10.1109/iciev.2019.8858520.

[21] Alrazzak, U., & Alhalabi, B. (2019, May). A Survey on Human Activity Recognition Using Accelerometer Sensor. *2019 Joint 8th International Conference on Informatics, Electronics & Vision (ICIEV) and 2019 3rd International Conference on Imaging, Vision & Pattern Recognition (IcIVPR)*. https://doi.org/10.1109/iciev.2019.8858578.

[22] Islam, M. S., Hossain, T., Ahad, M. A. R., & Inoue, S. (2020, December 24). Exploring Human Activities Using eSense Earable Device. *Smart Innovation, Systems and Technologies*, 169–185. https://doi.org/10.1007/978-981-15-8944-7_11.

[23] Faiz, F., Ideno, Y., Iwasaki, H., Muroi, Y., & Inoue, S. (2020, December 24). Multilabel Classification of Nursing Activities in a Realistic Scenario. *Smart Innovation, Systems and Technologies*, 269–288. https://doi.org/10.1007/978-981-15-8944-7_17.

[24] Gjoreski, H., Kiprijanovska, I., Stankoski, S., Kalabakov, S., Broulidakis, J., Nduka, C., & Gjoreski, M. (2020, December 24). Head-AR: Human Activity Recognition with Head-Mounted IMU Using Weighted Ensemble Learning. *Smart Innovation, Systems and Technologies*, 153–167. https://doi.org/10.1007/978-981-15-8944-7_10.

[25] Pias, T. S., Eisenberg, D., & Fresneda Fernandez, J. (2022, June 10). Accuracy Improvement of Vehicle Recognition by Using Smart Device Sensors. *Sensors*, 22(12), 4397. https://doi.org/10.3390/s22124397.

[26] Pias, T. S., Kabir, R., Eisenberg, D., Ahmed, N., & Islam, M. R. (2019, October). Gender Recognition by Monitoring Walking Patterns via Smartwatch Sensors. *2019 IEEE Eurasia Conference on IOT, Communication and Engineering (ECICE)*. https://doi.org/10.1109/ecice47484.2019.8942670.

[27] Pias, T. S., Eisenberg, D., & Islam, M. A. (2019, October). Vehicle Recognition Via Sensor Data From Smart Devices. *2019 IEEE Eurasia Conference on IOT, Communication and Engineering (ECICE)*. https://doi.org/10.1109/ecice47484.2019.8942799.

[28] Takeshita, R., Shoji, A., Hossain, T., Yokokubo, A., & Lopez, G. (2021, November 17). Emotion Recognition from Heart Rate Variability Data of Smartwatch While Watching a Video. *2021 Thirteenth International Conference on Mobile Computing and Ubiquitous Network (ICMU)*. https://doi.org/10.23919/icmu50196.2021.9638844.

[29] Takeshita, R., Shoji, A., Hossain, T., Yokokubo, A., & Lopez, G. (2021, November 17). Emotion Recognition from Heart Rate Variability Data of Smartwatch While Watching a Video. *2021 Thirteenth International Conference on Mobile Computing and Ubiquitous Network (ICMU)*. https://doi.org/10.23919/icmu50196.2021.9638844.

[30] Hasan, M., Rokhshana-Nishat-Anzum, Yasmin, S., & Pias, T. S. (2021, August 16). Fine-Grained Emotion Recognition from EEG Signal Using Fast Fourier Transformation and CNN. *2021 Joint 10th International Conference on Informatics, Electronics & Vision (ICIEV) and 2021 5th International Conference on Imaging, Vision & Pattern Recognition (IcIVPR)*. https://doi.org/10.1109/icievicivpr52578.2021.9564204.

[31] Matin, A., Bhuiyan, R. A., Shafi, S. R., Kundu, A. K., & Islam, M. U. (2019, May). A Hybrid Scheme Using PCA and ICA Based Statistical Feature for Epileptic Seizure Recognition from EEG Signal. *2019 Joint 8th International Conference on Informatics, Electronics & Vision (ICIEV) and 2019 3rd International Conference on Imaging, Vision & Pattern Recognition (IcIVPR)*. https://doi.org/10.1109/iciev.2019.8858573.

[32] Moctezuma, L. A., Abe, T., & Molinas, M. (2022). Two-dimensional CNN-based distinction of human emotions from EEG channels selected by multi-objective evolutionary algorithm. *Scientific Reports*, 12(1). https://doi.org/10.1038/s41598-022-07517-5.

[33] Mazumder, A., Ghosh, P., Khasnobish, A., Bhattacharyya, S., & Tibarewala, D. N. (2015). Selection of Relevant Features from Cognitive EEG Signals Using ReliefF and MRMR Algorithm. In S. Gupta, S. Bag, K. Ganguly, I. Sarkar, & P. Biswas (eds.), *Advancements of Medical Electronics* (pp. 125–136). Springer, New Delhi.

[34] Joshi, V. M., & Ghongade, R. B. (2020). Optimal Number of Electrode Selection for EEG Based Emotion Recognition using Linear Formulation of Differential Entropy. *Biomedical and Pharmacology Journal*, 13(02), 645–653. https://doi.org/10.13005/bpj/1928.

[35] Topic, A., Russo, M., Stella, M., & Saric, M. (2022). Emotion Recognition Using a Reduced Set of EEG Channels Based on Holographic Feature Maps. *Sensors*, 22(9), 3248. https://doi.org/10.3390/s22093248.

[36] Msonda, J. R., He, Z., & Lu, C. (2021). Feature Reconstruction Based Channel Selection for Emotion Recognition Using EEG. *2021 IEEE Signal Processing in Medicine and Biology Symposium (SPMB)*. https://doi.org/10.1109/spmb52430.2021.9672258.

[37] Jaroszewicz, L. R., Cyran, K. A., & Podeszwa, T. (2000). Optimized CGH-based pattern recognizer. *Optica Applicata*, 30(2/3), 317-334.

[38] Belouchrani, A., Abed-Meraim, K., Cardoso, J. F., & Moulines, E. (1997). A blind source separation technique using second-order statistics. *IEEE Transactions on Signal Processing*, 45(2), 434-444.

[39] Hasan, M., Rokhshana-Nishat-Anzum, Yasmin, S., & Pias, T. S. (2021). Fine-Grained Emotion Recognition from EEG Signal Using Fast Fourier Transformation and CNN. *2021 Joint 10th International Conference on Informatics, Electronics & Vision (ICIEV) and 2021 5th International Conference on Imaging, Vision & Pattern Recognition (icIVPR)*. https://doi.org/10.1109/icievicivpr52578.2021.9564204.

[40] Homan, R. W., Herman, J., & Purdy, P. (1987). Cerebral location of international 10–20 system electrode placement. *Electroencephalography and Clinical Neurophysiology*, 66(4), 376–382.

[41] Lobes of the brain. (2022). [Illustration]. Queensland Brain Institute. https://qbi.uq. edu.au/brain/brain-anatomy/lobes-brain

[42] Houssein, E. H., Hammad, A., & Ali, A. A. (2022). Human emotion recognition from EEG-based brain–computer interface using machine learning: a comprehensive review. *Neural Computing and Applications*, 34(15), 12527–12557. https://doi.org/10.1007/s00521-022-07292-4.

[43] Apu, M. R. H., Akter, F., Lubna, M. F. A., Helaly, T., & Pias, T. S. (2021). ECG Arrhythmia Classification Using 1D CNN Leveraging the Resampling Technique and Gaussian Mixture Model. *2021 Joint 10th International Conference on Informatics, Electronics & Vision (ICIEV) and 2021 5th International Conference on Imaging, Vision & Pattern Recognition (icIVPR)*. https://doi.org/10.1109/icievicivpr52578.2021.9564201.

[44] Wu, D., Wang, Y., Xia, S. T., Bailey, J., & Ma, X. (2020). Skip connections matter: On the transferability of adversarial examples generated with resnets. arXiv preprint arXiv:2002.05990.

CHAPTER 5

Translation-Delay-Aware Emotional Avatar System for Online Communication Support

Tomoya Suzuki, Akihito Taya, Yoshito Tobe, and Guillaume Lopez
Aoyama Gakuin University

5.1 INTRODUCTION

The development of the Internet has expanded and changed many of our daily activities, such as online shopping, call centers, and audio and video content via the Web and social networking services (SNS). In particular, online communication and conference have been around for some time, and the COVID-19 pandemic accelerated its global spread.

Online communication has the advantage of connecting the entire world, and information technology facilitates its continuous development. On one hand, machine translation software is one such system. Many machine translation systems are used, such as Google Translate [1], which can automatically translate websites in a browser and SNS messages. Besides, automatic translation subtitles [2] during streaming utilizing Application Programming Interfaces (APIs) [3] are also in use. Thus, machine translation systems are being used increasingly to break down language barriers and communicate online with foreigners. On the other hand, the quality of text-to-speech software also improved a lot. It reads aloud input texts using machine voices. Many are used in search systems such as Siri [4] and Google [5]. Recently, it has become possible to produce a voice that is so close to an actual human voice that it is hard to recognize it as a machine voice. This technology is used not only for interpersonal communication but also for announcements at train stations and for music. Furthermore, it is also possible to control emotions by

DOI: 10.1201/9781003371540-6

adjusting the volume of the voice, thus making it possible to produce a voice that is appropriate to the situation. Many foreign languages, including Japanese, English, and Chinese, are supported, making them suitable for a wide range of users.

With the development of various interpersonal communication technologies, there are growing expectations for the use of virtual avatars to substitute for the appearance of a speaker. A virtual avatar is a 3D model that performs speech and actions in place of a speaker. Recently, they have been used for streaming services [6] and guiding information on electronic bulletin boards [7]. The use of avatars allows for communication that differs from real appearance. Besides, since facial expressions can be adjusted in advance, smooth communication that reduces discomfort for the other party can be achieved [6]. In real-time use, it is also possible to express emotions based on the speaker's facial expressions and speech characteristics obtained from the camera and microphone [8].

However, there are several challenges when using avatars for communication, both domestically and internationally. One is that most current avatar facial expression creation methods involve tracking. Conventional avatar facial expression creation based on tracking and recognition of a speaker's face can only express facial expressions estimated in real-time from the speaker's face. Therefore, it is not possible to transfer the emotional expressions on the speaker's face to other elements such as voice and gestures. Trisha et al. [9] estimate emotion using not only facial expressions but also speech and text for a total of three factors. However, the accuracy is insufficient for multi-class classifications.

Furthermore, the automatic translation has a delay time. In this project, automatic translation is implemented for both domestic and international conversations. Niehues et al. [10] have created a low-latency neural speech translation system, but it has yet to be completely eliminated. These problems interfere with real-time conversation. Most current avatar-based communication systems use only visual and audio data to estimate emotions. In addition to the small number of emotion types that can be reflected in speech, many of them use monotone voice to account for the delay when real-time reflection is considered.

To solve these issues, we propose a system named speaker's face emotion to avatar's face and voice expression (F2FVep), which uses an emotion estimation method to adjust the estimated emotions and reflect them timely in the avatar's facial expressions. In a former study, we proposed VFep [8]. This communication tool uses the voice input from the microphone to generate emotion labels and generate facial expressions of 3D models suitable for the emotion labels. We extended VFep to add an automatic translation function, but the delay of the translation output became a problem. F2FVep considers the delay time before the avatar reads out the translated speaker's speech and appropriately reflects the speaker's emotion on the avatar's face by shifting the timing of emotion reflection.

The rest of this chapter is organized as follows. In Section 5.2, we explain the previous work related to this study. In Section 5.3, we show the design and implementation of F2FVep, respectively. In Section 5.4, we present the preliminary experiment and evaluation results of F2FVep.

5.2   RELATED WORKS

In this section, we describe the related work to this study. The work is divided into three sections related to this work: emotion recognition in communications, automatic translation systems, and dialogue systems.

5.2.1   Emotion Recognition in Communications

Internet communication often involves text-based conversations or voice-only conversations. Besides, even if a camera or other devices can be used to recognize facial expressions in a conversation. However, the person is not able to see all of the other person's appearance. These problems can cause discrepancies in awareness in conversation. Therefore, the consideration of emotion estimation is important for smooth communication through the Internet. In psychology, basic emotions have been identified, and several models of expression have been proposed [11,12]. Ekman [11] conducted many studies on category perception and proposed six basic emotions: joy, sadness, anger, fear, disgust, and surprise. Russell [12] presented emotional words to subjects and evaluated their reactions, revealing a circular structure with two dimensions: valence and arousal. Since then, emotion modeling has attracted researchers' attention [13] and has been continuously improved [14,15].

Based on this definition of emotion, models that can estimate human emotion from various information ranging from each biological information to textual information and reflect emotion in various applications have been studied. In the field of speech, there is a deep framework for real-time speech-driven 3D facial animation from raw speech signals [16]. It uses deep neural network (DNN) and convolutional neural network (CNN) to reflect the speaker's gender, accent, and language. For facial expressions, the Face API [17], an API provided by Microsoft, can detect facial expressions based on advanced facial recognition functions and also detect emotions based on functions that can analyze and detect facial feature point extraction. In the area of text, since the advent of Transformer [24], there has been an increase in research on emotion estimation from many texts. Varsha et al. have conducted emotion detection in sentences using bidirectional encoder representations from transformers (BERT) and efficiently learning an encoder that classifies token replacements accurately (ELECTRA)-based knowledge-embedding attention, which can estimate fine-grained emotions and from input text [19]. These studies also use emotion estimation by extracting a part of the information in various conversations, but they do not provide accurate emotion estimation. Human emotions are not the same and are a mixture of many emotions.

5.2.2   Automatic Translation Systems

Automatic translation is important for facilitating dialogue both domestically and internationally. Many machine translation tools have been developed to facilitate translation and understanding of other languages, including Google's machine translation technology [1], DeepL translate [20], and MiraiTranslate [21].

Roseline et al. have created an Android-based language translation application that can translate from English to other languages and vice versa [22]. Santosa et al. proposed an architecture for a speech translation system that uses an English-Bahasa Indonesian speech translation system based on "badan pengkajian dan penerapan teknologi" (BPPT)'s engineering capabilities and results and uses separate mobile terminals for each language in conversations on Android-based cell phones [23].

However, when such research uses mobile devices such as Android and communicates only through text and voice translation, there is a delay before the message is conveyed to the other party. This delay can make it difficult to accurately convey emotions.

5.2.3 Dialogue Systems

Dialogue systems are indispensable for many users, especially after the widespread use of telephones. With the spread of smartphones, dialogue systems can take the form not only of voice-based systems but also of systems that allow users to interact with each other while listening to facial expressions. Many text-based dialogue systems have also been developed, and they take the form of SNS. Many systems have been developed that use 3D avatars and robots in addition to people interacting with each other. At train stations and public facilities, 3D avatars are installed on electronic billboards, allowing users to listen to the information in a text-based interactive format. In the field of robotics, many humanoid robots are enriching communication with humans. Wan et al. developed a new model of a chat robot with interaction through facial expressions [24]. Unlike conventional voice assistants, it interacts with the user using specific role-play. Sakatani et al. designed and implemented a novel telecommunication system for interpersonal interaction, avatar-mediated communication (AMC) system [25]. AMC system is a system that allows a human user to enjoy a conversation through a software agent without directly interacting with a conversational partner. Using this system, we are examining how it contributes to the user's conversational experience and interpersonal relationship building.

In such research, the use of avatars and chatting with them has the problem of not taking emotions into account. 3D avatars can be used to present adjusted emotions, and taking emotions into account allows for smooth communication.

5.3 TRANSLATION-DELAY-AWARE EMOTION REFLECTION

5.3.1 Features of F2FVep and Comparison with Other Systems

This section describes the details of the proposed system and its functionality. There are many different types of dialogue systems. They range from voice translation to text translation, from image-based chatbots to facial expressions on avatars, and more. We compare the functions and target situations of our system and existing studies. The results are listed in Table 5.1.

TABLE 5.1 Comparison with Related Work

	F2FVep	VFep [8]	Midoriko Chatbot [24]	AMC System [25]	Emotion Reflection System [16]
Dialogue	Virtual voice	Voice	Text	Virtual voice	Voice
Real time	✓	✓	✓	✓	✓
Facial emotion recognition	✓	-	-	-	-
Voice emotion recognition	-	✓	-	-	✓
Text emotion recognition	-	-	✓	-	-
Emotion control of Avatar's face	✓	✓	✓	-	✓
Emotion control of Avatar's voice	✓	-	-	-	-
Auto translation	✓	-	-	✓	-

F2FVep acquires voice from a microphone, so it can use not only text-based speech sentences but also voice features. The spoken voice is recognized by the system and then translated to other languages. Furthermore, by using a camera, it is possible to utilize deep learning to estimate the speaker's emotions. Therefore, it is different from many chatbots in existing work. F2FVep can express intended emotions by using translated read-aloud voice that can reflect emotion rather than text-based dialogue. Besides, the estimated emotions are also reflected on the face of the avatar.

5.3.2 Modules of Processing Emotion Estimation and Reflection

F2FVep consists of the following four modules: (1) a speech recognition module (SRM), (2) an emotion estimation module (EEM), (3) a conversational text translation module (CTTM), and (4) a 3D avatar reading module (ARM). The speech input from the microphone is recognized as the speaker's speech sentences using existing speech recognition APIs. Images of the speaker's face from the web camera are also used to estimate the speaker's emotions based on deep learning. F2FVep reads out translated sentences from the speaker's speech using a combination of a 3D avatar and text-to-speech software. However,since translation usually takes time, the timing of reading aloud the translated sentence is delayed compared to the original speech. Therefore, the estimated speaker's emotion should not be reflected in the 3D avatar immediately. We will solve this problem by preserving emotion and delay-aware synchronization. Emotions are stored at the time of microphone input

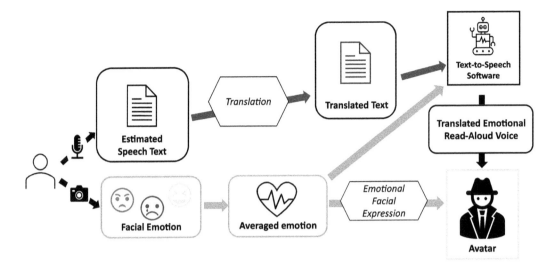

Figure 5.1 Schematic diagram of F2FVep overall process flow. Using cameras, the system extracts the speaker's emotions from image data and then reflects recognized emotions in the avatar. The system acquires translated sentences from the acquired text data and uses text-to-speech software to make the avatar speak the translated read-aloud.

and are delayed and reflected in the 3D avatar to convey the emotions. Figure 5.1 shows the overall process flow. Following are the details of F2FVep's four modules.

1. SRM uses existing speech recognition APIs. The recognized speech sentences are saved in a log file and used for translation in CTTM.

2. EEM estimates emotions from various modalities. The results are reflected in text-to-speech software and the avatar's facial expressions and are used to express emotions during the read-aloud of the avatar.

3. CTTM translates speech sentences recognized and stored by SRM and passes the translated sentences to ARM for activation. CTTM uses an existing translation system.

4. ARM uses a text-to-speech system to create a reading voice based on the translated text passed from the CTTM. The speech creation system will use the existing text-to-speech software. The created speech is used to perform the reading operation on the avatar. At this time, the avatar's facial expressions and the reading voice reflect the estimated emotions.

Since each module must run in parallel, each module is implemented as an independent program. Each module is implemented based on C# to combine the Unity implementation for the use of Avatar. We implemented a Python system according to the APIs and DLs installed in the speech recognition system and the emotion estimation system as external systems.

5.3.2.1 Speech Recognition Module

This module activates a system that recognizes speech input from a microphone. In this chapter, we used existing speech recognition APIs, Google Cloud Speech-to-Text [26]. Google Cloud Speech-to-Text is adopted as an external program in F2FVep, so it guesses the microphone-input speech sentence, determines the guessed sentence, and saves each sentence in a log file with a new line at that point. When the silent time exceeds a certain period, the system judges that the speech sentence is over and fixes the sentence.

5.3.2.2 Emotion Estimation Module

EEM performs emotion estimation from the speaker's facial expressions, and the combined results are input to the Avatar text-to-speech system. For the emotion estimation method, we use "Emotion detection using deep learning" provided by atulapra [27] is used for estimation. An image of the speaker's facial expression is captured every f seconds, and emotion estimation is performed using the captured image. In the evaluation, f is set to 1 second.

In Ref. [27], seven emotions can be estimated, "angry", "happy", "neutral", "sad", "surprised", "disgusted", and "fearless". However, the emotions to be used F2FVep are selected from the five types of "angry", "happy", "neutral", "sad", and "surprised". Therefore, we deleted the "disgusted" and "fearless" that cannot be set by the text-to-speech software.

5.3.2.3 Conversational Text Translation Module

CTTM translates sentences recognized by SRM. In this paper, we adopt Google Cloud Translation [28] as a translation system. The recognized speech sentences are translated to the spoken sentences logged by the speech recognition module from the original language to another one.

The recognized speech sentences are saved in a log file, and translation is performed for each line because each line contains a recognized sentence. The log file is checked for updates every n second, and after checking for updates, translation is performed for each updated sentence. In F2FVep, n is set to 0.01 second. If the timing of the update is not correct, there may be a delay in the translation process.

F2FVep translates a sentence to another, and we assume that the translated sentences are grammatically correct. Although currently available translation systems sometimes generate upset sentences, we do not focus on the translation performance in this paper.

5.3.2.4 3D Avatar Reading Module

ARM passes the translated sentences to the text-to-speech system for activation. At this time, ARM additionally sets the emotions estimated in EEM. ARM adopts "CeVIO AI Maki TSURUMAKI" [29] as a text-to-speech software in the evaluation.

"CeVIO AI Maki TSURUMAKI" supports both Japanese and English, and it can translate and read text from both Japanese to English and English to Japanese. In this paper, only the translation from Japanese to English is performed. The text is read out line by line from the log file memorized by SRM, and a speech file is created and saved as a WAV file. Here, ARM is running in the background. ARM searches for a sentence that has not yet been read from the saved text file of the translated speech every m second and executes the avatar's read-aloud. At this time, the avatar is set to emotional expressions. The data flow for each file and the timing of system startup are shown in Figure 5.2.

The emotions used are extracted from a log file of the ten most recent results estimated before the start of the reading, the percentage of each emotion is calculated from the average of these results. However, five emotions are pre-defined in the speech system used by CeVIO AI Maki TSURUMAKI: "fine", "angry", "sad", "calm", and "mild". Therefore, the emotions "angry", "happy", "neutral", "sad" and "surprised" to be used correspond to approximate emotions from the elements available in CeVIO AI. We reflected in "angry" and "sad" as the same emotions, and "happy" as "fine" because it approximates "fine". "neutral" is reflected in "calm". The "surprised" emotion is reflected in the "voice quality" and "inflection" changes since there is no emotion that approximates the pre-set.

The estimated emotion is also reflected to the avatar's facial expression. The emotion used for the avatar's emotion is selected from the most frequent emotion as a result of extracting the last 10 results estimated before the start of the read-aloud from the log file. This chapter uses Unity-Chan [30], an avatar provided by Unity Technologies Japan, LLC. Since each part of the face is modeled individually, it is possible to express more realistic facial expressions. F2FVep also employs lip-sync [31], an open library, to create a sense of realism as if the user were speaking. Figure 5.3 shows the facial expressions corresponding to each emotion from Unity-chan's facial expressions.

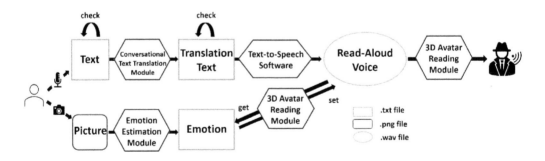

Figure 5.2 The data flow for each file and the timing of system startup. The speaker's text and translated speech sentences are input and output as text files, and the read speech is exchanged as WAV files.

Neutral   Happy   Angry

Sad   Surprised

Figure 5.3 Examples of avatar's expression. This paper reflects the five emotions "angry", "happy", "neutral", "sad", and "surprised" due to the limitations of the software used in F2FVep.

5.3.3 Delay-Aware Synchronization of Face and Voice

F2FVep works by a combination of translated text reading aloud and reflected facial expressions on a 3D avatar. Therefore, there is a problem that the delay in the translation process causes a gap in the timing between the translation of speech sentences and the reflection of facial expressions on the 3D avatar. Here, the considered delay times are that of estimation of speech texts and the speaker's emotions, translation speech texts, and making the read-aloud voice.

In order to synchronize the facial expression and reading aloud, four modules that are executed in parallel should work at the appropriate timing. The results of each module's operation are stored as text or data files to be shared with other modules when they need to reflect the results in the avatar.

The words spoken begin to recognize the speech text immediately after the end of the speech is recognized, and then translation and avatar reading are performed. Since it is a background process, it is possible to do the next word to be uttered in the meantime. A time frame of the speech recognition and reading aloud is shown in Figure 5.4. F2FVep makes it possible to use the data accumulated in the background where each module is running. Moreover, it is possible to reflect the

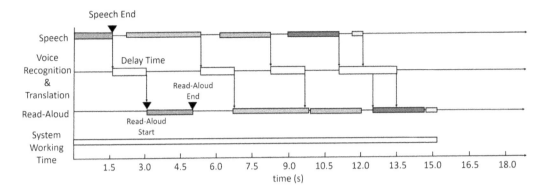

Figure 5.4 Time frame of speech recognition and reading aloud.

results to the avatar at the appropriate timing by shifting the timing of emotion reflection according to the delay times. In other words, emotions of the speaker and avatar are re-synchronized.

F2FVep reflects the individual facial expressions of avatars without using face tracking or other methods. Therefore, it is possible to reflect emotions in facial expressions at the appropriate time. Besides, individual movements are manipulated by modules in the background. Therefore, it is possible to start the next utterance after the end of the previous utterance. However, a certain percentage of file accesses may encounter failure because of file access conflict. This is evaluated in Section 5.4.2.

5.4 EXPERIMENT AND EVALUATION

5.4.1 Impression of Expressed Emotions

This section describes the evaluation results of F2FVep. First, we evaluated what users feel about the expressed emotions on the avatar's face and voice. In the experiment, subjects spoke the sentences listed in Table 5.2, and the spoken voice was input into the proposed system. Subjects expressed facial expressions like the specified emotion to the camera and said dialogues to the microphone based on the dialogues and assumed emotion labels that were set up in advance here. We then took a questionnaire after the experiment, focusing on the correspondence between the facial expressions on the camera and the expressions of the avatars on the screen (tone of speech and facial expressions of the avatars). We evaluated the questionnaire on a five-point scale from one to five. The pre-set dialogues and emotions are shown in Table 5.2 shows the results of the questionnaire after the experiment.

The questionnaire items are shown in Table 5.3 and the evaluation results in Figure 5.5. As can be seen from the results of the questionnaire, the ease of appearance varied greatly depending on the emotion. In particular, "Angry" and "Sad" were not easy to express. However, some experimenters answered that "Surprised"

TABLE 5.2 The Pre-set Dialogues and Emotions for Experiment

Dialogues	Emotion
We will now begin the experiment	Neutral
Enough is enough	Angry
Thank you!!	Happy
Wow! that was a surprise	Surprised
Good morning	Neutral
Why did you do this?	Sad
I always wanted that!	Happy
My test scores were terrible last time	Sad
Oh, you bought it!	Surprised
Don't run away, wait!	Angry
I won something good in the raffle today	Happy
I missed the candy.	Sad
You shouldn't have painted the wall like this!	Angry
Oh, it's coming down from above!	Surprised
Good work	Neutral

TABLE 5.3 The Questionnaire Items

Number	Questionnaire Items
Q.1	Did you feel the difference in emotion in each line?
Q.2	How well did avatar express "happy"?
Q.3	How well did avatar express "sad"?
Q.4	How well did avatar express "angry"?
Q.5	How well did avatar express "surprised"?
Q.6	Did you find the translation reading-out function convenient?
Q.7	How much do you want to use it in a conversation with someone you don't know?
Q.8	Would you like to use it in a conversation with a business associate?
Q.9	Would you use it in a conversation with friends?
Q.10	Would you like to use it in a conversation with your relatives?
Q.11	Do you think the number of facial expressions is appropriate?

and "Happy" were difficult to express, indicating individual differences. We believe that this is due to the use of the speaker's facial expressions for emotion estimation. The machine learning model used in the experiments to estimate speakers' emotions was based on a publicly available model and was not tuned for this experiment. The results also validate the convenience of the translation function of this system, as the reading-out function was highly rated overall.

We also conducted a questionnaire to determine whether the respondents would like to use this system from the perspective of "first-time users," "business associates," "friends," or "relatives". As a result, many respondents felt that they would like to use the system with "friends". Many were reluctant to use the system with "new acquaintances" or "business associates". We consider that this difference is due to their experience with avatar-based content. Since there are many activities

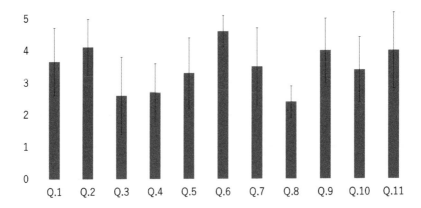

Figure 5.5 Evaluation results of the subjects' felt. The questionnaire focuses on whether the specified emotion is well expressed, the convenience of the read-out function, and whether the user would like to use it with a specific person.

on the Internet these days, and especially since anonymity is sometimes considered important, we believe that it can be used in some situations.

5.4.2 Delay Time of F2FVep

As we mentioned in Section 5.3.3, F2FVep is configured to run not only Unity-based ARM but also Python-based SRM, EEMC, and TTM as other modules, allowing parallel processing of the entire system. However, if the CTTM, which is accessed to translate the first time of utterance, and the SRM, which is accessed to store the next utterance, access the same log file at the same time, the system may fail. Therefore, we searched for the optimal file confirmation time by varying the confirmation time to minimize the delay, taking into account the timing when no failure occurs.

To evaluate the failure rate, the speaker said "good-bye" immediately after "hello" was uttered. This was repeated ten times. Access failure occurs when these two utterances are consecutive. The file confirmation periods to be checked are 1, 0.1, 0.01, 0.003, 0.002, and 0.001 seconds. The results are shown in Figure 5.6.

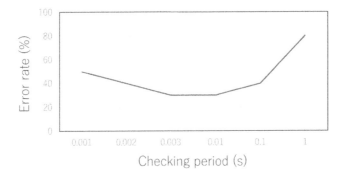

Figure 5.6 Error rate as a function of checking period.

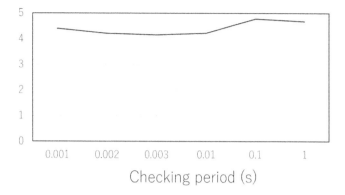

Figure 5.7 Delay time before reading-aloud of each checking period.

From this figure, it can be seen that the error rate is high at 1 second, but then the error rate decreases, and from then on the error rate increases again. This may be due to the relatively slow setting of 1 second, where the recording of speech sentences does not occur in time for translation, resulting in duplicate accesses. Duplicate accesses will also occur even if the timing is too early. Accelerating the timing prevents duplicate file access until the timing of the translation of the speech text. However, due to the time lag during read-aloud voice making, duplicate accesses occur between the writing of the speech text during recognizing the speech text and the confirmation of the speech text during read-aloud voice making. Figure 5.7. shows the measured delay time before reading aloud for each checking period. The results show that the delay time does not vary with the checking period. Therefore, a period with fewer access conflicts and faster checks should be selected. For this reason, this paper uses 0.01 seconds as the appropriate file confirmation time.

5.5 SUMMARY

F2FVep reflects emotions to a virtual avatar by considering the text translation delay time before the avatar reads out the translated speaker's utterance. In this paper, we examine a system that reflects emotions from a speaker's facial expressions to the avatar's facial expressions and to the speech software that reads out translated sentences. Emotions estimated from facial expressions could be used for read-aloud without any problems. As future prospects, we will also examine the use of voice and text emotions other than facial expressions. Besides, we will also study the improvement of the file access method to reduce the delay time.

BIBLIOGRAPHY

[1] Google. Google translate, accessed July 2022. https://translate.google.co.jp/.

[2] Ryota Nishimura. ninshikiChan, accessed July 2022. https://sayonari.coresv.com/ ninshikiChan/20210822_config.html.

[3] Google. Google cloud APIs, accessed July 2022. https://cloud.google.com/product-terms/.

[4] Apple. Siri, accessed July 2022. https://www.apple.com/siri/.

[5] Google. Google, accessed July 2022. https://www.google.com/.

[6] Zhicong Lu, Chenxinran Shen, Jiannan Li, Hong Shen, and Daniel Wigdor. More kawaii than a real-person live streamer: Understanding how the otaku community engages with and perceives virtual YouTubers. In *Proceedings of the 2021 CHI Conference on Human Factors in Computing Systems*, Japan, pp. 1–14, 2021.

[7] UsideU Co. Ltd. TimeRep, accessed July 2022. https://timerep.jp/.

[8] Tomoya Suzuki, Akihito Taya, and Yoshito Tobe. VFep: 3D graphic face representation based on voice-based emotion recognition. In *2021 IEEE International Conference on Pervasive Computing and Communications Workshops and other Affiliated Events (PerCom Workshops)*, Kassel pp. 74–79, 2021.

[9] Trisha Mittal, Uttaran Bhattacharya, Rohan Chandra, Aniket Bera, and Dinesh Manocha. M3er: Multiplicative multimodal emotion recognition using facial, textual, and speech cues. In *Proceedings of the AAAI Conference on Artificial Intelligence*, vol. 34, pp. 1359–1367, New York, USA, 2020.

[10] Jan Niehues, Ngoc-Quan Pham, Thanh-Le Ha, Matthias Sperber, and Alex Waibel. Low-latency neural speech translation. arXiv preprint arXiv:1808.00491, 2018.

[11] Paul Ekman. An argument for basic emotions. *Cognition & Emotion*, 6(3–4):169–200, 1992.

[12] James A. Russell. A circumplex model of affect. *Journal of Personality and Social Psychology*, 39(6):1161, 1980.

[13] Rolf Pfeifer. Artificial Intelligence models of emotion. In Vernon Hamilton, Gordon H. Bower, and Nico H. Frijda (eds.), *Cognitive Perspectives on Emotion and Motivation*, pp. 287–320. Springer, Berlin, 1988.

[14] Joao Dias and Ana Paiva. Feeling and reasoning: A computational model for emotional characters. In *Portuguese Conference on Artificial Intelligence*, pp. 127–140. Springer, University of Covilhã, Portugal, 2005.

[15] Stacy Marsella, Jonathan Gratch, Paolo Petta, et al. Computational models of emotion. *A Blueprint for Affective Computing: A Sourcebook and Manual*, 11(1):21–46, 2010.

[16] Tero Karras, Timo Aila, Samuli Laine, Antti Herva, and Jaakko Lehtinen. Audio-driven facial animation by joint end-to-end learning of pose and emotion. *ACM Transactions on Graphics (TOG)*, 36(4):1–12, 2017.

[17] Microsoft. Face API Microsoft Azure, accessed July 2022. https://azure.microsoft.com/ja-jp/services/cognitive-services/face/.

[18] Ashish Vaswani, Noam Shazeer, Niki Parmar, Jakob Uszkoreit, Llion Jones, Aidan N. Gomez, Łukasz Kaiser, and Illia Polosukhin. Attention is all you need. *Advances in Neural Information Processing Systems*, 30, pp. 6000–6010, 2017.

[19] Varsha Suresh and Desmond C. Ong. Using knowledge-embedded attention to augment pre-trained language models for fine-grained emotion recognition. In *2021 9th International Conference on Affective Computing and Intelligent Interaction (ACII)*, Nara, Japan, pp. 1–8. IEEE, 2021.

[20] DeepL GmbH. DeepL Translate, accessed July 2022. https://www.deepl.com/translator.

[21] Mirai Translate, Inc. MiraiTranslate, accessed July 2022. https://miraitranslate.com/.

[22] N. Sweety Surya, C. Babitha, M. Janaki, P. Jasmine Anitta, and S. Jerin. An android based language translator application. *Technix International Journal for Engineering Research*, 9(6):19–26, 2022.

[23] Agung Santosa, Asril Jarin, Lyla Ruslana Aini, Gita Citra Puspita, Muhammad Teduh Uliniansyah, Elvira Nurfadhilah, Harnum A. Prafitia, Made Gunawan, Andi Djalal Latief, Hammam Riza, et al. The architecture of speech-to-speech translator for mobile conversation. In *2019 22nd Conference of the Oriental COCOSDA International Committee for the Co-ordination and Standardisation of Speech Databases and Assessment Techniques (O-COCOSDA)*, Cebu, Philippines, pp. 1–6. IEEE, 2019.

[24] Yu-Ting Wan, Cheng-Chun Chiu, Kai-Wen Liang, and Pao-Chi Chang. Midoriko chatbot: LSTM-based emotional 3D avatar. In *2019 IEEE 8th Global Conference on Consumer Electronics (GCCE)*, pp. 937–940. IEEE, Osaka, Japan, 2019.

[25] Yoshihiro Sakatani, Junya Nakanishi, Takuya Yamada, Takahiro Komori, Shohei Fujii, Masataka Okubo, and Tadashi Nakano. An avatar-mediated communication system for the construction of interpersonal relationships. In *2018 IEEE International Conference on Systems, Man, and Cybernetics (SMC)*, pp. 2614–2619. IEEE, Miyazaki, Japan, 2018.

[26] Google. Google cloud speech-to-text, accessed July 2022. https://cloud.google.com/speech-to-text/.

[27] atulapra. Emotion etection using deep learning, accessed July 2022. https://github.com/atulapra/Emotion-detection.

[28] Google. Google cloud translation, accessed July 2022. https://cloud.google.com/translate.

[29] AHS Co. Ltd. CeVIO AI Maki TSURUMAKI, accessed July 2022. https://www.ah-soft.com/ commercial/cevio/.

[30] Unity Technologies Japan. UNITY-CHAN!, accessed July 2022. https://unity-chan.com/ contents/guideline/.

[31] Oculus. Oculus LipSync Unity, accessed July 2022. https://developer.oculus.com/downloads/package/oculus-lipsync-unity/.

CHAPTER 6

Touching with Eye Contact and Vocal Greetings Increases the Sense of Security

Miyuki Iwamoto

Kyoto Institute of Technology

Atsushi Nakazawa

Okayama University

6.1 INTRODUCTION

Contact is considered to be a type of emotional communication. Touching another person is the most direct act of communicating one's presence to the other person, and being touched is a means of communication through which we convey various feelings and thoughts to others and establish a relationship [1]. For example, it can be the first step in establishing a relationship with another person, as in a handshake, or it can be a means of communication to establish an intimate relationship, such as skin ship. In other words, physical contact is considered to be an opportunity to bridge the "psychological distance" between one person and another. Furthermore, the act of touching reduces anxiety and generates a sense of security [2]. There has been a lot of research on the emotions of security and anxiety associated with physical contact, as well as on the methods and ways of making contact.

Kennell states that the act of contact can strengthen the bond between mother and child [3]. Field stated that bilateral contact could reduce client anxiety [4], and Drescher found that in nursing and caregiving settings, the act of contact between the caregiver and the cared-for person reduced the anxiety of the cared-for person

DOI: 10.1201/9781003371540-7

[5]. Many positive results have been obtained, such as in the case of the caregiver's contact with the cared-for person in nursing and caregiving situations. However, many of these studies were conducted in special situations. Onozuka et al. also defined the degree of pleasure or displeasure with general physical contact as contact aversion and examined its relationship with the four attachment styles defined by Aikoshi: stable (positive sense of self and others), rejecting (positive sense of self, negative sense of others), ambivalent (negative sense of self, positive sense of others) and fearful (negative sense of self and others) [6]. The results showed that "the stable" and "ambivalent" types preferred to be contacted, and that a positive view of others (whether the attachment target responds immediately when help or protection is requested) was a factor in their preference for contact [7]. Yamaguchi and Haruki reported that being touched evokes feelings of "gladness," "calmness," and "feeling encouraged," suggesting that physical contact can be healing to people [8].

However, on the other hand, negative results and effects have also been reported: according to Whitcher et al., physical contact is reported to increase anxiety and discomfort in care settings when the gender of the caregiver and the care-receiver are different [9]. Furthermore, Yamaguchi says that the act of physical contact has both positive and negative aspects. In fact, Yamaguchi defined the resistance to physical contact as tactile resistance and examined the relationship between the toucher and the touched, tactile resistance and anxiety caused by physical contact, and found that the effect of physical contact on anxiety differed depending on the relationship between the two parties and the tactile resistance of the individual [10].

He also stated that blindly performing the act of contact on the contacted person does not feel good, but causes discomfort [11], and that there is a law of touching that feels good [12,13] As a method of contact, a slow speed of about 5 cm per second gives the most relaxing effect to the contacted person [12–14]. It has also been found that the most relaxing effect is obtained at a pressure of around 400–800 N during contact [15]. Furthermore, Akutsu et al. found that in contact care, the areas where a relaxing effect is obtained are the shoulders and the back of the hands [16]. Contact also plays an important role in communication to share one's feelings with others. Both Field and Spence showed that interpersonal contact plays an important role in controlling emotional well-being [17,18] . In addition, Jones and Yarbrough note that physical contact (such as a strong handshake, a push for attention, or a gentle pat on the shoulder) can sometimes convey more powerful vitality and immediacy than language [19].

Thus, much research has been conducted on contact, mostly on the emotions of the contacted person because of making contact, the method of contact, and the relationship between contact and communication. However, almost no mention has been made of pre-contact behavior. For example, in daily life, being touched suddenly from behind in a silent state causes discomfort and high arousal. This suggests that touching does not necessarily reduce anxiety or give a sense of security and that the situation of touching (from behind by another person, while talking to another person, etc.) may cause differences in the sense of anxiety or security of the touched person. In this study, physiological indices were subjectively evaluated and measured to clarify the effects of the combination of contact and other stimuli (visual and audio) on the arousal and discomfort of the contacted person.

6.2 RELATED WORK

This chapter describes research related to Electro Dermal Activity (EDA) and Anticipation and Peripheral Vision.

6.2.1 Electro Dermal Activity (EDA)

Electro Dermal Activity (EDA) measures the potential difference between two points on the skin. It is classified into the skin conductance level (SCL) of the low-frequency component and the skin conductance response (SCR) of the high-frequency component. SCL reflects the degree to which the nervous system is active; SCR is a transient, short-term fluctuation observed in a mixture of those occurring in response to emotion and those that are spontaneous. These two are also known as sympathetic cutaneous responses and are thought to reflect the function of the efferent nerve activity within the cutaneous sympathetic activity [20]. Ree et al. evaluated the arousal and emotional effects of soft contact, such as caressing, using participants' SCL, facial electromyography (EMG) responses, and subjective ratings of pleasure and intensity [21]. A further experiment was conducted by Bechara et al. using the Iowa Gambling Task. The results of this experiment showed that the physical responses of the experimental participants changed before they were consciously aware of the change in behavior [22]. Bauer et al. also conducted a pair presentation of human faces and names to subjects who had difficulty identifying human faces. High SCR was shown when the presented face and name were matched [23].

Thus, transient short-term tension and arousal can be measured. In our study, we also decided to use SCR because the experimenter touches the subject's shoulder and we wanted to measure the short-term response.

6.2.2 Anticipation and Peripheral Vision

Humans do not passively perceive unpleasant stimuli in the external world, but regulate their perception of unpleasant stimuli through active anticipation. For example, it is known that when unpleasant stimuli are predictable or unpredictable, stimulus processing is accelerated and emotional responses such as subjective unpleasant feelings and the autonomic nervous system are smaller when the stimuli are predictable [24]. There have also been studies investigating the reduction of anxiety in situations in which people ride in an automated vehicle by presenting information that enables them to anticipate the situation and behavior of the vehicle body (predictive cues). Mizunami et al. showed that presenting white lines indicating the direction of vehicle movement as augmented reality (AR) reduced the anxiety of young people in a situation simulating automated driving [25]. Inoue et al. showed that the presentation of auditory information to anticipate the arrival of a curve reduced the anxiety of young adults while riding in an automated vehicle, in addition to the re-examination of the effect of visual information by Mizunami et al. [26]. These findings suggest that anticipation may influence the reduction of discomfort and anxiety. Generally, it is said that the visual field narrows with advancing age, but in reality, there is no change in the range of vision, only a narrowing of the gazing range. The visual field is the area that can be seen without moving the eyes when looking straight ahead. The relatively clear and conscious area around the gazing point is called the peripheral visual field [27], and it is the visual field that can be perceptually processed even without attention [28]. It includes visual processing speed, light adaptation, dark adaptation, dynamic vision, near vision, peripheral vision, depth perception, and depth perception. Visual functions such as light adaptation, dark adaptation, dynamic vision, near vision, peripheral vision, depth perception, and contrast sensitivity decrease with age [29,30]. In addition, Ikeda et al. found that the peripheral visual field shrinks with increasing cognitive load [31]. In the present study, to reproduce the shrinkage of the peripheral visual field, the subjects' visual field was narrowed by physical means as a visual field limitation because it was difficult to conduct an experiment in which the subjects were continuously subjected to cognitive load.

6.3   EXPERIMENT

The purpose of this study was to clarify the relationship between the combination of stimuli and subjective evaluation including arousal and physiological indices during contact. The auditory and visual conditions were varied as stimuli, and subjective evaluation and physiological indices were measured. The auditory condition consisted of touching while talking to someone, henceforth "vocal greeting ", touching without talking to someone hereafter referred to as "no vocal greeting" and the visual condition consisted of "no contact person visible (from behind the subject)," "contact person visible (without eye contact)," and "contact person visible (with eye contact)". For the contact stimulus, the contactor's hand was placed on the contactee's shoulder for 3 seconds. Subjective evaluation was conducted on two axes: arousal-drowsiness and pleasantness-unpleasantness.

6.3.1   Experimental Overview

The experimental collaborators were 22 male undergraduate and graduate students in their 20s. The participant was asked to place the Empatica E4 on his non-dominant wrist, then moved to the experimental space in the same room, sat on a chair, and set up a camera to capture the experimental scene. To prevent the participant from moving the wrist-worn Empatica E4 during the stimulation, we asked the participant to place both hands on the desk (Figure 6.1). Before starting the experiment, we asked him to listen to the voice played during the voice call

Figure 6.1 Experimental scene.

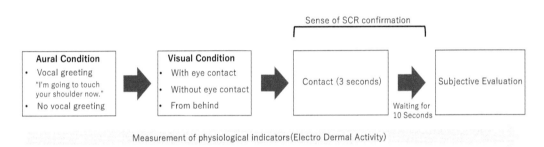

Figure 6.2 Experimental procedure.

once as an exercise and the following contact patterns: from behind, without eye contact, and with eye contact. After the practice, the experiment started. As shown in Figure 6.2, in the case of "vocal greeting, contact," we played the voice and made contact with the participant's shoulder for 3 seconds in accordance with the visual condition. After the contact, the subject waited for 10 seconds and then made a subjective evaluation. These were repeated in six patterns in random order for a total of two sets. Physiological indices were measured during the two sets, and the experiment was terminated when the Empatica E4 was removed after the participants completed the two sets and rated their rankings.

As the experimental environment, a desk and chair with partitions on both the front and side sides were set up in the laboratory as shown in Figure 6.3. A video camera was set up behind the chairs so that the subjects could observe the contact. The room temperature was 23°C.

6.3.2 Types of Stimuli

A contact person (male, 25 years old) touched the participant's right shoulder with his left hand for 3 seconds as a contact stimulus. The auditory condition consisted

Figure 6.3 Experimental environment.

TABLE 6.1 Pattern Classification

Pattern	Auditory Condition	Visual Condition
A	No vocal greeting	Out of sight of participants (from behind)
B	No vocal greeting	Without eye contact (forward)
C	No vocal greeting	With eye contact (forward)
D	Vocal greeting	Out of sight of participants (from behind)
E	Vocal greeting	Without eye contact (forward)
F	Vocal greeting	With eye contact (forward)

of two patterns immediately before the contact: vocal greeting and not vocal greeting. The visual condition consisted of six patterns of task combinations: not in participant's sight, in participant's sight but not making eye contact, and "in participant's sight but making eye contact" (Table 6.1). Hereafter, these will be denoted as "from behind," "without eye contact," and "with eye contact." A synthetic voice was played from a PC to call the participant to make contact in the auditory condition. The synthesized voice was a male voice saying, "I'm going to touch your shoulder now." The contact person wore a mask so that the participant could see the stimulator and his eyes when he walked around in front of the participant in the visual condition.

6.3.3 Subjective Evaluation

Russell's circle model was used as the subjective evaluation (Figure 6.4), with the horizontal axis representing valence as "pleasantness-unpleasantness" and the vertical axis representing arousal as arousal-drowsiness. The range of each evaluation value was from −1 to 1, with positive values indicating pleasantness or arousal and negative values indicating discomfort or drowsiness. As in the preliminary

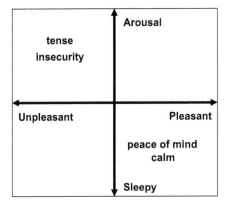

Figure 6.4 Russell's circle model.

experiment, the participants were asked to rank the six patterns in order of their discomfort after the experiment.

6.3.4 The Skin Conductance Response (SCR)

In this study, we measured EDA as a physiological index. The EDA is classified into the low-frequency component SPL and the high-frequency component SCR. In this experiment, we focused on SCR, which represents transient changes in skin electrical resistance that occur within a few seconds in response to external stimuli (Figure 6.5). The time from the stimulus to the apex of the waveform is expressed as latency, the time from the onset of a reaction to the time reaction reaches its apex as rise time, and the amplitude from the apex of the waveform to the rise time as amplitude. In this study, the amplitude was used as an index to measure the contact-induced stress response. In this study, the Empatica E4 wristband was used to measure physiological indices (Figure 6.6). Empatica E4 can be worn on the wrist

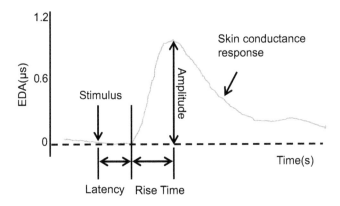

Figure 6.5 Skin conductance response.

Figure 6.6   Empatica E4.

to acquire real-time physiological data and can measure the heart rate, acceleration, EDA, and body temperature, with a sampling frequency of 4 Hz for EDA.

6.3.5   Parsing Method

In this study, we used Elan 6.2 to annotate video data from a fixed camera and EDA measured with Empatica E4 (Figure 6.7). Four types of annotations were made: visual condition, audio segment when a voice call was made, contact stimulus, and SCR response segment. Figure 6.7 shows the correspondence between latency, rise time, and amplitude shown in Figure 6.5. The raw data acquired with Empatica E4 were smoothed with a low-pass filter (moving average method) and standardized by Z-transformation for each Participant. First, a two-way ANOVA with repetition

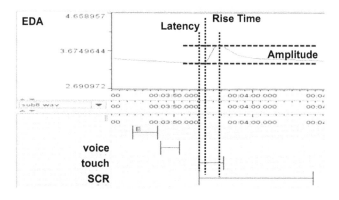

Figure 6.7   Examples of annotation.

was used to examine whether there was a main effect of the auditory, visual, or interaction conditions on both subjective ratings and physiological parameters. If a main effect was found, a two-tailed t-test was used to calculate the p-value for the auditory condition (2 groups), and a two-tailed t-test (Bonferroni's correction) was used to calculate the p-value for the visual condition (3 groups) to see if there were statistically significant differences.

6.4 RESULTS

The results of subjective evaluation and physiological indices are shown.

6.4.1 Subjective Evaluation

A two-way ANOVA revealed no main effect of interaction for each item, but main effects were found for the auditory and visual conditions for "pleasant-discomfort" ($p < 0.05$) and for the visual condition for "arousal-drowsiness" ($p < 0.05$). Therefore, we conducted t-tests for the auditory and visual conditions for "pleasant - unpleasant" and for the visual condition for "awake - drowsy." Figure 6.8 shows the evaluation values of "pleasantness-unpleasantness" in the auditory condition for the two patterns of "no vocal greeting" and "vocal greeting" ($N = 22$ people * 2 sets * 3 patterns). The graph shows the mean value and 95% confidence interval for each pattern, with higher and lower ratings indicating more pleasantness and discomfort, respectively. The results also show that the evaluation value was higher for the "vocal greeting" pattern than for the "no vocal greeting" pattern. Figure 6.9 summarizes the "pleasantness-displeasure" evaluation values for

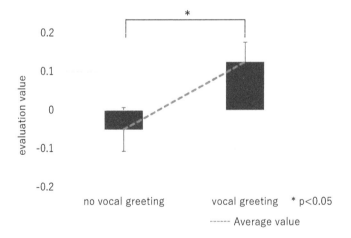

Figure 6.8 Evaluation values of "pleasantness-unpleasantness" in the auditory condition. The graph shows the mean value and 95% confidence interval for each pattern, with higher and lower ratings indicating more pleasantness and discomfort, respectively.

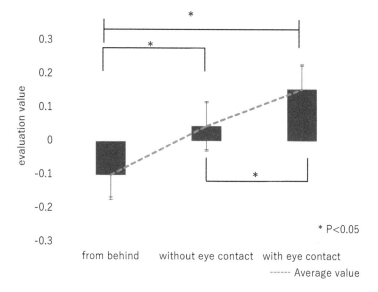

Figure 6.9 Evaluation values of "pleasantness-unpleasantness" in the visual condition. The graph shows the mean value and 95% confidence interval for each pattern, with higher and lower ratings indicating more pleasantness and discomfort, respectively.

the three patterns of visual conditions: from behind, without eye contact, and with eye contact ($N = 22$ persons*2 sets*2 patterns). It shows statistically significant differences among the three patterns ($p < 0.05$). The results also show that the evaluation values were higher for "without eye contact" or "with eye contact" than for "from behind." Furthermore, "with eye contact" has a higher evaluation value than "without eye contact."

Next, Figure 6.10 summarizes the evaluation values of "arousal-drowsiness" in the two patterns of auditory conditions: no vocal greeting and vocal greeting ($N = 22$ persons * 2 sets * 3 patterns). The graph shows the mean value and 95% confidence intervals for each pattern, with higher and lower values indicating greater arousal and drowsiness, respectively. Figure 6.11 summarizes the "arousal-drowsiness" ratings for the three visual conditions: from behind, without eye contact, and with eye contact ($N = 22$ subjects*2 sets*2 patterns). There was a statistically significant difference between "from behind" and "without eye contact" and between "from behind" and "with eye contact" ($p < 0.05$). The results also show that the evaluation values of "without eye contact" and "with eye contact" were lower than those of "from behind." Furthermore, the difference in evaluation values between "without eye contact" and "with eye contact" is smaller than that between "with eye contact" and "without eye contact."

In addition, Figure 6.12 shows a stacked graph of the rank of each pattern (N = 22). The darker/lighter the gradient, the more/less offended the user was. The horizontal axis shows the respective pattern. A indicates from behind + no

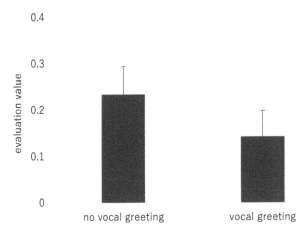

Figure 6.10 Evaluation values of "arousal-drowsiness" in the auditory conditions. The graph shows the mean value and 95% confidence intervals for each pattern, with higher and lower values indicating greater arousal and drowsiness, respectively.

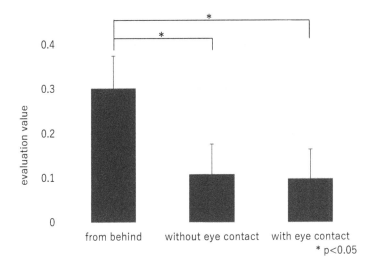

Figure 6.11 Evaluation values of "arousal-drowsiness" in the visual conditions. The graph shows the mean value and 95% confidence intervals for each pattern, with higher and lower values indicating greater arousal and drowsiness, respectively.

vocal greeting, B indicates without eye contact + no vocal greeting, C indicates with eye contact + no vocal greeting, D indicates from behind + vocal greeting, E indicates without eye contact + vocal greeting, and F indicates with eye contact + vocal greeting. Figure 6.12 shows that "with eye contact + vocal greeting" has the second widest gradient. Next, "without eye contact + vocal greeting" has the widest gradient, and "with eye contact + no vocal greeting" and "from behind + vocal greeting" have equally wide gradients.

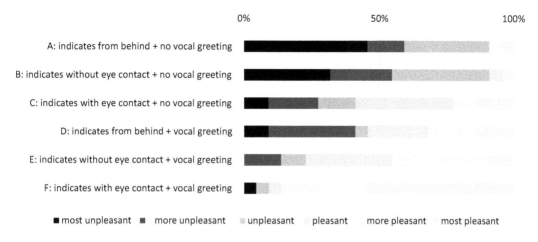

Figure 6.12 Stacked graph of the rank of each pattern. The darker/lighter the gradient, the more/less offended the user was.

6.4.2 Physiological Indicators (Skin Conductance Reaction)

A two-way ANOVA revealed no main effects for the visual condition or interaction, but a main effect for the auditory condition ($p < 0.05$). Therefore, a t-test was conducted for the auditory condition. Figure 6.13 summarizes the SCR response for the two patterns of auditory condition: no vocal greeting and vocal greeting ($N = 22$ participants * 2 sets * 3 patterns). The graph shows the mean value and 95% confidence interval for each pattern, and there was no statistically significant difference between the two patterns ($p < 0.05$). However, the graph shows that the amount of response was smaller for the "vocal greeting" pattern than for the "no vocal greeting" pattern. In addition, Figure 6.14 summarizes the amount of

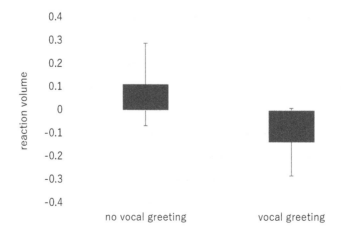

Figure 6.13 SCR response for the two patterns of auditory condition. The graph shows the mean value and 95% confidence interval for each pattern.

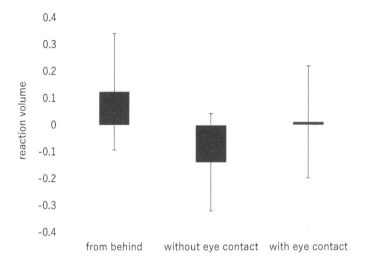

Figure 6.14 SCR response for the two patterns of visual condition. The graph shows the mean value and 95% confidence interval for each pattern.

SCR responses in the three patterns of visual conditions: from behind, without eye contact and with eye contact ($N = 22$ participants * 2 sets * 2 patterns). As in the auditory condition, the means and 95% confidence intervals for each pattern were shown. In the visual condition, no differences were found between the three patterns.

6.5 DISCUSSIONS AND FUTURE WORK

This study investigated the effects of stimulus combinations, especially contact and voice or eye contact, on arousal and discomfort. In addition, we also investigated the effects on the EDA of physiological indices. The results showed that vocal greeting before physical touch reduced the participant's discomfort and the amount of SCR response. This may be because the participants were able to anticipate the timing of the touch. In addition, the arousal and discomfort were reduced when the touch was made in a position that was visible to the participant, and the SCR response was also reduced. This is because the participant can confirm the aspect of the contactor and the timing of the contact by seeing the contactor and thus feels less discomfort, and the small CR response may have reduced the stress felt during touch. In addition, the participant's evaluation of comfort and discomfort was higher when eye contact was made while the contactor was visible to the participant than when eye contact was not made. On the other hand, when eye contact was made, the participants felt more comfortable. furthermore, the fact that the SCR response was greater when eye contact was made suggests that the participant was conscious of being watched and felt embarrassed, which may have caused the SCR response to be greater. These results indicate that the subjective evaluation and physiological indexes of the participants were greatly affected by the other stimuli (visual and audio) during the touch.

The changes may have been small in this experiment because both the contact person and the participant were males in their 20s. For example, looking at the results of Figure 6.10, there was a difference in the results between the arousal vocal greeting and the no vocal greeting, but the difference was not significant. This was also evident in the SCR response This could be due to the fact that both were males in their 20s. Therefore, it is necessary to conduct the same experiment with participant of various generations and genders to test whether the hypothesis is substantiated.

It is suggested that the same participant evaluation and physiological indicators of the contactee may be significantly affected when conducted with different generations and genders of contact person and participants, such as male and female, female and female, young and old, but the opposite may be true for the act of looking, such as eye contact. Therefore, it is considered necessary to conduct the same experiment with the contact person and participants of different generations and genders to test whether the hypothesis is substantiated.

In the present study, cutaneous electrical activity was used to investigate whether visual or auditory stimulation at the time of touch makes a difference to the contactee's response. Although it can be confirmed that there was a response with cutaneous electrical activity, it is not possible to measure the sense of security or anxiety at the time of touch. In the future, other physiological indices will need to be used to clarify which emotions (anxiety, relief, surprise, and fear) the contactee's reaction at the time of touch applies to, and which touch methods are perceived as pleasant or unpleasant.

ACKNOWLEDGEMENTS

This work was supported by JST CREST Grant Number JPMJCR17A5.

BIBLIOGRAPHY

[1] Hajime Yamaguchi, "Skin sensation and the brain", *Japanese Society of Oriental Physiotherapy*, 42(2), pp. 9–16, (2017).

[2] Alberto Gallace and Charles Spence, "The science of interpersonal touch: An overview", *Neuroscience & Biobehavioral Reviews*, 34(2), pp. 246–259, (2010).

[3] John H. Kennell and Marshall H. Klaus, *Parent-Infant Bonding*. Mosby: Maryland Heights, MI (1982)

[4] Tiffany Field, Susan Seligman, Frank Scafidi, and Saul Schanberg, "Alleviating post-traumatic stress in children following Hurricane Andrew", *Journal of Applied Developmental Psychology*, 17(1), pp. 37–50, (1996).

[5] Vincent M. Drescher, William Andrew Horsley Gantt, and William E. Whitehead, "Heart rate response to touch", *Psychosomatic Medicine*, 42(6), pp. 559–565, (1980).

[6] Mari Aikoshi, "Clinico-psychological effects of physical contact and its relationship to attachment styles in adolescents", Faculty of Humanities and Social Sciences of Iwate University 18, pp. 1–18, (2009).

[7] Ai Onoduka and Emiko Katsurada, "Relationships between University Student's attachment styles and their preference of touch", *Kwansei Gakuin University Bulletin of Psychological Science Research*, 45, pp. 31–35, (2019).

[8] Hajime Yamaguchi and Yutaka Haruki, "Effects of physical contact on mood", *The Japanese Psychological Association 62*, pp. 1039, (1998).

[9] Sheryle J. Whitcher and Jeffrey D. Fisher, "Multidimensional reaction to therapeutic touch in a hospital setting", *Journal of Personality and Social Psychology*, 37(1), pp. 87–96, (1979).

[10] Hajime Yamaguchi, "Effect of touch on one's anxiety : Relation to hesitation in touching", The Journal of J. F. Oberlin University. *Psychological and Educational Research*, 1, pp. 123–132, (2010).

[11] Francis Sue, Edmund T. Rolls, Bowtell Richard, McGlone Francis, O'Doherty John, Andrew Browning, Stuart Clare, and E. Smith, "The representation of pleasant touch in the brain and its relationship with taste and olfactory areas", *Neuroreport*, 10(3), pp. 453–459, (1999).

[12] Hajime Yamaguchi, "Healing power of the hand", *Soshisha*, pp. 74–77, (2012).

[13] Hajime Yamaguchi, "The wonders of skin sensation", pp. 156–161, (2006).

[14] Karen M. Grewen, Bobbi J. Anderson, Susan S. Girdler, and Kathleen C. Light, "Warm partner contact is related to lower cardiovascular reactivity", *Behavioral Medicine*, 29(3), pp. 123–130, (2003).

[15] Miguel A. Diego and Tiffany Field, "Moderate pressure massage elicits a parasympathetic nervous system response", *International Journal of Neuroscience*, 119(5), pp. 630–638, (2009).

[16] Hozumi Akutsu, Mika Inan, and Ayako Otake, "Consideration of effective touching areas", *Japan Nursing Association*, 36, pp. 35–37, (2005).

[17] Tiffany Field, "Touch", MIT Press: Cambridge, MA (2014).

[18] Charles Spence, "The ICI report on the secret of the senses", The Communication Group: London (2002).

[19] Stanley E. Jones and A. Elaine Yarbrough, "A naturalistic study of the meanings of touch", *Communications Monographs*, 52(1), pp. 19–56, (1985).

[20] Hiroko Mitani, "Physiology sympathetic skin reaction and its test method", *Clinical Laboratory Practice*, 22(1), pp. 25–29, (2004).

[21] Anbjørn Ree, Leah M. Mayo, Siri Leknes, and Uta Sailer, "Touch targeting C-tactile afferent fibers has a unique physiological pattern: A combined electrodermal and facial electromyography study", *Biological Psychology*, 140, pp. 55–63, (2019).

[22] Antoine Bechara, Hanna Damasio, Daniel Tranel, and Antonio R. Damasio, "Deciding advantageously before knowing the advantageous strategy", *Science*, 275(5304), pp. 1293–1295, (1997).

[23] Russell M. Bauer, "Autonomic recognition of names and faces in prosopagnosia: A neuropsychological application of the guilty knowledge test", *Neuropsychologia*, 22(4), pp. 457–469, (1984).

[24] Suzanne M. Miller, "Controllability and human stress: Method, evidence and theory", *Behaviour Research and Therapy*, 17(4), pp. 287–304, (1979).

[25] Tazuru Mizunami, Yuki Sakamura, Akitoshi Tomita, Kazuya Inoue, Itaru Kitahara, and Etsuko T. Harada, "Reduction of anxiety for an autonomous vehicle by augmented visual information", *The Japanese Psychological Association*, 82 pp. 3EV–056, (2018).

[26] Kazuya Inoue, Tazuru Mizunami, Yuki Sakamura, Akitoshi Tomita, Itaru Kitahara, and Etsuko T. Harada, "Predictive cues reduce younger- but not older passengers' anxiety in autonomous vehicles", *The Japanese Society for Cognitive Psychology*, 18, Volume 2020 OS24, pp. 9, (2021).

[27] Toshiaki Miura, "Visual perception in everyday situations", *Cognitive Science & Information Processing*, 3 pp. 100–141, (1993).

[28] Akira Ishiguchi, "Perception and attention", *Japanese Psychological Review*, Volume 26 Issue 3, pp. 180–201, (1983).

[29] William Kosnik, Laura Winslow, Donald Kline, Kenneth Rasinski, and Robert Sekuler, "Visual changes in daily life throughout adulthood", *Journal of Gerontology*, 43(3), pp. 63–70, (1988).

[30] Kiichi Nagashima, "Sensory and perceptual changes with aging", *The Society of Japanese Psychological Review*, 27(3), pp. 283–294, (1984).

[31] Mitsuo Ikeda and Tetsuji Takeuchi, "Influence of foveal load on the functional visual field", *Perception & Psychophysics*, 18, pp. 255–260, (1975).

CHAPTER 7

Challenges and Opportunities of Activity Recognition in Clinical Pathways

Christina Garcia and Sozo Inoue

Kyushu Institute of Technology

7.1 INTRODUCTION

A clinical pathway (CPW) or care map is a standardized document used as a tool to guide evidence-based healthcare [1]. CPWs detail a multidisciplinary management plan that outlines an appropriate sequence of clinical interventions including time-frames, milestones, expected outcomes [2], and other inventory of actions [1] in the course of treatment of a homogenous patient group. CPWs practiced per healthcare institution vary. The aim of CPWs is to translate clinical practice guideline recommendations into clinical processes to standardize care in a healthcare institution considering unique culture and environment [1,3]. CPWs are used to streamline and improve the quality of care as well as to maximize the outcomes for specific patient cohorts [4]. With CPWs, unjustified variations in clinical practices are monitored to achieve a more efficient, best-fit care while reducing the costs of health system [5].

Handling of a specific clinical problem of patients varies per hospital depending on the organization, local management, and resources of the institution [6]. Data from electronic health records (EHR) [7,8] and other hospital event logs [9] are the basis for drafting CPWs to serve as a guide for the patient journey with respect to the clinical condition. According to the Department of Health of Queensland, the care outlined in the document must be altered if deemed not clinically appropriate

DOI: 10.1201/9781003371540-8

for the individual patient. Clinical pathways are reviewed every two years or as required when clinical evidence changes or an emergent issue arises that requires a change in the clinical pathway content [2]. Another factor to consider is the limitation of EHR and hospital logs which can also affect the quality of CPWs.

The application of human activity recognition (HAR) in healthcare paved the way for real-time monitoring of patient activities. With the continuous technological advancement of smartphones, sensors, and wearable devices, the performance of HAR systems has also improved. EHR is usually used in HAR studies as supplementary data increasing system accuracy. Similarly, combining objective data from HAR with EHR can help refine the process of identifying variations in CPWs. There is an opportunity to use HAR in the development of better clinical pathways.

CPWs are still dependent on clinical judgment. Integrating HAR in CPWs can provide additional baseline and objective data regarding patients, medical professionals, and the use of hospital resources to support streamlining and validation of CPWs. The application of HAR in clinical pathways can extract supporting information to track and confirm activities and delivery of healthcare on time. Furthermore, the differences and commonalities between CPWs of various institutions can be reviewed systematically using HAR to improve multidisciplinary care.

A number of survey papers identifying the use of HAR in healthcare have been published in efforts to improve patient handling and delivery of healthcare. Table 7.1 shows the summary of relevant surveys on HAR related to healthcare we have collated from the search detailing the objectives and data presented by the authors. Previous surveys listed have focused on how wearable technology and sensor-based approaches are utilized to improve healthcare for patients with ADHD [10], cancer [11,12], Parkinson Disease (PD) [13], mental illnesses [14], and chronic diseases including cardiovascular disease [15,16].

The respective authors presented collated data with information about participant demographics [11,12] and data gathering site which we categorize under Dataset/Site (A); type of condition [11,12] and other comorbidities considered [10] tallied under Disease/Condition (B); Sensor and Device (C) including type [11,13], functionality, placement, consideration including pros and cons [11,12,15]; proposed framework and systems (D) for application in clinical practice [13]; Assessment tools and metrics (E) such as adherence to wearing device [11] and validation approach [10]; methods and algorithm (F) either machine learning or deep learning; and details of the activities (G) performed.

Previous studies cited in Table 7.1 have surveyed the application of HAR in healthcare specific to medical conditions. In this survey, we aim to map the landscape of how HAR is integrated into hospital processes specifically concerning patient journeys detailed in clinical pathways. Furthermore, we are interested in identifying the medical professionals participating in activity recognition as most surveys have focused on summarizing HAR with subjects mainly patients and

TABLE 7.1 Summary of Survey Papers on HAR in Healthcare

Paper	A	B	C	D	E	F	G	Focus of Survey
[11]	✓	✓	✓		✓		✓	Wearable technology for oncology
[13]			✓	✓				Sensor-based perspective in early-stage Parkinson's Disease
[12]	✓	✓	✓					Wearable accelerometers for Cancer
[15]	✓		✓					Smart wearables for cardiac monitoring beyond atrial fibrillation
[10]	✓	✓	✓		✓	✓		Automated detection of ADHD
[17]		✓		✓	✓	✓		Clinical decision support systems for chronic diseases
[16]	✓		✓		✓	✓	✓	Inertial sensor-based lower limb joint kinematics
[14]			✓				✓	Sensing technologies for monitoring serious mental illnesses

A, Dataset/Site; B, Disease/Condition; C, Sensor/Device; D, Framework/System; E, Assessment tools/Metrics; F, Algorithm/Methods; G, Activities.

healthy groups. We identify the challenges and opportunities for human activity recognition in CPWs by answering the three research questions. Specifically, the objectives of this chapter are:

- RSQ1: How is activity recognition used to validate the activities of medical professionals and patients? We identify the activities in clinical pathways where HAR is applied and the respective sensors used.

- RSQ2: How is activity recognition utilized in the clinical perspective of patient diseases? We identify the diseases and medical conditions studied with HAR and how data is collected from the subjects.

- RSQ3: Who are the focused participants in activity recognition? We identify subjects both medical professionals and patients taking part in activity recognition based on clinical pathways.

The rest of this chapter is structured starting with the Review Method elaborated in Section 7.2, followed by an overview of the clinical pathway in Section 7.3, a summary of HAR application in CPWs in Section 7.4; the discussion of identified challenges and opportunities will be presented in Section 7.5, and Section 7.6 gives the conclusion.

7.2 REVIEW METHOD

In this section, we describe the process of selecting the list of surveyed papers.

TABLE 7.2   Summary of Referenced Clinical Paths for Keyword Search

Paper	Participant	Activities
[18]	Doctors, nurses, laboratory staff	Consultation, diagnostic tests, drug treatment, prescription drugs, ward round, consultation, surgery, and administrative tasks
[7]	Patient	Patient admission, blood test, x-ray, and surgery
[9]	Patient, medical staff, physician, nurse	Nursing care, treatment, admission, operation, laboratory test, patient record, informed consent, discharge, medication, and examination
[8]	Patient, medical expert	Medication, diagnosis, and treatment

7.2.1   Keyword Selection

As the first step of the implemented search strategy, we collated a search string. We have reviewed clinical pathways and identified four reference papers listed in Table 7.2 from which we extracted activity-related keywords. Doctors from Kyushu Hospital and medical technicians from Kumamoto hospital were also interviewed, and a list of activities done by the respective medical professionals was obtained. For the final search string, the result of the interview was combined with extracted keywords from the four cited CPWs.

The respective CPWs cited include cardiovascular disease (CVD) care developed based on international guidelines [18], and bronchial lung cancer clinical pathway recommended by the Ministry of Health of China [9]. We also considered activities from data-driven clinical pathways based on EHR i.e. patient admission, blood test, X-ray, surgery [7], medication, diagnosis, and treatment [8].

After finalizing the activity list, we identified synonyms and alternative phrasings for clinical pathways. Seven synonyms of clinical pathways were used in the query combined with the activity-related keywords both from surveyed CPWs and interviews. A total of 27 keywords were used as filters. The collated keywords of the search string are listed in Table 7.3. We merged all synonyms using "OR" operations.

7.2.1.1   Search String

TITLE-ABS-KEY ("clinical pathway" OR "clinical path" OR "clinical decision" OR "care pathway" OR "integrated care pathway" OR "critical pathway" OR "care map") AND TITLE-ABS-KEY ("administrative task" OR "blood test" OR conference OR consultation OR "diagnostic test" OR discharge OR "drug treatment" OR feeding OR "home visits" OR "informed consent" OR "laboratory test" OR medication OR monitoring OR "nursing care" OR operation OR "patient admission" OR prescription OR "Report creation" OR surgery OR "ward rounds").

TABLE 7.3   Keyword Search with CWPs Synonyms and Clinical Activity Related Terms

Clinical Path Synonyms	AND	
"Clinical pathway"	"Administrative task"	"Blood test"
"Clinical path"	Conference	Consultation
"Clinical decision"	"Diagnostic test"	Discharge
"Care pathway"	"Drug treatment"	"Laboratory test"
"Integrated care pathway"	"Informed consent"	Feeding
"Critical pathway"	"Home visits"	Medication
"Care map"	Monitoring	"Nursing care"
	"Patient admission"	Operation
	"Report creation"	Prescription
	"Ward rounds"	Surgery

7.2.2   PRISMA Review

The Preferred Reporting Items for Systematic Reviews and Meta-Analyses (PRISMA) statement [19] was used as a guiding method in the search process. Applying the search string in Section 2.1 to filter the Scopus database, our query resulted in a total of 48,109 records filtered in terms of the article title, abstract, and keywords. The papers were further filtered by Subject area Computer Science within 5 years duration between 2018 and 2022 in the English language. Duplicate papers were removed. Books, erratum and editorials, and proceedings were also excluded.

In line with the research questions targeted by this survey, inclusion criteria (ICs) and exclusion criteria (ECs) were set to extract only publications relevant to the objective of this chapter. Eligible studies were limited to the following inclusion criteria (ICs):

7.2.2.1   Inclusion Criteria

IC1: Papers should include HAR application in relevant clinical pathway activities.

IC2: Papers should specify the disease or clinical pathway stage.

IC3: Papers should specify the subject focused if medical professionals and/or patients.

7.2.2.2   Exclusion Criteria

Studies that met any of the exclusion criteria were also not considered in this review:

EC1: Papers that consider HAR with images, and EHR data only.

EC2: Papers targeting the activities of medical directors and clinical managers.

EC3: Papers focusing on robot integration as well as proposal papers.

The 686 papers were screened initially based on titles and abstracts. Ninety-four studies were assessed further through full-text reading. A total of 22 full papers are obtained from the original 48,109 reports filtered according to the set criteria. Figure 7.1 shows a flowchart of the record retrieval process based on the PRISMA statement.

We sorted the final papers obtained according to publisher and year as shown in Figure 7.2. Institute of Electrical and Electronics Engineers (IEEE), Elsevier, and Multidisciplinary Digital Publishing Institute (MDPI) were the top three publishers producing the majority of the papers. A decreasing trend in the number of relevant papers published per year was observed. This can be attributed to the pandemic

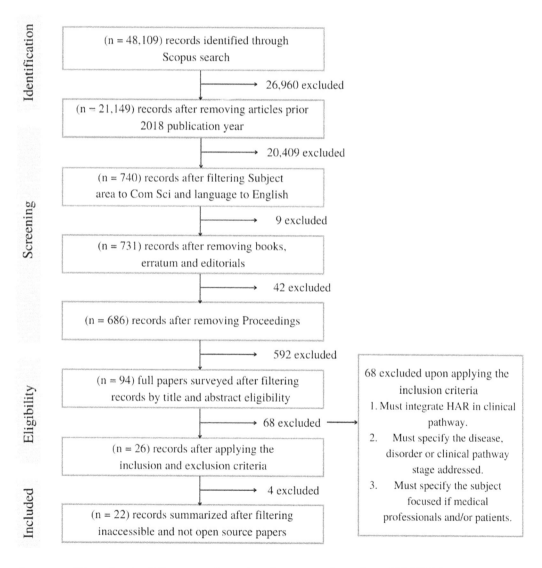

Figure 7.1 Flowchart of the record retrieval process based on PRISMA statement.

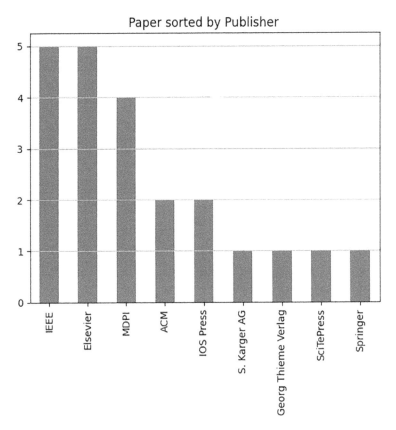

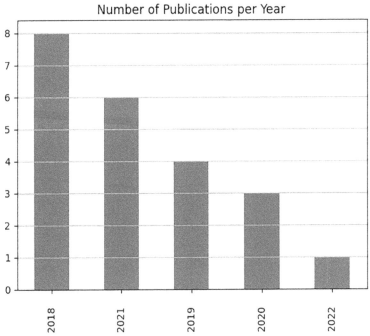

Figure 7.2 Final papers sorted by publisher and year.

situation in 2021 and 2022 where strict safety protocols were set and performing other activities in the hospital was restricted as there is a risk of COVID-19 [20]. Person-to-person contact was limited and several research facilities were closed with the work-from-home setup. Furthermore, the majority of medical professionals were focused on responding to patients with COVID-19; thus, there is difficulty in seeking clinical validation from available experts.

In 2018, 6 out of 8 studies focused on investigating patients with chronic disease mainly for assessment [21,22], monitoring [23,24], and rehabilitation [25,26]. Ostaszewski, M. and Pauk, J. [27] have studied plantar pressure insoles and wearable sensors for joint angle measurement mainly for clinical decision support. On the other hand, Nakawala, H. et al. [28] have limitations in surgical training systems and suggested a new context-aware software for decision-making during surgical training. The authors chose the Thoracentesis procedure as a prototypical scenario in their work. From 2020 onwards, all surveyed studies were focused on using wearables for continuous and objective real-life monitoring of chronic diseases, especially Parkinson [20,29,30].

7.3 OVERVIEW OF CLINICAL PATHWAYS

Clinical pathways (CPWs) are documents used as tools to guide evidence-based healthcare [1] and as a method for the patient-care management of specific patient groups during a well-defined period [31]. CPWs are known by other terms but 'clinical pathway' is internationally accepted in all settings of healthcare management [31]. CPWs have been implemented internationally since the 1980s and it was reported in 2003 that more than 80% of US hospitals in the USA had implemented clinical pathways representing a great resource commitment in the development of CPWs including training of staff, and implementation in the hospital setting [32]. Clinical pathways are proven to be useful guides for clinicians, especially new graduates with limited exposure to particular specialties, and for staff who, for some reason, are assigned in another workplace [2].

A clinical pathway is developed to find a systematic approach to monitoring patients considering a wide variety of chronic diseases and patient cohorts. Policymakers around the world view variations in health services as unacceptable and argue to encourage standardization of services for patients with identical problems undergoing similar pathways to receive the same access to clinicians, prescriptions, and the same operations to undergo for the same outcomes [33]. CPW is one of the main instruments for the implementation of clinical guidelines aiming to reduce duplication and reduce variation in health service process delivery [2].

Significant efforts are made in the health sector to create a level of interoperability and exchange of information between different systems [5]. Authors [5] have proposed a clinical pathway methodological and technological approach to reduce the general clinical complexity to improve the way patients are monitored, and to help physicians read the clinical picture in the best, most efficient way possible. The techniques commonly used to evaluate CPWs are data and process mining [7].

7.3.1 Variations in CPWs

There is an international difference in purpose in the way clinical pathways are developed, such as CPWs developed in the United Kingdom, which differ from those in the USA [31]. Handling of a specific clinical problem of patients varies per hospital depending on the organization, local management, and resources of the institution. Clinical pathways can vary in details of the patient journey. Furthermore, aside from the international differences in the purpose, existing alternative names to CPWs were found which has led to confusion [31].

Functional CPWs also contain clinical complexity considering the generalized context of an aging population and the diffusion of chronic diseases [5]. There is a big challenge in representing information streams to extract clinical path information from a varied dataset [5]. Moreover, clinical pathways are still dependent on clinical judgment. CPWs are reviewed every 24 months or as deemed necessary when an emergent issue arises or clinical evidence changes that require updating of clinical pathway content [2].

Variations in clinical pathways can cause confusion in understanding the concept and intended purpose of CPWs. Nonetheless, it is possible to identify a generic approach to representing healthcare pathways [33].

7.3.2 Activities in Clinical Pathways

Based on bronchial lung cancer CPW specification recommended by the Ministry of Health of China, researchers pointed out one feature of the clinical pathway is that it is typically arranged in a day-by-day format, enumerating the essential/critical medical behaviors or multidisciplinary clinical activities which are spread along a series of time intervals [9]. The authors mentioned that specific clinical activities such as medical orders and radiological examination tests are represented by the designated medical behaviors, which serve as checkpoints for the quality of care in various stages of the CPW.

Daily behaviors are characterized by repetitive patterns of mobility and location traces [14]. Common activities we have identified from various data-driven clinical pathways are patient admission, blood test, X-ray, surgery [7], medication, diagnosis, and treatment [8]. From the listed hospital service activities in the care map for cardiovascular disease (CVD)[18] we identified activities such as consultation, diagnostic tests, drug treatment, prescription drugs, ward round, consultation, surgery, and administrative tasks. The bronchial lung cancer clinical pathway recommended by the Ministry of Health of China [9] include activities i.e nursing care, treatment, admission, operation, laboratory test, patient record, informed consent, discharge, medication, and examination.

Researchers suggest that new ways to mitigate the cognitive overload for the clinicians have to be investigated and by using predictive analysis for CPWs starting from decision support to medical prescription, it is possible to guide the clinicians in dealing with complex pathology cases [5].

7.3.3 Patient and Medical Professionals

Clinical pathway, as defined, entails multidisciplinary clinical activities undergone by the patient. Successful clinical pathways are a collaborative effort of various medical professionals interacting with the patient at different time intervals for specific clinical activities. Based on the hospital service activities in the clinical pathway for CVD prevention care, we identified medical professionals including physicians, nurses [9], laboratory staff and pharmacy staff to be involved in the patient journey [18]. Among the primary and constant medical professional interacting with the patient are doctors and nurses for activities such as consultation, patient records, informed consent, medication, and examination. Patient journey in hospitals often involves laboratory visits; hence, better comprehension of activities involving technicians is also vital.

Clinical pathways are intended for a specific group of patients experiencing the same medical condition. It is important to designate respective CPWs to the intended patient cohort.

7.4 HAR IN CLINICAL PATH

Human Activity Recognition application in healthcare has continued to increase over the past decade understanding activity patterns of both patients and medical staff to improve patient care. The growing interest in HAR can be associated with the increasing demand and use of sensors especially wearable devices in daily life concerning health and well-being applications [34]. With patient-centered clinical care, self-reporting physical activity is often required and digital wearable tools solve the limitations of self-reporting offering advantages such as scalability and continuous real-world objective data capture [35,36].

HAR for healthcare has many potential use cases, including moving gait diagnosis, cognitive behavior monitoring and intervention, stroke-patient hospital direction, Epilepsy, and Parkinson's Disease study for doctor assistance for a better understanding of patients' recovery and interpreting disease-specific patterns to determine the patient's condition and progression [37,38]. HAR is also applied in physical activities to achieve more a accurate assessment of physical function which is a vital aspect of the clinical evaluation required to inform treatment decisions especially for cancer patients [35].

7.4.1 Data Collected

The initial step for HAR research is data management including the identification of data sources and data collection setup. Researchers in HAR either use public datasets or do data collection in a laboratory setting or in the field including hospitals, patient homes, or health clinics. Over the years, several datasets have been collected and shared by different research groups in an attempt to establish benchmark datasets for human activity recognition by simulating real-life scenarios, variabilities, and activities [34,39].

The limited medical professional-to-patient ratio is one of the driving factors of HAR studies with existing research efforts mostly targeting activities of healthy subjects, patients, and caregivers with the increasing aging population. Moreover, doctors and researchers are extremely interested in ICU patients' activities which when accurately recognized would allow clinicians to provide an optimal personalized dose of mobilities [37].

In this survey, we identified 17 papers (77.27%) that focus on activities performed by the patients and only one study with doctors as subject of interest. Other studies involved volunteers who perform activities intended to understand patterns relating to patient mobility. In Ref. [40], five healthy volunteers participated for validation of continuous ambulatory monitoring system for Epileptic users in outpatient settings. The only study involving medical professional as subject performing the activity is on surgical tasks with Thoracentesis procedure as the prototypical scenario for interpreting the current surgical situation [28]. Figure 7.3 shows the focused subjects in the surveyed research studies.

7.4.2 Sensors and Devices

The advances in sensors have enabled HAR studies to explore assisted living in health care and well-being using wearables such as inertial sensors, physical health sensors, and environment sensors [41]. Existing HAR systems can be broadly

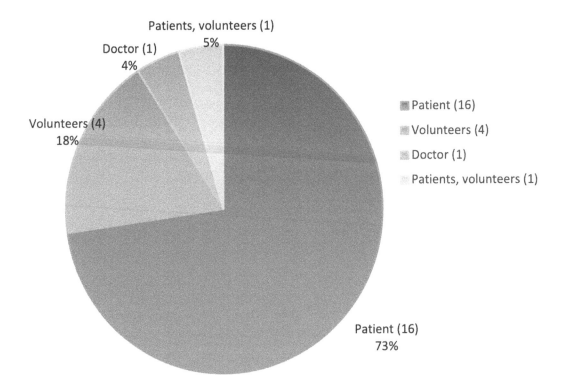

Figure 7.3 Focused subjects in the surveyed research studies.

categorized into three modalities either ambient-based, wearable-based, or hybrid depending on the sensors deployed [41]. Wearable sensors are mostly used in diagnostic and monitoring applications as these devices are capable of collecting physiological and movement data for health monitoring of patients [42]. Unlike vision-based HAR systems, wearable-based HAR systems do not suffer from severe privacy issues making wearable sensors suitable for healthcare applications [37].

With the complex nature of activities, the evaluation of the physical activity of cancer patients is challenging [12]. An accelerometer is the most common sensor applied in protocols of clinical trials involving monitoring activities of cancer patients [11] and in gait analysis to check micro and macro patterns such as variability in walking [12]. The most common types of sensors used in HAR are mainly due to their small size and low cost [34]. From the surveyed papers, we identified eight studies utilizing accelerometers among other sensors. Table 7.4 lists the sensors in the surveyed papers. From the surveyed papers, we have identified that fitness trackers, and accelerometer sensors are preferred for monitoring patients with chronic diseases such as Dementia [24], Diabetes [23,43], and PD [20,29,30] as the devices are easy to handle. Sensors are preferably integrated to wearable body vest [23,24,43,44], or worn on the wrist [25,29,40,44–47]. For gait monitoring gait, attaching sensors to insoles [27] or foot-mounted [48] is commonly practiced aside from using fitness tracking devices. Non-invasive placement of sensors is generally practiced as this allows comfort and ease of use.

7.4.3 Activities of Subjects

Studies on HAR aim to recognize human activities in controlled and uncontrolled settings [34] considering both simple and complex activities. Listed in Table 7.5 are the activities extracted from our surveyed papers with subject and clinical condition.

With human activity recognition, various sensing modalities and recognition techniques have been developed targeted towards simple, complex, or a specific set of activities by a single subject or a group. Activities can be approached with different recognition techniques depending on the type which can either be action-based such as gesture, posture, behavior, and activities of daily living (ADL), or motion-based such as tracking, and people counting [49]. HAR studies on multi-user activity recognition involve multiple people performing individual or joint actions and activities forming groups to achieve given common goals [50].

Wearable technology and HAR can help monitor activities including physical activity, sleep, and gait as well as the quality of life of cancer patients [12]. Objective monitoring of sleep cycle is important as sleep disturbance and insomnia impact the health of patients such as those with cancer [12] and ADHD [10]. On the other hand, understanding gate is important to assess markers of neurodegenerative diseases such as PD [12].

Simple activities performed by a single person involving the movement of the whole body such as walking, and sitting were studied to investigate mostly chronic

TABLE 7.4 Summary of Surveyed Papers Sensors and Placement

Medical Concern	Sensors/Devices	Placement
AxSpA [35]	Smartphone, wearables	Carried, worn
Bioimpedance[45]	Accelerometers, bioimpedance sensors	Ankle, feet, palm, wrist
Cancer, osteoporosis, Vascular disease [47]	Phone sensors	Carried, wrist
Cardiovascular [25]	Wristband device, depth camera	Wrist
Cerebral Palsy [51]	Motio capture, force plates	Camera, ground
Chronic obstructive Pulmonary disease [26]	Smart watch, noninvasive ventilator, pulse oximeter	
COVID-19 [52]	Temperature sensor, pressure sensor	Smart pillow
Dementia [24]	Fitness tracker	Vest
Diabetes [43]	ECG, breathing sensors, acceleration	Wearable body vest
Diabetes [23]	ECG, 3D acceleration, breathing sensors	Wearable body vest
Dysphagia [53]	Mechano-acoustic sensors acceleration	Near throat, ribcage side
Epilepsy [40]	ECG, PPG, EEG	Chest, wrist, back of ear
Gait quality [48]	Wearable IMU	Foot-mounted
Joint angle [27]	Plantar pressure insoles	Insole
Knee osteoarthritis, joint	Motion capture	Laboratory
Replacement surgery [21]		
Multiple sclerosis [22]	Wireless inertial sensors	Arm, forearm, hand
Musculoskeletal Disorder [46]	Accelerometer, gyroscope, magnetometer	Wrist, chest, ankle, hands, feet, head, hip, thigh, full body
Neonatal state[44]	Wearable stretching sensor, IMU, ECG	Smart vest, wrist
Parkinson [20]	Accelerometer, magnetometer, GPS	Carried smartphone
Parkinson [29]	Accelerometer, gyroscope	Wrists, necklace
Parkinson [30]	Wearable, accelerometer	Palm, belt, trousers pocket

TABLE 7.5 Summary of Surveyed Papers with Subject and Clinical Condition

Medical Concern	Subject A	B	C	Activity	Clinical Purpose
Chronic					
axSpA [35]	✓			Sleep, exercise, screen time	Monitoring
(COPD) [26]	✓			Medication, self-reporting, oxygen therapy, noninvasive ventilation, quit smoking, health education, pulmonary rehabilitation program	Rehabilitation
COVID-19 [52]	✓			In-bed situation, walking	Monitoring
Diabetes [43]	✓			Walking, steps, stairs	Early detection, monitoring
Diabetes [23]	✓			ADL, walking, steps, stairs	Monitoring
Dementia [24]	✓			Walking, gait	Monitoring
Dysphagia [53]	✓			Swallowing	Monitoring
Epilepsy [40]		✓		ADL	Monitoring
[a]Knee joint replacement [21]	✓			Gait, range of motion of knee, hip and ankle, walking	Assessment, surgery
Multiple sclerosis [22]	✓			Left/right arm finger-to-nose test	Assessment
Musculoskeletal [46]		✓		ADL, walking, running, sitting, stairs, standing, poses, jumping	Monitoring
Cerebral Palsy [51]	✓			Gait	Clinical decision support
Parkinson [29]	✓			ADL	Monitoring
Parkinson [20]	✓			Balance test, finger-tapping, walking, tracking	Monitoring
Parkinson [30]	✓			Walk, supine, finger tapping, hand and arm movements	Monitoring
Acute/Chronic					
Osteoporosis, vascular disease, cancer, [47]	✓			Running, walking, falling, climbing stairs, dropping the phone	Clinical decision support Monitoring
Cardiovascular disease [25]	✓			Exercise: walking, jumping, high knee running, side steps with arms	Rehabilitation

[a]Knee osteoarthritis joint replacement.

A, patient; B, volunteer acting as patient; C, doctor; COPP, Chronic Obstructive Pulmonary Disease'.

TABLE 7.5 (*Continued*) Summary of Surveyed Papers with Subject and Clinical Condition

Medical Concern	Subject A	B	C	Activity	Clinical Purpose
Others					
Bioimpedance [45]		✓		Standing, sitting, supine	Monitoring bioimpedance, posture detection real-time
Gait quality [48]	✓			Walking	Clinical decision support
Neonatal state [44]	✓	✓		Walking, sitting, turning, wrist movement (boxing, arm swing, arm tremble)	Monitoring
Joint angle [27]		✓		Walking	Clinical decision support
Thoracentesis [28]			✓	Surgical training	Surgery

A, patient; B, volunteer acting as patient; C, doctor.

such as Diabetes [23,43], Dementia [24], Cerebral Palsy [51] and Parkinson Disease [20,29]. Investigating walking movements was also used for studies on joint angle measurement [27].

7.5 DISCUSSION

In this section, we elaborate the challenges and opportunities for future research direction based on the limitations of the surveyed research works.

7.5.1 Challenges

In this subsection, we summarize the issues in integrating HAR into CPWs.

7.5.1.1 Data Gathering

HAR studies require the labeling of data, which can be done manually or using a mobile device. From the surveyed papers, a total of 16 papers involved patients as subjects. Data gathering done in the field such as in hospitals and in the patient home should be monitored in terms of device adherence. Device adherence can be affected by factors such as device placement, physical appearance, technical requirements, device handling such as charging [12], and encouragement from clinicians [35]. Widrawal rate can increase even after the recruitment process and participants' meeting [12]. Moreover, ease of usability and wearing comfort should be considered to increase participant retention rate. Hospital visit is part of life for patients with congenital heart disease, thus the design of a device intended for long-term use with ease should be considered [15]. Furthermore, data on evaluating physical activity are subject to possible user bias and limitations.

Introducing the system to participants and users, especially among the older population needs assistance. Appropriate training of participants, both patients and medical professionals, is necessary to bridge the gap between researchers and subjects. The effectiveness of training can affect the quality and efficiency of data gathered. User awareness and acceptance of both clinician and patient are key factors for accepting smart systems in healthcare [43]. Furthermore, interruption in data gathering and small sample size [20,52,53] should be considered as it may affect HAR system performance.

7.5.1.2 Integrating Sensors in Medical Facilities

Deployment of sensors in the field is subject to uncontrollable external factors such as signal interference, unstable connection, and unexpected battery failure if not properly monitored. Calibration and testing of devices with respect to the hospital setting should be considered especially with uncontrolled variables. Device consideration should include external factors in the setup. The accuracy of recorded activities such as step count varies between devices and manufacturers [15] and should be tested prior to deployment.

Furthermore, initial testing may mean an additional workload for medical professionals in terms of labeling, and interpretation of baseline data. Collaboration between researchers and medical professionals is dependent on the schedule and workload of medical professionals.

7.5.1.3 Regulatory Requirements

Ethics and approval of hospital management are considered in regulatory requirements [12]. Ethical standards regarding research on human subjects should be followed and approval of respective hospital research ethics committee should be confirmed in advance as much as possible as this will affect data gathering. Security and privacy of data containing information about the participants should be considered. Participant information sheets should be written for the respective cohort to ensure all participants understand the study.

7.5.1.4 Clinical Validation and Adoption of Machine Learning

Despite the advancement of AI, clinicians' concern about model stability and interpretability for discovering patient movement patterns specific to some symptoms [37] should also be clarified by researchers. In collaborative research work involving medical professionals, researchers need to represent data properly and reflect clinically meaningful results in the analysis. Problems with small sample size and interruption of data gathering due to unprecedented factors such as COVID-19 [20] can affect the quality of data.

Research on automated digital health systems is seldom implemented in the clinical setting and usually is in the proof-of-concept stage [53]. Currently, there is a challenge for researchers to communicate the results of simulations to the medical team. Efforts to address this gap include integrating web interfaces based on collected insights from medical professionals to reflect graphs they equally find meaningful. Ghods A, et al. [54] performed the participatory iterative design of visual interface and analytics involving clinicians. Personalized healthcare monitoring system with a mobile application designed for patient use such as for diabetes [55] and PD [20] monitoring is equally meaningful for both researchers and participants. The design of health systems should be driven by outcomes meaningful to researchers, end-user both medical professionals and patients.

7.5.2 Opportunities

In this subsection, we collated the suggested continuation of research work from the surveyed papers and identified future research directions.

7.5.2.1 Disease Focused

Current activity recognition research applied to clinical pathways is focused on chronic disease monitoring mainly on Parkinson's, Diabetes, and gait analysis. Figure 7.4 shows the classification of clinical conditions focused on in the surveyed papers. Chronic diseases are conditions that may get worse over time limiting daily

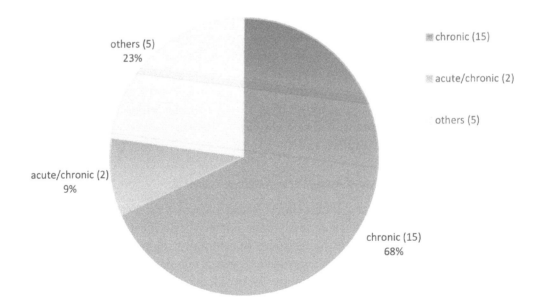

Figure 7.4 Classification of clinical condition focused in the surveyed papers.

activities that impact the lives of patients [56]. Heart disease, stroke, respiratory diseases, cancer, and diabetes are among the conditions falling under chronic diseases [17].

There is room for further study relating activity recognition to the clinical pathway of patients with disorders affecting movement such as

- Metabolic-syndrome, and musculoskeletal conditions i.e. paget's disease, stroke, carpal tunnel syndrome, and trauma.

- Neurological diseases including multiple system atrophy, progressive supranuclear palsy, and Wilson's disease.

- Psychological including depression, anxiety, and stress.

Sensing technologies of HAR with real-time data can bridge the need for an effective symptom monitoring for mental illness including granular tracking of behavioral, physiological, and social signals relevant to mental health [14].

Clinical implementation of the use of Inertial Measurement units (IMU) was surveyed with the increasing use for estimation of lower limb kinematics, but the clinical implementation is still lacking [16].

7.5.2.2 Persons of Interest and Activities

Human Activity Recognition application in healthcare has continued to increase over the past decade, understanding activity patterns of both patients and medical staff to improve patient care. Based on the survey, research efforts mostly target patients as persons of interest while less study can be found centered on medical professionals. Results of the survey indicate 17 papers on HAR studies related to CPWs have patients as subject of interest (77.27%).

Patient journey in hospitals often involves laboratory visits; hence, better comprehension of the routine of the laboratory technician and other medical staff is also vital. Research targeted on medical professionals such as medical staff, laboratory technician and doctor activities throughout the clinical pathway are to be studied further to review workload distribution, identify activity patterns affecting work performance, patient interaction, and delay of care delivery. A balanced workload distribution is important to maximize staff and optimize care delivery especially considering the shortage of medical professional.

Using HAR for clinical pathway-related activities will allow objective monitoring of patient activities, reduce self-reporting biases, and unload nurses and clinicians of data entry tasks.

7.5.2.3 Clinical Path Development

There is an opportunity to use objective data from HAR to reinforce electronic health records and support clinical decision-making. Clinical decision support systems is expected to provide a better clinical orientation, empower patient awareness

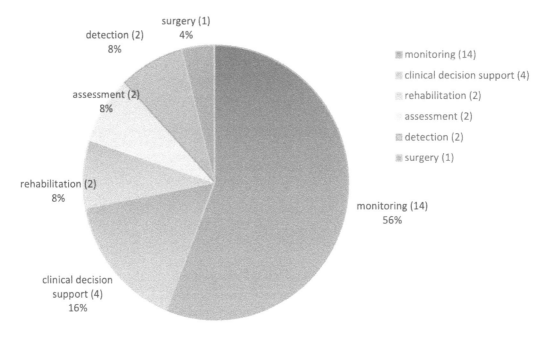

Figure 7.5 Clinical purpose of surveyed papers.

and instill deeper knowledge of their condition [17]. Understanding the interaction of patients in the stages elaborated in CPWs can help support decision-making related to the patient's clinical condition and streamline clinical pathways.

Based on our review, 56% of the studies use HAR as a tool for monitoring. Figure 7.5 shows the clinical purpose of the surveyed papers.

HAR can be used as a supplementary reference to event logs in the development of CPWs. There is room to explore activity recognition to monitor the quality of clinical pathways by identifying the frequency of hospital visits, length of stay, and admission; checking and confirmation of patient path and identity; checking conformity to guideline of institution supporting EHR and event logs; identifying activity performance on time; and validating usage of medical equipment to strengthen accountability and distribution.

7.6 CONCLUSION

In this chapter, we survey the application of HAR in clinical pathways identifying subjects, and activities performed, and focus on medical conditions of current works. We point out the challenges and opportunities for HAR in clinical pathways extending to activities of medical professionals, and to identify patient movement and clinical activities delivered to support electronic health records and other hospital logs as a basis for updating CPWs to streamline healthcare.

Based on an analysis of the filtered papers, our findings suggest that the majority of the current papers integrate HAR in the context of health-related interventions as a means to monitor patient status. There is an opportunity to study activities related to clinical conditions such as neurological, psychological, and musculoskeletal affecting patient movement.

7.6.1 Limitations to Validity

In this chapter, we have surveyed the literature according to our specific search string and targeted research questions. As a result, the literature query in the Scopus databases was narrowed down using the set criteria relevant to our objective. Also, the survey was queried from a single database and was limited to five years duration between 2018 and 2022. It is possible that other relevant papers were not included in this analysis.

BIBLIOGRAPHY

[1] Rotter, T., de Jong, R. B., Lacko, S. E., et al. (2019). Clinical pathways as a quality strategy. In Busse, R., Klazinga, N., Panteli, D., et al. (eds.), *Improving Healthcare Quality in Europe: Characteristics, Effectiveness and Implementation of Different Strategies [Internet]*, Health Policy Series, No. 53. European Observatory on Health Systems and Policies: Copenhagen (Denmark), p. 12.

[2] Clinical Excellence Queensland, Queensland Health (2021). Clinical Pathways, https://clinicalexcellence.qld.gov.au/resources/clinical-pathways.

[3] Hipp, R., Abel, E., & Weber, R. J. (2016). A primer on clinical pathways. *Hospital Pharmacy* 51(5), 416–421. doi: 10.1310/hpj5105-416.

[4] Lawal, A. K., Rotter, T., Kinsman, L., Machotta, A., Ronellenfitsch, U., Scott, S. D., Goodridge, D., Plishka, C., & Groot, G. (2016). What is a clinical pathway? Refinement of an operational definition to identify clinical pathway studies for a Cochrane systematic review. *BMC Medicine* 14, 35. doi: 10.1186/s12916-016-0580-z.

[5] Ardito, C., Bellifemine, F., Noia, T.D., Lofú, D., & Mallardi, G. (2020). A proposal of case-based approach to clinical pathway modeling Support. *2020 IEEE Conference on Evolving and Adaptive Intelligent Systems (EAIS)*, Bari, Italy, pp. 1–6.

[6] Schlieter, H., Benedict, M., Gand, K., & Burwitz, M. (2017). Towards adaptive pathways: Reference architecture for personalized dynamic pathways. *2017 IEEE 19th Conference on Business Informatics (CBI)*, pp. 359–368. doi: 10.1109/CBI.2017.55.

[7] Funkner, A. A., Yakovlev, A. N., & Kovalchuk, S. V. (2017). Data-driven modeling of clinical pathways using electronic health records. *Procedia Computer Science* 121, 835–842. doi: 10.1016/j.procs.2017.11.108.

[8] Zhang, Y., Padman, R., & Patel, N. (2015). Paving the COWpath: Learning and visualizing clinical pathways from electronic health record data. *Journal of Biomedical Informatics* 58, 186–197.

[9] Huang, Z., Lu, X., Duan, H., & Fan, W. (2013). Summarizing clinical pathways from event logs. *Journal of Biomedical Informatics* 46(1), 111–127. doi: 10.1016/j.jbi.2012.10.001.

[10] Loh, H. W., Ooi, C. P., Barua, P. D., Palmer, E. E., Molinari, F., Acharya, & U. R. (2022). Automated detection of ADHD: Current trends and future perspective. *Computers in Biology and Medicine*, 146, 105525. doi: 10.1016/j.compbiomed.2022.105525.

[11] Gresham, G., Schrack, J., Gresham, L. M., Shinde, A. M., Hendifar, A. E., Tuli, R., Rimel, B. J., Figlin, R., Meinert, C. L., & Piantadosi, S. (2018). Wearable activity monitors in oncology trials: Current use of an emerging technology. *Contemporary Clinical Trials*, 64, 13–21. doi: 10.1016/j.cct.2017.11.002.

[12] Dadhania, S. & Williams, M. (2022). *Wearable Accelerometers in Cancer Patients*. doi: 10.1007/978-3-030-83620-75.

[13] Krokidis, M. G., Dimitrakopoulos, G. N., Vrahatis, A. G., Tzouvelekis, C., Drakoulis, D., Papavassileiou, F., Exarchos, T. P., & Vlamos, P. (2022). A sensor-based perspective in early-stage Parkinson's disease: Current state and the need for machine learning processes. *Sensors (Basel, Switzerland)*, 22(2), 409. doi: 10.3390/s22020409.

[14] Abdullah, S. & Choudhury, T. (2018). Sensing technologies for monitoring serious mental illnesses. *IEEE MultiMedia* 25(1), 61–75. doi: 10.1109/MMUL.2018.011921236.

[15] Duncker, D., Ding, W. Y., Etheridge, S., Noseworthy, P. A., Veltmann, C., Yao, X., Bunch, T. J., & Gupta, D. (2021). Smart wearables for cardiac monitoring-real-world use beyond atrial fibrillation. *Sensors (Basel, Switzerland)*, 21(7), 2539. doi: 10.3390/s21072539.

[16] Weygers, I., Kok, M., Konings, M., Hallez, H., De Vroey, H., & Claeys, K. (2020). Inertial sensor-based lower limb joint kinematics: A methodological systematic review. *Sensors (Basel, Switzerland)*, 20(3), 673. doi: 10.3390/s20030673.

[17] Souza-Pereira, L., Pombo, N., Ouhbi, S., Felizardo, V., & Garcia, N. (2020). Clinical decision support systems for chronic diseases: A systematic literature review. *Computer Methods and Programs in Biomedicine*, 195, 105565. doi: 10.1016/j.cmpb.2020.105565.

[18] Hendriks, M. E., Kundu, P., Boers, A. C., Bolarinwa, O. A., Te Pas, M. J., Akande, T. M., Agbede, K., Gomez, G. B., Redekop, W. K., Schultsz, C., & Swan Tan, S. (2014). Step-by-step guideline for disease-specific costing studies in low- and middle-income countries: A mixed methodology. *Global Health Action*, 7, 23573. doi: 10.3402/gha.v7.23573.

[19] Moher, D., Liberati, A., Tetzlaff, J., Altman, D. G., & The PRISMA Group. (2009). Preferred reporting items for systematic reviews and meta-analyses: The PRISMA statement. *PLoS Medicine* 6(7), e1000097. doi: 0.1371/ journal.pmed.1000097.

[20] Bouça-Machado, R., Pona-Ferreira, F., Leitão, M., Clemente, A., Vila-Viçosa, D., Kauppila, L. A., Costa, R. M., Matias, R., & Ferreira, J. J. (2021). Feasibility of a mobile-based system for unsupervised monitoring in Parkinson's disease. *Sensors* 21, 4972. doi: 10.3390/s21154972.

[21] Ro, D. H., Lee, J., Lee, J., Park, J. Y., Han, H. S., Lee, & M. C. (2019). Effects of knee osteoarthritis on hip and ankle gait mechanics. *Advances in Orthopedics* 2019, 9757369. doi: 10.1155/2019/9757369.

[22] Daunoraviciene, K., Ziziene, J., Griskevicius, J., Pauk, J., Ovcinikova, A., Kizlaitiene, R., & Kaubrys, G. (2018). Quantitative assessment of upper extremities motor function in multiple sclerosis. *Technology and Health Care : Official Journal of the European Society for Engineering and Medicine* 26(S2), 647–653. doi: 10.3233/THC-182511.

[23] Baig, M., Mirza, F., GholamHosseini, H., Gutierrez, J., & Ullah, E. (2018). Clinical decision support for early detection of prediabetes and type 2 diabetes mellitus using wearable technology. *2018 40th Annual International Conference of the IEEE Engineering in Medicine and Biology Society (EMBC)*, pp. 4456–4459. doi: 10.1109/EMBC.2018.8513343.

[24] Banerjee, T., Peterson, M., Oliver, Q., Froehle, A., & Lawhorne, L. (2018). Validating a commercial device for continuous activity measurement in the older adult population for dementia management. *Smart Health* 5–6, 51–62. doi: 10.1016/j.smhl.2017.11.001.

[25] Triantafyllidis, A., Filos, D., Buys, R., Claes, J., Cornelissen, V., Kouidi, E., Chatzitofis, A., Zarpalas, D., Daras, P., Walsh, D., Woods, C., Moran, K., Maglaveras, N., & Chouvarda, I. (2018). Computerized decision support for beneficial home-based exercise rehabilitation in patients with cardiovascular disease. *Computer Methods and Programs in Biomedicine* 162, 1–10. doi: 10.1016/j.cmpb.2018.04.030.

[26] Yang, G., Kong, C., & Xu, Q. (2018). A home rehabilitation comprehensive care system for patients with COPD based on comprehensive care pathway. *2018 IEEE Fourth International Conference on Big Data Computing Service and Applications (BigDataService)*, Bamberg, Germany, pp. 161–168.

[27] Ostaszewski, M., & Pauk, J. (2018). Estimation of ground reaction forces and joint moments on the basis on plantar pressure insoles and wearable sensors for joint angle measurement. *Technology and Health Care : Official Journal of the European Society for Engineering and Medicine* 26(S2), 605–612. doi: 10.3233/THC-182507.

[28] Nakawala, H., Ferrigno, G., & De Momi, E. (2018). Development of an intelligent surgical training system for thoracentesis. *Artificial Intelligence in Medicine* 84, 50–63. doi: 10.1016/j.artmed.2017.10.004.

[29] Habets, J. G. V., Heijmans, M., Leentjens, A. F. G., Simons, C. J. P., Temel, Y., Kuijf, M. L., Kubben, P. L., & Herff, C. (2021). A long-term, real-life Parkinson monitoring database combining unscripted objective and subjective recordings. *Data* 6(2), 22. doi: 10.3390/data6020022.

[30] Saez-Pons, J., Stamate, C., Weston, D., & Roussos, G. (2019). PDkit: An open source data science toolkit for Parkinson's disease. In *Adjunct Proceedings of the 2019 ACM International Joint Conference on Pervasive and Ubiquitous Computing and Proceedings of the 2019 ACM International Symposium on Wearable Computers (UbiComp/ISWC '19 Adjunct)*. Association for Computing Machinery, New York, pp. 939–943. doi: 10.1145/3341162.3346277.

[31] De Bleser, L., Depreitere, R., De Waele, K., Vanhaecht, K., Vlayen, J., & Sermeus, W. (2006). Defining pathways. *Journal of Nursing Management*, 14(7), 553–563. doi: 10.1111/j.1365-2934.2006.00702.x

[32] Kinsman, L., Rotter, T., James, E. et al. (2010). What is a clinical pathway? Development of a definition to inform the debate. *BMC Medicine* 8, 31. doi: 10.1186/1741-7015-8-31.

[33] Keen, J. (2012). What is a care pathway? *2012 4th International Workshop on Software Engineering in Health Care (SEHC)*, pp. 15–18. doi: 10.1109/SEHC.2012.6227000.

[34] Demrozi, F., Pravadelli, G., Bihorac, A., & Rashidi, P. (2020). Human activity recognition using inertial, physiological and environmental sensors: A comprehensive survey. *IEEE Access : Practical Innovations, Open Solutions*, 8, 210816–210836. doi: 10.1109/access.2020.3037715.

[35] Jones, S. L., Hue, W., Kelly, R. M., Barnett, R., Henderson, V., & Sengupta, R. (2021). Determinants of longitudinal adherence in smartphone-based self-tracking for chronic health conditions: Evidence from axial spondyloarthritis. *The Proceedings of the ACM on Interactive, Mobile, Wearable and Ubiquitous Technologies (IMWUT)*, vol. 5, 24 p. doi: 10.1145/3448093.

[36] Prince, S. A., Adamo, K. B., Hamel, M. E., Hardt, J., Gorber, S. C., & Tremblay, M. A. (2008). Comparison of direct versus self-report measures for assessing physical activity in adults: A systematic review. *International Journal of Behavioral Nutrition and Physical Activity* 5(1), 1.

[37] Liu, R., Ramli, A.A., Zhang, H., Henricson, E., & Liu, X. (2022). An overview of human activity recognition using wearable sensors: Healthcare and artificial intelligence. In Tekinerdogan, B., Wang, Y., & Zhang, L. J. (eds.), *Internet of Things: ICIOT 2021*. Lecture Notes in Computer Science, vol. 12993. Springer: Cham. doi: 10.1007/978-3-030-96068-11.

[38] Fikry, M., Hamdhana, D., Lago, P., & Inoue, S. (2021). Activity recognition for assisting people with ementia. *Intelligent Systems Reference Library*, 271–292. doi: 10.1007/978-3-030-68590-410.

[39] Schrader, L., Vargas Toro, A., Konietzny, S. et al. (2020). Advanced sensing and human activity recognition in early intervention and rehabilitation of elderly people. *Population Ageing* 13, 139–165. doi: 10.1007/s12062-020-09260-z.

[40] Zambrana-Vinaroz, D., Vicente-Samper, J. M., & Sabater-Navarro, J. M. (2022). Validation of continuous monitoring system for epileptic users in outpatient settings. *Sensors (Basel, Switzerland)*, 22(8), 2900. doi: 10.3390/s22082900.

[41] Wang, Y., Cang, S., & Yu, H. (2019). A survey on wearable sensor modality centred human activity recognition in health care. *Expert Systems with Applications* 137, 167–190. doi: 10.1016/j.eswa.2019.04.057.

[42] Dinarević, E. C., Husić, J. B., & Baraković, S. (2019). Issues of human activity recognition in healthcare. *2019 18th International Symposium INFOTEH-JAHORINA (IN-FOTEH)*, pp. 1–6. doi: 10.1109/INFOTEH.2019.8717749.

[43] Baig, M. M., GholamHosseini, H., Gutierrez, J., Ullah, E., & Lindén, M. (2021). Early detection of prediabetes and T2DM using wearable sensors and internet-of-things-based monitoring applications. *Applied Clinical Informatics* 12(1), 1–9. doi: 10.1055/s-0040-1719043.

[44] Chen, H. et al. (2020). Design of an integrated wearable multi-sensor platform based on flexible materials for neonatal monitoring. *IEEE Access* 8, 23732–23747. doi: 10.1109/ACCESS.2020.2970469.

[45] Dutt, A. G., Verling, M., & Karlen, W. (2020). Wearable bioimpedance for continuous and context-aware clinical monitoring. *2020 42nd Annual International Conference of the IEEE Engineering in Medicine & Biology Society (EMBC)*, pp. 3985–3988. doi: 10.1109/EMBC44109.2020.9175298.

[46] Wijekoon, A., Wiratunga, N., Sani, S., & Cooper, K. (2020). A knowledge-light approach to personalised and open-ended human activity recognition. *Knowledge-Based Systems* 192, 105651. doi: 10.1016/j.knosys.2020.105651.

[47] Richardson, A., Perl, A., Natan, S., & Segev, G. (2019). A clinical decision support system based on an unobtrusive mobile app. *ICT4AWE*. doi: 10.5220/0007587001670173.

[48] Qiu, S. et al. (2019). Body sensor network-based gait quality assessment for clinical decision-support via multi-sensor fusion. *IEEE Access* 7, 59884–59894. doi: 10.1109/ACCESS.2019.2913897.

[49] Hussain, Z., Sheng, Q. Z., & Zhang, W. (2019). Different approaches for human activity recognition: A survey. ArXiv, abs/1906.05074.

[50] Li, Qimeng, et al. (2020). Multi-user activity recognition: Challenges and opportunities. *Information Fusion* 63, 121–135.

[51] Zhang, Y. & Ma, Y. (2019). Application of supervised machine learning algorithms in the classification of sagittal gait patterns of cerebral palsy children with spastic diplegia. *Computers in Biology and Medicine* 106, 33–39. doi: 10.1016/j.compbiomed.2019.01.009.

[52] Li, S. & Chiu, C. (2021). Improved smart pillow for remote health care system. *Journal of Sensor and Actuator Networks* 10(1), 9. doi: 10.3390/jsan10010009.

[53] O'Brien, M. K., Botonis, O. K., Larkin, E., Carpenter, J., Martin-Harris, B., Maronati, R., Lee, K., Cherney, L. R., Hutchison, B., Xu, S., Rogers, J. A., & Jayaraman, A. (2021). Advanced machine learning tools to monitor biomarkers of dysphagia: A wearable sensor proof-of-concept study. *Digital Biomarkers* 5(2), 167–175. doi: 10.1159/000517144.

[54] Ghods, A., Caffrey, K., Lin, B., Fraga, K., Fritz, R., Schmitter-Edgecombe, M., Hundhausen, C., & Cook, D. J. (2019). Iterative design of visual analytics for a clinician-in-the-loop smart home. *IEEE Journal of Biomedical and Health Informatics* 23(4), 1742–1748. doi: 10.1109/JBHI.2018.2864287.

[55] Alfian, G., Syafrudin, M., Ijaz, M. F., Syaekhoni, M. A., Fitriyani, N. L., & Rhee, J. (2018). A personalized healthcare monitoring system for diabetic patients by utilizing BLE-based sensors and real-time data processing. *Sensors* 18(7), 2183. doi: 10.3390/s18072183.

[56] Benkel, I., Arnby, M., & Molander, U. (2020). Living with a chronic disease: A quantitative study of the views of patients with a chronic disease on the change in their life situation. *SAGE Open Medicine* 8. doi: 10.1177/2050312120910350.

II

Mental Health

CHAPTER 8

Anxolotl, an Anxiety Companion App - Stress Detection

Nuno Gomes
Instituto Politécnico de Lisboa

Matilde Pato
Instituto Superior de Engenharia de Lisboa Instituto Politécnico de Lisboa and LASIGE, FCUL
Universidade de Lisboa

Pedro Santos
Instituto Politécnico de Lisboa

André Lourenço
Instituto Politécnico de Lisboa and CardioID Technologies

Lourenço Rodrigues
Instituto Politécnico de Lisboa and CardioID Technologies

8.1 INTRODUCTION

Stress is a term that describes bodily reactions to perceived physical or psychological threats [1]. Since the start of stress level recording among the population, these values have been on the rise, and the pandemic had a significant impact on them. There is a consistent increase of stress-related mental symptoms (anxiety, depression, general psychological distress) in the general population during the pandemic compared to before [2].

While these facts are dire, stress in its inception is a good evolutionary response to dangerous situations, allowing our bodies to be better prepared to perform in the face of a "fight-or-flight" situation. An example of such a situation could be an encounter with a tiger. Nowadays, it is unusual to find tigers in a person's

DOI: 10.1201/9781003371540-10

day-to-day life, and so, it is more prevalent in the case of deadlines or responsibilities, and its purpose is to help humans to be better prepared to deal with such events, using biological changes to face a recognized threat. It still can be beneficial, keeping us alert in dangerous situations and focused to meet challenges [1].

On the other side, if such situations keep adding up and stress does not subside, it stops being classified as an acute stress response, and it starts entering the chronic stress realm. At this stage, our bodies are producing hormones to keep the stress response up, but the outcome starts being more negative than positive. This chronic stress can lead to the atrophy of the brain mass and decrease in its weight. These structural changes bring about differences in the response to stress, cognition and memory [3]

Mental health problems exist along a continuum, from mild, time-limited stress, to severe mental health conditions, and while mental illnesses and stress are not the same, they are closely related. Stress and anxiety affect most people at some point in their lives, but the regularity at which that happens is one of the key points of classifying such events as a disease. Focusing on the anxiety and anxiety disorders, they are the most common type of mental illness in the world, affecting 264 million people worldwide as of 2017, with an increase of 14.9% per decade [4]. While the rise of both stress and anxiety is related, so are their symptoms.

Anxiety is one of the most pervasive and ubiquitous human emotions, in all cultures [5]. It is considered a basic negative emotion, such as sadness, anger, worry, and fear. Anxiety, fear, and stress all share similarities and might even overlap to some extent, but they are different states: Stress has a clear cause, which is called a stress-causing factor or a stressor, such as the tiger mentioned before. Fear also shares some similarities to stress, but it is classified as an emotion and might trigger a stress response. It is associated with danger and/or insecurity, and it is also focused on immediate present danger. Anxiety, by contrast, corresponds to a state of uncertainty, and it is more closely related to a future-oriented mood state associated with preparation for possible, upcoming negative event.

Measuring anxiety and stress has a big overlap, due to a propensity of one to cause the other, common risk factors, as well as the bodily reactions being similar. Choosing which biological data to capture and analyze to target each situation becomes paramount for detection. Nevertheless, the reason for the association between these psychological syndromes is yet to be established [6]. Regarding their monitorization, context is likely to be utterly important since it allows for a better evaluation of the data, and questionnaires can fill the gap in distinguishing both, as presented in Ref. [7].

The symptoms of these conditions can be divided into Somatic (physical) and Psychic. For the most part, the symptoms most commonly associated with each are:

- Anxiety

    - Somatic: tremors, palpitations (increased or irregular heart rate), dizziness, nausea, shortness of breath, sweating, muscle tension, etc.;

  – Psychic: difficulty concentrating, nervousness, Insomnia, constant worry, etc.

- Stress

  – Somatic: aches and pains, palpitations, muscle tension, digestive problems, etc.;
  – Psychic: anxiety, irritability, depression, sadness, panic attacks, etc.

Looking at the symptoms, we can see some overlap. Given that stress can cause an anxiety response, then all the symptoms present in anxiety become targetable on stress detection. Current consumer wearables are not yet capable of distinguishing data with such precision, yet they are the most accessible way of monitoring both cases.

The production of smart devices to help individuals monitor components of their health has been on the rise during the last few years [8]. The presence of smartphones among the population is almost universal, and these two tools could be used as a way of bringing comfort and quality of life to people suffering from mental illnesses such as anxiety or chronic stress.

8.1.1 Contributions

The Anxolotl project focuses on trying to supplement a more nuanced solution to a very nuanced problem, which is the management of mental health and follow-up of mental illnesses, namely General Anxiety Disorder (GAD) and Panic Disorder (PD). By taking advantage of consumer-grade wearables, which are already very present worldwide, and using them to allow patients to better manage their mental health and well-being. The big focus is to provide a support tool, one mainly used to keep track of their mental health data and allow them to intervene before an acute crisis settles, or chronic state in the case of stress.

8.1.2 Anxolotl: An Anxiety Companion App

The Anxolotl — An anxiety companion app — presents a system that can reliably detect anxiety and stress levels, detect panic attacks (PAs) as long as a wearable is being used. Ideally, upon the detection of abnormal anxiety or stress levels, a notification would pop up, and in the case of detection of PAs, the user will be able to choose which mechanisms to use, such as automatically calling a selected person, buzzing or suggesting breathing exercises. The app is intended to run on the background and auto-start to be as frictionless as possible to use.

The main idea is to give users control over their mental health situation. This would translate into being able to check anxiety and stress levels on a smartphone, as well as being warned by a notification in the case of consistently high stress or anxiety levels. Short-term solutions such as meditation, or wellness exercises could be suggested, but the main point is the detection. As long as the user leaves the app on the background, and wears the wearable, these mental health statistics can be recorded, and the user can live his/her life ignoring the app, until the time the app detects an abnormality.

Finally, there are some non-nuclear objectives, such as the presentation of the data to a validated medical professional, and stress detection. The last one is discussed in this chapter, as well as the algorithm used. It is intended to work along the anxiety detection in the way of giving users control over their situation. As stated before, anxiety and stress share symptoms, and to address this issue, questionnaires will be used such as the GAD questionnaire (GAD-7), and for stress the Perceived Stress Questionnaire (PSS).In this chapter, we focus on the stress detection without context, which is tougher, given the lack of truly unique symptoms.

8.1.2.1 Environment

The Anxolotl project starts by capturing data from the wearable. That data is sent in real time to a smartphone via Bluetooth Low Energy. The app is developed in Flutter to allow interoperability between iOS and Android, having a wider reach.

As shown in the Figure 8.1, filtering is applied (low-pass) on the mobile app, removing any erroneous data, and some data processing is done as well. Then, the data is synced every 10 minutes to the data center via HTTPS. The datacenter contains the models on an initial stage, where they are trained. On a later iteration, these trained models could be loaded and applied on the smartphone to reduce latency and have a real time response. The data center is responsible of receiving the biological data and training classifier models with it, giving the mental health statistics in return. A response is then sent to the smartphone identifying stress levels and presenting them to the user. The user can then check their mental health levels on their smartphone, as well as receive notifications when the models detect unusually high levels.

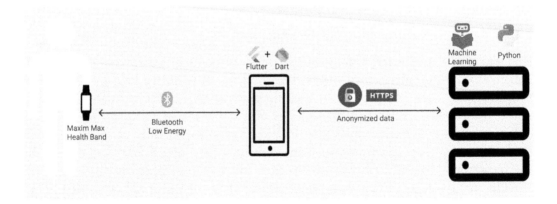

Figure 8.1   Anxolotl solution designed environment.

8.1.3 Organization

The remainder of this chapter is structured as follows: in Section 8.2 we give an overview of the current existing research on the stress subject, as well as mention some relevant scientific projects. Section 8.3 describes the technical context needed for an easier understanding of our solution. Section 8.4 describes the methodology we use for the model design, as well as iterates on the different options. Section 8.5 presents the results and discusses some of the limitations associated with our work. Finally, Section 8.6 wraps up all the work, and presents our findings as well as the next steps.

8.2 RELATED WORK

Lately, there has been a push toward a better mental health maintenance, since it is detrimental to an individual's quality of life. This section will focus on the papers that, as of late, provided good results with wearable compatible sensors in measuring stress, anxiety, or panic attacks. Given the focus of this chapter, a good collection of sensors data to measure each of this metrics will bring immense value, since it will allow for more combinations of sensors to be picked. The pioneers in this field were Healey and Picard who showed, in 2005, that stress could be detected using physiological sensors [10].

The purpose of Healey and Picard [10] was to distinguish between 3 base levels (*low*, *medium* and *high*) of stress in drivers, with an accuracy rate of around 97%. The stress addressed here was the stress with a negative bias, namely distress. Four types of physiological sensors were used during the experiment: electrocardiogram (ECG), electromyography (EMG), skin conductivity (also known as SC, electroder-mal activation (EDA) or galvanic skin response (GSR)), and respiration (through chest cavity expansion). Their algorithm included the mean and variance of the EMG taken in the hand, respiration and the mean of the heart rate (HR) over one second intervals throughout a drive. In this chapter, the best correlating signals with stress levels were the mean of the skin conductivity (0.47), followed by the L100 (frequency domain HR Variability (HRV)) (0.41) and finally the HR (0.30). According to this chapter, using the HR and GSR with intervals of 5 minutes, stress levels could accurately be predicted 97.4% of the time.

Hee Han et al. [11] focused on measuring the stress levels from a population of 17 subjects on an everyday setting and on a laboratory setting, while binarily accessing their stress condition (stressed or not-stressed). This chapter focused on using three sensors, photoplethysmography (PPG), ECG and GSR. In a lab setting, this chapter provided a 94.6% accuracy in distinguishing the stress levels, while that figure dropped to 81.82% on an everyday setting. One of the outcomes was finding that in the everyday setting, GSR + ECG group showed the best everyday accuracy, which was 90.91% [11]. Another finding was that the sensors from the wearables tend to perform worse in an everyday setting, since data capture noise became a real problem when it came to measuring data in an ordinary setting.

Finally, an overlook of the current situation in measuring stress, we can see value in all the presented sensors. While HRV and PPG are relatively recent, they are also promising, as HRV was identified as the most useful physiological metric for the detection of stress and anxiety [8], it was also observed that HR and GSR were the most regularly used sensory signals because they gave the most promising results and high-accuracy for detecting stress and its levels [12].

8.3 BACKGROUND

Here we present the context we think is necessary to understand both parts of this work, both the more medical, as well as the more technological. Stress can be measured by monitoring physiological indicators such as heart activity, blood activity, skin response (GSR) or skin temperature (ST), and we address this problem with a strong theoretical background. While measuring stress on itself is tricky, we can measure indicators of such, and such events must be explained and theoretically correlated with stress itself. Regarding the machine learning (ML), we will also present the algorithms and methods we consider important. While the development is highly empirical, given a ML context, it highly relies on a basic understanding of the human body, and the relations between stress and stress-related physiological data.

8.3.1 Measuring Biological Data

Given that stress is a bodily response to a *stimulus*, or multiple *stimuli* with somatic symptoms, those same symptoms can be measured. Multiple types of symptoms allow the existence of multiple different ways of measuring, and while the most promising data seems to be heart activity and galvanic activity related [9,11,13] there is also value in the monitoring of ST. All these factors play a role in the physical manifestation of stress on the human body, and these studies presented good results with accuracies of more than 90% using the presented physiological data.

GSR refers to electrical changes that arise when the skin receives specific signals from the brain. These changes may be due to emotional activation, cognitive workload or physical exertion [9]. While these changes can be subtle, stress can also cause sweat to happen, and as such, increase the level of GSR, which can be used for detection.

Heart activity is the most known of these biological signals, and most wearable devices can capture HR and HRV. While the HR increases upon stress, it also increases on many other ordinary phenomena, such as a scare, on the other hand, HRV has a tighter relation with stress. Usually, HRV is extrapolated from PPG and highly related to HR, and time-domain indices of HRV can quantify the amount of variability in measurements of the period between successive heartbeats, the Inter-Beat-Interval (IBI) [12].

The "fight-or-flight" response restricts the blood flow from the extremities and increases the blood flow to vital organs. This peripheral vasoconstriction produces changes in ST on the extremities including hands, which can indicate stress and its intensity [9]. While rises and drops in temperature are normal body functions, when correlated with other signals, ST might be a good indicator of a stress response, by using mean temperature or the slope of the temperature during a certain time frame.

It was observed that when stress occurs, HR, blood pressure, respiration rate, and GSR tend to increase while HRV and ST decrease [12]. This is not much different from a physical exercise session, and here is where context can make or break a model. But with this in mind, a good amount of features will bring better results to a model, given not a single feature can accurately detect stress.

8.3.2   Machine Learning

In a complex problem such as stress detection, the application of some type of machine learning (ML) algorithms makes sense. The vast amount of data in a context where multiple variables, such as HR, HRV, GSR, and ST, might have different outputs based on each other, makes it a prime target for the ML approach. It is no wonder it has already been applied to it and continues to be used and researched to this day.

8.3.2.1   Feature Selection

Machine learning algorithms are built with data that is fed to them, so it is easy to assume that the quality of the models is proportional to the amount and quality of information that is consumed. To take out any irrelevant information, it is common to apply a pre-processing step known as feature selection, in order to improve the model's performance. Following, are some of the techniques used.

Recursive feature elimination (RFE) with cross-validation is one of the algorithms used to achieve this feature selection. Recursion is the process of repeating a process multiple times. In the case of *RFE*, the process consists in generating a different model, and for each iteration, different features are taken away based on the generated metrics. While this process takes place, the impact of the removal of each feature is observed in the model's accuracy, to find the optimum set of features to use for the maximum results.

Sequential Feature Selector adds (forward selection) or removes (backward selection) features to form a feature subset in a greedy fashion. At each step, this estimator chooses the best feature to add or remove based on the cross-validation score of an estimator.

8.3.2.2 *Classifiers*

Classification consists in predicting the class of a set of given data points; classes are sometimes called targets/labels or categories. Classification is the task of approximating a mapping function from input variables (X) to discrete output variables (Y). There are a lot of classification algorithms available, however, what dictates whether they perform accurately or not depends on the nature of the given data set and the relationships between data. Some of the most common classification algorithms are Support Vector Machines (SVM), K-Nearest Neighbours (K-NN), Random Forests (RF), Decision Trees, and Naive Bayes (NB).

8.3.2.3 *Classifiers in Stress Detection*

Many studies have applied multiple methods in feature selection and classification, but no universal algorithm has been developed for stress. With that in mind, it is a good idea to look at what came before to have a clear perspective on where to start regarding this subject.

In Gjoreski et al. [9], the best result for context stress detection, regarding F1-Score was the Decision Tree with 90%, followed by Random Forest with 74%, SVM with 69% and K-NN with the same result. All these results were made in an aggregation-window with 10 seconds. The no-context events had lower precision scores, around 7% for true positives in the best model.

Memar and Mokaribolhassan [13] present a table, with a stress analysis review. Here, for data sets without context and using the data available in our dataset (HR, GSR, and ST), the best results in terms of accuracy were from a SVM with 80%, K-NN with 88.6% and Logistic Regression with 91.4%. On the other side, the measurements had a large number of sensors, which we do not have.

Finally, Han et al. [11], had success using PPG, ECG, and GSR, while classifying the stress with K-NN (multiple variables) and SVM, with accuracies ranging from 85%–95%, coming closer to 85% on contextless stress detection on day-to-day tasks. Feature selection was used to reach those results, and classifiers were tested along the development as well.

8.4 METHODOLOGY

The approach we use in this challenge is heavily influenced by current literature. Instead of a traditional heuristic approach based on a machine learning (ML) problem, this challenge is interpreted as a data problem. Since the provided data is not unprocessed, we opt to interpret the problem this way to try and connect the data we already have with the results we are aiming for.

While the influence of the literature is going to be relevant, another relevant feature of our work is the usage of the SKlearn framework, which brings some limitations, namely not having implementations of the most technically advanced algorithms, such as deep neural networks. With that said, we have to forfeit some of the more advanced algorithms and focus on long established algorithms.

This section regards our analysis of the data set, features, and their selection as well as an introduction to our ML algorithm choices.

8.4.1   Data

Our solution uses the SMILE data set [14], and by extension it is designed to work well with it. A total of 45 healthy adult Belgian participants (39 females and 6 males) were recruited for SMILE. Among participants, the average age was 24.5 years old and the standard deviation was 3.0 years. On average, each participant contributed 8.7 days of data. Two types of sensors were used for the data set, one for HR, and another one for GSR and ST.

Regarding the data set itself, the data is not the original recorded data. It is anonymous and was reconstructed from a model based on the original data, and this process was made for the continuous portion of data by the data set providers. For the handcrafted portion of the data, we have 60 minutes of measurements *per* stress label, which means the data has to be processed to fit into a 1-1 model — one data point to one label.

The data also comes normalized from 0 to 1 and contains masking, that identifies when the captured data was unreliable, or the user was not wearing the device, and so it can be discarded. Regarding the data set organization, it is divided into deep features, in which the features are presented as close to raw as possible, while still being normalized, and handcrafted features which were calculated from not normalized features, but are presented and normalized as well.

8.4.1.1   Data Filtering

Regarding filtering the data to achieve more representative results, we opt to filter out entries presenting more than half the data as unreliable (in one minute). Not removing these points could impact our output, given that each valid point would have twice the impact on the label result. Another reason for this choice are the experimental results, given that ratio presents the best results as shown in Table 8.1.

TABLE 8.1   Accuracy and F1-Score Metrics in Ratio of Non-Zero Values on the Training Data Set

Non-Zero Ratio	Accuracy	F1 Score
0.3	0.54	0.58
0.4	0.54	0.58
0.5	**0.56**	**0.60**
0.6	0.53	0.57
0.7	0.53	0.56

Note: The bold values indicate the best results.

8.4.1.2 Testing

Testing is also an important part of dealing with the data set since it is the way we validate or discard the hypothesis. For these tests, we searched and found k-fold split and the k-fold stratified to be a good compromise between good output and low complexity.

We choose k-fold, since k-fold stratified removes entries to balance classes, and in the case of stress detecting, the order by which the entries are removed is important since a timeline exists. Our solution is to balance the data set ourselves while using k-fold. We are sticking with three splits, to try and avoid overfitting while keeping the relation between train set and test set sizes near the real size relation between the train data set (2060 entries) and the test data set (960 entries).

8.4.2 Features

The supplied data set contains features extrapolated from the original data set via ML and reassembling, as well as features based on HR, GSR, and ST that were extracted from the data and presented as byproducts of the original data. The handcrafted features contain some lost granularity, but the deep features are normalized, and so it would be impossible to recalculate new features from them. With that in mind, our choice is to use only the handcrafted features.

8.4.2.1 Feature Selection

From the provided 20 features on the handcrafted part of the data set, we have tried and tested some and ended up processing them to create our own features. Here we present 16 features, some with a scientific paper support, which we cite, and some of them with an empirical evidence basis. Below we present our selected features, with citations in the case they are inspired by another paper.

- Heart Rate

    - Mean HR [9],
    - HR standard deviation [9],
    - HR quartile deviation (Percentile 75 to 25) [9],
    - HRV standard deviation variability [15],
    - HRV mean standard deviation [15],
    - HRV mean of root mean square of R-R differences,
    - Percentile 90 of low frequency signal,
    - Percentile 90 of low and high frequency ratio,
    - Mean of low and high frequency ratio.

- Galvanic Skin Response

  - Mean GSR [15],
  - GSR quartile deviation (Percentile 75 to 25) [15].

- Skin Temperature

  - Mean ST [9],
  - Mean ST Variability,
  - Max ST slope value,
  - ST Mean Slope [9],
  - Percentile 90 of ST slope.

In the case of heart activity, the unreferenced features, are added because low and high frequencies, as well as the ratio between them, are good measures of stress-related activity [15]. The non-cited data on ST is used because increases and decreases in ST values can be indicators of stress, and the rate of increase is the biggest indicator, which is why both variability of the mean and three slope values are present.

All of these and more features are passed through a ridge correlation between each feature and the label, and none of them had smaller absolute correlations than 20% or bigger than 200%, to keep balance. The data with low correlations are kept because they are often referred in literature as good indicators, and since we are still applying a feature extractor tool, not much harm can be done.

8.4.2.2 Feature Extraction

Since the provided data set contains a minute of data per label, features must be downsampled, but by doing that we would be losing granularity. In response, our group opted to use research features while downsampling said data. To try and have the most important features, we tried two feature extractors, that are used with the classifier as algorithm since we assume the same algorithm is the best feature extractor for itself.

The two tried and tested feature extractors are the recursive feature elimination with cross-validation (RFECV) [16], and the sequential feature selector, which are both provided by the SKLearn framework. They both have been positively used in the literature and are currently regarded as trustworthy. The Table 8.2 presents their results using Linear-SVC (C-Support Vector Classification) as the classifier, and being tested with the k-fold split. We use five features minimum, as we think that is the best relation between features and the size of the data set.

RFECV gives, on average, more features according to the Figures 8.2 and 8.3 with higher correlations between them; we believe that the data set is not big

TABLE 8.2 Results from Different Classifiers, Using the Train and Test Data Set

Methods	K-fold Acc	K-fold F1	Test Acc	Test F1
Linear-SVC	0.57	0.56	**0.64**	0.54
Random forest	0.47	**0.58**	0.51	**0.58**
Decision tree	0.51	0.55	0.49	0.50
5-NN	0.54	**0.58**	0.48	0.51
7-NN	0.53	**0.58**	0.52	0.54
9-NN	0.52	0.57	0.53	0.55
NB	**0.58**	0.57	0.54	0.41

Note: The bold values indicate the best results.

```
        f0    f1    f2    f3    f4    f5   ...    f8    f9   f10   f11   f12   f13
f0    1.00  0.91  0.91  0.23  0.20  0.28   ... -0.01 -0.00  0.01  0.01 -0.02 -0.01
f1    0.91  1.00  0.89  0.24  0.26  0.23   ... -0.02 -0.03  0.04  0.04  0.01  0.02
f2    0.91  0.89  1.00  0.19  0.23  0.26   ... -0.02 -0.06  0.06  0.05  0.01  0.02
f3    0.23  0.24  0.19  1.00  0.84 -0.04   ... -0.01 -0.05  0.04  0.12  0.10  0.11
f4    0.20  0.26  0.23  0.84  1.00  0.02   ... -0.09 -0.05  0.04  0.16  0.15  0.16
f5    0.28  0.23  0.26 -0.04  0.02  1.00   ... -0.01  0.06 -0.05 -0.04 -0.02 -0.02
f6    0.19  0.19  0.18  0.58  0.57  0.17   ... -0.02 -0.05  0.01 -0.00 -0.02 -0.02
f7    0.19  0.20  0.17  0.57  0.54  0.26   ...  0.01 -0.08  0.04  0.05  0.05  0.05
f8   -0.01 -0.02 -0.02 -0.01 -0.09 -0.01   ...  1.00  0.09 -0.03 -0.10 -0.09 -0.09
f9   -0.00 -0.03 -0.06 -0.05 -0.05  0.06   ...  0.09  1.00 -0.30 -0.15  0.00 -0.01
f10   0.01  0.04  0.06  0.04  0.04 -0.05   ... -0.03 -0.30  1.00  0.39  0.04  0.09
f11   0.01  0.04  0.05  0.12  0.16 -0.04   ... -0.10 -0.15  0.39  1.00  0.86  0.88
f12  -0.02  0.01  0.01  0.10  0.15 -0.02   ... -0.09  0.00  0.04  0.86  1.00  0.99
f13  -0.01  0.02  0.02  0.11  0.16 -0.02   ... -0.09 -0.01  0.09  0.88  0.99  1.00
```

Figure 8.2 Screenshot of the RFECV Feature correlation results.

```
         f0    f1    f2    f3    f4
f0     1.00  0.23  0.19 -0.02 -0.01
f1     0.23  1.00  0.58 -0.02  0.11
f2     0.19  0.58  1.00  0.01  0.05
f3    -0.02 -0.02  0.01  1.00 -0.10
f4    -0.01  0.11  0.05 -0.10  1.00
```

Figure 8.3 Screenshot of the sequential feature selector results.

enough for so many features. On the other hand, after testing both options on the test page, the results from the RCEV are 0.59 accuracy with 0.51 F1-score against the results from the sequential feature selector which are around 0.62 accuracy with 0.54 F1-score, making the sequential feature selector a more suitable choice.

8.4.3   Machine Learning Classification

Physiological data varies from individual to individual, and while classifying data on a per subject basis can give the ML a personal approach, our data does not have personal identifiers. With that in mind, the error rate is going to be higher, since the values that identify stress in a person are not exactly the same that identify stress on a group.

Furthermore, we approach this challenge using ML algorithms, such as K-NN with multiple neighborhoods (i.e., 5-NN, 7-NN, and 9-NN), SVM, NB, Random Forest and Decision Trees, since those have been fairly covered in the literature, as stated before. K-NN is a method that uses k-nearest data points and does a majority vote to predict the result, and k is used to identify the number of data-points. SVM finds hyper-planes to divide data points into different classes [11]. We use the SKlearn implementation of SVM, and mostly Linear-SVC. NB classifier predicts the result based on the probabilities of each feature's probabilistic knowledge, and Random Forest and Decision Trees work by iterating trees of questions and ending with a conclusion in the end.

The model testing evaluation is done with the training data set, as we opt to keep that variable constant. This choice was made in an effort to reduce the complexity of the system, since not having labels for the test data set proved to be a challenge, since its results do not completely correlate with our train data set results.

8.5   RESULTS

In this chapter, the features without context are used to classify stress. While we have some limitations regarding the data set, we designed a machine learning flow to receive the data and output a label a list of labels classifying stress with a binary classification. Our final algorithm is presented in Algorithm 8.1.

Algorithm 8.1 Pseudo-Code of the Workflow

---

filterDatasetZeros(p=0.5,trainDataset)
discretizeDataset(trainDataset)
balanceDataset(trainDataset)
clf = Classifier
selector = SequentialFeatureSelector
pickedFeatures = selector.selectFeatures(clf,trainDataset)
clf.fit(pickedFeatures)
clf.predict(testDataset)
output(answer.txt)

Given that, we will now change the classifier for each of the suggested classifiers and access its viability for the challenge. Our findings are presented in Table 8.1. Regarding the testing, we perform it on the train data set using k-fold, as well as tests on the challenge submission page.

Given this, our pick is using the Linear-SVC, since it presents the best results. The Random Forest is also used initially with a varying degree of success, even allowing us to achieve an accuracy of 0.62 with specialized parameters. But after tuning, the Linear-SVC provides the best consistent results. While the score, is not high enough to be used in a real setting, it proves promising, given the limitations.

The code is fully available at https://github.com/matpato/CfP-Workshop-and-Challenge-Wellbeing.git, a sample of the data set is available too.

8.5.1 Discussion

Given the complexity of a stress monitoring solution, better can always be achieved; even though our result is notable among our peers, some things could have been better. The data set being open, and having a test page was a good way of avoiding data overfit, but regarding the data set, some things could be improved.

The data set not having real data was a slight inconvenient, since a lot of nuance was lost, but that did not make it impossible to achieve good predictions. On the other hand, the data being normalized is a problem, since we could not extract features from the data, and features that can be interesting could not be used. Examples of this are, inter beat interval (IBI), and its variance on a different time window, the low and high frequencies at full granularity and even the zero of the temperature slope. Those values could have made the scores better, and are commonly used in research, yet we can not calculate them with full precision.

Regarding our work, the usage of SKLearn alone is a problem, since it restricts our access to machine learning tools. It is possible that deep neural networks can provide better results, but since the time was little to learn a new framework, the group made the choice to play it safe on the framework. More feature tuning and classifier tuning can also have be used to improve results, but this suggestion had issues with computational power when it was tried.

8.6 CONCLUSION

In this chapter, we propose a stress monitoring system to be applied on the Anxolotl project. While we can adapt the algorithm to different data, namely from the wearable, new data sets need to be tested to assert its viability. Our results show a 64% accuracy score, which is not high for real life application, but that can be a result of the data set. More research is needed on that regard. While this result is not the best, we are confident that this model has potential to achieve viability on real world classification after improvements.

BIBLIOGRAPHY

[1] J. Choi, B. Ahmed, and R. Gutierrez-Osuna, "Development and evaluation of an ambulatory stress monitor based on wearable sensors," *IEEE Transactions on Information Technology in Biomedicine*, vol. 16, no. 2, pp. 279–286, 2012.

[2] A. M. Kunzler, N. Röthke, K. Lieb, T. Rigotti, and M. Coenen, "Mental health and resilience amid the covid-19 pandemic in the eu," European Parliamentary Research Service, Technical Report, 2021. [Online]. Available: https://www.europarl.europa.eu/RegData/etudes/STUD/2022/697217/EPRS_STU(2022)697217_EN.pdf

[3] H. Yaribeygi, Y. Panahi, H. Sahraei, T. P. Johnston, and A. Sahebkar, "The impact of stress on body function: A review," *EXCLI Journal*, 2017. [Online]. Available: https://www.excli.de/vol16/Sahebkar_Panahi_21072017_proof.pdf.

[4] M. Elgendi and C. Menon, "Assessing anxiety disorders using wearable devices: Challenges and future directions," *Brain Sciences*, vol. 9, p. 50, 2019.

[5] I. G. Sarason and B. R. Sarason, Test anxiety. In H. Leitenberg, Ed., *Handbook of Social and Evaluation Anxiety*, pp. 475–495. Boston, MA: Springer US, 1990. [Online]. Available: https://doi.org/10.1007/978-1-4899-2504-6_16.

[6] E. Ramón-Arbués, V. Gea-Caballero, J. M. Granada-López, R. Juárez-Vela, B. Pellicer-García, and I. Antón-Solanas, "The prevalence of depression, anxiety and stress and their associated factors in college students," *International Journal of Environmental Research and Public Health*, vol. 17, no. 19, 2020. [Online]. Available: https://www.mdpi.com/1660-4601/17/19/7001.

[7] L. Bickman, "Improving mental health services: A 50-year journey from randomized experiments to artificial intelligence and precision mental health," *Administration and Policy in Mental Health and Mental Health Services Research*, vol. 47, pp. 795–843, 2020.

[8] B. A. Hickey, T. Chalmers, P. Newton, C.-T. Lin, D. Sibbritt, C. S. McLachlan, R. Clifton-Bligh, J. Morley, and S. Lal, "Smart devices and wearable technologies to detect and monitor mental health conditions and stress: A systematic review," *Sensors*, vol. 21, no. 10, p. 3461, 2021. [Online]. Available: http://dx.doi.org/10.3390/s21103461.

[9] M. Gjoreski, M. Luštrek, M. Gams, and H. Gjoreski, "Monitoring stress with a wrist device using context," *Journal of Biomedical Informatics*, vol. 73, pp. 159–170, 2017. [Online]. Available: https://www.sciencedirect.com/science/article/pii/S1532046417301855.

[10] J. Healey and R. Picard, "Detecting stress during real-world driving tasks using physiological sensors," *IEEE Transactions on Intelligent Transportation Systems*, vol. 6, pp. 156–166, 2005.

[11] H. J. Han, S. Labbaf, J. Borelli, N. Dutt, and A. M. Rahmani, "Objective stress monitoring based on wearable sensors in everyday settings," *Journal of Medical Engineering & Technology*, vol. 44, pp. 177–189, 2020.

[12] S. Gedam and S. Paul, "A review on mental stress detection using wearable sensors and machine learning techniques," *IEEE Access*, vol. 9, pp. 84045–84066, 2021.

[13] M. Memar and A. Mokaribolhassan, "Stress level classification using statistical analysis of skin conductance signal while driving," *SN Applied Sciences*, vol. 3, no. 1, p. 64, 2021. [Online]. Available: https://doi.org/10.1007/s42452-020-04134-7.

[14] C. W. Group, "Momentary stress labels with electrocardiogram, skin conductance, and acceleration dataset," Computational Wellbeing Group, Technical Report, 2022. [Online]. Available: https://compwell.rice.edu/workshops/embc2022/challenge.

[15] Y. S. Can, N. Chalabianloo, D. Ekiz, and C. Ersoy, "Continuous stress detection using wearable sensors in real life: Algorithmic programming contest case study," *Sensors*, vol. 19, no. 8, p. 1849, 2019. [Online]. Available: https://doi.org/10.3390/s19081849.

[16] A. Iranfar, A. Valdés, and D. Atienza, "Relearn: A robust machine learning framework in presence of missing data for multimodal stress detection from physiological signals," *2021 43rd Annual International Conference of the IEEE Engineering in Medicine & Biology Society (EMBC)*, Mexico, vol. 2021, pp. 535–541, 2021.

CHAPTER 9

Detection of Self-Reported Stress Level from Wearable Sensor Data Using Machine Learning and Deep Learning-Based Classifiers: Is It Feasible?

Atzeni Michele, Cossu Luca, Cappon Giacomo, and Vettoretti Martina

University of Padova

9.1 INTRODUCTION

Persons' mental health is at the root of almost every interaction that a person can have, from daily living, relationships, to physical health. Positive mental health helps an individual to work productively, achieve their full potential and augmenting their emotional, psychological, and social well-being. According to the "Global Burden of Disease Study", the global prevalence of mental health disorders has always been above 10%, and about 450 million people have mental health disorders [1,2]. Specifically, mental health can be disrupted from numerous factors such as social anxiety, depression, psychological disorders, drug addiction, workplace issues, and, more commonly, stress. Indeed, most individuals are prone to stress, which is the reaction that people may have when they are subject to demands and pressures that do not correspond to their knowledge and abilities and that can challenge their handling capabilities. The body can react to stress in different ways, hence an individual can experience headaches, shallow breathing or hyperventilating, sweating,

DOI: 10.1201/9781003371540-11

and heart palpitations [3]. In this context, the wide spread of wearable devices, e.g., smartwatches and portable sensors, bring the potential of identifying stress episodes by monitoring body changes and, more specifically, vital signs such as body and skin temperature, blood pressure, heart rate, electrocardiogram (ECG) or the galvanic skin response (GSR) [4]. Therefore, the possibility of leveraging portable smart devices for monitoring and, ultimately, preserving mental health welfare via automatic algorithms and systems, has received increasing attention worldwide. While various methods for the purpose have been proposed in the literature [5–7], effective stress episode detection is still an open challenge. In this chapter, we preliminary explore the feasibility of adopting four different machine learning (ML) and deep learning (DL) models (based on logistic regression (LR), support vector machines (SVM), and long-short term memory (LSTM)), fed by deep learning-based and handcrafted features extracted from wearable sensor raw data, to detect stress. The manuscript is structured as follows. Section 9.2 presents the details of the dataset. Section 9.3 describes the methods for model development. Section 9.4 defines the metrics used for model evaluation and comparison and reports the obtained results. Finally, Section 9.5 draws the final conclusions and discusses possible future work.

9.2 THE SMILE DATASET

The dataset used in this work has been provided by the Computational Wellbeing Group of Rice University from Houston, Texas in the context of an open challenge during the 44th IEEE Engineering in Medicine and Biology Society Conference [8]. The SMILE dataset is composed of 45 healthy adult participants (39 females and 6 males) from Belgium, with an average age of 24.5 years old, with a standard deviation of 3.0 years. Each participant contributed to an average of 8.7 days of data. Two types of wearable sensors were used for data collection: a wrist-worn device (Chillband, IMEC, Belgium) designed for the measurement of skin conductance (SC), skin temperature (ST), and acceleration data (ACC), a chest patch (Health Patch, IMEC, Belgium) to measure ECG and ACC. Participants were also asked to report their stress levels and received reminders on their mobile phones. The dataset provides for each stress level data-point 60-minute sequences of ECG, GSR, and ST features to be used for the stress level prediction. Table 9.1 shows the detail of the provided features. These features were computed from ECG, GSR and TS signals with 5-minute sliding windows with 4-minute overlapping segments. Besides the handcrafted features, the dataset provides some deep features which have been extracted through unsupervised machine learning on the whole SMILE dataset with different backbones such as Conv-1D and Transformer-based Autoencoders. In total, the dataset contains 2070 samples, each with corresponding self-reported stress labels ranging from 0 ("not at all") to 6 ("very") with a proportion of about 50% for the 0 label. Labels greater than 0 have been set to 1 which led to work in a binary classification setting.

TABLE 9.1   List of Handcrafted Features in the SMILE Dataset

Signal	Feature
ECG	Mean heart rate
ECG	Standard deviation of heart rate variability's R-R intervals
ECG	Root mean square of successive R-R differences
ECG	Low frequency signal (power in the 0.04–0.15 Hz band)
ECG	High frequency signal (power in the 0.15–0.40 Hz band)
ECG	Ration of low and high frequency
ECG	Ratio of the very low (0.0033–0.04 Hz) and low frequency
ECG	Heart rate cycle
GSR	Average GSR level
GSR	Phasic GSR - signal power of the pahsic GSR signal (0.16–2.1 Hz)
GSR	GSR response rate - number of GSR responses in window divided by the total length of the window (i.e. responses per second)
GSR	GSR second difference - signal power in second difference from the GSR signal
GSR	GSR magnitude - the sum of the magnitudes of GSR responses
GSR	GSR duration - the sum of the durations of GSR responses
GSR	GSR area the sum of the area of GSR responses in seconds. The area is defined using the triangular method ($1/2 \times$ GSR magnitude $\times$ GSR duration)
ST	Mean ST
ST	Standard deviation of the ST
ST	Slope of the ST - slope of a straight line fitted through the data
ST	Median ST

9.3   MODEL DEVELOPMENT

9.3.1   General Model Structure Definition

In this work, we defined and experimented four different model structures which we chose and optimized following a trial-and-error approach. Figure 9.1 shows the scheme of the general model structure. It consists of two layers. The preprocessing layer prepares and processes the original SMILE dataset for subsequent model training by performing common operations, such as feature extraction, and data

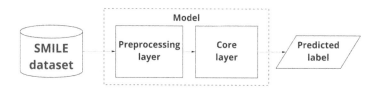

Figure 9.1   General model structure scheme.

cleaning. The core layer incorporates and trains the ML/DL model of choice using the data provided by the preprocessing layer and outputs the stress label inferred from each data sample. All the pipelines were based on a common preprocessing layer and a personalized core layer at first; however, it seemed that each model was performing better in some scenarios than others. For this reason, it was chosen to tune each core layer with their best preprocessing layer. Below the details of each model structure are reported. Hereafter, we labeled each model as A, B, C, and D for the sake of simplicity.

9.3.1.1 Model A

In model A, we explored the use of LSTMs to solve the stress classification problem at hand.

9.3.1.1.1 Preprocessing Layer
The aim being simplifying the feature set at hand, the preprocessing layer of model A limits to removing from the SMILE dataset all handcrafted features extracted from ECG and ST data. Additionally, the layer also removes the deep features extracted using the Conv-1D backbone.

9.3.1.1.2 Core Layer
The core layer of model A leverages the simplified dataset provided by the preprocessing layer to train a composite model made of two LSTMs each consisting of two hidden layers of 64 and 32 units. The first LSTM is fed using only the GSR-related handcrafted features, while the second LSTM uses the remaining deep features extracted using the Transformer based autoencoder. The two LSTMs' outputs are then flatten and provided as input to a dense output layer composed of a single unit with a sigmoid activation function. Finally, the output of the model is set to 1 when the predicted probability is greater or equal to 0.6, 0 otherwise.

9.3.1.2 Model B

Model B is an optimized SVM model.

9.3.1.2.1 Preprocessing Layer
The feature extraction is a time-consuming and complex task, which poses challenges on such a significant and important step of the machine learning stack. For the purpose, we used the Time Series Feature Extraction Library (TSFEL), a Python package that provides support for fast exploratory analysis supported by an automated process of feature extraction on multidimensional time series [9]. The TSFEL features can be grouped into three categories according to the domain where they are calculated: temporal, statistical and spectral domain. During the work, all the three types of variables were extracted and further evaluated. However, since

TABLE 9.2   List of TSFEL Extracted Feature

Feature	Description
Histogram	Frequency of data points with a value within the corresponding histogram bin
Interquartile range (IQR)	Q3 − Q1, where Q3 and Q1 represent the first and third quartile, respectively
Mean absolute deviation	Average of the absolute deviations from the mean
Median absolute deviation	Median of the absolute deviation from the median
Root mean square	Square root of the mean square
Standard deviation	Square root of feature variance
Variance	Expectation of the squared deviation of a variable from its sample mean
ECDF percentile count	Cumulative sum of samples that are less than the percentile
ECDF slope	Slope of the ECDF between the two percentiles
Kurtosis	Heavy-tailed or light-tailed relative to a normal distribution measure
Skewness	Measure of the asymmetry of a distribution
Maximum	Peak value of the feature
Minimum	Valley value of the feature
Mean	Feature mean value
Median	Feature median value

considering all the extracted features drove to poorer performances, we decided to keep only the statistical type of features for each of the handcrafted features of the SMILE dataset, for a total of 298 new derived features. Some features were dropped based on Pearson's correlation (correlation threshold equal to 0.95). The statistical domain computed features are shown in Table 9.2. The feature extraction has been done mainly to extract the information related to the handcrafted features signals in order to have a 1-D set of features (specifying in the algorithm a window-size equal to the length of the feature signal) in a machine learning task fashion. New extracted features of the training and test sets were scaled based on standard scaler formula from scikit-learn library. The standard score of a sample x is calculated as:

$$\frac{x - u}{s} = z \tag{9.1}$$

where u is the mean of the training samples or zero if with mean = False, and s is the standard deviation of the training samples or one if with std=False.

9.3.1.2.2   Core Layer

The core layer utilizes this new preprocessed dataset to train a simplified and tuned SVM model with linear kernel. The building procedure foresees two sequential sub-steps, a feature reduction step using an importance weighted criteria for a

Recursive Feature Elimination (RFE) approach and a fine-tuning step using the cross-validated grid search method. The feature selection procedure is recursively repeated on the shrinked set until the desired number of features to select is eventually reached. In this work, the desired number of features was set to five based on the predicting performances. The grid search method is focused mainly on the regularization parameter C. The cross-validation was done using a 5-fold cross-validation.

9.3.1.3 Model C

In model C we explored the use of an ensemble of three LR models to solve the stress classification problem.

9.3.1.3.1 Preprocessing Layer

The SMILE dataset provides some masking matrices where a zero means that the specific signal was missing or not good enough to extract the raw features for the specific label. Using these masks we have created three different sub-datasets to work with:

- The first dataset comes with both ECG and GSR raw features but only where the ECG masking matrix has at least one point where the features have been extracted. Moreover all labels with missing values of the ECG signal have been removed.

- The second dataset comes with both ECG and GSR raw features but only where the GSR masking matrix has at least one point where the features have been extracted.

- The third dataset is the intersection of the previous ones, it contains labels where both ECG and GSR signals where complete and without missing values.

On each of these datasets, a feature extraction step has been performed using the TSFEL library. On the extracted features we have performed a feature selection with ANOVA F-value as score and selecting all features with a p-value<0.05.

9.3.1.3.2 Core Layer

These three datasets have been exploited in a multi-model approach. Each of the datasets has been used to train a LR model. These three models are combined together during the prediction phase in order to use the best model according to the available input features. This means that if the input features we are trying to classify did not have missing values, they would have been ingested to the third model, the one trained on the dataset with the same characteristics (no missing values and all features available). Instead, if either EGC or GSR features were missing, the prediction was performed using either the first or the second model. If the input features did not respect any of the three models characteristics, the predicted value was arbitrarily set to 1.

9.3.1.4 Model D

Model D represents a more naive approach to the preprocessing layer, with simpler features extracted from the SMILE dataset.

9.3.1.4.1 Preprocessing Layer

Exploiting the masks provided in the dataset, we have selected the handcrafted features with ones in both ECG and GSR signals, resulting in the same dataset as the third one created in the preprocessing layer of model C. On this dataset, a manual feature extraction step has been developed to extract for each 60-minute time series its mean, standard deviation, median, maximum absolute value and maximum first-order differences value. These features have been chosen from a preliminary visual inspection of the dataset, which showed the presence of peaks and smaller variability in the data with the stress labels with respect to the no-stress labels. Then, a selection step based on the chi-squared score function, which computes chi-squared stats between each feature and class, was performed to select the 15 most significant features.

9.3.1.4.2 Core Layer

The core layer of model D uses this set of 15 features to perform a LR to classify the stress level.

9.4 MODEL EVALUATION

9.4.1 Performance Metrics

Accuracy (ACC) and F1-score (F1) were chosen as performance metrics to assess models' prediction capabilities.

9.4.2 Results

In Table 9.3 the Accuracy and F1-score of each model are presented. Model A has reached performances of 0.57 and 0.52 for ACC and F1 respectively. A possible limitation could be the focus only on DL features. Further developments could be based on training LSTMs also on handcrafted features and adding them to the last flattened and dense layers in order to contribute to the output predicted probability. Model B has reached performances of 0.56 and 0.6 for ACC and F1 respectively.

TABLE 9.3 Accuracy and
F1-Score for the Proposed Models

Model	Accuracy	F1-Score
A	0.5720	0.5248
B	0.5639	0.6004
C	0.499	0.6229
D	0.5639	0.3445

The final group of variables included in the model are from either ECG, GSR, and ST handcrafted features. In particular, one ECG-related (*Mean heart* rate Estimated Empirical Cumulative Distribution Function (ECDF)), one GSR-related (*GSR duration* maximum value) and three ST-related (*median* ECDF percentile count, *median* ECDF Percentile and median Histogram) were included in the final model. From a grid of C values ([0.01, 0.1, 1, 1.5, 10, 100]), the best coefficient selected by the cross-validation is equal to 1. There are two main limitations of this approach. First, the missing rows of data are still considered in the model development. Second, the TSFEL extracted features are based on already extracted feature signals smoothed by the sliding window mean. Model C has reached an accuracy of 0.499 and F1-score of 0.6229. The final group of included variables for each individual model counts about 200 of them which is very high considering the number of available samples. The limitation of this approach is that the performed feature selection was univariate, which may explain the high number of selected features. Model D has reached an accuracy of 0.5639 with an F1-score of 0.3445. The final 15 features included in the model are from the pool of five extracted features for each raw feature. In particular, the selected features included none of the GSR-related features, only three of the ST-related (maximum absolute value of the slope, maximum absolute first-order difference of the median and maximum absolute value of the median) and most of the ECG features (mean of the mean, maximum absolute first-order difference of the mean, median of the mean, mean, maximum absolute value and median of the high-frequency power and mean and maximum absolute value of the hearth rate cycle). The main limitation of this model is its accuracy, showing that simpler models such as LR could not be suitable for the hard task of self-reported stress detection.

9.5 CONCLUSIONS

Classification of a person stress level from wearable devices is a complex task which has an increasing interest among the scientific community, but still has a lot of room for future improvements. In the setting of an open challenge for the 44th IEEE Engineering in Medicine and Biology Society Conference, a sample dataset has been publicly released to inspire new ideas and collaborations and drive the research frontier. In this work we have proposed four different approaches to investigate such problem, but the task is far from being solved. The overall classification performance was low, with slightly better performance achieved by the model using SVM and RFE. These results evidence that the problem of stress detection from wearable sensor data is a complex problem, difficult to address, whose feasibility proof still requires some research effort. One possible problem could be related to the subjective nature of the self-reported stress level, which was used as an outcome in the current work. The use of more objective approaches to report stress level may help overcome this issue. Other difficulties could be related to the fact that each individual may manifest stress in his/her own personalized way. This could be addressed by the development of personalized models, in which a different model is learned for each individuals. Finally, another possible margin for improvement could be the collection of new variables or signals that could better discriminate among stress levels.

Resource

All code sources are available at: https://github.com/gcappon/no-stress.

ACKNOWLEDGEMENT

This work was supported by MIUR (Italian Minister for Education).

REFERENCES

[1] E. D. Vecchia, M. M. Costa, and E. Lau, "Urgent mental health issues in adolescents," *The Lancet Child & Adolescent Health*, vol. 3, no. 4, pp. 218–219, 2019. [Online]. Available: https://www.sciencedirect.com/science/article/pii/S2352464219300690.

[2] M. L. Wainberg, P. Scorza, J. M. Shultz, L. Helpman, J. J. Mootz, K. A. Johnson, Y. Neria, J.-M. E. Bradford, M. A. Oquendo, and M. R. Arbuckle, "Challenges and opportunities in global mental health: A research-to-practice perspective," *Current Psychiatry Reports*, vol. 19, no. 5, p. 28, 2017. [Online]. Available: https://doi.org/10.1007/s11920-017-0780-z.

[3] B. McEwen and R. Sapolsky, "Stress and your health," *The Journal of Clinical Endocrinology & Metabolism*, vol. 91, no. 2, pp. E2–E2, 2006. [Online]. Available: https://doi.org/10.1210/jcem.91.2.9994.

[4] D. Dias and J. Paulo Silva Cunha, "Wearable health devices-vital sign monitoring, systems and technologies," *Sensors (Basel)*, vol. 18, no. 8, p. 2414, 2018.

[5] H. Yang, H. Yu, K. Sridhar, T. Vaessen, I. Myin-Germeys, and A. Sano, "More to Less (M2L): Enhanced health recognition in the wild with reduced modality of wearable sensors,"arXiv e-prints, p. arXiv:2202.08267, 2022.

[6] H. Yu, T. Vaessen, I. Myin-Germeys, and A. Sano, "Modality fusion network and personalized attention in momentary stress detection in the wild," arXiv e-prints, p. arXiv:2107.09510, 2021.

[7] H. Yu and A. Sano, "Semi-supervised learning and data augmentation in wearable-based momentary stress detection in the wild," arXiv e-prints, p. arXiv:2202.12935, 2022.

[8] Computational Wellbeing Group, Rice University. "EMBCW: Workshop and challenge on detection of stress and mental health using wearable sensors." [Online]. Available: https://compwell.rice.edu/workshops/embc2022/challenge.

[9] M. Barandas, D. Folgado, L. Fernandes, S. Santos, M. Abreu, P. Bota, H. Liu, T. Schultz, and H. Gamboa, "TSFEL: Time series feature extraction library," *SoftwareX*, vol. 11, p. 100456, 2020. [Online]. Available: https://www.sciencedirect.com/science/article/pii/S2352711020300017.

CHAPTER 10

A Multi-Sensor Fusion Method for Stress Recognition

Leonardo Alchieri, Nouran Abdalazim, Lidia Alecci, Silvia Santini, and Shkurta Gashi

Università della Svizzera Italiana (USI)

10.1 INTRODUCTION

According to the World Health Organization, stress is a *"state of worry or mental tension caused by a difficult situation"*.[1] People may experience stress frequently, e.g., in their work environment [1]. While stress can have a positive effect – e.g., help individuals to focus and temporary increase their work performance – long periods of stressful events can impact mental and physical health [2].

Automatic stress detection techniques have been proposed as an instrument to enable the monitoring and management of stress levels, with the goal of helping people reduce stress-related health risks [3]. The use of physiological signals for stress detection is particularly promising. This is because stress induces – through the action of the autonomic nervous system [2,4] – known patterns in human physiological parameters. Such parameters include, e.g., blood volume pulse (BVP), galvanic skin response (GSR) – also known as electrodermal activity (EDA) – and skin temperature (ST). They can all be captured continuously and unobtrusively using wearable devices [1].

Building upon this existing knowledge, we propose a novel multi-sensor method to detect whether a user is experiencing "stress" or "no stress". Specifically, we utilize a two-stage approach that combines two sensory inputs: an electrocardiogram (ECG) signal and an ST signal. Two separate Gaussian Process (GP) classifiers are first used to process features computed from each of the signals separately.

DOI: 10.1201/9781003371540-12

Then, we employ a quadratic discriminant analysis (QDA) algorithm to combine the individual predictions and gauge whether the user should be classified as experiencing "stress" or "no stress". Our results show that this method can outperform baseline classifiers by 10% points when using F1-score as evaluation metrics. The implementation of our approach is publicly available on GitHub (https://github.com/LeonardoAlchieri/MUSE).

10.2 RELATED WORK

There exist several stress detection techniques in the literature. Some of them rely on a single sensor modality to perform the estimate, while others rely on multiple modalities. Holder et al. [5] refer to them as *unimodal* and *multimodal* approaches, respectively.

Unimodal approaches include, e.g., [5–8]. Rashid et al. [6] use a convolutional neural network (CNN) to distinguish between stress and non-stress states using BVP data collected with wristbands. Greco et al. [7] presented a stress detection approach based on extensive preprocessing of EDA traces and support vector machine classifier. In Ref. [8] a method that combines artificial intelligence and fuzzy logic to analyze complex systems is proposed for stress detection, based on HR. These approaches show the feasibility of using physiological signals for stress detection.

There exist also several examples of multimodal methods [9–12]. Gil-Martin et al. [9], for instance, proposed a binary stress detection system that relies on CNNs, along with inertial signals such as accelerometer (ACC) and physiological signals such as BVP, EDA, ECG, electromyogram (EMG) and respiration from two wearable devices. Wu et al. [11] leverage transfer learning along with handcrafted and deep features extracted from EDA, PPG and ST to detect stress. In Ref. [12], a real-time binary stress detection system is proposed, where heart rate variability (HRV) and GSR features, collected using wrist-worn devices, were employed, along with a voting and similarity-based fusion (VSBF) method. In Ref. [10], the authors utilize unlabeled physiological and behavioral data to support the robustness of the stress classification problem, in a semi-supervised framework for stress detection, consisting of data augmentation, auto-encoders, and consistency regularization.

Building upon the work mentioned above, we also leveraged multiple sensors to recognize stress. In particular, we focused on understanding the most effective strategy to fusion sensor data and the overall impact of a sensor on stress detection.

10.3 DATA ANALYSIS

In this section, we describe the dataset used and our data analysis approach for stress detection.

10.3.1 Dataset

To evaluate our approach, we employed the **SMILE** (momentary stress labels with ECG, GSR, and ST data) dataset presented by Yu and Sano [10]. This dataset was made available to the participants of the *EMBC 2022 Workshop and Challenge on Detection of Stress and Mental Health Using Wearable Sensors*. In the version shared for the challenge, the dataset includes features computed from physiological data collected from 45 healthy participants (39 female, 6 male), along with a total of 2070 stress labels.

Two wearable devices were used to collect the physiological data: A *Chillband*[2] (IMEC), which collects GSR, ST and ACC; and a *Health Patch* (IMEC),[3] which captures a raw ECG signal along with ACC data.

Participants reported their stress levels, on a scale from 1 (no stress) to 7 (extreme stress), several times during the day. The self-reported stress score was then assigned to the 60-minute segment of physiological data preceding the time at which the label was reported.

The pre-computed features included in the dataset were extracted over 5-minute windows, with 4 minutes overlap. Since every labeled data segment is 60 minutes long, each segment provides 60 samples of each feature. There are in total 20 features extracted from three different signals. The features extracted from the ECG signal are: mean heart rate, heart rate cycle, low- and high-frequency signal, and their ratios, the ratio between low and very low frequency, the root mean square error of R-R differences and the standard deviation of the R-R intervals. The features extracted from the GSR are: the mean, the signal power of the phasic component, the response rate, the second difference, the response, the magnitude, the duration and the area. Finally, the features extracted from the ST signal are: the mean, the standard deviation, the median and the slope of the fitted linear regression. The dataset further includes a set of so-called *deep features* extracted using autoencoders, which we, however, did not use in our work.

While the dataset contains stress score labels from 1 to 7, the task of the challenge requested a binary classification between "stress" and "no stress" states. For our analysis, we thus followed the method suggested by Yu and Sano [10] and assigned scores 1 to the class "no tress" and scores from 2 to 7 to the class "stress". This way, the dataset results balanced, with 52% of the data samples in the positive class (stress) and 48% in the negative class (no stress).

A test set of 986 data points was later used to evaluate the performance obtained by the stress classification methods proposed by the teams that participated to the challenge. Our team, *MUSE-USI*, using the method described below, ranked second in the challenge.

10.3.2 Exploration of the SMILE Dataset

We explore the presence of missing values in the dataset and the relationship between stress and extracted features.

10.3.2.1 Missing Values

The dataset contains two types of missing data. The first group refers to the missing values of some of the features (27.25% of the cases), which were imputed by dataset authors with 0s. A smaller case, i.e., around 0.05% of the whole dataset, also present some instances where, in a whole feature's sequence, one or more values are empty. We solved this issue by inputting the average of all other available values in the affected timeseries.

10.3.2.2 Correlation

We then performed correlation analysis to investigate the relationship between features and stress labels. To this goal, we explored the correlation using Pearson's ρ, Kendall's τ and Spearman's ρ [13]. We found no significant difference between the correlation measures; for this reason, we report only the first one. Figure 10.1 shows the correlation between the features and stress labels. We observe that the ECG features have the highest correlation with respect to the stress label, which is in line with the results reported in Ref. [14]. Some ST features have high correlation as well. The GSR features do not show any correlation with the stress label. These results suggest that the ECG and ST signals may lead to better stress-detection performance. We discuss this point further in Section 10.4.1.

10.3.3 Classification Procedure

To recognize stress from the physiological data, we tested different machine learning algorithms. We implemented the approach using `Python` and the `Scikit-learn` library [15].

10.3.3.1 Five-Minute Window Selection

Each stress label and its corresponding feature have 60 associated values, with each corresponding to a 5-minute window, allowing for information as far back as 60 minutes before the label was collected. However, previous work in the literature, e.g., [16], uses shorter time intervals, such as, e.g., 10 minutes before. Saliency maps

Figure 10.1 Pearson's correlation coefficient for all of the features. The p-value threshold was set to 0.05.

in Ref. [10] also suggest that values closer in time to the stress label, particularly those within 10 minutes before, are more important in the SMILE dataset. Based on these considerations, the number of 5-minute windows used was reduced to only those within 10 minutes before the stress label. This resulted in having only ten values associated with each stress label and its feature. Experiments were conducted using data with other thresholds, such as, e.g., 30 minutes before the stress label, and the 10-minute threshold produced the highest results.

10.3.3.2 Classifiers

For all sensors and modalities, i.e., multimodal or unimodal, we implemented a series of "classical" Machine Learning models: Gaussian Process (GP), Quadratic Discriminant Analysis (QDA), Support Vector Machine (SVM), Gaussian Naïve Bayes (NB), K-Nearest Neighbours (KNN), Decision Tree (DT) and some ensemble variations, like XGBoost (DT-XG), AdaBoost (DT-Ada) and Random Forest (RF).

10.3.3.3 Single-Sensor Models

We first investigated the use of only one sensor modality to recognize stress, to which we refer to as *unimodal* approach. However, since the data provided consists of two dimensions for each label, i.e., each feature is assigned to a 5-minute window, a few important considerations had to be made: most traditional machine learning algorithms cannot deal with multi-dimensional inputs. For simplicity, single label's data can be defined as $x \in \mathbb{R}^{T \times F}$, where T is the number of 5-minute windows considered ($T = 10$) and F is the number of features such as, e.g., 8 for the ECG data. The approach used to solve this, which we called *feature unravelling*, assigned the ground truth to each of the T 5-minute windows; in this case the number of total labels over which a classifier is trained is going to be T times more; $x \mapsto \{x'_j \in \mathbb{R}^F\}_{j=1}^T$. This approach is assumed fair given the shorter threshold of 10 minutes before the label collection: going further back in time, e.g., 60 minutes, might create problems.

We then performed feature selection using the mutual information [17], which measures the mutual dependence of two variables. We did not observe any performance improvement when adopting it. Accordingly, we used all the features in the classification pipeline.

10.3.3.4 Multi-Sensor Models

We then investigated the use of multiple sensors to detect stress. The other objective laid out, in this setting, was to aid the explainability of the detection model. Based on this, we trained N independent models, where N is either 2 or 3 sensors, over the "unravelled" labels; and then used a *fusion method* to join the $N \cdot T$ predictions, i.e., $T = 10$ predictions per sensor, for each of the 5-minute windows. Figure 10.2 shows the multimodal approach applied in more detail. Different combinations of ML sensor models, as well as fusion methods, both ML-based or not, were tested.

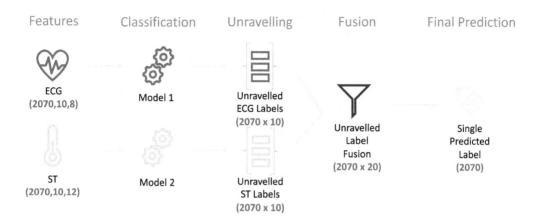

Figure 10.2 Overview of our multi-sensor approach.

As for the fusion modality, it was also tested whether using *probabilities*, i.e., instead of a label, the confidence that the classifier gives for the prediction, might give better performance compared to using binary predictions. Feature selection was tested here was well, but no results are shown since performance improvements were not observed.

10.3.3.5 Evaluation Procedure

All models were trained and tested on the "train set", as provided for the competition, using a **10-fold cross validation** procedure, with **accuracy** as performance metric, and standard errors with 68% confidence. We further evaluated the performance of our approach on the "test set" through the automatic platform CodaLab (https://codalab.org/). This was used only to confront the best models, identified through the cross validation procedure, as to avoid introduction of bias, e.g., overfitting on the test set [18].

For the model identified as best, as obtained in Section 24.4, a description of its results shall be provided, based on simple explainable AI practices [19]. Namely, which features bear the most importance; and which 5-minute window and sensor, during the model fusion, is more important. Both were obtained using an accuracy-based *feature permutation* [20] metric. We also calculated a confusion matrix, averaged over the cross validation folds, to identify how the model performs.

10.4 RESULTS AND DISCUSSION

10.4.1 Single-Sensor Models

As mentioned before, different techniques to deal with the dimensionality of the input data were tested. Table 10.1 shows the accuracy of the classifiers in comparison to the baseline, using the unraveling technique. The accuracy level is modest for all models, even though it is above a random baseline, but nonetheless in line with

TABLE 10.1   Accuracy (%) for Some Classifiers and Sensors (Single-Sensor)

ML Model\Sensor	ECG	GSR	ST
Gaussian Process	**58 ± 3**	40 ± 3	**60 ± 3**
SVM	58 ± 3	44 ± 4	59 ± 4
Naïve Bayes	54 ± 3	49 ± 6	57 ± 5
AdaBoost	54 ± 3	**50 ± 3**	56 ± 3
KNN	50 ± 2	49 ± 1	51 ± 2
QDA	51 ± 2	48 ± 6	59 ± 4
Uniform random baseline		*50 ± 2*	
Biased random baseline		*52.75 ± 0.06*	

Note: The bold values indicate the best results.

the results obtained by Ref. [10]. Some classifiers performed better than others, e.g., SVM and GP, with somewhat consistency among sensors. As for sensors, ECG and ST have similar results, while GSR models are not statistically different than the random baseline, as might have been expected from the correlation analysis (Figure 10.1).

10.4.2   Multi-Sensor Models

In the multimodal approach, we used only the GP and SVM models, as they showed to perform best for the single sensor experiments. As for the combination of sensors, while all were tested, meaningful results were possible only when using ECG and ST together, given the low performance of GSR-based models in Section 10.4.1.

A decision to use the probability predictions, for the fusion phase, was taken, as opposed to the label predictions. During our tests, no discernible difference could be found between the two, when using cross-validation over the train set. However, from some performance benchmarks over the test set, we found that the probability predictions did indeed perform slightly better, given the same initial conditions.

Table 10.2 reports the classification results using the multi-sensor fusion technique applied on the prediction probabilities. In this case, since the results over the cross-validation technique were, most of the time, not statistically significant with one another, the accuracy over the test set is also reported. The models used for the ECG and ST features were always the same together; some tests with different combinations were constructed, but at best the same results were obtained, and at worst a decrease in performance. From this analysis, the best model can be identified as the one which uses a Gaussian Process for the first phase, over both ECG and ST features, and a Quadratic Discriminant Analysis for the fusion modality.

10.4.3   Best Model Analysis

Figure 10.3 presents the feature importance for the ECG and ST sensor using the Gaussian Process model. The most important features for the ST are slope fitted, the average of the signal and the standard deviation. As for the ECG data, all but 3 have high importance, i.e., the two ratios, between low and high and low

TABLE 10.2 Accuracy (%) for Combination of ML Models and Fusion Techniques for the ECG+ST Multi-sensory Approach

Single-Sensor Model	SVM		GP	
Fusion Technique	CV	Test	CV	Test
Average	59 ± 3	51.52	60 ± 3	54.67
Gaussian process	$\mathbf{60 \pm 3}$	52.74	$\mathbf{61 \pm 3}$	52.33
SVM	$\mathbf{60 \pm 3}$	53.14	59 ± 3	51.42
AdaBoost	59 ± 3	**54.56**	60 ± 3	51.72
QDA	55 ± 3	54.16	57 ± 5	**56.19**
Uniform random baseline		50 ± 2		
Biased random baseline		52.75 ± 0.06		

Note: Test accuracy is with two decimals, as provided by CodaLab. All others are rounded according to their standard error.
The bold values indicate the best results.

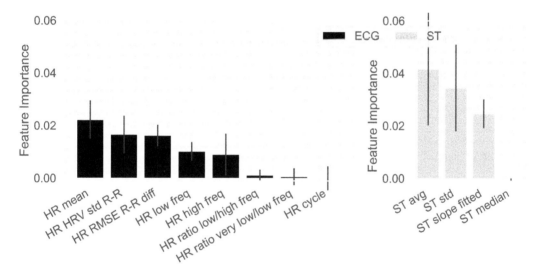

Figure 10.3 Feature importance (over 10-fold cross validation), for the two models that make up the multi-modal approach, i.e. SVM for ECG and SVM for ST. Confidence intervals at 68% confidence are also shown.

and very low frequencies in HR signal, the high frequency values, the HR cycle and the standard deviation of the R-R peaks. The others were not statistically different than 0.

Figure 10.4a shows the importance of each 5-minute window for ECG and ST, from the fusion model. The fusion method, over the train set, considers the ST data as more important, for almost all 5-minute windows. This means that, according to the QDA fusion method, the ST-model predictions are more discriminative. On the other hand, there is no pattern for what concerns how far back is important before the stress label collection: this could be either due to the decision of using only 10 minutes before the label, and as such all values are already somewhat important, or

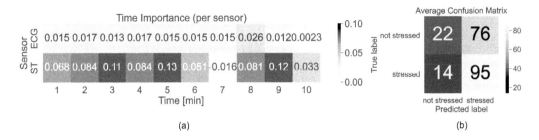

Figure 10.4 (a) Heatmap with the feature importance, calculated with feature permutation. (b) Confusion matrix (10-fold cross validation).

the incapacity, on the fusion model side, in discriminating this. Future works could explore more in details this factor.

Figure 10.4b shows the averaged confusion matrix: the model can compute more accurately true labels (*stress*) than false ones (*no stress*). The approach is capable of detecting one a person is stressed more often than when it is not: in a real world application, this behaviour could be desired for such a system.

10.5 CONCLUSION

In this chapter, we proposed a multi-sensor approach for stress detection. Our method relies on handcrafted features extracted from the ECG and ST signals, processed using machine learning algorithms, and achieves an F1-score of 61.84% and accuracy of 56.19%. Our work shows the potential of multimodal approaches for stress detection.

ACKNOWLEDGMENTS

This work is partially supported by the Swiss National Science Foundation (SNSF) through the grant 205121_197242 for the project *PROSELF: Semi-automated Self-Tracking Systems to Improve Personal Productivity*.

Note

1. https://www.who.int/news-room/questions-and-answers/item/stress.
2. https://drupal.imec-int.com/sites/default/files/2017-02/CHILL%20BAND_0.pdf.
3. https://www.imec-int.com/sites/default/files/imported/HEALTH%2520PATCH.pdf.

REFERENCES

[1] A. Sano and R. W. Picard, "Stress recognition using wearable sensors and mobile phones," in *2013 Humaine Association Conference on Affective Computing and Intelligent Interaction (ACII)*. IEEE, Geneva, Switzerland, 2013, pp. 671–676.

[2] L. D. Sharma, V. K. Bohat, M. Habib, A.-Z. Ala'M, H. Faris, and I. Aljarah, "Evolutionary inspired approach for mental stress detection using EEG signal," *Expert Systems with Applications*, vol. 197, p. 116634, 2022.

[3] S. Gedam and S. Paul, "Automatic stress detection using wearable sensors and machine learning: A review," in *11th International Conference on Computing, Communication and Networking Technologies (ICCCNT 2020)*. IEEE, Kharagpur, India, 2020, pp. 1–7.

[4] P. Schmidt, A. Reiss, R. Dürichen, and K. Van Laerhoven, "Wearable-based affect recognition: A review," *Sensors*, vol. 19, no. 19, p. 4079, 2019.

[5] R. Holder, R. K. Sah, M. Cleveland, and H. Ghasemzadeh, "Comparing the predictability of sensor modalities to detect stress from wearable sensor data," in *2022 IEEE 19th Annual Consumer Communications & Networking Conference (CCNC)*. IEEE, Las Vegas, NV, USA, 2022, pp. 557–562.

[6] N. Rashid, L. Chen, M. Dautta, A. Jimenez, P. Tseng, and M. A. Al Faruque, "Feature augmented hybrid CNN for stress recognition using wrist-based photoplethysmography sensor," in *2021 43rd Annual International Conference of the IEEE Engineering in Medicine & Biology Society (EMBC)*. IEEE, Virtual Conference, 2021, pp. 2374–2377.

[7] A. Greco, G. Valenza, J. Lázaro, J. M. Garzón-Rey, J. Aguiló, C. De-la Camara, R. Bailón, and E. P. Scilingo, "Acute stress state classification based on electrodermal activity modeling," *IEEE Transactions on Affective Computing*, Volume: 14, Issue: 1, Page(s): 788–799, 2021.

[8] Q. Lin, T. Li, P. M. Shakeel, and R. D. J. Samuel, "Advanced artificial intelligence in heart rate and blood pressure monitoring for stress management," *Journal of Ambient Intelligence and Humanized Computing*, vol. 12, pp. 3329–3340, 2021.

[9] M. Gil-Martin, R. San-Segundo, A. Mateos, and J. Ferreiros-Lopez, "Human stress detection with wearable sensors using convolutional neural networks," *IEEE Aerospace and Electronic Systems Magazine*, vol. 37, no. 1, pp. 60–70, 2022.

[10] H. Yu and A. Sano, "Semi-supervised learning and data augmentation in wearable-based momentary stress detection in the wild," arXiv preprint arXiv:2202.12935, 2022.

[11] J. Wu, Y. Zhang, and X. Zhao, "Stress detection using wearable devices based on transfer learning," in *2021 IEEE International Conference on Bioinformatics and Biomedicine (BIBM)*.IEEE, Virtual Conference, Houston, TX, USA, 2021, pp. 3122–3128.

[12] S. A. Khowaja, A. G. Prabono, F. Setiawan, B. N. Yahya, and S.-L. Lee, "Toward soft real-time stress detection using wrist-worn devices for human workspaces," *Soft Computing*, vol. 25, pp. 2793–2820, 2021.

[13] M. Kendall and A. Stuart, *The Advanced Theory of Statistics*, 3rd ed. London: Griffin, 1973.

[14] M. Elgendi and C. Menon, "Machine learning ranks ecg as an optimal wearable biosignal for assessing driving stress," *IEEE Access*, vol. 8, pp. 34362–34374, 2020.

[15] F. Pedregosa, G. Varoquaux, A. Gramfort, V. Michel, B. Thirion, O. Grisel, M. Blondel, P. Prettenhofer, R. Weiss, V. Dubourg et al., "Scikit-learn: Machine learning in python," *the Journal of Machine Learning Research (JMLR)*, vol. 12, pp. 2825–2830, 2011.

[16] Y. S. Can, B. Arnrich, and C. Ersoy, "Stress detection in daily life scenarios using smart phones and wearable sensors: A survey," *Journal of Biomedical Informatics*, vol. 92, p. 103139, 2019.

[17] C. E. Shannon, "A mathematical theory of communication," *ACM Sigmobile Mobile Computing and Communications Review*, vol. 5, no. 1, pp. 3–55, 2001.

[18] V. Feldman, R. Frostig, and M. Hardt, "The advantages of multiple classes for reducing overfitting from test set reuse," in *International Conference on Machine Learning*. PMLR, 2019, Long Beach, California, pp. 1892–1900.

[19] R. R. Hoffman, S. T. Mueller, G. Klein, and J. Litman, "Metrics for explainable AI: Challenges and prospects," arXiv preprint arXiv:1812.04608, 2018.

[20] L. Breiman, "Random forests," *Machine Learning*, vol. 45, pp. 5–32, 2001.

CHAPTER 11

Classification of Stress via Ambulatory ECG and GSR Data

Zachary Dair, Muhammad Saad, Urja Pawar, and Ruairi O'Reilly

Munster Technological University

Samantha Dockray

University College Cork

11.1 INTRODUCTION

Stress is a psychophysiological reaction in response to internal or external stressors. In psychological models of behaviour, stress can be represented by considerations of arousal, as the level of activation, and valence, as the negative or positive dimension of the emotional state [1]. A moderate stress level can support people to develop resilience and respond to the demands of the situation. However, high acute or prolonged stress can present a risk to mental health and is linked to physical illness. While high stress over a prolonged period can lead to harmful effects such as depression, mental disorders, reduced job productivity, and enhanced risk of various somatic and mental illnesses [2,3].

These conditions can degrade physical and mental health if not treated; however, effective and timely treatment may rely on detection via accurate monitoring. Providing individuals with accessible, continuous stress monitoring delivers greater awareness and insights into daily stress enabling self-moderation, distancing from stressors, and ultimately leading to reduced levels of daily stress.

Biomedical healthcare devices, such as wearable sensors, provide individuals with physiological monitoring capabilities. These devices contain multiple sensors capable of recording various physiological signals, such as electrocardiograms (ECG) and galvanic skin response/electrodermal activity (GSR/EDA).

ECG measures the heart's electrical activity, commonly utilised in a medical setting for arrhythmia detection [4]. Additionally, ECG signals have been used to

DOI: 10.1201/9781003371540-13

indicate psychological states based on the relationship of the psychological state to the autonomic nervous system, as articulated in the Polyvagal Theory [5], which is responsible for involuntary physiological responses due to psychological processes.

GSR measures the skin's electrical activity variances due to fluctuating sweat levels that originate from the autonomic activation of sweat glands. GSR commonly represents an individual's level of activation (Arousal), making it suitable for detecting stress and other high arousal psychological states[6]. These signals have demonstrated high efficacy for fitness tracking applications, physical health monitoring and are beginning to show potential for mental health monitoring [7,8]. Such signals are often collected and analysed in widely available commercial wearable health monitors such as Samsung Galaxy Smartwatches, Fitbit, Apple Watch and research devices such as Empatica.

This work contributes a high-performing stress detection approach using ambulatory physiological data. This is achieved by (1) assessing the most suitable features indicative of stress for hourly and per-minute stress detection, (2) approximating missing data to reduce the impact on classification performance due to simulated sensor detachment, and by (3) investigating disparity between training and testing data impeding the generalisability of a model.

11.2 CHALLENGES

The SMILE [17] dataset highlights several commonly encountered challenges for conducting stress detection from wearable data gathered in an ambulatory setting. The most prominent challenge is the complexity of accurately detecting a fluctuation in psychological states based on physiological signals, which may fluctuate as a correlate of psychological states, including stress or other factors. This requires a granular analysis of physiological signals, in this case, ECG and GSR, to identify the baseline values for the individual and, subsequently, any fluctuations that could originate from involuntary reactions to stressors. Additionally, these fluctuations may originate from factors other than stress, such as movement artefacts, sensor error, or other psychological reactions requiring further modelling to avoid misclassification.

An additional challenge relates to the labelling of the data, specifically using one label per hour. Detecting psychological states from physiological signals commonly utilises shorter data windows to provide a granular analysis of the individual. With an hourly label of stress, it is unclear as to the actual duration of the stress reaction of the individual. As such, the classifier may train or predict features indicative of a neutral state that instead contain a stress label or inversely. Without knowing the ground truth label per minute, an approximation based on the hour can lead to potential miss-classifications.

Finally, missing data is a significant issue in the ambulatory assessment of individuals, often stemming from sensor detachment or movement artefacts. SMILE demonstrates this issue through the absence of certain features throughout the train and test data. Interestingly, both portions of the dataset include several instances

(Train: 19 of 2070, Test: 2 of 986) with no data. Missing data is a significant aspect of this dataset. In the training set, a mere 17 of 2070 instances contain features for the entire hour, emphasising a requirement to use each modality and potential feature imputation to replace missing values.

11.3 METHODOLOGY

The adopted methodology is depicted in Figure 11.1; two distinct workflows are denoted, the proposed approach and the challenge approach. In addition, the diagram demonstrates the components which contributed to the optimal approach for stress detection on SMILE data.

11.3.1 Dataset

This study uses the SMILE dataset [17], which contains physiological data and self-reported stress annotations from 45 healthy participants (39 females and 6 males). Physiological data originates from two sensors - a wrist-worn device for GSR/EDA and Skin Temperature (ST) and a chest-worn device for ECG. Each dataset annotation is a self-reported stress level on a scale of 0 (not at all) to 6 (very) collected via a mobile phone application with random notifications prompting a report.

SMILE provides three categories of features, all extracted from 5-minute sliding windows with 4-minute overlapping segments: Eight handcrafted ECG features are provided, consisting of a range of statistical and frequency measures, commonly known as heart rate variability measures. Handcrafted GSR features

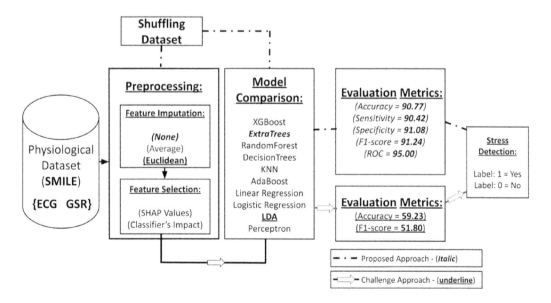

Figure 11.1 A detailed overview of the methodology for stress detection using physiological data.

TABLE 11.1   Percentage of Data Missing Per Hour and Per Minute in SMILE

Data Split	Feature	Minutes (%)	Full Hours (%)
Train	ECG HC	11.75	10.96
Train	GSR HC	12.59	12.22
Train	Deep ECG	20.67	9.56
Train	All features	1.27	0.91
Test	ECG HC	5.00	4.15
Test	GSR HC	6.79	6.49
Test	Deep ECG	24.72	9.83
Test	All features	0.25	0.20

are eight similar statistical and frequency measures derived from the GSR signal, and included in this category are four statistical measures of skin temperature (Table 11.1).

There are two categories distinguished as deep features, and both originate from using an ECG signal in conjunction with a deep model, specifically a convolutional neural network and a transformer. These deep features are reconstructed portions of the original ECG signal for that period. Notably, the SMILE dataset provides specific training and testing portions of data. However, the testing set contains no labels, requiring the usage of an 80:20 split of training data to enable model evaluation. Subsequently, high-performing models are re-trained on the entire training set before classifying the test data.

11.3.2   Feature Imputation

In ambulatory physiological data recording, missing values due to sensor detachment is a common issue and causes significant issues for ML training and classification. Therefore, various methods of feature imputation are utilised to replace the missing data with appropriate values. A primitive method is to compute the average value of the missing feature across the entire dataset and substitute missing values with this average. However, this approach loses the inherent links between that feature and its label. A more complex method utilises Euclidean distance or other similarity measures on an existing feature to find a similar instance. Once a similar instance based on a single feature or combination of features is identified, the previously missing features are replaced with values found from the similar instance. This approach also has limitations, such as requiring a minimum of a single feature to be present to act as a comparator.

11.3.3   Feature Selection

Feature selection is a pre-processing procedure to identify the most performant features in the data. For this work, an initial classification is conducted using the baseline classifiers and each feature individually to provide insights on per-feature performance for stress detection. However, as the dataset contains instances of missing data for all features, an ensemble of independent feature classifiers enables leveraging the individual potential of each feature. Furthermore, aggregating predictions and using a voting mechanism can compensate for missing data. Subsequently, each permutation of features is analysed to assess the potential for a high-performing combination of features. Finally, a feature vector containing all features is utilised to ensure that any latent patterns between features are captured and leveraged for stress detection.

Another technique to perform feature selection is via feature importance. Feature importance techniques assign a score to participating features based on their impact on the model's classification process and have been used in modelling many medical datasets [10,11]. In this work, SHAP values[12] are used to analyse the importance of different features. SHAP values are based on the concept of Shapley, which is a game theory approach to identify the contribution of each player participating in a game towards achieving a goal [12].

11.3.4 Baseline Classifiers

A battery of machine learning models of various architectures provides the initial baseline results of each new experimental procedure. Additionally, the variation in architectures generates insights into the most appropriate classifier type for stress detection from ECG and GSR features.

- Linear regression: A regression algorithm used to predict target value based on a set of independent features. This algorithm assumes a linear relationship between dependent and independent variables. Therefore, not suited for modelling non-linear relationships.

- Logistic regression: A classification algorithm used to predict binary outcomes from a set of independent features. It is based on a logarithmic link function that enables modelling non-linear associations in a linear way. While it does not assume a linear relationship between dependent and independent variables, it assumes a linear relationship between link function and independent variables that limits the effectivity of this algorithm in real-world non-linear data.

- K-Nearest Neighbours (KNN): Is used to predict the target class based on the existing samples in the training data by utilising different distance metrics (Euclidean, Manhattan, Hamming, Minkowski) in order to classify similar samples to a particular class. As the algorithm is based on finding similar samples, it does not perform well with too many features as it becomes harder to find similar samples as per a given distance metric. Also, it's required to have homogeneous (same scale) features in the data.

- Linear Discriminant Analysis (LDA): A dimensionality reduction algorithm that can be used as a robust classification algorithm as it reduces high dimensional data to low dimensions that leads to an increase in classification performance by avoiding the curse of dimensionality. While normalised data is assumed for this algorithm to work well, there are ways to arrive at the same LDA features without normalised data. However, the algorithm constructs a linear decision boundary for classification, limiting its application to non-linear classification problems.

- Extra trees: Extra trees is a tree ensemble algorithm that uses many trees to classify an input and decide classification based on majority voting. Each tree is a decision tree that learns to classify data upon conditioning on features. Each tree in the extra trees algorithm uses original training inputs of data with randomly assigned split conditions that enable a fast and effective classification process.

- Random forest: Random forest is also a tree ensemble algorithm that utilises many decision trees to classify an input instance. Random forest uses different replicas of the original training input with data replacement and optimum split conditions to train the trees. Therefore, random forests often perform better than other ML classifiers.

- AdaBoost: Adaptive boosting is a boosting algorithm that combines a number of weak classifiers to generate one strong classifier. Initially, data is passed to the first model. Then, the incorrectly classified instances are assigned higher weights and passed to a second model in series to decrease their chance of being incorrectly classified. This is repeated with a limited number of models until the combination classifies with sufficient accuracy. However, this algorithm has reduced performance on noisy datasets.

- XGBoost: A boosting technique that combines weak tree-based classifiers to create a strong classifier. Incorrectly classified samples from one decision tree are passed to another after increasing their weights (the penalty for misclassifying). This algorithm has built-in regularisation that makes it less prone to overfitting.

- Multi-Layer Perceptron (MLP): A classic neural-networks-based classifier that passes input to layers of operations to learn granular information about the data that enables it to identify complex non-linear decision surfaces for classification purposes. Classifiers based on neural networks perform well with large input data. However, these classifiers are computationally expensive to train and require considerable model-tuning to achieve high performance.

11.3.5 Evaluation Criteria

Several metrics, such as accuracy, precision, recall, sensitivity, specificity, F-measure, receiver operating characteristic curve (ROC), and area under the curve (AUC) scores, are used to assess the performance of ML classifiers for the stress detection tasks. Additional metrics are utilised as solely utilising classification accuracy lacks class-specific information of the approach evaluated [13]. Therefore, recall, sensitivity, specificity, and F1 scores are recommended to assess the number of positive and negative predictions made for the targeted classes. Furthermore, classifiers can be fine-tuned using the ROC and AUC metrics as they provide reasonable compensation between the true positive rate (TPR) and the false-positive rate (FPR). This work uses accuracy, F1-measure, sensitivity, specificity, and ROC metrics to evaluate the ML classifiers for detecting stress from the physiological dataset.

11.3.6 Per Minute Classification

Commonly used approaches for detecting stress or other psychological states use a reduced signal duration, ranging from seconds to several minutes [14–16]. This provides the distinct advantage of requiring less data, reducing computational complexity. Additionally, a smaller duration enables more frequent classifications of stress or other emotions, reducing lag and providing greater momentary insights into an individual. As such, the hourly instances of data provided in SMILE are converted into per-minute samples. However, as the annotation frequency of SMILE remains at one stress label per hour, it is unclear whether every minute of data within the hour truly reflects the associated label. Specifically, the per-hour label can add to classification confusion, as certain portions of data within an hour are likely to be neutral, with sporadic and limited instances of stress, due to the nature of stress and daily occurrences.

Once converted into per-minute instances of data, classification is conducted as normal. However, the original testing labels are provided per hour, indicating the aggregation method requirement. Several voting mechanisms were created to combine per-minute classifications into hourly accurately. The first utilises the mean classification per hour with a dynamic threshold enabling the weighting of predictions. The second is a highly sensitive approach, which monitors for any classification of stress within an hour, and, if detected, reports the entire hour as stress. The final method utilises an isolated LDA classifier using 60 classifications as features to return a single per-hour binary result indicating the presence or absence of stress.

11.3.7 Covariate Shift

The similarity of training and testing data was analysed using the baseline classifiers. First, each data instance is relabelled with a new label distinguishing each data portion as training (1) or testing (0) data. Subsequently, the newly labelled portions of data are combined into a single dataset, which is shuffled to ensure randomisation. Finally, the combined dataset is split into 80% training and 20% testing, and each of the classifiers aims to detect whether the data originates from training or testing splits. Using this method, high performance from the classifiers indicates substantial variance between training and testing data, typically called covariate shift. An issue arises when the distribution of subsets of data is

TABLE 11.2 Feature Selection Classification Metrics Hourly and per Minute Grouped by Feature Type

Features	Best Classifier	Duration	Accuracy	F1-Score
All	RandForest	H	0.65	0.65
All	Extra Trees Ens.	II	0.60	0.71
All	XGBoost	M	0.69	0.73
ECG	**ExtraTrees**	**H**	**0.73**	**0.71**
ECG	ExtraTrees	M	0.69	0.68
ECG, GSR	XGBoost	H	0.65	0.70
ECG, GSR	**LogReg**	**M**	**0.70**	**0.72**
ECG, GSR, ECG_T	ExtraTrees	H	0.69	0.70
ECG, GSR, ECG_T	RandForest	M	0.68	0.71
ECG_C	LogReg	H	0.59	0.61
ECG_C	LogReg	M	0.62	0.71
ECG_T	XGBoost	H	0.59	0.60
ECG_T	LDA	M	0.61	0.69
GSR	ExtraTrees	H	0.63	0.69
GSR	LogReg	M	0.65	0.74

Note: The bold values indicate the best results.

TABLE 11.3 Top Three Models for Binary Classification of Data Origin (Train or Test) Indicating Covariate Shift

Model	Accuracy	F1 Score	Sensitivity	Specificity
XGBoost	0.99	0.99	0.97	1.00
RandomForest	0.98	0.98	0.94	1.00
DecisonTrees	0.97	0.98	0.96	0.98

varied. Often covariate shifts will lead to substantial negative impacts on testing and production classifications, requiring weighting, normalisation or combining the training and testing data to provide the classifier with a broader perspective of data when training [17] (Tables 11.2 and 11.3).

11.4 RESULTS AND DISCUSSION

11.4.1 Feature Selection

Conducting an initial performance analysis enables an evaluation of the suitability of individual features to detect instances of stress from physiological data. From this analysis, ECG demonstrates the highest stress detection accuracy using the hourly data denoted in Table 11.2, which aligns with the frequent usage of ECG in psychological state detection approaches found in related literature [6,8,18]. In addition, the inherent links between ECG and the ANS likely attribute the signal's performance to indicating stress. Due to the prevalence of GSR in stress detection approaches [6,16], higher classification accuracy was expected. The reduced

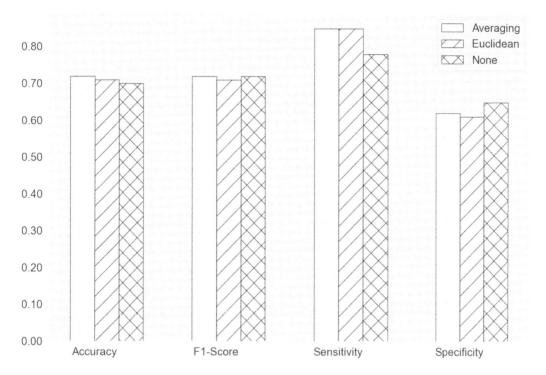

Figure 11.2 Impact of feature imputation methods on logistic regression.

performance compared with other approaches may stem from using different GSR features, recording methods or dataset normalisation operations (Figure 11.2).

Notably, the individual performance of deep ECG features achieves reduced classification accuracy and F1 scores. Likely as these features consist of reconstructed raw ECG signals, which provide a more granular perspective of ECG but may obscure the physiological changes associated with stress due to the number of data points and lack of a statistical summary highlighting the signals' fluctuations.

A combined analysis utilising all features in a single input vector achieves moderate classification accuracy, lower than solely using ECG features, likely resulting from confusion caused by the Deep ECG features.

11.4.2   Feature Importance

The feature importance scores were calculated using SHAP based on the selected features that achieved good performance scores, namely handcrafted ECG and GSR features (Figure 11.3). The scores can be positive or negative based on whether the feature value positively or negatively impacted the positive classification (binary class = 1). A bee swarm plot in Figure 11.4 depicts the positive and negative importance scores assigned to the 20 handcrafted features in a logistic regression model. The plot shows the importance scores assigned across multiple instances in the data. The red-to-blue colour transition represents their high to low importance.

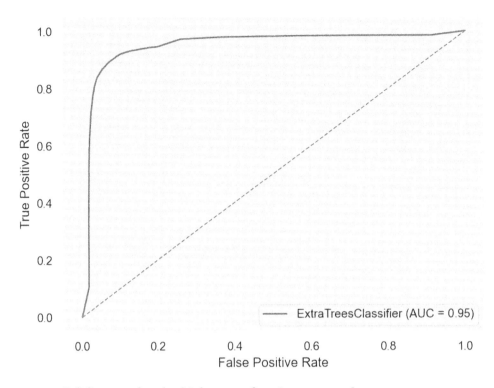

Figure 11.3 ROC curve for the highest performing approach.

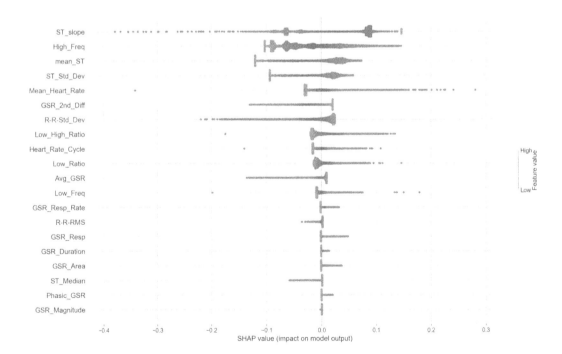

Figure 11.4 Summary of how the top features in a dataset impact the model's output.

It can be observed that there are many handcrafted features heavily impacting classification, the top five being the slope of the ST, high-frequency ECG signal, mean ST, the standard deviation of ST, and mean heart rate. Furthermore, the plot shows that the high slope of ST contributed towards negative stress classification. Contrastingly, high values of high frequency present in the ECG signal contributed toward positive classification as intuitively, heart rate might increase during stress. It was also observed that low mean ST and heart rate values contributed to negative classifications.

11.4.3   Per-Minute Classification

Per-minute classification reduces the data required to conduct momentary stress detection and provides a more granular analysis of the individual. Feature selection was also conducted on a per-minute basis. All features demonstrated an increased performance for stress detection, except for ECG, which exhibited a slightly reduced accuracy, Table 11.2.

Interestingly, the most performant features in per-minute classifications combine handcrafted ECG and GSR features. This is a result of the reduced dimensionality of the features, which places greater importance on the individual values comprising the ECG and GSR features, such as mean heart rate, heart rate cycle and skin temperature.

The increased performance can be attributed to per-minute instances providing isolated portions of data less likely to contain features indicative of both stress and neutral states. Furthermore, comparing each minute enables more significant distinctions between fluctuating data due to the granularity of the analysis. However, the reduced performance compared to hourly classifications can be explained by the greater importance placed on the individual features, emphasising the effect of missing values on classification.

11.4.4   Feature Imputation

Substantial portions of the SMILE dataset are missing features as denoted in Table 11.1. These missing values replicate a commonly occurring challenge in ambulatory assessments of physiological signals collected using wearable devices. Hence, warranting the adoption of two methods for feature imputation to approximate the missing values. The comparative performance of conducting feature imputation is demonstrated in Figure 11.2. Both methods result in a 1%–2% increase in accuracy for the combined ECG/GSR features, additionally sensitivity increases by 7%, while a 3%–4% decrease in sensitivity occurs. While the performance on the training set shows a minor improvement, the Euclidean method contributed to the higher scoring achieved on the challenge data subset, with accuracy increasing by 3.75% from 55.48%–59.23%. Furthermore, the sustained performance using these methods indicates suitability to enable the replacement of missing data without negatively impacting the classifier, which provides a method for reducing the impact of sensor detachment in real ambulatory analysis.

11.4.5 Generalisability

A significant aspect of ML classification problems is achieving a generalisable and robust solution. Shuffling the training data enables the classifier to train on data randomly, originating from various individuals and reflecting stress and neutral instances. This method reduces bias and ultimately leads to a performant classifier, as demonstrated by the proposed approach in Figure 11.1 and the ROC curve in Figure 11.3. This proposed approach achieved high scores in all evaluation metrics: 90.77% classification accuracy, 91.24 F1-Score, 90.42 Sensitivity and 91.08 Specificity. However, the same approach used to detect stress from the challenge dataset leads to 55.78% classification accuracy. This substantial-performance disparity indicates significant variance between the training and testing data. Evidence of covariate shift is indicated by the high performance demonstrated for classifying between dataset splits denoted in Table 11.3. This occurrence could arise in real-life applications for many reasons, such as physiological differences, noisy data, sensor variation, or nuanced physiological stress indicators. Therefore, emphasising the importance of comprehensive and balanced data collection for accurate psychophysiological analysis is critical.

11.4.6 Challenge Approach

The highest performing challenge approach achieves 59.23% and is denoted in Figure 11.1. Achieved using the Euclidean feature imputation method on ECG and GSR features and an LDA model for per-minute classifications, with a second LDA classifier voting mechanism to provide hourly results.

11.5 CONCLUSIONS

An empirical evaluation aided the construction of a stress detection approach using physiological data collected from wearable technology in an ambulatory environment. The proposed approach leverages ECG and GSR features with dataset shuffling to ensure a random data distribution for training. The classifier utilised is ExtraTrees, which achieves high performance on a subset of SMILE training data across all evaluation metrics (90.77% Accuracy, 91.24 F1-Score, 90.42 Sensitivity, 91.08 Specificity). Additionally, evaluated high-performing feature imputation methods are adopted to approximate missing data, which reduces the impact of issues such as uncontrolled sensor movement and possible detachment in ambulatory data-gathering settings. Source code is available - https://github.com/ZacDair/EMBC_Release.

11.6 FUTURE WORK

Due to the substantial performance disparity between SMILE training and testing data, future work will attempt to reduce covariate shift through multiple methods.

An initial method relies on integrating a subset of testing data into the training dataset to evaluate the proposed approach's capabilities for learning features of the test distribution. Subsequently, normalisation and re-weighting methods will be adopted to reduce the variance between the data.

REFERENCES

[1] Alan Kim Johnson and Erling A. Anderson. Stress and arousal. In John T. Cacioppo and Louis G. Tassinary (Eds.), *Principles of Psychophysiology: Physical, Social, and Inferential Elements.* Cambridge University Press: Cambridge, pp. 914, 1990.

[2] Han Yu and Akane Sano. Semi-supervised learning and data augmentation in wearable-based momentary stress detection in the wild. arXiv preprint arXiv:2202.12935, 2022.

[3] Prerna Garg, Jayasankar Santhosh, Andreas Dengel, and Shoya Ishimaru. Stress detection by machine learning and wearable sensors. In *26th International Conference on Intelligent User Interfaces-Companion*, College Station, TX, USA, 2021.

[4] Eduardo José da S. Luz, William Robson Schwartz, Guillermo Cámara-Chávez, and David Menotti. ECG-based heartbeat classification for Arrhythmia detection: A survey. *Computer Methods and Programs in Biomedicine*, 127:144–164, 2016.

[5] Stephen W. Porges. The polyvagal theory: New insights into adaptive reactions of the autonomic nervous system. *Cleveland Clinic Journal of Medicine*, 76(Suppl 2):S86, 2009.

[6] Jorn Bakker, Mykola Pechenizkiy, and Natalia Sidorova. What's your current stress level? Detection of stress patterns from GSR sensor data. In *2011 IEEE 11th International Conference on Data Mining Workshops*, Vancouver, Canada, pp. 573–580, 2011.

[7] André Henriksen, Martin Haugen Mikalsen, Ashenafi Zebene Woldaregay, Miroslav Muzny, Gunnar Hartvigsen, Laila Arnesdatter Hopstock, Sameline Grimsgaard, et al. Using fitness trackers and smartwatches to measure physical activity in research: Analysis of consumer wrist-worn wearables. *Journal of Medical Internet Research*, 20(3):e9157, 2018.

[8] Akane Sano, Sara Taylor, Andrew W. McHill, Andrew J. K. Phillips, Laura K. Barger, Elizabeth Klerman, Rosalind Picard, et al. Identifying objective physiological markers and modifiable behaviors for self-reported stress and mental health status using wearable sensors and mobile phones: Observational study. *Journal of Medical Internet Research*, 20(6):e210, 2018.

[9] Huiyuan Yang, Han Yu, Kusha Sridhar, Thomas Vaessen, Inez Myin-Germeys, and Akane Sano. More to Less (M2L): Enhanced health recognition in the wild with reduced modality of wearable sensors. arXiv preprint arXiv:2202.08267, 2022.

[10] Urja Pawar, Donna O'Shea, Susan Rea, and Ruairi O'Reilly. Incorporating explainable artificial intelligence (XAI) to aid the understanding of machine learning in the healthcare domain. In *AICS*, Seattle, WA, USA, pages 169–180, 2020.

[11] Urja Pawar, Christopher T. Culbert, and Ruairi O'Reilly. Evaluating hierarchical medical workflows using feature importance. In *2021 IEEE 34th International Symposium on Computer-Based Medical Systems (CBMS)*, Aveiro, Portugal, pp. 265–270. IEEE, 2021.

[12] Scott M. Lundberg and Su-In Lee. A unified approach to interpreting model predictions. *Advances in Neural Information Processing Systems*, 30, 2017.

[13] Samriti Sharma, Gurvinder Singh, and Manik Sharma. A comprehensive review and analysis of supervised-learning and soft computing techniques for stress diagnosis in humans. *Computers in Biology and Medicine*, 134:104450, 2021.

[14] Nilava Mukherjee, Sumitra Mukhopadhyay, and Rajarshi Gupta. Real-time mental stress detection technique using neural networks towards a wearable health monitor. *Measurement Science and Technology*, 33(4):044003, 2022.

[15] Aneta Lisowska, Szymon Wilk, and Mor Peleg. Catching patient's attention at the right time to help them undergo behavioural change. In *19th International Conference on Artificial Intelligence in Medicine, AIME 2021*, pp. 72–82. Springer International Publisher: New York, 2021.

[16] Alberto de Santos Sierra, Carmen Sanchez Avila, Javier Guerra Casanova, and Gonzalo Bailador del Pozo. A stress-detection system based on physiological signals and fuzzy logic. *IEEE Transactions on Industrial Electronics*, 58(10):4857–4865, 2011.

[17] Geeta Dharani, Nimisha G. Nair, Pallavi Satpathy, and Jabez Christopher. Covariate shift: A review and analysis on classifiers. In *2019 Global Conference for Advancement in Technology (GCAT)*, Bangaluru, India, pp. 1–6, 2019.

[18] Foteini Agrafioti, Dimitris Hatzinakos, and Adam K. Anderson. ECG pattern analysis for emotion detection. *IEEE Transactions on Affective Computing*, 3(1):102–115, 2012.

CHAPTER 12

Detection and Classification of Acute Psychological Stress in Free-Living: Challenges and Achievements

M. Sevil, M. Rashid, and R. Askari

Illinois Institute of Technology

L. Sharp and L. Quinn

University of Illinois Chicago

A. Cinar

Illinois Institute of Technology

12.1 INTRODUCTION

Detecting acute psychological stress (APS) events in daily life can enable preventive measures to mitigate APS-instigated risks. For APS detection and classification in free-living, we are constrained to use signals generated from the sensors of wearable devices, such as wristbands, that can be worn in daily life. The physiological response to various types of APS can be user-dependent and may not have a distinctly unique signature. Furthermore, physical activity (PA), including structured exercise, unexpected/unplanned physical activities, and activities of daily-living, can also cause physiological responses that affect many of the same variables measured by wearable device sensors. Simultaneous occurrences of APS and PA in free-living provides more complex situations. Several devices and algorithms can characterize APS and PA in clinical environments with high accuracy. In free-living, the sensors

DOI: 10.1201/9781003371540-14

are limited to those in fashionable devices that can be worn comfortably. Recent advances in wearable devices provided wristbands with sensors for measuring electrodermal activity, blood volume pulse, skin temperature, and 3-axis accelerometers. The data reported by these sensors can be refined and interpreted to detect and classify APS and PA. Both APS and PA lead to the activation of the sympathetic nervous system. The sympathetic division of the autonomic nervous system responds to PA by increasing the heart rate, blood pressure, and respiration rate, and by stimulating the release of glucose from the liver for energy. The general physiological response of APS is similar to PA, though exercise normally elicits a larger response. The physical fitness level, individual traits, and personal experiences affect transient physiological responses to APS. These factors make it challenging to reliably monitor APS and PA by using only the measured variables and necessitates the use of detection and classification techniques based on meticulously selected features derived from the measurements [1–8].

Change in secretion levels of stress hormones such as cortisol would be a marker of APS and its intensity. Many physiological variables, such as eye-tracking [9], speech wave analysis [10], and lactate and cortisol levels can help distinguish APS from PA in clinical experiments. However, continuous and noninvasive monitoring of these variables is not practical in free-living. Data from wearable devices provide an alternative solution. Advances in wristband-based technologies provide data collection at high-frequency and real-time streaming of several physiological variables from a single device [11] (Table 12.1, Figure 12.1). These conveniently measured biosignals include: galvanic skin response (GSR) also called electrodermal activity, an indicator of perspiration rate; blood volume pulse (BVP) used for estimating heart rate (HR) and extracting HR variability features; and skin temperature (ST) that captures abrupt changes in skin functions, which are indicative of thermoregulation, insulation, sweating, and control of blood flow. All three variables are correlated with both PA intensity and APS level. 3D Accelerometer (ACC) plays a key role in distinguishing PA from APS, since there is no correlation between ACC and APS, though a strong association exists with PA (Table 12.1).

Due to the multifaceted response of APS, a multivariable measurement and assessment approach is required for the robust and reliable detection of APS in free-living, especially in the presence of PA. Previous studies indicate that APS can be accurately detected using wristband devices [1,5–8,12–16]. A few studies report the classification of different types of APS, such as mental stress and emotional anxiety [1–5,17]. Detecting the concurrent presence and the type of APS is further complicated by the presence of different types and intensities of physical activities. For example, metabolic and physiologic responses during training for a race are different from the variations before and during the competitive race. Accidents while bicycling, running to catch a bus, or hearing the screams of a young child while doing house chores are examples of co-existence of APS and PA.

Signals for discriminating APS from PA (italics) can be measured by Empatica E4 [5] (Figure 12.1). We focused on detecting the presence of PA, APS and their simultaneous occurrence, and on determining their types and intensities, through the

TABLE 12.1   Biosensor, Biosignals and Example Indicators

Sensor	Measurement	PI	PA	APS
GSR	Electrical conductance of the skin, sweat gland activation	Sympathetic nervous system (SNS) activation	Increase due to the sweating	Increase due to sweat gland stimulus as a result of SNS activation
BVP	Absorption of light by the blood flowing through the vessels	Heart rate variability (HRV) is affected by SNS activation	HRV altered due to SNS activation	HRV altered due to SNS activation
ST	Measurement of skin surface temperature	Response of systemic vasoconstriction and thermoregulation	Drop due to segmental vasoconstriction caused by a reflex in the spinal cord	Temperature of thermoregulatory tissues drop
3-D ACC	Acceleration in 3 orthogonal directions	Movement, speed, acceleration, stability, position	PA intensity is highly correlated with ACC signal variations	No correlation exists, except jolting of the body, arm motion
HR	Derived from BVP inter-beat (interval)	Individual cardiovascular condition	PA intensity is highly correlated with increase in HR	APS intensity is highly correlated with increase in HR

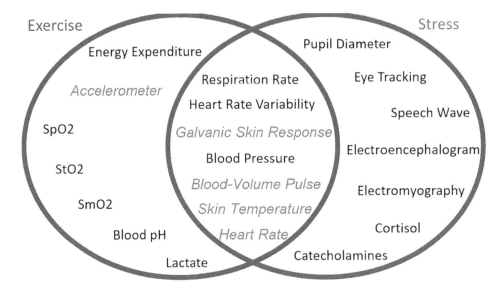

Figure 12.1 Signals for discriminating APS from PA (italics) can be measured by Empatica E4.

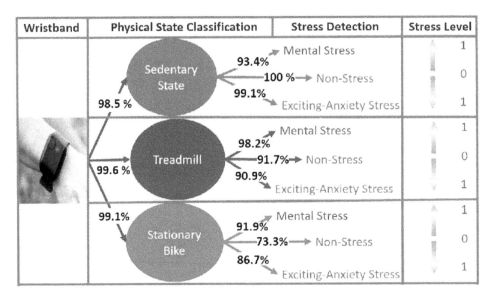

Figure 12.2 Structure and results of the proposed method (stress level: normalized APS estimates [0–1]), (numerical information: percentage classification accuracies (with testing data).

interpretation of physiological signals measured by a wristband (Figure 12.2). We discriminate various types of APS (non-stress state [NS], mental stress [MS], and emotional-anxiety stress [EAS]) and concurrent PA (sedentary state [SS], treadmill run [TR], stationary bike [SB]). To enable the simultaneous detection and clas-

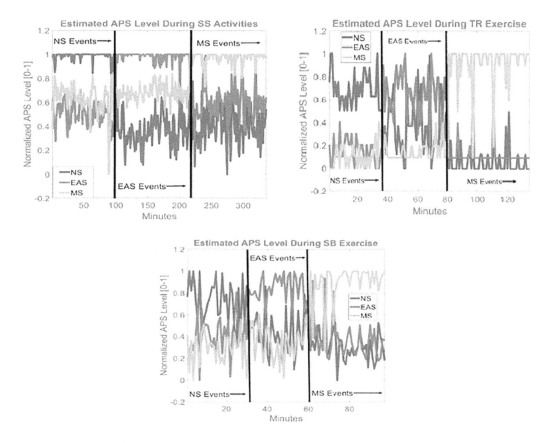

Figure 12.3 APS (NS, EAS, MS) level estimation during different physical activities.

sification of APS and PA, we rely on data reported by Empatica E4 wristband (Figure 12.3) [1,6,7]. Empatica E4 reports five variables: ACC, BVP, GSR, ST, and HR computed by an internal algorithm in E4 from BVP [11]. E4 can stream data in real-time or store multiple days of collected data and upload it as a batch. The measured physiological variables are used to generate features that are interpreted by machine learning (ML) algorithms.

12.2 METHODS AND DATA

12.2.1 Data Collection

Thirty-four subjects consented and completed 166 experiments that included staying in SS or performing a PA (TR, SB) without psychological stressors (NS), or with APS inducements (MS, EAS). The experiments were approved by the IRB of the university. The SS experiments include NS episodes where participants watch neutral videos, read books, or surf the internet; EAS inducement where data are collected during research meetings with supervisors, driving a car, and solving test problems in the allotted time; and MS inducement where a subject undergoes the

Stroop test, IQ test, mental arithmetic test, mathematics exam, or puzzle games. The APS inducements utilized in the experiments are recognized as standard techniques in the literature [5–10,17–20].

TRs include NS events such as watching nature videos or listening to music; EAS (watching surgery or car crash videos); and MS inducement (mental multiplication of two-digit numbers) during TR. Energy expenditure (EE) is measured and compared across the NS, EAS, and MS experiments to ensure the PA is consistent for all experiments. A portable indirect calorimetry system (Cosmed K5, Rome, Italy [21]) is used for EE estimation to determine PA intensity. In some experiments EE estimates are also computed from wristband data [4]). The subjects performed similar intensity PA during TR and SB. The SB experiments had the same APS inducements as the TR bouts. Table 12.2 lists all experiments. Demographic information of participants and experiment information (EE and E4 data, APS and PA types, duration, start time), are recorded for all experiments.

TABLE 12.2   Experiments Conducted for Data Collection

Physical State Classification			
Physical Activity	**Number of Exp.**	**Number of Subjects**	**Total Time (*Minutes*)**
Sedentary state	89	10	3172
Treadmill	57	20	2164
Stationary bike	61	19	1973
SS Experiments with APS Inducements			
Stress Inducement	**Number of Exp.**	**Number of Subjects**	**Total Time (*Minutes*)**
Non-stress	28	6	849
Exciting-anxiety stress	29	9	1129
Mental stress	32	6	1197
TR Experiments with APS Inducements			
Stress Inducement	**Number of Exp.**	**Number of Subjects**	**Total Time (*Minutes*)**
Non-stress	28	20	1162
Exciting-anxiety stress	12	12	679
Mental stress	17	8	326
SB Experiments with APS Inducements			
Stress Inducement	**Number of Exp.**	**Number of Subjects**	**Total Time (*Min*)**
Non-Stress	29	19	891
Exciting-Anxiety Stress	24	12	585
Mental Stress	8	7	237

The State-Trait Anxiety Inventory (STAI) [22–24] self- reported questionnaire data is collected both before and after each NS and EAS inducement experiments to assess the EAS response of participants. STAI-T (Trait) scores indicate the feelings of stress, anxiety or discomfort that one experiences on a day-to-day basis. STAI-S (State) scores indicate temporal fear, nervousness, discomfort, and the arousal of the autonomic nervous system that are perceived as stressful states [22–24].

12.2.2 Data Processing

Empatica E4 collects biosignals at high frequency (ACC: 32 Hz, BVP: 64 Hz, GSR: 4 Hz, ST: 4 Hz and HR: 1 Hz) [11]. The raw signals collected from E4 are corrupted by noise and motion artifacts. Various signal processing techniques are used to denoise them. The Savitzky–Golay filter [25] is used for denoising ACC, ST, HR, and GSR data. The BVP signal and the motion artifacts corrupting the BVP data have similar signatures and frequencies. We utilize sequential signal processing with an initial bandpass filter (Butterworth filter, cut off frequencies: [0.3 Hz, 3.5 Hz]) followed by an adaptive noise cancellation algorithm based on nonlinear recursive least squares filtering and wavelet decomposition (Symlets 4 wavelet function, 4 level decomposition) [26–28] to eliminate the effects of artifacts.

12.2.3 Feature Extraction

Features are extracted from the filtered biosignals at one-minute intervals. The features generated include statistical features (mean, standard deviation, kurtosis, skewness, etc.), mathematical features (derivative, area under the curve, arccosine, etc.), and data-specific features (maximum amplitude of the low-frequency BVP variations, zero-cross of ACC readings, etc.) [5,29–34]. The ratios of extracted features can be valuable in discriminating APS and PA. For example, during a stressful SS episode, the ACC readings are relatively stable (mean magnitude of ACC), while the GSR (mean magnitude of GSR) values increase because of the incremental increase in sweating rate in response to APS, and the ratio of the mean magnitudes of ACC and GSR is informative for detecting APS. We extracted additional secondary features as the ratios of various primary features. A total of 2068 feature variables are obtained, with 718 primary features (225 from 3D-ACC, 148 from processed and denoised BVP, 98 from HR, 111 from ST, 136 from GSR) and 1350 secondary features. Some features are highly correlated and do not provide additional information. They are pruned using principal components analysis (PCA) [35]. Due to the lack of PA during most of the experiment, the SS experiments are longer in duration than PA, which causes an imbalance in the number of samples among the classes. Since imbalances in class sizes may result in bias and poor classification accuracy, a combination of up-sampling (Adaptive Synthetic Sampling (ADASYN) [36]) and down-sampling methods are used. The impact of up-sampling the minor class is reduced by simultaneously down-sampling the major class by retaining the unique samples as determined by the similarity measure of k-means clustering.

We also studied what effect different levels of up-sampling the minor class has on the accuracy of the PA and APS classification. The highest accuracy is achieved with 25% up- sampling of the minor class. The balanced data set is divided into training (90%), and testing (10%), and 10-fold cross-validation is utilized for validation and hyperparameter optimization.

12.2.4   Feature Reduction

We compute the p-values for the feature variables between pairs of PA classes and the feature variables are retained at 1% confidence level, resulting in 1750 retained features. All feature variables were normally distributed, and outliers in the extracted feature variables are removed by retaining only the values that lie within the 1st and 99th percentiles for the distribution of the values. PCA is used to reduce the 1750 retained features down to a fewer number of uncorrelated latent variables. After reducing the dimension of the feature variables, we retain only the selected principal components (PC) for building the ML models for classification. The number of PCs to retain is determined through explicit enumeration by optimizing the classification accuracy using 10-fold cross-validation, and the number of retained components are varied between explaining 70% and 99% of the variance in feature variables data, with 250 PCs retained for training the PA classification models to discriminate SS, TR, and SB (90% variance explained). The number of PCs retained for training the APS discrimination (SS, TR, and SB) are 300, 250, and 200, corresponding to 92%, 92%, and 95% of variances explained, respectively. Since there is no rational link between APS and ACC data, the primary ACC features are not used for APS classification, but secondary features that include ACC can be used because they will capture an increase in a particular variable relative to the primary ACC features.

12.2.5   Machine Learning (ML) Algorithms

The normalized PCs are used with various ML algorithms, including k-nearest neighbors (k- NN), naive Bayes (NB), ensemble learning (EL), support vector machines (SVM), linear discriminant (LD), decision tree (DT), and deep-learning (DL). Four different classification models are developed, one for PA classification, and three for APS classification (SS, TR, SB) (Figure 12.2). Each classification node has its own unique classification algorithm selected as the best performing algorithm from among the seven different algorithms based on validation data.

   Bayesian optimization with expected improvement acquisition function is used to optimize the hyperparameters for each algorithm. Distance and number of neighbors (k-NN), box-constraints and kernel scale (SVM), number of ensemble learning cycle, ensemble aggregation method, minimum leaf size, and learning rate (EL), lambda and learner (LR), distribution and width (NB), and minimum leaf size (DT) are optimized for 100 iterations with 10-fold cross-validation to achieve the minimum value of the objective function.

12.3 RESULTS

12.3.1 Physical Activity Classification

SVM performed slightly better than the other algorithms with more than 99% classification accuracy with testing data. Achieving high accuracy for PA classification is important because classification inaccuracies in PA can have an effect on APS detection and classification. Instances of TR exercise are classified with high accuracy (99.6%), while a few SS activities are misclassified as SB exercise. The ACC readings can readily distinguish between TR and SB exercises, but a few subjects held the treadmill bar during TR, which caused the patterns in physiological variables during TR to resemble SB, and led to misclassifications (1%).

12.3.2 Acute Psychological Stress Classification

During SS episodes, NS is distinguished from MS/EAS with up to 100% accuracy. The MS detection achieves slightly lower accuracy at 93%. During TR exercise, all instances of NS are accurately identified. The SVM algorithm is able to distinguish different types of APS with 84% accuracy during SB exercise. APS classification during SS had best accuracy (97.3%) with LD algorithms, with SVM a close second (with testing data). The SVM algorithm had best accuracy in APS classification in the presence of both TR and SB. Since the score scales and calculations are different for each ML algorithm, SVM is chosen as the sole algorithm to be used for consistent APS level estimation. It provides good accuracy (PA: 99.19%, APS-SS: 94.07%, APS-TR: 94.17%, and APS-SB: 86.21%). We evaluated the commonly used performance metrics (recall, precision, and F-score values) for the best three algorithms and various APS types. The F-scores are given in Table 12.3. We presented only the most accurate three ML algorithms (SVM, EL, and LD). SVM performs slightly better with all indexes.

The normalized APS levels are analyzed for nine different permutations of PA and APS (Figure 12.3), each of the three PA with each of the APS categories.

TABLE 12.3 F Scores for APS Classifications with Various ML Algorithms During Various PA States (SS, SB, TR)

PA	Algorithm	NS	EAS	MS	Mean
SS	LD	0.974	0.953	0.964	0.963
SS	EL	0.973	0.966	0.974	0.971
SS	SVM	0.972	0.951	0.956	0.960
SB	EL	0.855	0.837	0.935	0.875
SB	LD	0.858	0.777	0.920	0.851
SB	SVM	0.858	0.777	0.920	0.851
TR	SVM	0.837	0.865	0.939	0.880
TR	EL	0.845	0.862	0.927	0.878
TR	LD	0.834	0.859	0.936	0.876

NS, EAS, and MS categories are statistically evaluated using a two-way analysis of variance (ANOVA) and estimated APS level, and the classifications are found to be statistically significant (p-values ¡ 0.05). Hence, the proposed approach has good potential to distinguish different types of PA and various types of APS in the presence or absence of PA.

12.4 CONCLUSIONS

Detection and classification of acute psychological stress necessitates algorithms that can discriminate APS in the presence of other confounding factors affecting the biosignals. The biosignals are limited to measurements generated from sensors of wearable devices that can be worn in daily living.

The biosignals from wearable devices used to detect and assess APS are susceptible to various confounding factors such as various physical activities. These biosignals must be filtered to eliminate noise and artifacts and subsequently used to generate features processed by machine learning algorithms for APS detection, classification, and intensity estimation. The ML algorithms developed for detecting APS in the possible presence of various physical activities are successful in detecting and discriminating various types of APS.

ACKNOWLEDGEMENT

Financial support from the NIH under grants 1DP3DK101075 and 1R01DK130049, and JDRF under grant 2-SRA-2017-506-M-B made possible through collaboration between the JDRF and The Leona M. and Harry B. Helmsley Charitable Trust.

REFERENCES

[1] M. Sevil, I. Hajizadeh, S. Samadi, J. Feng, C. Lazaro, N. Frantz, X. Yu, R. Brandt, Z. Maloney, and A. Cinar, "Social and competition stress detection with wristband physiological signals," in *2017 IEEE 14th International Conference on Wearable and Implantable Body Sensor Networks (BSN)*. Eindhoven, Netherlands, IEEE, 2017, pp. 39–42.

[2] T. Nakayama, Y. Ohnuki, and K. Niwa, "Fall in skin temperature during exercise," *The Japanese Journal of Physiology*, vol. 27, no. 4, pp. 423–437, 1977.

[3] K. A. Herborn, J. L. Graves, P. Jerem, N. P. Evans, R. Nager, D. J. McCafferty, and D. E. McKeegan, "Skin temperature reveals the intensity of acute stress," *Physiology & Behavior*, vol. 152, pp. 225–230, 2015.

[4] M. Sevil, M. Rashid, Z. Maloney, I. Hajizadeh, S. Samadi, M. R. Askari, N. Hobbs, R. Brandt, M. Park, L. Quinn, et al., "Determining physical activity characteristics from wristband data for use in automated insulin delivery systems," *IEEE Sensors Journal*, vol. 20, no. 21, pp. 12 859–12 870, 2020.

[5] M. Sevil, M. Rashid, I. Hajizadeh, M. R. Askari, N. Hobbs, R. Brandt, M. Park, L. Quinn, and A. Cinar, "Discrimination of simultaneous psychological and physical stressors using wristband biosignals," *Computer Methods and Programs in Biomedicine*, vol. 199, p. 105898, 2021.

[6] M. Sevil, M. Rashid, M. R. Askari, Z. Maloney, I. Hajizadeh, and A. Cinar, "Detection and characterization of physical activity and psychological stress from wristband data," *Signals*, vol. 1, no. 2, pp. 188–208, 2020.

[7] F.-T. Sun, C. Kuo, H.-T. Cheng, S. Buthpitiya, P. Collins, and M. Griss, "Activity-aware mental stress detection using physiological sensors," in *International Conference on Mobile Computing, Applications, and Services*. Springer, Santa Clara, CA, USA, 2010, pp. 282–301.

[8] Y. S. Can, B. Arnrich, and C. Ersoy, "Stress detection in daily life scenarios using smart phones and wearable sensors: A survey," *Journal of Biomedical Informatics*, vol. 92, p. 103139, 2019.

[9] A. Sanchez, C. Vazquez, C. Marker, J. LeMoult, and J. Joormann, "Attentional disengagement predicts stress recovery in depression: An eye-tracking study." *Journal of Abnormal Psychology*, vol. 122, no. 2, p. 303, 2013.

[10] B. Schuller, G. Rigoll, and M. Lang, "Hidden markov model-based speech emotion recognition," in *2003 IEEE International Conference on Acoustics, Speech, and Signal Processing, 2003 (ICASSP'03)*, vol. 2. IEEE, Hong Kong, China, 2003, pp. II–1.

[11] C. McCarthy, N. Pradhan, C. Redpath, and A. Adler, "Validation of the empatica e4 wristband," in *2016 IEEE EMBS International Student Conference (ISC)*. IEEE, Ottawa, Canada, 2016, pp. 1–4.

[12] M. T. Imboden, M. B. Nelson, L. A. Kaminsky, and A. H. Montoye, "Comparison of four fitbit and jawbone activity monitors with a research-grade actigraph accelerometer for estimating physical activity and energy expenditure," *British Journal of Sports Medicine*, vol. 52, no. 13, pp. 844–850, 2018.

[13] S. Ollander, C. Godin, A. Campagne, and S. Charbonnier, "A comparison of wearable and stationary sensors for stress detection," in *2016 IEEE International Conference on Systems, Man, and Cybernetics (SMC)*. IEEE, Budapest, Hungary, 2016, pp. 004 362–004 366.

[14] V. Sandulescu, S. Andrews, D. Ellis, N. Bellotto, and O. M. Mozos, "Stress detection using wearable physiological sensors," in *International Work-Conference on the Interplay between Natural and Artificial Computation*. Springer, Elche, Spain, 2015, pp. 526–532.

[15] B. Cvetković, M. Gjoreski, J. Šorn, P. Maslov, M. Kosiedowski, M. Bogdański, A. Stroiński, and M. Luštrek, "Real-time physical activity and mental stress management with a wristband and a smartphone," in *Proceedings of the 2017 ACM International Joint Conference on Pervasive and Ubiquitous Computing and Proceedings of the 2017 ACM International Symposium on Wearable Computers*, Maui, Hawaii, 2017, pp. 225–228.

[16] J. Minguillon, E. Perez, M. A. Lopez-Gordo, F. Pelayo, and M. J. Sanchez-Carrion, "Portable system for real-time detection of stress level," *Sensors*, vol. 18, no. 8, p. 2504, 2018.

[17] P. Karthikeyan, M. Murugappan, and S. Yaacob, "A review on stress inducement stimuli for assessing human stress using physiological signals," in *2011 IEEE 7th International Colloquium on Signal Processing and Its Applications*. IEEE, Penang, Malaysia, 2011, pp. 420–425.

[18] Y. Shi, M. H. Nguyen, P. Blitz, B. French, S. Fisk, F. De la Torre, A. Smailagic, D. P. Siewiorek, M. al'Absi, E. Ertin, et al., "Personalized stress detection from physiological measurements," in *International Symposium on Quality of Life Technology*, Las Vegas, USA, 2010, pp. 28–29.

[19] P. Rani, J. Sims, R. Brackin, and N. Sarkar, "Online stress detection using psychophysiological signals for implicit human-robot cooperation," *Robotica*, vol. 20, no. 6, pp. 673–685, 2002.

[20] A. de Santos Sierra, C. S. Ávila, G. B. Del Pozo, and J. G. Casanova, "Stress detection by means of stress physiological template," in *2011 Third World Congress on Nature and Biologically Inspired Computing*. IEEE, Salamanca, Spain, 2011, pp. 131–136.

[21] I. Perez-Suarez, M. Martin-Rincon, J. J. Gonzalez-Henriquez, C. Fezzardi, S. Perez-Regalado, V. Galvan-Alvarez, J. W. Juan-Habib, D. Morales-Alamo, and J. A. Calbet, "Accuracy and precision of the cosmed k5 portable analyser," *Frontiers in Physiology*, vol. 9, p. 1764, 2018.

[22] T. M. Marteau and H. Bekker, "The development of a six-item short-form of the state scale of the spielberger state: Trait anxiety inventory (STAI)," *British Journal of Clinical Psychology*, vol. 31, no. 3, pp. 301–306, 1992.

[23] C. D. Spielberger, S. J. Sydeman, A. E. Owen, and B. J. Marsh, *Measuring Anxiety and Anger with the State-Trait Anxiety Inventory (STAI) and the State-Trait Anger Expression Inventory (STAXI)*. Lawrence Erlbaum Associates Publishers, Mahwah, NJ, 1999.

[24] C. D. Spielberger and E. C. Reheiser, "Measuring anxiety, anger, depression, and curiosity as emotional states and personality traits with the STAI," in M. J. Hilsenroth and D. L. Segal (eds.), *Comprehensive Handbook of Psychological Assessment, Volume 2: Personality Assessment*, vol. 2, p. 70. John Wiley & Sons, Hoboken, NJ, 2003.

[25] Q. Li, X. Chen, and W. Xu, "Noise reduction of accelerometer signal with singular value decomposition and savitzky-golay filter," *Journal of Information &Computational Science*, vol. 10, no. 15, pp. 4783–4793, 2013.

[26] Z. Zhang, "Photoplethysmography-based heart rate monitoring in physical activities via joint sparse spectrum reconstruction," *IEEE Transactions on Biomedical Engineering*, vol. 62, no. 8, pp. 1902–1910, 2015.

[27] Z. Zhang, Z. Pi, and B. Liu, "Troika: A general framework for heart rate monitoring using wrist-type photoplethysmographic signals during intensive physical exercise," *IEEE Transactions on Biomedical Engineering*, vol. 62, no. 2, pp. 522–531, 2014.

[28] M. R. Askari, M. Rashid, M. Sevil, I. Hajizadeh, R. Brandt, S. Samadi, and A. Cinar, "Artifact removal from data generated by nonlinear systems: Heart rate estimation from blood volume pulse signal," *Industrial & Engineering Chemistry Research*, vol. 59, no. 6, pp. 2318–2327, 2019.

[29] G. Zhou, J. H. Hansen, and J. F. Kaiser, "Nonlinear feature based classification of speech under stress," *IEEE Transactions on Speech and Audio Processing*, vol. 9, no. 3, pp. 201–216, 2001.

[30] A. Mannini and A. M. Sabatini, "Machine learning methods for classifying human physical activity from on-body accelerometers," *Sensors*, vol. 10, no. 2, pp. 1154–1175, 2010.

[31] R. San-Segundo, J. M. Montero, R. Barra-Chicote, F. Fernández, and J. M. Pardo, "Feature extraction from smartphone inertial signals for human activity segmentation," *Signal Processing*, vol. 120, pp. 359–372, 2016.

[32] I.-V. Bornoiu and O. Grigore, "A study about feature extraction for stress detection," in *2013 8th International Symposium on Advanced Topics in Electrical Engineering (ATEE)*. IEEE, Bucharest, Romania, 2013, pp. 1–4.

[33] F. Seoane, I. Mohino-Herranz, J. Ferreira, L. Alvarez, R. Buendia, D. Ayllón, C. Llerena, and R. Gil-Pita, "Wearable biomedical measurement systems for assessment of mental stress of combatants in real time," *Sensors*, vol. 14, no. 4, pp. 7120–7141, 2014.

[34] T. F. Bastos-Filho, A. Ferreira, A. C. Atencio, S. Arjunan, and D. Kumar, "Evaluation of feature extraction techniques in emotional state recognition," in *2012 4th International Conference on Intelligent Human Computer Interaction (IHCI)*. IEEE, Kharagpur, India, 2012, pp. 1–6.

[35] I. T. Jolliffe and J. Cadima, "Principal component analysis: A review and recent developments," *Philosophical Transactions of the Royal Society A: Mathematical, Physical and Engineering Sciences*, vol. 374, no. 2065, p. 20150202, 2016.

[36] H. He, Y. Bai, E. A. Garcia, and S. Li, "Adasyn: Adaptive synthetic sampling approach for imbalanced learning," in *2008 IEEE International Joint Conference on Neural Networks (IEEE World Congress on Computational Intelligence)*. IEEE, Hong Kong, China, 2008, pp. 1322–1328.

CHAPTER 13

IEEE EMBC 2022 Workshop and Challenge on Detection of Stress and Mental Health Using Wearable Sensors

Huiyuan Yang, Han Yu, Alicia Choto Segovia, and Maryam Khalid
Rice University

Thomas Vaessen
University of Twente

Akane Sano
Rice University

13.1 MOTIVATION AND GOALS

Mental health and well-being are one of the most challenging issues in modern society[1,2]. For example, moderate stress can help a person in many beneficial ways to confront a challenge [3]. On the other hand, excessive stress, a common phenomenon in our society, can cause overall negative health and well-being impact [4], such as increasing susceptibility to infection and illness[5–7], affecting a diverse range of physical, psychological, and behavioral conditions (i.e., anxiety, depression, sleep disorders, or decreasing job productivity)[8–11]. Furthermore, mental disorders such as depression and schizophrenia, if not monitored and treated timely, can lead to further degradation of the person's mental health and well-being. The ability to measure stress levels or mental health could enable better self-management of one's behavioral choices in ways that might be intervened timely.

While various methods [2,12–18] have been proposed for automatic stress or mental health detection using wearable or mobile phone data, it is far from solved.

DOI: 10.1201/9781003371540-15

Besides, it is an understudied research question of reproducibility, due to the lack of a proper publicly accessible dataset and baselines. This workshop introduces to the research community the publicly accessible datasets with both anonymized handcrafted features and deep features for in the wild stress and mental health sensing challenges.

The goals of this workshop are to inspire ideas and collaborations, to raise awareness of reproducibility problems in modeling wearable data in the wild, and to drive the research frontier. Sharing the datasets, including both features and baselines, will facilitate research activity such as multimodal wearable/mobile sensor data processing and modeling, handling missing data, and personalization.

13.2   DATASET

The SMILE dataset was collected from 45 healthy adult participants (39 females and 6 males) in Belgium. The average age of participants was 24.5 years old, with a standard deviation of 3.0 years. Each participant contributed to an average of 8.7 days of data. Two types of wearable sensors were used for data collection. One was a wrist-worn device (Chillband, IMEC, Belgium) designed for the measurement of skin conductance (SC), skin temperature (ST), and acceleration data (ACC). The second sensor was a chest patch (Health Patch, IMEC, Belgium) to measure ECG and ACC. It contains a sensor node designed to monitor ECG at 256 Hz and ACC at 32 Hz continuously throughout the study period. Participants could remove the sensors while showering or before doing intense exercises. Also, participants received notifications on their mobile phones to report their momentary stress levels daily.

In addition to the physiological data collected by sensors, participants received notifications on their mobile phones to report their momentary stress levels ten times at random timing per day for eight consecutive days. In total, 3056 stress labels were collected across all participants (80% compliance). The stress scale ranged from 0 ("not at all") to 6 ("very"). The portions of each stress level's labels were 48.9%, 19.2%, 13.2%, 8.3%, 6.8%, 2.5%, and 1.0% from no stress at all to the highest stress level, respectively. For our challenge, we designed a binary classification problem (*stress vs non-stress*) by treating any stress scale larger than 1 as positive, and others as negative examples.

13.3   FEATURE EXTRACTION

The data were split into individual samples based on the timestamp of labels. Each sample was 60-minute sequence, from which the binary prediction (*stress vs non-stress*) was made. Next, we split the examples into two groups based on participant ID, resulting in 2070 training examples ($\mathcal{D}_{\text{train}}$) and 986 testing examples ($\mathcal{D}_{\text{test}}$). Note that there was no overlap of participants between the two groups. To build machine learning algorithms on those wearable data, a set of features were extracted from both ECG and GSR signals, including both handcrafted features and deep features (Figure 13.1).

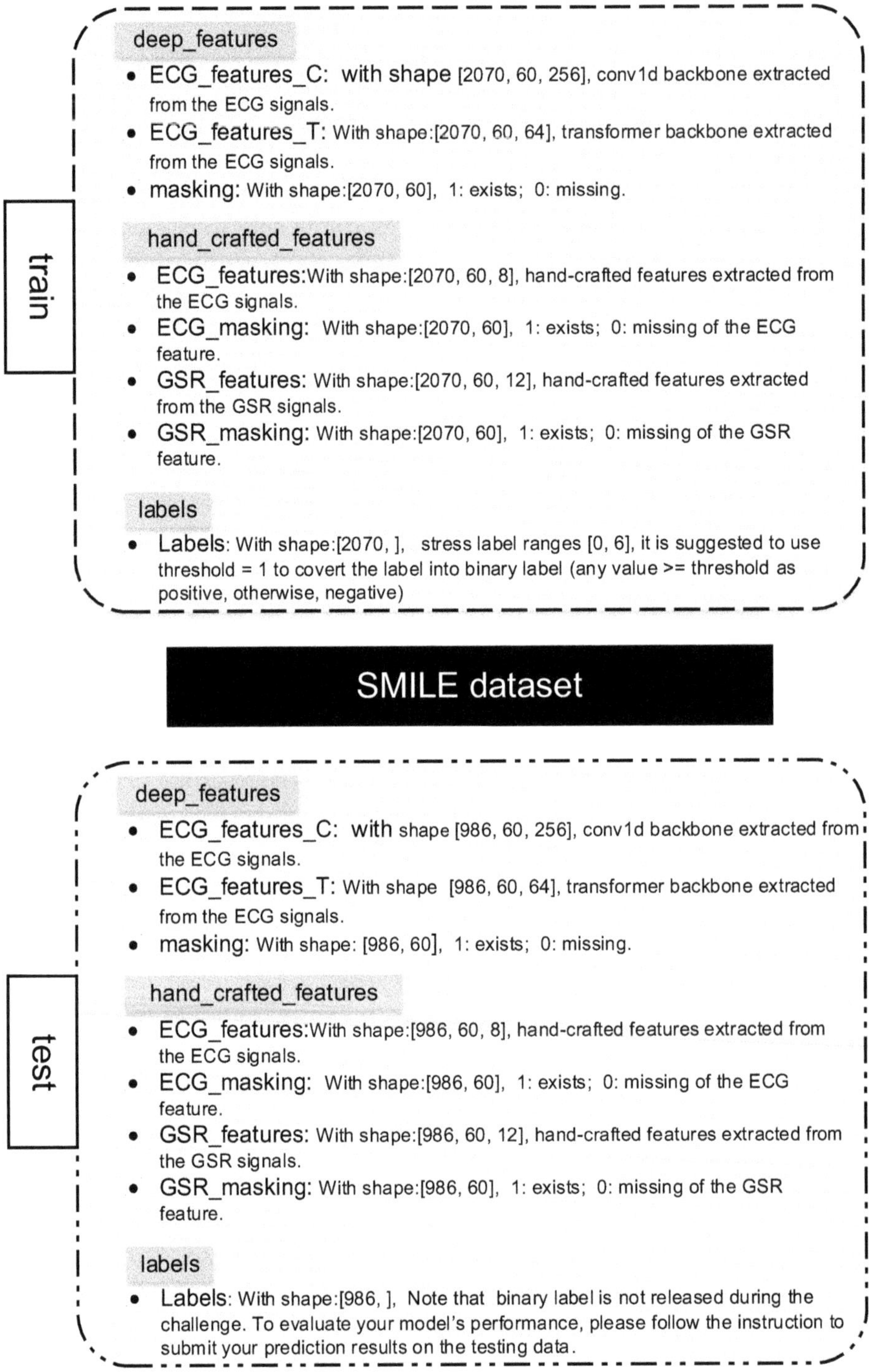

train

deep_features
- ECG_features_C: with shape [2070, 60, 256], conv1d backbone extracted from the ECG signals.
- ECG_features_T: With shape:[2070, 60, 64], transformer backbone extracted from the ECG signals.
- masking: With shape:[2070, 60], 1: exists; 0: missing.

hand_crafted_features
- ECG_features:With shape:[2070, 60, 8], hand-crafted features extracted from the ECG signals.
- ECG_masking: With shape:[2070, 60], 1: exists; 0: missing of the ECG feature.
- GSR_features: With shape:[2070, 60, 12], hand-crafted features extracted from the GSR signals.
- GSR_masking: With shape:[2070, 60], 1: exists; 0: missing of the GSR feature.

labels
- Labels: With shape:[2070,], stress label ranges [0, 6], it is suggested to use threshold = 1 to covert the label into binary label (any value >= threshold as positive, otherwise, negative)

SMILE dataset

test

deep_features
- ECG_features_C: with shape [986, 60, 256], conv1d backbone extracted from the ECG signals.
- ECG_features_T: With shape [986, 60, 64], transformer backbone extracted from the ECG signals.
- masking: With shape: [986, 60], 1: exists; 0: missing.

hand_crafted_features
- ECG_features:With shape:[986, 60, 8], hand-crafted features extracted from the ECG signals.
- ECG_masking: With shape:[986, 60], 1: exists; 0: missing of the ECG feature.
- GSR_features: With shape:[986, 60, 12], hand-crafted features extracted from the GSR signals.
- GSR_masking: With shape:[986, 60], 1: exists; 0: missing of the GSR feature.

labels
- Labels: With shape:[986,], Note that binary label is not released during the challenge. To evaluate your model's performance, please follow the instruction to submit your prediction results on the testing data.

Figure 13.1 Feature structure of the SMILE dataset, including both the deep features and handcrafted features for the training and testing dataset. Note that the label is not shared for the testing dataset, and participants are instructed to submit predictions on the testing data to the CodaLab platform for performance evaluation.

13.3.1   Handcrafted Features for Both ECG and GSR Signals

Following previous work [19], a set of handcrafted features were extracted from both ECG and GSR signals with 5-minute sliding windows and 4-minute overlapping, leading to 60 segments for each 60-minute sample. We used $\mathcal{D} = \{x_1^{i,m}, x_2^{i,m}, \dots, x_{60}^{i,m}\}, i = 1, 2, \dots, N, m \in \{\text{GSR}, \text{ECG}\}$ to represent the features for the whole dataset, where $x_t^{i,\text{EGC}} \in \mathbb{R}^8$ represent the 8 hand-crafted features extracted from ECG signals, and $x_t^{i,\text{GSR}} \in \mathbb{R}^{12}$ represent the 12 hand-crafted features extracted from the GSR signals. A detailed description of the handcrafted features can be found in Table 13.1.

13.3.2   Deep Features for ECG Signals

Inspired by the great success of deep models on wearable data [20–23], we also used deep models for feature extraction from ECG signals. Two reconstruction-based self-supervised learning frameworks, namely Conv-1D-based Autoencoder and Transformer [24], were used for feature extraction, as shown in Figure 13.2.

TABLE 13.1   Features: Electrocardiogram (ECG), Galvanic Skin Response (GSR), Skin Temperature (ST)

No	Feature	Source
1	Mean heart rate	ECG
2	Standard deviation of heart rate variability's R-R intervals	ECG
3	Root mean square of successive R-R differences	ECG
4	Low frequency signal (power in the 0.04–0.15 Hz band)	ECG
5	High frequency signal (power in the 0.15–0.40 Hz band)	ECG
6	Ratio of low and high frequency	ECG
7	Ratio of very low (0.0033–0.04 Hz) and low frequency	ECG
8	Heart rate cycle	ECG
9	GSR level - average GSR	GSR
10	Phasic GSR - signal power of the phasic GSR signal (0.16–2.1 Hz)	GSR
11	GSR response rate - number of GSR responses in window divided by the total length of the window (i.e. responses per second)	GSR
12	GSR second difference - signal power in second difference from the GSR signal	GSR
13	GSR response - number of GSR responses	GSR
14	GSR magnitude - the sum of the magnitudes of GSR responses	GSR
15	GSR duration - the sum of the magnitudes of GSR responses	GSR
16	GSR area - the sum of the area of GSR responses in seconds. The area is defined using the triangular method (1/2 x GSR magnitude x GSR duration)	GSR
17	Mean ST	ST
18	Standard deviation of the ST	ST
19	Slope of the ST - slop of a straight line fitted through the data	ST
20	Median ST	ST

Note that ST features are also available for the GSR data.

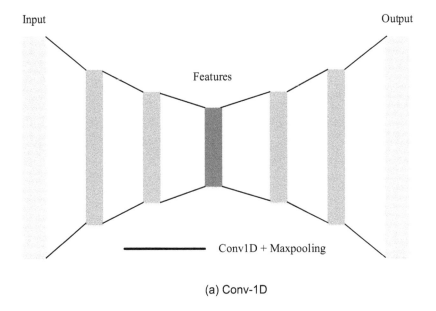

(a) Conv-1D

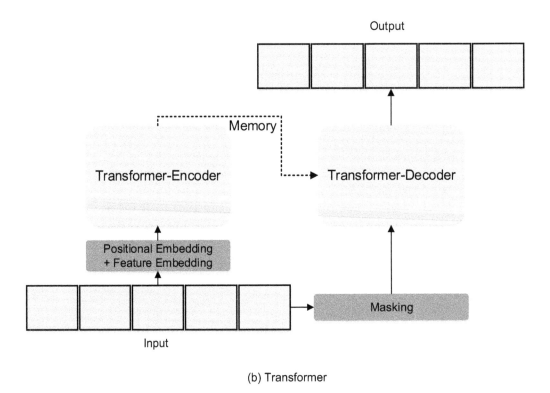

(b) Transformer

Figure 13.2 Framework of unsupervised Autoencoder. (a) Conv-1D is used as backbone. (b) Transformer framework.

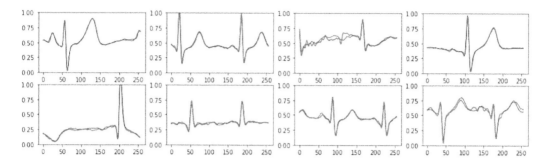

Figure 13.3 Examples of reconstruction error from the Conv-1d-based autoencoder. Note that **dotted** lines represent the raw ECG signals, while **solid** lines indicate the reconstructed signals. vertical: normalized magnitude; horizontal: data points sampled at 256 Hz.

As the raw ECG signal from 60-minute continuous observation at 256 Hz was too long to be directly fed into a deep model, we first split the data samples into 60-second segment, resulting in $\mathbf{s}^i = \{s_1^i, s_2^i, \ldots, s_t^i\}, t \in \{1, 2, \ldots, 60\}$. Then, we focused on extracting features from the individual segment $s_t^i \in \mathbb{R}^{15360}$.

Both frameworks were trained by minimizing reconstruction loss, which was calculated as the difference between the raw ECG signal and the reconstructed signal. Formally, it was defined as $\mathcal{L} = \text{MSE}(s, \hat{s})$, where MSE means the mean square error, s is the raw ECG signal and $\hat{s}$ is the reconstructed signal. Through minimizing the loss function $\mathcal{L}$, we hoped the deep models to learn rich information from the raw signals, which can then be used for machine learning algorithms.

The illustration of reconstructed examples is shown in Figure 13.3. As we can see, both conv-1d-based autoencoder and Transformer frameworks were able to reconstruct the raw ECG signals, even the areas with significant changes (*i.e., peaks*). In addition, we also found that the reconstructed signals show some robustness to noise (*i.e., third column in first row* in Figure 13.3).

13.4 BASELINE MODELS

Three baseline models, including Dense layers, Conv-1D and LSTM, were evaluated on both hand-crafted features and deep learning-based features. Their performances are listed in Table 13.2.

13.5 CHALLENGES

The goal of the challenge is to improve the performance of stress detection using wearable sensors. Participants developed stress detection models using the provided features, including both hand-crafted features from GSR and ECG, and deep features from ECG (Figure 13.4).

TABLE 13.2   Three Models Are Evaluated on Both Hand-Crafted Features and Deep Learning-Based Features

Model	Deep Learning-Based Features		Hand-Crafted Features		
	ECG (C)	ECG (T)	ECG	GSR	ECG+GSR
Dense	0.50/0.64	0.47/0.38	0.54/0.59	0.55/0.55	0.55/0.55
Conv-1D	0.55/0.40	0.53/0.57	0.51/0.44	0.52/0.48	0.56/0.53
LSTM	0.51/0.43	0.48/0.42	0.57/0.51	0.45/0.48	0.53/0.52

The corresponding performance (Accuracy/F1-score) is reported. Note that *ECG + GSR* means early fusion. C and T indict the features extracted by conv-1D-based autoencoder and transformer respectively.

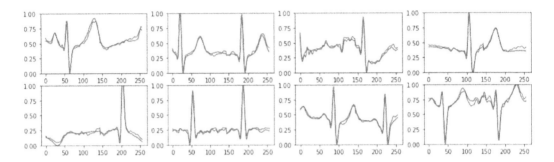

Figure 13.4 Examples of reconstruction error from the transformer-based Autoencoder. Note that **dotted** lines represent the raw ECG signals, while **solid** lines indicate the reconstructed signals. vertical: normalized magnitude; horizontal: data points sampled at 256 Hz.

For fair comparisons, we shared training data (*with labels*) and testing data (*w/o labels*), and participants were required to submit their model prediction on the testing data to the online competition platform, CodaLab[1] for performance evaluation.

To evaluate the performance, both accuracy and F1-score on the testing data were reported.

13.5.1   Challenge Rules

The requirements for each participant/team are:

- Multiple teams from a single entity (such as a company, university, or university department) are allowed as long as the teams are truly independent and do not share team members (at any point), code, or any ideas. Multiple teams from the same research group or company unit are not allowed because of the difficulty of maintaining independence in those situations. If there is any question on independence, the teams will be required to supply an official letter from the company that indicates that the teams do not interact at any point (socially or professionally) and work in separate facilities, as well as the location of those facilities.

- Participants can join an existing team before the abstract deadline as long as they have not belonged to another team or communicated with another team about the current Challenge. You may update your author list by completing this form again (check the 'Update team members' box on the form).

- The machine learning algorithms can be a traditional machine learning algorithm, deep model, or a mix of the two. There are no restrictions on the model.

- Participants may use any open-source code.

- Participants may not make your challenge code publicly available during the Challenge, or use any code from another participant that was shared (intentionally or not) during the course of the Challenge.

- The testing dataset will be made available to the participants along the release of training data, but the label is not shared for the testing data.

- To evaluate performance, participants should submit their prediction results to the Codalab platform, [2] and both F1-score and accuracy will be calculated.

- The performance evaluation is based on the sum of F1-score and accuracy on the testing dataset.

- To be eligible for prizes, participants must: (1) register for the Challenge; (2) submit source code that can be run directly on the dataset; (3) submit a paper describing your algorithm by the deadline; (4) attend and present at the EMBC 2022 workshop.

13.5.2 Timeline

- Challenge site opens: April 04, 2022

- Training data and blind testing data release: April 30, 2022

- Testing phase begins: May 16, 2022

- Competition registration ends: June 1, 2022

- Competition ends: June 30, 2022

- Paper/technical report submission deadline: June 30, 2022

- Workshop date: July 11 , 2022

Figure 13.5 Codelab submission history from the beginning to the end of this challenge.

13.5.3 Challenge Participants and Results

There were 23 registered teams from 21 institutions from 8 countries for the challenge. Figure 13.5 shows codelab submission activities during the challenge.

Six groups submitted their manuscripts including both challenge and research tracks, and each submission was reviewed by at least two reviewers and one meta reviewer. Among the submissions, five papers were selected to present during the conference. The top three submitted methods are summarized in Table 13.3.

TABLE 13.3 Summary of the Top Three Submitted Methods in the Challenge

Rank	Team	Performance		
		F1	Acc	Sum
First	Anxolotl	0.5496	0.641	1.1906
		The authors introduced the Anxolotl – an anxiety companion app– a system that can reliably detect anxiety levels, detect and predict panic attacks. The best result is obtained through usingthe hand-crafted features from ECG and GSR with Linear-SVC algorithm.		
Second	MUSE_USI	0.6184	0.5619	1.1803
		The authors focused on understanding the most effective strategy to fuse information from different sensors, and propose a multi-model fusion method for stress detection. The best result is reported by fusing the most important features from both ECG and GSR features with a Gaussian Process model.		

(*Continued*)

TABLE 13.3 (*Continued*) Summary of the Top Three Submitted Methods in the Challenge

Rank	Team	Performance		
		F1	Acc	Sum
Third	DEI_UNIPD	0.6004	0.5369	1.1373
		The authors implemented 4 different machine learning algorithms (LSTM, SVM and logistic regression) for stress detection using both hand-crafted features and deep features, finding the SVM model with the hand-crafted features achieved the highest performance.		

The rank is based on the sum of Acc and F1-score. Team Anxolotl from the *Instituto Politécnico de Lisboa and Universidade de Lisboa* , team MUSE_USI from the *Università della Svizzera Italiana* , and team DEI_UNIPD from the *University of Padova.*

13.6 CONCLUSION

Automatic detection of stress and mental health using wearable sensors is becoming increasingly more popular, due to its unobtrusive, privacy-preserving, very affordable, and user-convenient attributes. Inspired by the great success of deep models on various tasks, including computer vision, natural language processing, speech analysis, and so on, researchers started embracing deep learning-based methods for wearable data-based applications. However, we may find that conventional machine learning algorithms and traditional hand-crafted features are still widely used, and even beat the state-of-the-art deep models (i.e.,*LSTM, CNN, and Transformer*).

To benefit from the advance in deep models, researchers are encouraged to: (1) investigate how to combine the domain knowledge with deep models, rather than directly adapt the deep models to wearable data; (2) publicly share their collected datasets, as deep models are data-hungry, and massive well-annotated data will facilitate the development of new algorithms.

ACKNOWLEDGEMENT

This work was supported by National Science Foundation under the grant number #1840167 and #2047296 and Rice University. We would also thank the IEEE EMBC 2022 conference organizers, reviewers, workshop keynote speakers, and workshop/challenge participants for their efforts to make this workshop and challenge an successful event.

Notes

1. https://codalab.lisn.upsaclay.fr.
2. https://codalab.lisn.upsaclay.fr/competitions/4759?secret_key=8fc6ba6745a64b11a913457c6 6895a1b.

BIBLIOGRAPHY

[1] J. Campion, A. Javed, N. Sartorius, and M. Marmot, "Addressing the public mental health challenge of Covid-19," *The Lancet Psychiatry*, vol. 7, no. 8, pp. 657–659, 2020.

[2] Y. S. Can, N. Chalabianloo, D. Ekiz, and C. Ersoy, "Continuous stress detection using wearable sensors in real life: Algorithmic programming contest case study," *Sensors*, vol. 19, no. 8, p. 1849, 2019.

[3] F. S. Dhabhar, "Effects of stress on immune function: The good, the bad, and the beautiful," *Immunologic Research*, vol. 58, no. 2, pp. 193–210, 2014.

[4] K. Aschbacher, A. O'Donovan, O. M. Wolkowitz, F. S. Dhabhar, Y. Su, and E. Epel, "Good stress, bad stress and oxidative stress: Insights from anticipatory cortisol reactivity," *Psychoneuroendocrinology*, vol. 38, no. 9, pp. 1698–1708, 2013.

[5] S. Cohen, D. A. Tyrrell, and A. P. Smith, "Psychological stress and susceptibility to the common cold," *New England Journal of Medicine*, vol. 325, no. 9, pp. 606–612, 1991.

[6] J. Schaubroeck, J. R. Jones, and J. L. Xie, "Individual differences in utilizing control to cope with job demands: Effects on susceptibility to infectious disease," *Journal of Applied Psychology*, vol. 86, no. 2, p. 265, 2001.

[7] K. Kario, S. M. Bruce, and G. P. Thomas, "Disasters and the heart: A review of the effects of earthquake-induced stress on cardiovascular disease," *Hypertension Research*, vol. 26, no. 5, pp. 355–367, 2003.

[8] R. Beiter, R. Nash, M. McCrady, D. Rhoades, M. Linscomb, M. Clarahan, and S. Sammut, "The prevalence and correlates of depression, anxiety, and stress in a sample of college students," *Journal of Affective Disorders*, vol. 173, pp. 90–96, 2015.

[9] N. Bayram and N. Bilgel, "The prevalence and socio-demographic correlations of depression, anxiety and stress among a group of university students," *Social Psychiatry and Psychiatric Epidemiology*, vol. 43, no. 8, pp. 667–672, 2008.

[10] I. Donald, P. Taylor, S. Johnson, C. Cooper, S. Cartwright, and S. Robertson, "Work environments, stress, and productivity: An examination using asset," *International Journal of Stress Management*, vol. 12, no. 4, p. 409, 2005.

[11] M. Partinen, "Sleep disorders and stress," *Journal of Psychosomatic Research*, vol. 38, pp. 89–91, 1994.

[12] A. Sano and R. W. Picard, "Stress recognition using wearable sensors and mobile phones," in *2013 Humaine Association Conference on Affective Computing and Intelligent Interaction*, pp. 671–676, IEEE, 2013.

[13] A. Muaremi, B. Arnrich, and G. Troster, "Towards measuring stress with smartphones and wearable devices during workday and sleep," *BioNanoScience*, vol. 3, no. 2, pp. 172–183, 2013.

[14] J. Chen, M. Abbod, and J.-S. Shieh, "Pain and stress detection using wearable sensors and devices: A review," *Sensors*, vol. 21, no. 4, p. 1030, 2021.

[15] Y. S. Can, B. Arnrich, and C. Ersoy, "Stress detection in daily life scenarios using smart phones and wearable sensors: A survey," *Journal of Biomedical Informatics*, vol. 92, p. 103139, 2019.

[16] E. Smets, E. Rios Velazquez, G. Schiavone, I. Chakroun, E. D'Hondt, W. De Raedt, J. Cornelis, O. Janssens, S. Van Hoecke, S. Claes, et al., "Large-scale wearable data reveal digital phenotypes for daily-life stress detection," *NPJ Digital Medicine*, vol. 1, no. 1, pp. 1–10, 2018.

[17] H. Yang, H. Yu, K. Sridhar, T. Vaessen, I. Myin-Germeys, and A. Sano, "More to Less (M2L): Enhanced in the wild recognition on wearable data with reduced modality through multimodal training.," *The 44th International Conference of the IEEE Engineering in Medicine and Biology Society*, Glasgow, Scotland, 2022.

[18] H. Yu, T. Vaessen, I. Myin-Germeys, and A. Sano, "Modality fusion network and personalized attention in momentary stress detection in the wild," in *2021 9th International Conference on Affective Computing and Intelligent Interaction (ACII)*, pp. 1–8, IEEE, Virtual Conference, Nara, Japan, 2021.

[19] E. Smets, "Towards large-scale physiological stress detection in an ambulant environment," PhD Thesis, 2018.

[20] A. Sathyanarayana, S. Joty, L. Fernandez-Luque, F. Ofli, J. Srivastava, A. Elmagarmid, T. Arora, S. Taheri, et al., "Sleep quality prediction from wearable data using deep learning," *JMIR mHealth and uHealth*, vol. 4, no. 4, p. e6562, 2016.

[21] A. Natarajan, Y. Chang, S. Mariani, A. Rahman, G. Boverman, S. Vij, and J. Rubin, "A wide and deep transformer neural network for 12-lead ECG classification," in *2020 Computing in Cardiology*, Rimini, Italy, pp. 1–4, IEEE, 2020.

[22] B. Behinaein, A. Bhatti, D. Rodenburg, P. Hungler, and A. Etemad, "A transformer architecture for stress detection from ECG," in *2021 International Symposium on Wearable Computers*, Virtual Conference, USA, pp. 132–134, 2021.

[23] S. Gedam and S. Paul, "A review on mental stress detection using wearable sensors and machine learning techniques," *IEEE Access*, vol. 9, pp. 84045–84066, 2021.

[24] A. Vaswani, N. Shazeer, N. Parmar, J. Uszkoreit, L. Jones, A. N. Gomez, L. Kaiser, and I. Polosukhin, "Attention is all you need," *Advances in Neural Information Processing Systems*, vol. 30, pp. 5998–6008, 2017.

CHAPTER 14

Understanding Mental Health Using Ubiquitous Sensors and Machine Learning: Challenges Ahead

Tahia Tazin
Kyushu Institute of Technology

Tahera Hossain
Aoyama Gakuin University

Shahera Hossain
University of Asia Pacific

Sozo Inoue
Kyushu Institute of Technology

14.1 INTRODUCTION

Mental health issues, such as mood swings, personality changes, an inability to handle stress or daily problems, withdrawal from friends and activities, etc., are widespread around the world. In this regard, the prevention and treatment of mental illnesses are a public health priority due to the rise in the prevalence and burden of mental illness worldwide [1,2]. According to the World Health Organization (WHO), mental problems are the reason for more than 90% of suicides. The WHO considers mental illness as a worldwide crisis as well as an economic issue.

Mental illness affects our emotions, behaviors, and thoughts. It also affects our decision-making, interpersonal interactions, and stress management. Every stage of life, from childhood to adulthood, involves mental health. Mental illnesses can have a significant effect not only on the patients but also on their families, friends, and society as a whole because it is stressful to live with the consequences of someone close to you having a mental illness. There are a wide variety of ailments identified

DOI: 10.1201/9781003371540-16

as mental diseases such as anxiety disorders, depression, stress, mood disorders, psychotic disorders, eating disorders, impulse control and addiction disorders, personality disorders, obsessive-compulsive disorder, post-traumatic stress disorders, stress response syndromes, dissociative disorders, factitious disorders, sexual and gender disorders, somatic symptom disorders, and tic disorders. Because they are so common in today's society, stress, anxiety, and frustration are seen as necessary components of working life.

On the other hand, due to the ongoing global pandemic of coronavirus disease 2019 (COVID-19), ongoing and essential public health initiatives put many individuals in situations where they might suffer from effects connected to poor mental health, such as isolation and job loss. Because of online education and financial losses during the pandemic, many young adults face mental health-related problems including depression and anxiety. Moreover, as a result, young people are more likely to report drug use than older people. Before the pandemic, there was already a high chance that young adults would have poor mental health or addiction problems, but many of them did not get proper help.

In this regard, in the last 20 years, one of the most important ways that measurement science has been used is to get different physiological signals from the human body so that they can be analyzed automatically. Microelectronics, very large-scale integration, embedded computing, and sensing technology have all made important contributions to the creation of wearable, smart measurement devices. These devices have made it possible for a new kind of health monitoring called "e-healthcare," in which smart machines can spot health problems early on and people don't have to go to clinics as often to get expert diagnoses. Due to its significance for overall health, productivity, and personal well-being, data scientists have been interested in how to measure mental stress for a certain period of time.

In the last few decades, sensor technology has also changed quickly, with sensors getting smaller, lighter, and more accurate. They are also becoming more common and more integrated into networks, so they can give out huge amounts of data almost anywhere and almost instantly. Sensors keep track of everything about people today. Numerous sensors on mobile phones are used to track multiple factors, including position, movement, social interaction, light, sound, nearby digital devices, and more. Smartwatches and other wearable gadgets with sensors that can monitor body function and activity are rising in popularity. This digital exhaust that sensors produce contains a wealth of knowledge about how people behave and possible insights into their thoughts, feelings, and mental well-being.

There is evidence that smartphones and other similar technologies could be used to deliver mental health interventions [3,4]. A wide range of embedded sensors are present in wearable technology including smartphones, smartwatches, and fitness bands. A few examples of these include communication signals (WiFi, Bluetooth, etc.), inertial sensors (accelerometer, gyroscope), physiological sensors (heart rate, dermal activity, etc.), and environmental sensors (ambient pressure, temperature, etc.). This opens the possibility of multimodal sensing applications in the healthcare domain [5]. Contextual information, including physical activity [6], location [7], mood [8], and social interactions [9], among others, can be inferred by integrating the data from subsets of those sensors. In this context, machine learning is crucial in this situation because manually analyzing a lot of sensor data is difficult. It is feasible to extract useful information from sensor data using machine learning techniques and to use that knowledge to continuously monitor the present status of the users. Reviews of the literature and research surveys emphasizing ML applications for mental well-being have started to emerge in the fields of medicine and clinical psychology in recent years.

In this paper, we review recent studies on sensor-based, mostly machine learning-based mental health monitoring systems. Research on mental health disorders such as depression, anxiety disorders, bipolar disorder, stress, etc. was our main focus. The objective of this research is to review pertinent literature that demonstrates how technology (multimodal sensing and machine learning) is being used for autonomous and adaptive mental health monitoring.

The following significant aspects of mental health detection are examined in this review paper:

- An overview of current research in the field of machine learning models and applications being created for mental health.

- A survey on the methods used (and difficulties faced) in developing and assessing ML models.

- An overview of sensors and the workflow of sensor-based mental health monitoring systems and

- A list of research challenges and opportunities in the field.

This paper lists the following findings based on the aforementioned inspections:

- Principally, mental health monitoring systems collected and analyze behavioral and physiological data in order to correlate them with the signs of mental disorders and perform digital phenotyping.

- Thereby, a variety of environmental, wearable, and mobile phone sensors have been used to track physiological variables like heart rate variability (HRV), skin temperature (ST), electromyography (EMG), blood volume pulse (BVP), blood pressure (BP), etc. As well as behavioral information, such as how much sleep a person gets, their social interactions, and their voice characteristics, etc. data analyzed as important factors for mental health disorders.

- The predicted emotional states were frequently compared to self-reports and monitoring systems.

- In the majority of studies, there have also been recommendations for specific relationships between the behavioral and physiological collected data related to mental disorder, but the majority of developed technologies have not yet undergone a thorough validation of their applicability in clinical settings.

- In addition, the vast majority of monitoring systems do not evaluate the actual patient data and instead focus on the general public and healthy individuals for health and fitness applications which need to address in future research. Small sample sizes and quick follow-up times are additional important issues.

- When introducing a predictive model, the user-independent (general) models may also need to consider diversities like age and ethnicity.

- Furthermore, there is an urgent need for open communication and a cooperative relationship between healthcare professionals and patients because the acceptability of sensing systems is largely dependent on patient and provider confidence in the data collection organization and its goals.

The remaining part of this chapter proceeds as follows. First, Section 14.2 begins with motivations for applying ML to mental health. Section 14.3 explains thoroughly the types of mental health problems discussed in this paper, the obtained physiological signals and mental health correlation, and impact of wearable, ambient, and smartphone-based sensors on mental health. Section 14.4 describes the methods of mental health understanding which covers a brief of data labeling approach, data analysis and reprocessing, and machine learning model training details. Section 14.5 covers research challenges and opportunities and the conclusions drawn are presented in Section 14.6.

14.2 MOTIVATIONS FOR IMPLEMENTING ML TO MENTAL HEALTH

COVID-19 has influenced the vast majority of people worldwide. According to several studies, COVID-19 affected patients might have symptoms of depression [10–12], anxiety [11–14], post traumatic stress disorder [13,14], and insomnia [11]. Cross-sectionally, 22.5% of COVID-19-affected patients also had neuropsychiatric diagnoses [15]. CORONERVE, a UK-wide surveillance program, found 23 people with a psychiatric disorder who had been infected with severe acute respiratory syndrome coronavirus 2 (SARS-CoV-2) [16]. A meta-analysis of pooled data showed that a coronavirus-infected person might have delirium, depression, anxiety, manic symptoms, insomnia, and poor memory [17]. Based on the electronic health records of patients in the United States, a large case-control study found that the chances of being diagnosed with COVID-19 were higher for people with bipolar disorder, depression, and schizophrenia [18]. Research on past economic downturns shows that losing a job is linked to depression, anxiety, stress, and low self-esteem. It may also lead to more people using drugs or attempting suicide. During the pandemic, adults who have lost their jobs or have lower incomes report more signs of mental illness than those who have not lost their jobs or incomes.

According to the WHO, a healthy individual possesses both physical and mental health [19]. The standard way to diagnose depression is with the Patient Health Questionnaire (PHQ). The Depression, Anxiety, and Stress Scale (DASS-21), which has 21 questions, is used to look for signs of these mental illnesses [20,21]. From a clinical perspective, the main signs of depression are forgetfulness, inability to concentrate, difficulty making decisions, loss of interest in pastimes and hobbies, including sex, overeating, weight gain, skipping meals and weight loss, guilt, worthlessness, helplessness, restlessness, and irritation, as well as suicidal thoughts. These symptoms had a major impact on the person's life, including their ability to learn, work, and engage in social activities. This finding is crucial in developing a clinical diagnosis. Generalized anxiety disorder (GAD) causes people to be irritable, anxious, tired, unable to sleep, have stomach problems, panic, feel like they are in immediate danger, sweat a lot, breathe quickly, and have trouble focusing. Inability to relax, poor energy, frequent overreaction, feeling disturbed or irritated, and recurring colds or illnesses are all signs of stress. Thus, stress, anxiety, and depression share symptoms, such as chest discomfort, weariness, an elevated heart rate, and difficulty focusing, making machine categorization difficult. In response to the need for better mental health services, digital technology is increasingly important in making therapy more accessible, engaging, and effective.

To build more reliable systems that can automatically learn from data, the area of ML extends statistical and computational methodologies [22]. These methods hold promise for aiding in comprehending massive amounts of health data and have been effectively used in gaming and recommend systems. ML has led to significant advances by enabling speedy and scalable analysis of complex data [23,24]. These analytical methods are also being investigated for use with mental health data, with the potential to significantly improve patient outcomes as well as the general public's knowledge of psychological illnesses and how to manage them. ML methods are being investigated more and more in the context of mental health because they provide fresh avenues for enhancing our understanding of human behaviors and predicting or optimizing outcomes [25–27].

14.3 BASIC STRUCTURE OF MENTAL HEALTH PREDICTION SYSTEMS

In this section, we will discuss the common types of mental health, physiological signal, and its relation with mental health, and wearable, ambient, and smartphone-based sensors used in mental health prediction.

14.3.1 Types of Mental Health Problems

People suffering from mental illnesses can experience changes in cognition, emotion, and behavior. In addition, persons with mental illnesses may experience difficulties at home, at work, and in society. Schizophrenia, depression, stress, bipolar disorder, and anxiety are just a few of the many different types of mental illnesses that exist (Figure 14.1). For understanding such mental health states researchers mostly focus on 'detection' of particular mental health condition labels (high, low, or moderate) for experiment.

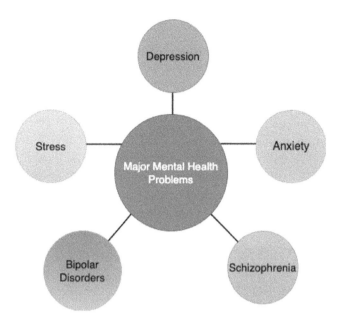

Figure 14.1 Mental disorders.

The most prevalent psychotic condition is schizophrenia, which affects up to 20 million people globally and accounts for more than 13.4 million years of life spent with a disability [28]. The disorder is severely incapacitating and frequently has negative effects on social interactions, economic opportunities, and education. Compared to the general population, those with schizophrenia are at an elevated risk of early death [29]. Because of this, it's critical to manage and properly treat schizophrenia in order to lessen the disorder's detrimental effects on the person's life.

One of the most prevalent and crippling health issues of our time is clinical depression, often known as major depressive disorder (MDD). More than 260 million people worldwide suffer from depression, which is a common mental condition [30, 31]. People who have depression frequently have recurrent episodes of symptoms, which can include sorrow, guilt, agitation, odd sleep patterns, low energy, social and physical isolation, and loss of interest in regular activities [30,32]. The main sign of depression is a disruption in mood, which is typically very severe sadness. If depression is not identified and treated, it may result in negative health outcomes or even suicide. It is urgently important to provide early and effective mental health interventions because depression is the primary cause of disease, disability, and morbidity worldwide.

Bipolar disorder is another mental disorder which is characterized by recurrent periods of both mania and depression [33]. In general, bipolar disorder, commonly referred to as pendulum sickness, is a form of mood disorder that includes both manic and depressed periods. An anxiety disorder is another prevalent mental illness that is characterized by an inability to control concern or fear. Anxiety is recognized as a highly complicated emotional integrity component of the person. According to an American Psychological Association study, 18% of Americans have anxiety problems. However, stress is the most common mental illness in Europe, afflicting 16% of the population [34]. Stress is another important term used in psychology to describe the mental state of feeling tired and anxious. It is typically brought on by changes in the environment or an underlying desire [35].

A significant amount of research revealed the relationship between behavior and mental health. To evaluate mental wellness, it is crucial to infer relevant behaviors. Depression is known to cause a decrease in social contact, emotional reactivity, and physical activity. Reduced social engagement in schizophrenia may be an indication of relapse and an aggravation of psychotic symptoms, along with anxious and depressive mood states. Speech volume and changes in speaking rate are behavioral signs of manic and depressed phases in bipolar disorder.

Symptomatic behavior can be tracked via passive sensing, as shown in Table 14.1. For sensing physical activity, a smartphone's accelerometer data can be used to describe how the user moves physically [36,37]. It is possible to use distinct patterns in the data to automatically identify various activities like running, walking, and standing. It is more common and can be mostly regarded as a research

TABLE 14.1   Behaviors Associated with Severe Mental Disorders That Can Be Monitored with Sensing

Domain	Behaviors	Sensors	Behavior Change Goals
Physical activity	Active versus inactive lifestyles (for example, walking, running, biking, stationary biking)	Accelerometer, GPS/location, gyroscope, barometer, compass	Increasing exercise while maintaining a healthy weight/body mass index (BMI)
Social interaction	Changes in geographic range, social interactions, turn-taking during conversations, voice volume, pace, intonation, and emotion	Microphone, accelerometer, GPS/location	Increase the number of social interactions; remove or alter conditions that worsen stress, anxiety, depressive symptoms, or distress related to psychotic symptoms
Sleep patterns	Time of sleep, interrupted versus uninterrupted sleep	Microphone, accelerometer, GPS/location, light, phone usage	Control sleep cycles and synchronize internal body clock

challenge solved to identify physical activity, especially for simpler activities, using onboard phone sensors or external wearables like Fitbit. On the other hand, computer vision, speech recognition, machine learning, and ubiquitous computing communities are still working to continuously capture social behaviors which is also an important symptomatic behavior for mental illness. The length of a person's speech, their speech tempo, and their pitch can also be important factors to understand mental disorders. Researchers agree that stress affects human vocal production and should use this information to monitor stress. The fundamental frequency of vocal cord vibration during speech production is pitch, the most researched acoustic trait for stress.

In another way, numerous habits, including sleep and insomnia, are important behavioral cues may also aid researchers in their understanding of internal mental health processes. It has been demonstrated that sleep problems, including insomnia, hypersomnia, and irregular sleep and wake times, are frequent signs of mental illnesses [38,39]. For instance, a relapse into a manic phase of bipolar disorder may be associated with an increase in the frequency of utilizing the phone's browser to search for information.

14.3.2 Physiological Signals and Mental Health Correlation

Heart Rate (HR) [40–42], HRV, ST [40,43], and Skin Conductance Level (SCL) are the physiological markers most frequently utilized in stress detection methods. BP [43,44], Respiration Rate (RR) [44–46]. Beat-to-beat variability, or HRV, can be analyzed using time-domain, frequency-domain, and non-linear domain indices. Inter-Beat-Interval (IBI) time-domain HRV indices evaluate the degree of variability in measurements of the time between subsequent heartbeats (IBI). During the observation period, the HRV measurement time may range from more than one minute to less than 24 hours [47].

Low Frequency (LF), High Frequency (HF), Ultra-low Frequency (ULF), and Very Low Frequency (VLF) are the four frequency bands that make up frequency-domain indices that evaluate the distribution of absolute or relative power (VLF). HRV frequency-band measurements are limited by the length of the recording period, which is advised to be at least 24 hours (ULF), 5 minutes to 24 hours (VLF), 2 minutes (LF), and 1 minute (HF). The power of the LF component to the power of the HF component in the Power Spectral Density is measured as the LF/HF ratio (PSD). As it depicts the balance of the autonomic nervous system, the LF/HF ratio is a crucial marker of the harmony between sympathetic and parasympathetic nerve activity [48].

Stress was found to cause an increase in HR, BP, RR, and GSR while a decrease in HRV and ST. In most cases, HRV is calculated using the Electrocardiogram (ECG), Electroencephalography (EEG), and Photoplethysmography (PPG) devices. The typical locations for wearable sensors and devices on the human body are shown in Figure 14.2. A study by Jang et al. [49] uses 60 different emotional stimuli to examine the consistency of changes in bio-signals as physiological reactions

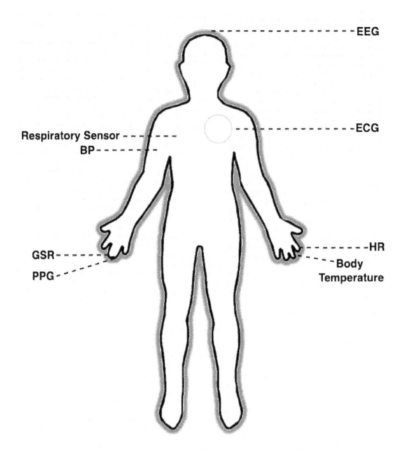

Figure 14.2 Illustrating typical locations for wearable sensors on the human body.

generated by the six basic emotions of happiness, sorrow, anger, fear, disgust, and surprise in order to achieve emotion detection using sensor data. Before and during the presentation of the stimuli, measurements of HR, SCL, mean of ST (meanSKT), and mean of Photoplethysmograph (meanPPG) were taken. The physiological responses to six emotions were consistent across time, which suggests that biosensors are useful instruments for emotion recognition. In particular, physiological parameters including SCL, HR, and PPG are found to be quite trustworthy [49].

14.3.3   Wearable, Ambient, and Smartphone-Based Sensors in Mental Health

The medical sciences and associated fields rely heavily on sensors nowadays because several wearable technology devices have been created to track emotional data. Thus, the emotional moods of people can be tracked using sensor data. The signals, however, should be consistent and dependable when they are associated with physiological reactions to different emotional states.

To understand different emotional states, the correlation between physical activity and depression has been discovered using data from accelerometer-based wearables [50]. It was shown that a decline in mobility and social interactions is a sign of more severe depressive symptoms. In addition, physiological sensing has demonstrated promising outcomes in the monitoring of schizophrenia, such as the use of HRV data as a sign of decompensation. In addition, physiological markers that respond to emotional events and can be used to identify stress and other emotional states include HRV, respiratory sinus arrhythmia (RSA), electrodermal activity (EDA), ST, EMG, BVP, BP, and cortisol levels [51].

On the other hand, the increasing field of mental health research has resulted in the identification of digital biomarkers [52] for the symptoms of mental diseases (Major depressive disorder, Bipolar disorder, Seasonal affective disorder, Post-traumatic stress disorders, and others). For example, location-based biomarkers derived from GPS, WiFi, and Bluetooth sensors, such as circadian rhythm [53,54], location regularity [55,56], time spent at home, time spent at specific place clusters, and location variance [54], have been linked to depression symptoms.

However, mobile phones are frequently used and include a lot of inbuilt sensors that may detect behavioral indicators like sleep, social environment, mood, and stress. As a result, many studies on personal sensing in mental health have also used mobile phone sensors. Numerous mental diseases, such as schizophrenia [57], bipolar disorder, and depression, have been studied by the use of smartphone sensors for detecting their existence and severity [54,58–60]. In addition, environmental or ambient sensors are typically deployed in a single room or a house to comprehend the context of that environment by gathering data from sensors and aiding the occupants. For the purpose of identifying cognitive impairment, ambient sensors have been studied in certain research on mental health monitoring [61].

An inconspicuous activity assessment system with motion sensors and contact sensors has been installed in Ref. [62] to monitor the activities of elderly people in their homes in an effort to research early diagnosis of cognitive deterioration. In addition, passive infrared motion sensors have been used in smart homes to monitor long-term depression and the everyday activities of older people [63]. Finally, a smart home test bed was created at Washington State University and consisted of an apartment that was outfitted with motion detectors on the ceiling, sensors on the cupboards and doors, as well as sensors on a few kitchen appliances. To evaluate each person's cognitive health, the work quality of smart home activities was measured [64].

For instance, sensor data from mobile phones, GPS, and accelerometers can be utilized to identify physiological patterns linked to bipolar disorder-related depression or low mood states. In addition, physiological markers that respond to emotional events can be tracked using HR and EDA sensors, enabling the identification of emotions as well as the measurement of stress levels. Schizophrenia monitoring variables include sleep, movement habits, and speech frequency and patterns. Last but not least, cognitive help is frequently provided by microphone, visible light, accelerometer, temperature, and digital compass sensors. Table 14.2 lists the wearable, physiological and emotional monitoring systems with research targets. Most of the research experiment duration was 1–10 weeks [11,24,37,65–67].

TABLE 14.2 Mental Health Monitoring Research Prototypes

Research Target	Participants(N)	Sensor/Module	Data
Office workers mental health identification [68]	100 office workers	Fitbit, self reported data, and mobile application	Activity data, questionnaires data, weather information and behavior information
Understanding bipolar disorder through depression prediction [69]	40 individuals	Kye press entry time and accelerometer	Kye press entry time data and accelerometer movement data
Stressful event detection [70]	Real life data ($N = 5$) and laboratory data ($N = 21$)	Empatica wrist device and smart phone application	Questionary data
Forecasting daily life stress [71]	Students ($N = 142$)	Self-reported data, and affectiva Q sensors	Self-reported questionnaire data, physiological data, accelerometer data
Academic performance, sleep patterns, stress levels, and awareness of mental health [72]	Students ($N = 66$)	Affectiva Q sensors, smart phone application	Pittsburgh sleep quality index data, questionnaire data, physical and mental health composite scale data
Anxiety and stress identification [73]	Students ($N = 21$)	Galvanic skin response (GSR) sensor, Oximeter sensor, breathing sensor and Arduino	Body temperature data, skin response data, heart rate and oxygen saturation data, breath rate data
Mental state prediction for suicide risk reconnaissance [61]	X	Electro-dermal activity (EDA) sensor and Electroencephalography (EEG) sensor	Stress level and emotional state data, blood flow and heart rate data, alcohol consumption and irritation level data, family history data and medical history data

(*Continued*)

TABLE 14.2 (*Continued*) Mental Health Monitoring Research Prototypes

Research Target	Participants(N)	Sensor/Module	Data
Mental and psychosocial stress identification [74]	Worker ($N = 39$)	ECG sensor, nine axis accelerometer, and body temperature sensor	ECG data, respiration signals, self-reported data
Emotion recognition [75]	University students and staff ($N = 23$)	EEG Electrode Cap Starter Kit, Shimmer3 GSR+module, Intel Realsense camera, Logitech webcam	EEG data, GSR data, Photoplethysmography (PPG) data, audio and video data
Mental illness identification [76]	4612 individuals	Fitbit, self reported data	Sleep data, activity data, resting heart rate data, alcohol use data, and medical examination data
Depressive symptoms prediction [63]	106 individuals	Mobile application, Accelerometer, Gyroscope, GPS	Self-reported questionary data, accelerometer data, gyroscope data, GPS data, Screen on/off record data, call logs data, SMS logs data, activity transition data, facial expression data
Stress level identification [77]	14 individuals	Vital Jacket, Trier Social Stress Test (TSST)	Electrocardiogram (ECG) data, self-reported data, HRV data
Mental stress detection [78]	Student ($N = 206$)	Questionnaire data	Self reported questionnaire data
Risk of depression identification [79]	600 individuals	Twitter streaming API	Twitter post data
Depression and anxiety prediction [80]	College students ($N = 217$)	Smart phone sensing app, patient health	Locations visited, distance traveled, phone usage duration, phone unlocks, sleep duration, and self-reported questionnaire data

(*Continued*)

TABLE 14.2 (*Continued*) Mental Health Monitoring Research Prototypes

Research Target	Participants(N)	Sensor/Module	Data
Real time mental stress detection [81]	Laboratory person (N = 15)	RespiBAN device, Empatica E4 device	Photoplethysmogram (PPG) signal data, ECG data, EDA data, EMG data, respiration (RESP) data, skin temperature (ST) data, 3-axis accelerometer data
Depression level prediction [82]	55 individuals	Smart phone sensors and fitbit, patient health questionnaire data, mobile application	Call data, conversation data, location data, heart rate data, questionary data, screen use data, heart rate data, sleep data, step data
Depression status prediction [83]	60 individuals	Oura ring, mobile application	Mood changing data, sleep data, physical activity data, phone usage data, GPS data, eye movement data, heart rate data
Stress prediction [84]	Office worker (N = 25)	Mobi (TMSI) device, Kinetic 3D sensor	Computer use pattern, facial expression data, body posture data, ECG data and skin conductance level data
Schizophrenia patient's psychotic relapse identification [85]	Schizophrenia patients (N = 63)	Smart phone sensor, clinical questionnaires	Light exposure data, volume data, conversation data, distance data, accelerometer data, screen usage data, questionnaire data
Psychotic relapse prediction in schizophrenia patients [86]	Schizophrenia patients (N = 63)	Smart phone sensor, mobile application	Ambient light data, sound data, conversation data, accelerometer data, distance traveled data, phone unlock duration data, call log data, SMS text data, app use data
Bipolar disorder [33]	Patients (N = 12)	Smart phone, mobile application	Self-reported mood, sleep and alcohol consumption data, stress data

Also, few research experiment duration was long such as 55 days [87], 2276 days [2] (Using a total of 2276 days, with 1231 overlapping 8-day sequences of data from 142 participants) and 1980 days [39]. Some of the research continuously conducted from 1.5 years to 3.5 years [8,10,85].

14.4 METHODS OF MENTAL HEALTH UNDERSTANDING

The major five types of mental health issues discussed in this paper are schizophrenia, anxiety and depression, bipolar disorder, and stress disorder. Deep learning, neural networks, ensemble learning, supervised learning, and unsupervised learning are just a few of the machine learning techniques shown in Figure 14.3 that are used to identify specific patterns and relationships from the massive amount of collected data and ultimately produce the right predictive model(s).

14.4.1 Data Labeling

Training data is used by machine learning algorithms to identify trends and create predictive models. To properly train the final prediction models, the data labeling phase—which includes associating the sensor data with the matching ground truth state—is crucial. The data labeling phase may take place on-site, at the hospital or clinic, or off-site while the participants go about their daily lives at home, at work, etc. Data tagging can be done through recurring assessments by a specialist or doctor on-site or over the phone [88,89], using self-reports, which are frequently displayed by a mobile application at regular intervals and the participant is in charge of the labeling process [90,91], or in response to an event, such as labeling stress in an exam situation [92].

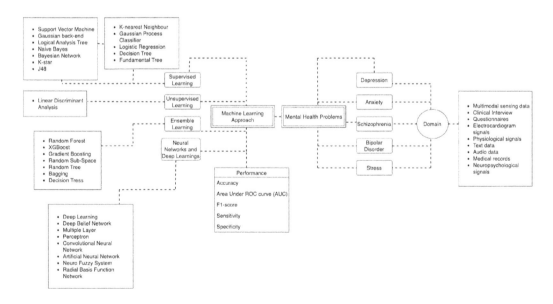

Figure 14.3 Overview of mental health prediction using ML.

14.4.2 Data Analysis and Preprocessing

To better understand and interpret the data and identify outliers, exploratory data analysis and preprocessing are done after the data has been collected. To remove outliers and minimize noise, preprocessing involves adding filters and changes to the raw data, such as scaling, quantization, binarization, and so on. One of the most popular preprocessing methods is dimensionality reduction, which includes techniques like multidimensional scaling [93] and principal component analysis. The raw sensor data is then utilized to create feature vectors via feature extraction. Machine learning algorithms need feature vectors since they are representations of the underlying data. The arithmetic mean, standard deviation, min, max, skewness, kurtosis, root mean square, power spectrum density, energy, and correlation coefficient are all common features retrieved for the purpose of detecting mental states [94].

14.4.3 Machine Learning Model Training

To accomplish more straightforward, understandable formats for basic tasks like finding the relationship and pattern recognition in high-dimensional datasets, a variety of ML approaches, including classification, regression, association, and clustering, can be used. In supervised learning, labels are applied to the data before they are used to train a model that can forecast the label for fresh data. In this case, the dataset includes both the desired inputs and outputs. Supervised learning was mostly used for classification tasks. In these tasks, a set of previously classified training instances is used to build a model that can, for example, predict a binary class label (e.g., presence or absence of a symptom) or a small set of class labels (e.g., mental health condition) of unseen instances. Most of the previous research employed supervised learning and frequently discussed the use of one or more of the following methods: Support Vector Machines, Random Forest, Decision Trees, k-Nearest Neighbors, supervised LDA, Lasso, and Logistic Regression [67,70,79,87,95–109]. A list of ml models/techniques is described in Table 14.3.

In unsupervised learning, data are clustered using mathematical methods to provide new information. Since there are no desired output labels in this dataset, it just contains inputs. Clustering approaches react to the existence or absence of commonalities in each data set to find patterns and aid in data structuring. of information. Only one of the publications clearly mentioned the use of semi-supervised learning methods that blend labeled and unlabeled data in their model. To predict mental health, deep learning (DL) techniques [18,56] and reinforcement learning (RL) techniques are also used to develop individualized recommendations for stress-management strategies [110].

It should be mentioned that many times, different algorithms are integrated to produce the final predictive models. But there is a difference between some training approaches, like user-dependent and user-independent (generic) models. Although they require more data training, user-dependent models that capture each

TABLE 14.3   ML Models/ Techniques

Supervised	Unsupervised	Semi-Supervised	Novel Methods
Support Vector Machines (SVM) k-Nearest neighbors (k-NN) Naïve Bayes (NB)Regression analysis, e.g., Logistic Regression (LR), Lasso Supervised Latent Dirichlet Allocation Decision Trees (DT) Random Forests (RF) Supervised Hidden Markov Models (HMM) Supervised Neural networks (NN)	k-means clustering Hierarchical clustering Unsupervised Hidden Markov Models (HMM) Latent Dirichlet Allocation (LDA) Unsupervised Neural networks (NN) Association rule techniques	Semi-supervised ML Self-training Mixture models Co-training + multi-view learning Graph-based methods	Deep learning (DL) Active learning, i.e., Reinforcement Learning (RL)

user's unique behavior and are trained using data from that user produce superior outcomes. User-independent models, which do not need data for the target user but are trained with data from all other users but the target user, may not perform well for unusual users.

14.4.3.1 *Machine Learning Approaches in Predicting Schizophrenia*

Schizophrenia is a severe mental disorder. It impacts people's relationships with others and their thinking, acting, and emotional expressions. Despite not being as common as other severe mental disorders, schizophrenia can be the most severe and disabling. According to neuroscientists, schizophrenia is related to the brain network. Researchers have recently used artificial intelligence (AI) and machine learning to predict, classify, and monitor various disorders, including schizophrenia, because machine learning methods are highly effective at identifying a link between disease symptoms and the disease. There are significant connections between different parts of the brain and schizophrenia symptoms. Machine learning is capable of identifying these relationships. Logistic regression is a well-known technique for categorizing binary problems. The goal of the binary categorization is to identify patients who have schizophrenia. In numerous studies, Logistic regression has been used to identify schizophrenia. In Ref. [111], the authors used Logistic regression to pick essential variables in schizophrenia patients' recovery stages among 75 Hong Kong adults. Data on sociodemographic variables, stages of recovery, and recovery-related components were gathered. Stage 3 recovery, or "living with disability," could be identified by Logistic regression with an accuracy of 75.45%, and stage 4 recovery, or "living beyond disability," with an accuracy of 75.50%.

The authors in Ref. [112] proposed a relapse prediction model based on machine learning and mobile sensing data. A support vector machine (SVM)-based relapse prediction model uses various features, including activity, distance, the number of communications, etc. The supervised classifier known as Naive Bayes is based on Bayes theory. The independence of features is the primary presumption of Naive Bayes. A Naive Bayes classifier is a traditional ML model that performs admirably in classification tasks. In one study [113], Naive Bayes was used to collect and classify data for 48 schizophrenia patients and 24 healthy people. The Wisconsin Card Sorting Test, full-scale IQ, positive and negative syndrome scale, age, and sex were among the features of the dataset. With a 67% accuracy rate, the Naive Bayes model could identify schizophrenia. Authors in Ref. [114] used EEG signals to predict schizophrenia using a Random forest classifier. The dataset contained 32 healthy and 49 schizophrenia patients. Event-related potentials (ERPs) from fundamental sensory tasks were included in the dataset. Only ERP averages from nine electrodes were employed in the dataset for training the random forest.

14.4.3.2 Machine Learning Approaches in Predicting Depression and Anxiety

Many studies have concentrated on gathering and classifying data from blog posts using machine learning algorithms like Random Forest Tree (RFT), Support Vector Machine (SVM), and Convolution Neural Network (CNN). The authors in Ref. [115] concentrated on the factors that influence depression and Post Traumatic Stress Disorder (PTSD) in Twitter users. The probability of PTSD increasing was identified using the Hidden Markov Model. Depression and PTSD were present in 31.4% and 24% of the total sample. The authors used decision tree classification to assess the risk of suicide by gathering tweets from 135 participants hired through Amazon Mechanical Turk [116]. The rate of accuracy for predicting suicide rates was found to be 92%. In Ref. [110], depression was predicted using big data techniques based on a person's reading preferences. To create a book classifier, the features of Chinese text were extracted, and naive Bayes was found to be the most suitable classifier after applying five classifications.

Machine learning algorithms can be used in the field of anxiety disorders in various ways, including detecting anxiety disorders, predicting their future risk, and predicting how well they will respond to medical treatment. Authors in Ref. [117] used five machine learning algorithms to identify anxiety risks for early intervention and treatment, including Logistic Regression, Naive Bayes, Random Forest, Support Vector Machine, and Catboost. Interviews with 740 subjects resulted in a data set with 14 features used for classification. On the testing set, the Catboost model performs the best, with a classification accuracy of 89.3%.

14.4.3.3 Machine Learning Approaches in Predicting Bipolar Disorder

Many researchers have used machine learning algorithms to predict bipolar disorder early. Using Naive Bayes, RFT, and a SVM, the authors in Ref. [118] proposed a predictive model to detect bipolar disorder among students. They achieved 92.1% accuracy by using the Support vector machine algorithm. The authors in Ref. [65] collected EEG data and used the extreme applied gradient boosting (XGB) technique to identify patients with bipolar disorder. For the comparative analysis, the authors have also used additional machine learning classifiers, including Naive Bayes (NB), Decision Tree (DT), KNN, and SVM. According to the study, XGB performs better than other machine learning classifiers in terms of accuracy, recall, and precision.

14.4.3.4 Machine Learning Approaches in Predicting Stress

The majority of people experience stress regularly and at various times. However, continuous stress or high stress will threaten our safety and cause trouble with our regular activities. Many physical issues linked to stress can be avoided by early detection of mental stress. Stress levels can be determined utilizing different biosignals, such as thermal, electrical, impedance, acoustical, and optical changes that occur when a person is under stress. Adnan Ghaderi et al. used biological signals based on sensors, such as heart rate, respiration rate, hand and foot movements, etc., to present the user's stress level [45]. Different features were extracted at various intervals of time. KNN and SVM methods were used for classification to determine the precise stress level. Naive Bayes, decision trees, and SVM were utilized to identify relaxed states (non-stress) contrasted to stressed states (stress) using signal processing techniques on the physiological signals that were being monitored in Ref. [119]. Support vector machine (SVM) classifiers, K-means clustering, and decision trees were proposed in Ref. [120]. In Ref. [121], stress was predicted using a KNN classifier using body temperature, GSR, and RR interval data.

14.4.3.5 Performance Evaluation of ML Models

The capacity of developed classification models to generalize classifications or predictions to new cases is often evaluated, which means how correctly a classifier predicts the actual class labels for new data for which the desired output is known. The papers reported evaluation strategies such as Leave-one-user-out (LOSO) or k-fold cross-validation for this [69,122–126]. Through majority of previous research used 10–fold cross–validation for data splitting [65,122,124] but few research studies also used 80%/20% splitting or 70%/30% splitting ratio for training and test samples [61,125,127]. Table 14.4 presents a summary of performance evaluation.

The majority of articles presented accuracy, precision, recall, and F1-scores to describe the performance of constructed classifiers [86,125–131]. In a few cases, Log Loss was utilized, which takes into of the uncertainty of a forecast depending on how much it differs from the actual label. Precision shows how valuable a forecast is

TABLE 14.4 Performance Evaluation

Research Target	Model/System	Results/Accuracy
Mental state prediction [34]	Tree Ensemble (RF)	90% accuracy
Suicidal risk prediction [132]	Linear classifier	20.5% F1 score
Work stress [31]	SVM	84% accuracy
Real time mental stress [133]	SVM (Kernel Linear)	99% accuracy
Workload prediction [94]	AdaBoost	97% accuracy
Stress level prediction [11]	LSTM	62.83% accuracy
Stress prediction [87]	DeepMood	83% accuracy

(low false positive rate) and recall tells how complete it is (low false negative rate). The F1 score is a calculated weighted harmonic mean of the classifiers precision and recall, and it measures how many samples or individuals are properly classified out of the total number classified.

The area under the ROC curve (AUC) metric was frequently employed for unbalanced datasets with unequal error costs and was suggested as a more suitable evaluation technique [98,100,134,135]. To identify any unexpected values, outlier sensitivity, and dangers of over- or underestimating erroneous predictions, measures of mean error (e.g., MSE, MAE, RMSE, SMAPE) were employed in a few regression tasks [67,69,102,106,136,137]. A list of commonly used evaluation metrics is described in Table 14.5.

14.5 FUTURE RESEARCH CHALLENGES AND OPPORTUNITIES

Mental health monitoring systems primarily gather and analyze behavioral and physiological data in order to relate it to the symptoms of mental diseases in order to accomplish digital phenotyping. Variables like HRV, ST, EMG, BVP, BP, and other parameters have been tracked in order to do this using a range of ambient, wearable, and mobile phone sensors. The self-reported status along with the monitoring systems were regularly contrasted to the anticipated mood states. The majority of earlier studies suggested specific connections between behavioral and physiological information and the patient's mental health status. It is important to note that the majority of such technologies have not had their suitability for use in clinical settings sufficiently evaluated. It's important to think about how monitoring systems measure emotional states because most of them are not approved as medical devices. Instead, they are made for the general public and healthy people to use in health and fitness applications. Therefore, there are still many technical and practical challenges in digital approaches to mental disorders identification that need to be resolved, such as issues with maintaining compliance over time, battery limitations, manufacturing, durability, integration, challenges with information analysis and interpretation, data accuracy, ethics/privacy concerns, acceptability, and engagement issues.

TABLE 14.5 Definitions of the Most Commonly Used Performance Measures for Classification

Evaluation Metric		Description
$\text{Accuracy} = \dfrac{TP + TN}{TP + FP + FN + TN}$	(14.1)	Accuracy is the measure of correct classified test samples against the total number of test samples. Averaged for each of the classes; it provides the measure of the accuracy of the entire classifier
$\text{Precision} = \dfrac{TP}{TP + FP}$	(14.2)	Precision is the classifiers' ability to not label a sample as positive; of it should be negative. It is calculated as the ratio between true positives, divided by the sum of true positives and false positives
$\text{Recall} = \dfrac{TP}{TP + FN}$	(14.3)	Recall represents the percentage of positive samples that were correctly labeled as positives
$\text{F1} = \dfrac{2 * \text{Precision} * \text{Recall}}{\text{Precision} + \text{Recall}}$	(14.4)	F1 score is calculated as a weighted harmonic mean of the classifiers' precision and recall ($F1 = 1$ is best)

In the equation, the meanings of TP, TN, FP, and FN are stated as: TP, True Positive; TN, True Negative; FP, False Positive; and FN, False Negative.

14.5.1 Data Access Challenges

Enabling effective ML modeling requires access to the availability of high-quality, relevant, and extensive data, which is linked to the challenges of identifying essential health and care needs. This can be particularly challenging in the field of mental health due to the ethical and privacy issues involved in (1) recruiting people who might be more vulnerable to research and (2) the time-consuming and labor-intensive nature of data acquisition, which frequently necessitates multidisciplinary partnerships with healthcare providers and is not easily scale-able [98].

The requirement for rich, personal data in order to construct effective ML models and treatments raises the challenge of how to ensure that people generally agree to and can trust academics and data applications with the collection and processing of their sensitive information. This will almost certainly necessitate rigorous balances between data requirements for algorithmic purposes and how associated data activities are justifiable in terms of benefit [66]. For example, while sensitive data such as a person's gender, age, or clinical diagnosis might help distinguish health-behavior patterns and groups and enable testing for diversity in a dataset [138,139], we must evaluate how comfortable people are submitting such data.

14.5.2 Data Labeling

Data labeling, or the process of connecting a set of sensor data to the matching genuine mental state at that moment, is one of the largest hurdles in the development of mental monitoring systems. To train the machine learning models, this is also referred to as the ground truth data. Depending on how well the ground truth data are collected, the models' final performance will vary. It takes a lot of time and effort to obtain proper labeled data. For instance, bipolar illness sufferers need an expert evaluation to determine their current status, which necessitates a visit to the hospital. Transfer learning is one approach that may be employed when there is a lack of sufficient labeled data. Also, the use of semi-supervised learning techniques is one solution that might be used to solve this issue.

The statistics for self-reported assessments' subjectivity is another problem. Participants in off-site research could be asked to answer a questionnaire about their current situation, which relies on their view of themselves and is prone to bias and data capture problems (e.g., mislabeling a state). Predictive models will be significantly impacted by these kinds of inaccuracies. There are ways [140] to cope with label noise, but they haven't often been investigated for monitoring mental status.

14.5.3 User Variance

Physiological and behavioral habits will differ amongst users because everyone is different and unique. The study for stress detection by Muaremi et al. [141], in which they achieved a 53% and 61% accuracy for the user-independent and user-dependent models, can be used to understand performance variations between user-independent and user-dependent models. Another illustration comes from the study of Zenonos et al. [91] on mood recognition, where they attained an average accuracy of 62% for the user-independent model and 70% for the user-dependent model. The strengths of both types of hybrid models have been combined in various hybrid models that have been proposed in earlier works on mental state detection [90,132, 133]. However, there is still a need for advancement in this area of hybrid models that can adjust to the unique needs of each user.

14.5.4 Mental Health Constructs and Clinical Validity of ML Results

The development of interpretable and (clinically) meaningful outputs for mental health care providers or target users is a fundamental challenge in the design of ML-enabled systems. Many medical professionals continue to have concerns about the consistency and challenge of implementing machine learning predictive systems to actual medical procedures, as well as the accuracy of automated techniques like machine learning. According to Dang et al., there is no established method for gathering high-quality data, it is challenging to obtain labels, which results in inconsistent supervised learning approaches, and there is also a lack of recognition for best practices when handling machine learning models [142]. These difficulties and factors may limit the use of machine learning models in the field of mental health.

The validity of the mental health components must therefore be confirmed by additional study. Additionally, it is necessary to guarantee that ML outputs are applicable and prediction robust for usage in "practice" (reliability). Future research needs to start evaluating how well ML model findings can be applied because they are meant to be employed in and integrated into actual mental health interventions. Clinical specialists, for example, can provide critical perspectives on construct validity, assessments of ground truth and biases, and critical context details that can aid in the interpretation of data findings, increase rigor, and manage deployment risks and trade-offs.

14.5.5   Considerations of Ethics

Data on mental health is considered to be more sensitive than other types of health information data. That's why the user's consent and ethical approvals are crucial factors for a mental health monitoring system before the data gathering phase even begins. The fundamental rule for carrying out medical research with human beings is that all procedures must adhere to the ethical standards. Data can only be provided willingly by patients who agree to be studied, and formal informed consent is required. Therefore, prior to signing the consent form, it is crucial that all involved participants have received adequate information about the study's objectives, methods, foundational information, potential negative effects, and other pertinent aspects. They should also be made aware of their right to revoke their consent at any time.

14.6   CONCLUSION

Physiological and behavioral sensing systems have the potential to improve the management and monitoring of mental health. The use of these devices can enhance patients' self-awareness, which can have a positive impact on the management of their condition. This awareness of one's mental state can inhibit the deterioration and progression of a number of mental disorders. In this research, we summarize how technology (multimodal sensing and machine learning) is being used for autonomous and adaptive mental health monitoring. In the mental health-related research, it's important to keep in mind that sensors don't actually sense the mental state itself, but rather a behavior that results from an underlying physiological change when considering physiological and behavioral data as indicators of mental health. Therefore, technology must be established in mental health, as it has been in other fields of medicine, in order to provide convenient and point-of-care devices for those affected.

BIBLIOGRAPHY

[1] Ronald Kessler, Matthias Angermeyer, James Anthony, Ron Graaf, Koen Demyttenaere, Isabelle Gasquet, Giovanni de Girolamo, Semyon Gluzman, Oye Gureje, Josep Maria Haro, Norito Kawakami, Aimee Karam, Daphna Levinson, Maria Medina-Mora, Mark Oakley Browne, Jose Posada-Villa, Dan Stein, Sergio Aguilar-Gaxiola, and Tevfik Ustun. Lifetime prevalence and age-of-onset distributions of mental disorders in the who world mental health (WMH) surveys. *World Psychiatry: Official Journal of the World Psychiatric Association (WPA)*, 6:168–176, 2007.

[2] Ronald Kessler, Steven Heeringa, Matthew Lakoma, Maria Petukhova, Agnes Rupp, Michael Schoenbaum, Philip Wang, and Alan Zaslavsky. Individual and societal effects of mental disorders on earnings in the united states: Results from the national comorbidity survey replication. *The American Journal of Psychiatry*, 165:703–711, 2008.

[3] Joseph Firth, John Torous, Jennifer Nicholas, Rebekah Carney, Simon Rosenbaum, and Jerome Sarris. Can smartphone mental health interventions reduce symptoms of anxiety? A meta-analysis of randomized controlled trials. *Journal of Affective Disorders*, 218:15–22, 2017.

[4] John Torous, Rohn Friedman, and Matcheri Keshavan. Smartphone ownership and interest in mobile applications to monitor symptoms of mental health conditions. *JMIR mHealth uHealth*, 2(1):e2, 2014.

[5] Debraj De, Pratool Bharti, Sajal Das, and Sriram Chellappan. Multimodal wearable sensing for fine-grained activity recognition in healthcare. *IEEE Internet Computing*, 19:1–1, 09 2015.

[6] Oscar D. Lara and Miguel A. Labrador. A survey on human activity recognition using wearable sensors. *IEEE Communications Surveys & Tutorials*, 15:1192–1209, 2013.

[7] Ramon Brena, Juan García-Vázquez, Carlos Galván Tejada, David Muñoz-Rodriguez, Cesar Vargas-Rosales, James Fangmeyer Jr, and Alberto Palma. Evolution of indoor positioning technologies: A survey. *Journal of Sensors*, 2017, 2017.

[8] Robert Likamwa, Yunxin Liu, Nicholas D. Lane, and Lin Zhong. Can your smartphone infer your mood? *Proceedings of ACM Workshop on Sensing Applications on Mobile Phones (PhoneSense)*, Seattle, Washington, USA, 2011.

[9] Nathan Eagle and Alex (Sandy) Pentland. Reality mining: Sensing complex social systems. *Personal and Ubiquitous Computing*, 10(4):255–268, 2005.

[10] Zhang Jie, Huipeng Lu, Haiping Zeng, Shining Zhang, Qifeng Du, Tingyun Jiang, and Baoguo Du. The differential psychological distress of populations affected by the Covid-19 pandemic. *Brain, Behavior, and Immunity*, 87:49–50, 2020.

[11] Mario Mazza, Rebecca De Lorenzo, Caterina Conte, Sara Poletti, Benedetta Vai, Irene Bollettini, Elisa Melloni, Roberto Furlan, fabio ciceri, Patrizia Rovere-Querini, and Francesco Benedetti. Anxiety and depression in covid-19 survivors: Role of inflammatory and clinical predictors. *Brain Behavior and Immunity*, 89:594–600, 2020.

[12] Clara Paz, Guido Mascialino, Lila Adana, Alberto Rodriguez, Katherine Simbaña-Rivera, Lenin Gomez, Maritza Troya, María Paez, Javier Cardenas, Rebekka Gerstner, and Esteban Ortiz-Prado. Anxiety and depression in patients with confirmed and suspected Covid-19 in ecuador. *Psychiatry and Clinical Neurosciences*, 74, pp. 554–555 2020.

[13] Hai-Xin Bo, Wen Li, Yuan Yang, Yu Wang, Zhang Qinge, Teris Cheung, Xinjuan Wu, and Yu-Tao Xiang. Posttraumatic stress symptoms and attitude toward crisis mental health services among clinically stable patients with COVID-19 in China. *Psychological Medicine*, 51:1–7, 2020.

[14] Stephen Halpin, Claire McIvor, Gemma Whyatt, Anastasia Adams, Olivia Harvey, Lyndsay McLean, Christopher Walshaw, Steven Kemp, Joanna Corrado, Rajinder Singh, Tamsin Collins, Rory O'Connor, and Manoj Sivan. Postdischarge symptoms and rehabilitation needs in survivors of Covid-19 infection: A cross-sectional evaluation. *Journal of Medical Virology*, 93, pp. 1013–1022 2020.

[15] Krishna Nalleballe, Sanjeeva Reddy Onteddu, Rohan Sharma, Vasuki Dandu, Aliza Brown, Madhu Jasti, Sisira Yadala, Karthika Veerapaneni, Suman Siddamreddy, Akshay Avula, Nidhi Kapoor, Kamran Mudassar, and Sukanthi Kovvuru. Spectrum of neuropsychiatric manifestations in Covid-19. *Brain, Behavior, and Immunity*, 88, pp. 71–74 2020.

[16] Varatharaj Mrcp, Ian Galea, Thomas Mrcpch, Mustafa Sultan, Rhys H Thomas, Ellul Mrcp, Tom Solomon, Michael Phd, Mark A Ellul, Easton Phd, Laura Benjamin, Rachel Kneen, Benedict Michael, Aravinthan Varatharaj, Naomi Thomas, Mark Ellul, Nicholas Davies, Thomas Pollak, Elizabeth Tenorio, and Wing Chou. Neurological and neuropsychiatric complications of Covid-19 in 153 patients: A UK-wide surveillance study. *The Lancet Psychiatry*, 7(10):875–882, 2020.

[17] Jonathan Rogers, Edward Chesney, Dom Oliver, Thomas Pollak, Philip McGuire, Paolo Fusar-Poli, Michael Zandi, Glyn Lewis, and Anthony David. Psychiatric and neuropsychiatric presentations associated with severe coronavirus infections: A systematic review and meta-analysis with comparison to the Covid-19 pandemic. *The Lancet Psychiatry*, 7:611–627, 2020.

[18] Quan Qiu Wang, Rong Xu, and Nora Volkow. Increased risk of Covid-19 infection and mortality in people with mental disorders: Analysis from electronic health records in the United States. *World Psychiatry: Official Journal of the World Psychiatric Association (WPA)*, 20:124–130, 2020.

[19] Arkaprabha Sau and Ishita Bhakta. Predicting anxiety and depression in elderly patients using machine learning technology. *Healthcare Technology Letters*, 4:223–248, 2017.

[20] Kurt Kroenke, Robert L. Spitzer, and Janet Williams. The PHQ-9 validity of a brief depression severity measure. *Journal of General Internal Medicine*, 16:606–613, 2001.

[21] Tian Po Oei, Sukanlaya Sawang, Yong Goh, and Firdaus Mukhtar. Using the depression anxiety stress scale 21 (DASS-21) across cultures. *International Journal of Psychology : Journal International de Psychologie*, 48:1018–1029, 2013.

[22] Adrian Shatte, Delyse Hutchinson, and Samantha Teague. Machine learning in mental health: A scoping review of methods and applications. *Psychological Medicine*, 49: 1–23, 2019.

[23] Glen Coppersmith, Kim Ngo, Ryan Leary, and Anthony Wood. Exploratory analysis of social media prior to a suicide attempt. *Proceedings of the Third Workshop on Computational Linguistics and Clinical Psychology*, pp. 106–117, San Diego, CA, 2016.

[24] Michael Jordan and Tom M. Mitchell. Machine learning: Trends, perspectives, and prospects. *Science (New York, N.Y.)*, 349:255–60, 2015.

[25] Munmun Choudhury, Emre Kiciman, Mark Dredze, Glen Coppersmith, and Mrinal Kumar. Discovering shifts to suicidal ideation from mental health content in social media. *Proceedings of the 2016 CHI Conference on Human Factors in Computing Systems*, 2016: 2098–2110, 2016.

[26] Natasha Jaques, Sara Taylor, Ehimwenma Nosakhare, Akane Sano, and Rosalind W. Picard. Multi-task learning for predicting health , stress , and happiness. In *Proceedings of NIPS Workshop on ML in Health*, Barcelona, Spain, 2016.

[27] Koustuv Saha, Benjamin Sugar, John Torous, Bruno Abrahao, Emre Kiciman, and Munmun Choudhury. A social media study on the effects of psychiatric medication use. *International AAAI Conference on Web and Social Media (ICWSM 2019)*, Munich, Germany, 2019.

[28] Fiona J. Charlson, Alize J. Ferrari, Damian F. Santomauro, Sandra Diminic, Emily Stockings, James G. Scott, John J. McGrath, and Harvey A. Whiteford. Global epidemiology and burden of schizophrenia: Findings from the global burden of disease study 2016. *Schizophrenia Bulletin*, 44(6):1195–1203, 2018.

[29] Mark Olfson, Tobias Gerhard, Cecilia Huang, Stephen Crystal, and T. Scott Stroup. Premature mortality among adults with schizophrenia in the United States. *JAMA Psychiatry*, 72(12):1172–1181, 2015.

[30] Who, World Health Organisation — Depression. https://www.who.int/newsroom/fact-sheets/detail/depression, 2020. Accessed: 2022-07-01.

[31] Hannah König, Hans-Helmut König, and Alexander Konnopka. The excess costs of depression: A systematic review and meta-analysis. *Epidemiology and Psychiatric Sciences*, 29:e30, 2020.

[32] Rui Wang, Weichen Wang, Alex daSilva, Jeremy F. Huckins, William M. Kelley, Todd F. Heatherton, and Andrew T. Campbell. Tracking depression dynamics in college students using mobile phone and wearable sensing. *Proceedings of ACM Interactive, Mobile, Wearable and Ubiquitous Technologies*, 2(1):26, 2018.

[33] Jakob E. Bardram, Mads Frost, Károly Szántó, Maria Faurholt-Jepsen, Maj Vinberg, and Lars Vedel Kessing. Designing mobile health technology for bipolar disorder: A field trial of the monarca system. In *Proceedings of the SIGCHI Conference on Human Factors in Computing Systems, CHI'13*, pp. 2627–2636, New York, 2013. Association for Computing Machinery.

[34] Hans-Ulrich Wittchen, Frank Jacobi, Jurgen Rehm, Anders Gustavsson, Mikael Svensson, Bengt G. Jónsson, Jes Olesen, Christer R. Allgulander, Jordi Alonso, Carlo Faravelli, Laura Fratiglioni, Poul Jørgen Jennum, Roselind Lieb, Andreas Maercker, Jim van Os, Martin A. Preisig, Luis Salvador-Carulla, Roland Simon, and Hans-Christoph Steinhausen. The size and burden of mental disorders and other disorders of the brain in europe 2010. *European Neuropsychopharmacology: The Journal of the European College of Neuropsychopharmacology*, 21:655–79, 2011.

[35] Philip Schmidt, Attila Reiss, Robert Duerichen, and Kristof Van Laerhoven. Wearable affect and stress recognition: A review. arXiv:1811.08854 , 2018.

[36] Sozo Inoue, Paula Lago, Tahera Hossain, Tittaya Mairittha, and Nattaya Mairittha. Integrating activity recognition and nursing care records: The system, deployment, and a verification study. *Proceedings of the ACM on Interactive, Mobile, Wearable and Ubiquitous Technologies (IMWUT)*, 3(3):1–24, 2019.

[37] Nicholas D. Lane, Emiliano Miluzzo, Hong Lu, Daniel Peebles, Tanzeem Choudhury, and Andrew T. Campbell. A survey of mobile phone sensing. *IEEE Communications Magazine*, 48(9):140–150, 2010.

[38] Anda Gershon, Wesley Thompson, Polina Eidelman, Eleanor McGlinchey, Katherine Kaplan, and Allison Harvey. Restless pillow, ruffled mind: Sleep and affect coupling in interepisode bipolar disorder. *Journal of Abnormal Psychology*, 121:863–873, 2012.

[39] Ihori Kobayashi, Jessica M. Boarts, and Douglas L. Delahanty. Polysomnographically measured sleep abnormalities in PTS: A meta-analytic review. *Psychophysiology*, 44(4):660–669, 2007.

[40] Anthonette Cantara and Angie Ceniza. Stress sensor prototype: Determining the stress level in using a computer through validated self-made heart rate (HR) and galvanic skin response (GSR) sensors and fuzzy logic algorithm. *International Journal of Engineering Research & Technology*, 5:28–37, 2016.

[41] Jongyoon Choi, Beena Ahmed, and Ricardo Gutierrez-Osuna. Development and evaluation of an ambulatory stress monitor based on wearable sensors. *IEEE Transactions on Information Technology in Biomedicine: A Publication of the IEEE Engineering in Medicine and Biology Society*, 16:279–86, 2011.

[42] Alberto Sierra, Carmen Sánchez Ávila, Javier Casanova, and Gonzalo Bailador. A stress-detection system based on physiological signals and fuzzy logic. *IEEE Transactions on Industrial Electronics*, 58:4857–4865, 2011.

[43] Martin Gjoreski, Mitja Luštrek, Matjaž Gams, and Hristijan Gjoreski. Monitoring stress with a wrist device using context. *Journal of Biomedical Informatics*, 73:159–170, 2017.

[44] Monika Chauhan, Shivani V. Vora, and Dipak Dabhi. Effective stress detection using physiological parameters. In *2017 International Conference on Innovations in Information, Embedded and Communication Systems (ICIIECS)*, Coimbatore, India, pp. 1–6, 2017.

[45] Adnan Ghaderi, Javad Frounchi, and Alireza Farnam. Machine learning-based signal processing using physiological signals for stress detection. In *2015 22nd Iranian Conference on Biomedical Engineering (ICBME)*, Tehran, Iran, pp. 93–98, 2015.

[46] María Viqueira, Begoña Zapirain, and Amaia Mendez. A stress sensor based on galvanic skin response (GSR) controlled by zigbee. *Sensors (Basel, Switzerland)*, 12:6075–101, 2012.

[47] Fred Shaffer and Jack Ginsberg. An overview of heart rate variability metrics and norms. *Frontiers Public Health*, 5:1–17, 2017.

[48] Szymon Siecinski, Pawel Kostka, and Ewaryst Tkacz. Heart rate variability analysis on electrocardiograms, seismocardiograms and gyrocardiograms on healthy volunteers. *Sensors*, 20:4522, 2020.

[49] Eun-Hye Jang, Ah-Young Kim, Sang-Hyeob Kim, Han-Young Yu, and Jin-Hun Sohn. Internal consistency of physiological responses during exposure to emotional stimuli using biosensors. In *Proceedings of the 6th International Joint Conference on Pervasive and Embedded Computing and Communication Systems, PECCS 2016*, pp. 110–115, Setubal, PRT, 2016. SCITEPRESS - Science and Technology Publications, Lda.

[50] Jeff K. Vallance, Elisabeth A. H. Winkler, Paul A. Gardiner, Genevieve N. Healy, Brigid M. Lynch, and Neville Owen. Associations of objectively-assessed physical activity and sedentary time with depression: Nhanes (2005–2006). *Preventive Medicine*, 53(4):284–288, 2011. Special Section: Epidemiology, Risk, and Causation.

[51] Mohammed Taj-Eldin, Christian Ryan, Brendan O'Flynn, and Paul Galvin. A review of wearable solutions for physiological and emotional monitoring for use by people with autism spectrum disorder and their caregivers. *Sensors*, 18:4271, 2018.

[52] Kennedy Opoku Asare, Isaac Moshe, Yannik Terhorst, Julio Vega, Simo Hosio, Harald Baumeister, Laura Pulkki-Råback, and Denzil Ferreira. Mood ratings and digital biomarkers from smartphone and wearable data differentiates and predicts depression status: A longitudinal data analysis. *Pervasive and Mobile Computing*, 83:101621, 2022.

[53] Prerna Chikersal, Afsaneh Doryab, Michael Tumminia, Daniella K. Villalba, Janine M. Dutcher, Xinwen Liu, Sheldon Cohen, Kasey G. Creswell, Jennifer Mankoff, John David Creswell, Mayank Goel, and Anind K. Dey. Detecting depression and predicting its onset using longitudinal symptoms captured by passive sensing: A machine learning approach with robust feature selection. *ACM Transactions on Computer-Human Interaction*, 28(1):3, 2021.

[54] Sohrab Saeb, Mi Zhang, Mary Kwasny, Christopher J. Karr, Konrad Kording, and David C. Mohr. The relationship between clinical, momentary, and sensor-based assessment of depression. In *2015 9th International Conference on Pervasive Computing Technologies for Healthcare (PervasiveHealth)*, pp. 229–232, 2015.

[55] Luca Canzian and Mirco Musolesi. Trajectories of depression: Unobtrusive monitoring of depressive states by means of smartphone mobility traces analysis. In *Proceedings of the 2015 ACM International Joint Conference on Pervasive and Ubiquitous Computing, UbiComp'15*, pp. 1293–1304, New York, 2015. Association for Computing Machinery.

[56] Sandrine Muller, Heinrich Peters, Sandra Matz, Weichen Wang, and Gabriella Harari. Investigating the relationships between mobility behaviours and indicators of subjective well-being using smartphone-based experience sampling and GPS tracking. *European Journal of Personality*, 34:714–732, 2020.

[57] Dror Ben-Zeev, Rui Wang, Saeed Abdullah, Rachel Brian, Emily Scherer, Lisa Mistler, Marta Hauser, John Kane, Andrew Campbell, and Tanzeem Choudhury. Mobile behavioral sensing for outpatients and inpatients with schizophrenia. *Psychiatric Services*, 67:58–561, 2015.

[58] Maria Faurholt-Jepsen, Maj Vinberg, Mads Frost, Ellen Christensen, Jakob Bardram, and Lars Kessing. Daily electronic monitoring of subjective and objective measures of illness activity in bipolar disorder using smartphones- the monarca II trial protocol: A randomized controlled single-blind parallel-group trial. *BMC Psychiatry*, 14:309, 2014.

[59] Sohrab Saeb, Christopher Zhang, Miand Karr, Stephen M. Schueller, Marya E. Corden, Konrad P. Kording, and David C. Mohr. Mobile phone sensor correlates of depressive symptom severity in daily-life behavior: An exploratory study. *Journal of Medical Internet Research*, 17(7):e175, 2015.

[60] Rui Wang, Min S. H. Aung, Saeed Abdullah, Rachel Brian, Andrew T. Campbell, Tanzeem Choudhury, Marta Hauser, John Kane, Michael Merrill, Emily A. Scherer, Vincent W. S. Tseng, and Dror Ben-Zeev. Crosscheck: Toward passive sensing and detection of mental health changes in people with schizophrenia. In *Proceedings of the 2016 ACM International Joint Conference on Pervasive and Ubiquitous Computing, UbiComp'16*, pp. 886–897, New York, 2016. Association for Computing Machinery.

[61] Md Golam Rabiul Alam, Eung Jun Cho, Eui-nam Huh, and Choong Seon Hong. Cloud based mental state monitoring system for suicide risk reconnaissance using wearable bio-sensors. *ICUIMC'14: Proceedings of the 8th International Conference on Ubiquitous Information Management and Communication*, Siem Reap, Cambodia, 2014.

[62] Tamara Hayes, Francena Abendroth, Andre Adami, Misha Pavel, Tracy Zitzelberger, and Jeffrey Kaye. Unobtrusive assessment of activity patterns associated with mild cognitive impairment. *Alzheimer's & Dementia : The Journal of the Alzheimer's Association*, 4:395–405, 2008.

[63] Juyoung Hong, Jiwon Kim, Sunmi Kim, Jaewon Oh, Deokjong Lee, San Lee, Jinsun Uh, Juhong Yoon, and Yukyung Choi. Depressive symptoms feature-based machine learning approach to predicting depression using smartphone. *Healthcare*, 10:1189, 2022.

[64] Prafulla Dawadi, Diane Cook, Maureen Schmitter-Edgecombe, and Carolyn Parsey. Automated assessment of cognitive health using smart home technologies. *Technology and Health Care : Official Journal of the European Society for Engineering and Medicine*, 21:323–343, 2013.

[65] Jorge Mateo Sotos, Monique Torres, J. Santos, Oscar Quevedo-Teruel, and C. Basar. A machine learning-based method to identify bipolar disorder patients. *Circuits, Systems, and Signal Processing*, 41:2244–2265, 2022.

[66] Susan Michie, Lucy Yardley, Robert West, Kevin Patrick, and Felix Greaves. Developing and evaluating digital interventions to promote behavior change in health and health care: Recommendations resulting from an international workshop. *Journal of Medical Internet Research*, 19:e232, 2017.

[67] Vikramjit Mitra, Andreas Kathol, Elizabeth Shriberg, Colleen Richey, and Martin Graciarena. The SRI AVEC-2014 evaluation system. *AVEC 2014 - Proceedings of the 4th International Workshop on Audio/Visual Emotion Challenge, Workshop of MM 2014*, Orlando Florida, USA, pp. 93–101, 2014.

[68] Yusuke Nishimura, Tahera Hossain, Akane Sano, Shota Isomura, Yutaka Arakawa, and Sozo Inoue. Toward the analysis of office workers' mental indicators based on wearable, work activity, and weather data. In Md Atiqur Rahman Ahad, Sozo Inoue, Daniel Roggen, and Kaori Fujinami, editors, *Sensor-and Video-Based Activity and Behavior Computing*, pp. 1–26. Springer Nature: Singapore, 2022.

[69] Bokai Cao, Lei Zheng, Chenwei Zhang, Philip Yu, Andrea Piscitello, John Zulueta, Olusola Ajilore, Kelly Ryan, and Alex Leow. Deepmood: Modeling mobile phone typing dynamics for mood detection. *Proceedings of the 23rd ACM SIGKDD International Conference on Knowledge Discovery and Data Mining*, pp. 747–755, Halifax, NS, Canada, August 13–17, 2017.

[70] Martin Gjoreski, Hristijan Gjoreski, Mitja Lustrek, and Matjaz Gams. Continuous stress detection using a wrist device: in laboratory and real life. *Proceedings of the 2016 ACM International Joint Conference on Pervasive and Ubiquitous Computing: Adjunct*, Heidelberg, Germany, pp. 1185–1193, 2016.

[71] Terumi Umematsu, Akane Sano, Sara Taylor, and Rosalind Picard. Improving students' daily life stress forecasting using LSTM neural networks. *IEEE International Conference on Biomedical and Health Informatics (BHI)*, pp. 1–4, Chicago, IL, 2019.

[72] Akane Sano, Andrew Phillips, Amy Yu, Andrew Mchill, Sara Taylor, Natasha Jaques, Charles Czeisler, Elizabeth Klerman, and Rosalind Picard. Recognizing academic performance, sleep quality, stress level, and mental health using personality traits, wearable sensors and mobile phones. *The International Conference on Wearable and Implantable Body Sensor Networks*, Cambridge, MA, USA, pp. 1–6, 2015.

[73] Jorge Rodríguez-Arce, Liliana Lara-Flores, Otniel Portillo-Rodríguez, and Rigoberto Martinez Mendez. Towards an anxiety and stress recognition system for academic environments based on physiological features. *Computer Methods and Programs in Biomedicine*, 190:105408, 2020.

[74] Lu Han, Qiang Zhang, Xianxiang Chen, Qingyuan Zhan, Ting Yang, and Zhan Zhao. Detecting work-related stress with a wearable device. *Computers in Industry*, 90:42–49, 2017.

[75] Nastaran Saffaryazdi, Yenushka Goonesekera, Nafiseh Saffaryazdi, Nebiyou Hailemariam, Ebasa Temesgen, Suranga Nanayakkara, Elizabeth Broadbent, and Mark Billinghurst. Emotion recognition in conversations using brain and physiological signals. *IUI'22: 27th International Conference on Intelligent User Interfaces*, pp. 229–242, 2022.

[76] Tomoki Saito, Hikaru Suzuki, and Akifumi Kishi. Predictive modeling of mental illness onset using wearable devices and medical examination data: Machine learning approach. *Frontiers in Digital Health*, 4:861808, 2022.

[77] Tania Pereira, Pedro Almeida, João Paulo Cunha, and Ana Aguiar. Heart rate variability metrics for fine-grained stress level assessment. *Computer Methods and Programs in Biomedicine*, 148:71–80, 2017.

[78] Ravinder Ahuja and Alisha Banga. Mental stress detection in university students using machine learning algorithms. *Procedia Computer Science*, 152:349–353, 2019.

[79] Xuetong Chen, Martin Sykora, Thomas Jackson, and Suzanne Elayan. What about mood swings: Identifying depression on twitter with temporal measures of emotions. *Companion of the Web Conference 2018 on the Web Conference 2018, WWW 2018*, pp. 1653–1660, , Lyon, France, 2018.

[80] Jeremy Huckins, Alex Dasilva, Weichen Wang, Elin Hedlund, Courtney Rogers, Subigya Nepal, Jialing Wu, Mikio Obuchi, Eilis Murphy, Meghan Meyer, Dylan Wagner, Paul Holtzheimer, and Andrew Campbell. Mental health and behavior during the early phases of the Covid-19 pandemic: A longitudinal mobile smartphone and ecological momentary assessment study in college students. *Journal of Medical Internet Research*, 22(6):e20185, 2020.

[81] Nilava Mukherjee, Sumitra Mukhopadhyay, and Rajarshi Gupta. Real-time mental stress detection technique using neural networks towards wearable health monitor. *Measurement Science and Technology*, 33(4):044003, 2021.

[82] Tahsin Mullick, Ana Radovic, Sam Shaaban, and Afsaneh Doryab. Predicting depression in adolescents using mobile and wearable sensors: Multimodal machine learning–based exploratory study. *JMIR Formative Research*, 6:e35807, 2022.

[83] Kennedy Opoku Asare, Isaac Moshe, Yannik Terhorst, Julio Vega, Simo Hosio, Harald Baumeister, Laura Pulkki-Råback, and Denzil Ferreira. Mood ratings and digital biomarkers from smartphone and wearable data differentiates and predicts depression status: A longitudinal data analysis. *Pervasive and Mobile Computing*, 83:101621, 2022.

[84] Ane Alberdi, Asier Aztiria, Adrian Basarab, and Diane Cook. Using smart offices to predict occupational stress. *International Journal of Industrial Ergonomics*, 67:13–26, 2018.

[85] Bishal Lamichhane, Joanne Zhou, and Akane Sano. Psychotic relapse prediction in schizophrenia patients using a mobile sensing-based supervised deep learning model. arXiv:2205.12225v1, 2022.

[86] Joanne Zhou, Bishal Lamichhane, Dror Ben-Zeev, Andrew Campbell, and Akane Sano. Psychotic relapse in schizophrenia: Routine clustering of mobile sensor data facilitates relapse prediction (preprint). *JMIR mHealth and uHealth*, 10(4):e31006, 2021.

[87] Ramakanth Kavuluru, María Ramos-Morales, Tara Holaday, Amanda Williams, Laura Haye, and Julie Cerel. Classification of helpful comments on online suicide watch forums. *ACM BCB*, Seattle, WA, vol. 2016, pp. 32–40, 2016.

[88] Maria Faurholt-Jepsen, Maj Vinberg, Mads Frost, Sune Debel, Ellen Christensen, Jakob Bardram, and Lars Kessing. Behavioral activities collected through smartphones and the association with illness activity in bipolar disorder. *International Journal of Methods in Psychiatric Research*, 25:309–323, 2016.

[89] Michael Riegler, Mathias Lux, Carsten Griwodz, Concetto Spampinato, Thomas de Lange, Sigrun L. Eskeland, Konstantin Pogorelov, Wallapak Tavanapong, Peter T. Schmidt, Cathal Gurrin, Dag Johansen, Håvard Johansen, and Pål Halvorsen. Multimedia and medicine: Teammates for better disease detection and survival. In *Proceedings of the 24th ACM International Conference on Multimedia, MM'16*, pp. 968–977, New York, 2016. Association for Computing Machinery.

[90] Enrique Garcia Ceja, Venet Osmani, and Oscar Mayora. Automatic stress detection in working environments from smartphones' accelerometer data: A first step. *IEEE Journal of Biomedical and Health Informatics*, 20:1–8, 2016.

[91] Alexandros Zenonos, Aftab Khan, Georgios Kalogridis, Stefanos Vatsikas, Tim Lewis, and Mahesh Sooriyabandara. Healthyoffice: Mood recognition at work using smartphones and wearable sensors. *2016 IEEE International Conference on Pervasive Computing and Communication Workshops (PerCom Workshops)*, pp. 1–6, Sydney, NSW, Australia, 2016.

[92] Gerald Bauer and Paul Lukowicz. Can smartphones detect stress-related changes in the behaviour of individuals? In *2012 IEEE International Conference on Pervasive Computing and Communications Workshops*, Lugano, Switzerland, pp. 423–426, 2012.

[93] John C. Gower. Some distance properties of latent root and vector methods used in multivariate analysis. *Biometrika*, 53:325–338, 1966.

[94] Alban Maxhuni, Angélica Muñoz-Meléndez, Venet Osmani, Humberto Perez, Oscar Mayora, and Eduardo F. Morales. Classification of bipolar disorder episodes based on analysis of voice and motor activity of patients. *Pervasive and Mobile Computing*, 31:50–66, 2016.

[95] Orianna Demasi and Benjamin Recht. A step towards quantifying when an algorithm can and cannot predict an individual's wellbeing. *UbiComp'17: Proceedings of the 2017 ACM International Joint Conference on Pervasive and Ubiquitous Computing and Proceedings of the 2017 ACM International Symposium on Wearable Computers*, pp. 763–771, Maui, HI, 2017.

[96] Joachim Diederich, Aqeel Ajmi, and Peter Yellowlees. Ex-ray: Data mining and mental health. *Applied Soft Computing Journal*, 7:923–928, 2007.

[97] Afsaneh Doryab, Mads Frost, Maria Faurholt-Jepsen, Lars Kessing, and Jakob Bardram. Impact factor analysis: Combining prediction with parameter ranking to reveal the impact of behavior on health outcome. *Personal and Ubiquitous Computing*, 19:355–365, 2014.

[98] Sindhu Kiranmai Ernala, Michael L. Birnbaum, Kristin A. Candan, Asra F. Rizvi, William A. Sterling, John M. Kane, and Munmun De Choudhury. Methodological gaps in predicting mental health states from social media: Triangulating diagnostic signals. In *Proceedings of the 2019 CHI Conference on Human Factors in Computing Systems, CHI'19*, pp. 1–16, New York, 2019. Association for Computing Machinery.

[99] Iram Fatima, Hamid Mukhtar, Hafiz Ahmad, and Kashif Rajpoot. Analysis of user-generated content from online social communities to characterise and predict depression degree. *Journal of Information Science*, 44:016555151774083, 2017.

[100] Chaonan Feng, Huimin Gao, Bruce Ling, Jun Ji, and Yantao Ma. Shorten bipolarity checklist for the differentiation of subtypes of bipolar disorder using machine learning. *ICBCB 2018: Proceedings of the 2018 6th International Conference on Bioinformatics and Computational Biology*, Chengdu, China, pp. 162–166, 2018.

[101] Joakim Frogner, Farzan Majeed Noori, Pål Halvorsen, Steven Hicks, Enrique Garcia Ceja, Jim Torresen, and Michael Riegler. One-dimensional convolutional neural networks on motor activity measurements in detection of depression. *Proceedings of the 4th International Workshop on Multimedia for Personal Health & Health Care*, Nice, France, pp. 9–15, 2019.

[102] Adria Mallol-Ragolta, Svati Dhamija, and Terrance Boult. A multimodal approach for predicting changes in PTSD symptom severity. *ICMI'18: Proceedings of the 20th ACM International Conference on Multimodal Interaction*, pp. 324–333, Boulder, CO, 2018.

[103] Thin Nguyen, Bridianne O'Dea, Mark Larsen, Dinh Phung, Svetha Venkatesh, and Helen Christensen. Using linguistic and topic analysis to classify sub-groups of online depression communities. *Multimedia Tools and Applications*, 76:10653–10676, 2017.

[104] Ehimwenma Nosakhare and Rosalind Picard. Probabilistic latent variable modeling for assessing behavioral influences on well-being. *KDD'19: Proceedings of the 25th ACM SIGKDD International Conference on Knowledge Discovery & Data Mining*, Anchorage, AK, USA, pp. 2718–2726, 2019.

[105] John Pestian, Pawel Matykiewicz, Jacqueline Grupp-Phelan, Sarah Lavanier, Jennifer Combs, and Robert Kowatch. Using natural language processing to classify suicide notes. *AMIA ... Annual Symposium Proceedings/AMIA Symposium*, Washington, DC, USA, pp. 1091, 2008.

[106] Anupama Ray, Siddharth Kumar, Rutvik Reddy, Prerana Mukherjee, and Ritu Garg. Multi-level attention network using text, audio and video for depression prediction. *9th International Audio/Visual Emotion Challengeand Workshop (AVEC'19)*, pp. 81–88, Nice, France, October 21, 2019.

[107] Koustuv Saha and Munmun Choudhury. Modeling stress with social media around incidents of gun violence on college campuses. *Proceedings of the ACM on Human-Computer Interaction*, 1:92, 2017.

[108] Dimitris Spathis, Sandra Servia-Rodríguez, Katayoun Farrahi, Cecilia Mascolo, and Jason Rentfrow. Passive mobile sensing and psychological traits for large scale mood prediction. *Pervasive Health*, 2019:272–28105, 2019.

[109] Egon L. van den Broek, Frans Sluis, and Ton Dijkstra. Cross-validation of bimodal health-related stress assessment. *Personal and Ubiquitous Computing*, 17:1–13, 2012.

[110] Hou Yujiao, Jingjing Xu, Yixin Huang, and Xiaofeng Ma. A big data application to predict depression in the university based on the reading habits. *2016 3rd International Conference on Systems and Informatics (ICSAI)*, pp. 1085–1089, Shanghai, China, 2016.

[111] Stefan Borgwardt, Nikolaos Koutsouleris, Jacqueline Aston, Erich Studerus, Renata Smieskova, Anita Riecher-Rössler, and Eva Meisenzahl. Distinguishing prodromal from first-episode psychosis using neuroanatomical single-subject pattern recognition. *Schizophrenia Bulletin*, 39:1105–1114, 2012.

[112] Rui Wang, Weichen Wang, Mikio Obuchi, Emily Scherer, Rachel Brian, Dror Ben-Zeev, Tanzeem Choudhury, John Kane, Martar Hauser, Megan Walsh, and Andrew Campbell. On predicting relapse in schizophrenia using mobile sensing in a randomized control trial. *2020 IEEE International Conference on Pervasive Computing and Communications (PerCom)*, Austin, TX, USA, pp. 1–8, 2020.

[113] Young Jo, Sung Joo, Seung-Hyun Shon, Harin Kim, Yangsik Kim, and Jungsun Lee. Diagnosing schizophrenia with network analysis and a machine learning method. *International Journal of Methods in Psychiatric Research*, 29:e1818, 2020.

[114] Lei Zhang. EEG signals classification using machine learning for the identification and diagnosis of schizophrenia. *2019 41st Annual International Conference of the IEEE Engineering in Medicine and Biology Society (EMBC)*, vol. 2019, pp. 4521–4524, Berlin, Germany, 2019.

[115] Andrew Reece, Andrew Reagan, Katharina Lix, Peter Dodds, Christopher Danforth, and Ellen Langer. Forecasting the onset and course of mental illness with twitter data. *Scientific Reports*, 7:13006, 2017.

[116] Scott Braithwaite, Christophe Giraud-Carrier, Josh West, Michael Barnes, and Carl Hanson. Validating machine learning algorithms for twitter data against established measures of suicidality. *JMIR Mental Health*, 3:e21, 2016.

[117] Arkaprabha Sau and Ishita Bhakta. Screening of anxiety and depression among seafarers using machine learning technology. *Informatics in Medicine Unlocked*, 16:100228, 2019.

[118] Shebbeer Peerbasha and M. Mohamed Surputheen. A predictive model to identify possible affected bipolar disorder students using naïve baye's, random forest and SVM machine learning techniques of data mining and building a sequential deep learning model using keras. *International Journal of Computer Science and Network Security*, 21(5):267–274, 2021.

[119] Armando Barreto, Jing Zhai, and Malek Adjouadi. Non-intrusive physiological monitoring for automated stress detection in human-computer interaction. *HCI'07: Proceedings of the 2007 IEEE International Conference on Human-Computer Interaction*, Berlin Heidelberg, German, pp. 29–38, 10 2007.

[120] Hari Kurniawan, Alexandr Maslov, and Mykola Pechenizkiy. Stress detection from speech and galvanic skin response signals. *Proceedings of the 26th IEEE International Symposium on Computer-Based Medical Systems*, Porto, Portugal, pp. 209–214, 2013.

[121] Lucio Ciabattoni, Francesco Ferracuti, Sauro Longhi, Lucia Pepa, Luca Romeo, and Federica Verdini. Real-time mental stress detection based on smartwatch. *2017 IEEE International Conference on Consumer Electronics (ICCE)*, Las Vegas, NV, USA, pp. 110–111, 2017.

[122] Marios Adamou, Grigoris Antoniou, Elissavet Greasidou, Vincenzo Lagani, Paulos Charonyktakis, and Ioannis Tsamardinos. Mining free-text medical notes for suicide risk assessment. *SETN '18: Proceedings of the 10th Hellenic Conference on Artificial Intelligence*, Patras, Greece, pp. 1–8, 2018.

[123] Jesús Aguilar-Ruiz, Raquel Costa, and Federico Divina. Knowledge discovery from doctor-patient relationship. *2004, Proceedings of the 2004 ACM Symposium on Applied Computing: SAC'04*, New York, NY, United States, vol. 1, pp. 280–284, 2004.

[124] Md Golam Rabiul Alam, Eung Jun Cho, Eui-nam Huh, and Choong Seon Hong. Cloud based mental state monitoring system for suicide risk reconnaissance using wearable bio-sensors. *Event8th International Conference on Ubiquitous Information Management and Communication, ICUIMC 2014*, Siem Reap, Cambodia, 2014.

[125] Asif Salekin, Jeremy Eberle, Jeffrey Glenn, Bethany Teachman, and John Stankovic. A weakly supervised learning framework for detecting social anxiety and depression. *Proceedings of the ACM on Interactive, Mobile, Wearable and Ubiquitous Technologies (IMWUT)*, 2:81, 2018.

[126] M. Srividya, Subramaniam Mohanavalli, and Natarajan Bhalaji. Behavioral modeling for mental health using machine learning algorithms. *Journal of Medical Systems*, 42:1–12, 2018.

[127] Mashfiqui Rabbi, Shahid Ali, Tanzeem Choudhury, and Ethan Berke. Passive and in-situ assessment of mental and physical well-being using mobile sensors. *Proceedings of the ACM International Joint Conference on Pervasive and Ubiquitous Computing*, Beijing, China, 2011:385–394, 2011.

[128] Manas Gaur, Ugur Kursuncu, Amanuel Alambo, Amit Sheth, Raminta Daniulaityte, Krishnaprasad Thirunarayan, and Jyotishman Pathak. "Let me tell you about your mental health!": Contextualized classification of reddit posts to DSM-5 for web-based intervention. *CIKM'18: Proceedings of the 27th ACM International Conference on Information and Knowledge Management*, Turin, Italy, pp. 753–762, 2018.

[129] Alicia Nobles, Jeffrey Glenn, Kamran Kowsari, Bethany Teachman, and Laura Barnes. Identification of imminent suicide risk among young adults using text messages. *Proceedings of the 2018 CHI Conference on Human Factors in Computing Systems*, Montreal, QC, Canada, vol. 2018, 2018.

[130] Thomas Quisel, Wei-Nchih Lee, and Luca Foschini. Observation time vs. performance in digital phenotyping. *DigitalBiomarkers'17: Proceedings of the 1st Workshop on Digital Biomarkers*, pp. 33–36, 2017.

[131] Truyen Tran, Dinh Phung, Wei Luo, Richard Harvey, Michael Berk, and Svetha Venkatesh. An integrated framework for suicide risk prediction. *Proceedinngs of the ACM International Conference on Knowledge Discovery and Data Mining (SIGKDD)*, San Francisco, California, 2013.

[132] Qianli Xu, Tin Lay Nwe, and Cuntai Guan. Cluster-based analysis for personalized stress evaluation using physiological signals. *IEEE Journal of Biomedical and Health Informatics*, 19:275–281, 2015.

[133] Hong Lu, Denise Frauendorfer, Mashfiqui Rabbi, Marianne Schmid Mast, Gokul T. Chittaranjan, Andrew T. Campbell, Daniel Gatica-Perez, and Tanzeem Choudhury. Stresssense: Detecting stress in unconstrained acoustic environments using smartphones. In *Proceedings of the 2012 ACM Conference on Ubiquitous Computing, UbiComp'12*, pp. 351–360, New York, 2012. Association for Computing Machinery.

[134] Theodor Panagiotakopoulos, Dimitrios Lyras, Miltos Livaditis, Kyriakos Sgarbas, George Anastassopoulos, and Dimitrios Lymberopoulos. A contextual data mining approach toward assisting the treatment of anxiety disorders. *IEEE Transactions on Information Technology in Biomedicine: A Publication of the IEEE Engineering in Medicine and Biology Society*, 14:567–81, 2010.

[135] Camellia Zakaria, Rajesh Balan, and Youngki Lee. Stressmon: Scalable detection of perceived stress and depression using passive sensing of changes in work routines and group interactions. *Proceedings of the ACM on Human-Computer Interaction*, 3:1–29, 2019.

[136] Mehrab Bin Morshed, Koustuv Saha, Richard Li, Sidney D'Mello, Munmun Choudhury, Gregory Abowd, and Thomas Ploetz. Prediction of mood instability with passive sensing. *Proceedings of the ACM on Interactive, Mobile, Wearable and Ubiquitous Technologies*, 3:1–21, 2019.

[137] Konstantinos Tsiakas, Lynette Watts, Cyril Lutterodt, Theodoros Giannakopoulos, Alexandros Papangelis, Robert Gatchel, Vangelis Karkaletsis, and Fillia Makedon. A multimodal adaptive dialogue manager for depressive and anxiety disorder screening: A wizard-of-oZ experiment. *PETRA*, 82:1–82, 2015.

[138] Hoda Heidari, Claudio Ferrari, Krishna P. Gummadi, and Andreas Krause. Fairness behind a veil of ignorance: A welfare analysis for automated decision making. In *Proceedings of the 32nd International Conference on Neural Information Processing Systems, NIPS'18*, pp. 1273–1283, Red Hook, 2018. Curran Associates Inc.

[139] Ayanna Howard, Cha Zhang, and Eric Horvitz. Addressing bias in machine learning algorithms: A pilot study on emotion recognition for intelligent systems. In *2017 IEEE Workshop on Advanced Robotics and Its Social Impacts (ARSO)*, Austin, Texas, pp. 1–7, 2017.

[140] Benoît Frénay and Michel Verleysen. Classification in the presence of label noise: A survey. *IEEE Transactions on Neural Networks and Learning Systems*, 25:845–869, 2014.

[141] Amir Muaremi, Bert Arnrich, and Gerhard Tröster. Towards measuring stress with smartphones and wearable devices during workday and sleep. *BioNanoScience*, 3:172–183, 2013.

[142] Yingnong Dang, Qingwei Lin, and Peng Huang. Aiops: Real-world challenges and research innovations. In *2019 IEEE/ACM 41st International Conference on Software Engineering: Companion Proceedings (ICSE-Companion)*, Montreal, QC, Canada, pp. 4–5, 2019.

III

Nurse Care Records

Improving Complex Nurse Care Activity Recognition Using Barometric Pressure Sensors

Muhammad Fikry
Kyushu Institute of Technology

Christina Garcia, Vu Nguyen Phuong Quynh, and Sozo Inoue
Kyushu Institute of Technology

Shintaro Oyama
Nagoya University

Keiko Yamashita
Nagoya University

Yuji Sakamoto
Carecom Co., Ltd

Yoshinori Ideno
Nagoya University
Carecom Co., Ltd

15.1   INTRODUCTION

Recent developments in the smartphone industry, electronic devices and fitness trackers have contributed to increasing research works centered on Human Activity Recognition. Different sensors, wearable devices and mobile applications are

DOI: 10.1201/9781003371540-18

generally used to obtain data regarding activities of daily life (ADL) including sedentary behavior, postural transitions, and dynamic behavior [23] to routine activities done by office workers or nurses [15]. The application of machine learning and deep learning algorithms allowed researchers to grasp action, interaction, and motion patterns from an individual or group of people. The focus of activity recognition varies from simple activities such as walking, standing, and sitting to complex activities performed by medical staff to assist patients in hospitals.

With the increasing aging population, activities by the elderly, caregivers, and nurses are being further studied to improve care delivery. HAR serves as an assistive tool to improve elderly life support, monitoring both cognitive and physical functions [6]. Nurse activities are studied with the wearable approach where users carry the sensors with them as they perform any activity [14,15]. However, challenges on data collection due to environmental factors and noise, especially in the hospital setting, still limit research studies on HAR. To overcome these challenges, various types of sensors are integrated in the data collection from inertial, physiological, to environmental sensors. Accelerometer is the most prevalent sensor used for activity recognition and is oftentimes deployed together with other sensors such as body temperature sensors, compasses, electromyography, electrocardiograph, gyroscopes, magnetometers, barometric pressure sensors, and oximetry sensors [6].

A survey on the challenges and potential of barometric sensors for human activity tracking pointed out altitude, climate, and air velocity as common factors considered in the integration [20] of the device in data gathering. Even so, HAR researchers found solutions to these limitations and used various barometric pressure sensors to distinguish sitting and standing activities [23], predict driving behavior [13], and locating floor level of users [12] considering elevation changes. Barometric sensors can detect any pressure or temperature changes. Additional information from barometric sensor overcomes inter-patient variability of kinematic patterns, which often limits the performance of initial sensors in detecting transitions between different activities and postures [22].

Barometric pressure sensor can be useful for complex activity recognition. However, using barometric pressure sensors for nursing activities in hospitals is a challenge because, to identify nurse activities, we need to get the pressure value from the care movement without being influenced by other factors. While the barometric sensor will capture every change in movement, temperature and wind in the environment might affect the pressure reading.

In this study, we integrated sensors in a hospital to collect data for activity recognition and obtain nursing records without interfering with nursing activities. Our research aims to extract features from the barometric pressure sensor and Quppa sensors for activity classifiers. We examine the relationship between timestamp extensions and pressure features. We introduce features specific to the barometric pressure sensor to explore how the pressure feature works well for nursing activities in the real world and compare it with data collected from the lab. We show the characteristics of the pressure feature, such as identifying activity classes, which can be improved when we use the barometric pressure sensor. With timestamp extension, we investigate which pressure feature works better when we extend the label of complex nurse care activity recognition.

15.2 RELATED WORK

This section is to highlight work done by others that tie in with our work. We describe reviews of work related to the problem we are attempting to solve.

15.2.1 Nurse Care Activities

The first super-aging society in the world is Japan. According to the International Forum on the Super Aging Challenge 2021, Japan has one elderly in every three people. The staggering increase of elderly paved the way for more research works targeting to improve the delivery of nursing care. Nursing care activities in hospitals are provided directly to patients, therefore to ensure patient safety and happiness, nursing practices must constantly be good. Every nursing activity must record documentation clearly and accurately so that the evaluation of nursing care can be optimal [1]. Activity recognition of nurse activities varies from single tasks done per time duration to multiple activities delivered synchronously. Among the challenges of HAR on nursing care is activity labeling which sometimes does not match the expected duration. There is skew in the timestamps of activity labels, and there are instances where the duration is shorter than the actual activities. Modification of labels like extending durations can improve nursing activity recognition [15]. However, it is also necessary to investigate how differences in the sensor data can affect the extended duration and performance of the system.

15.2.2 Data Collection and Sensors

Sensors, wearables, and smartphones are commonly used to collect data for activity recognition. Wearable devices can capture activity recognition attributes such as motion, location, temperature, and ECG, among others. Smartphones are preferable over other wearables considering the integrated sensors and software capability allowing the device to collect various types of data, possibly, all day long [8]. In nursing care activity recognition, smartphones are often used for labeling and recording other patient data in efforts to overcome manual writing and pave the way to readily accessible collated information.

Other studies reveal that data from pressure sensor depending on its placement can extract more relevant information regarding the activities performed. Smart-surface pressure sensor placed on-body could detail pressure generated by muscle movement, body posture or direct user input [5]. Additional information from pressure sensor is used for activity recognition of sitting, standing, lying, running, walking, climbing stairs [9,22,23,29] and gait [11].

Elevation is one factor considered in pressure sensors as this generally affects sensor data. It has been observed that both temperature and air or atmospheric pressure gets lower as you climb. Considering latency problem and air conditioning, built-in pressure sensor in mobile phones can still be used to determine heights indoors for positioning and navigation if specific requirements are met [19].

15.2.3 Pre-Processing and Segmentation

The performance of HAR studies is dependent on the quality of data processed. Data cleaning, normalization, and transformation are examples of data preparation [18]. Among the critical steps of data handling are pre-processing and segmentation, which enables feature extraction needed by machine learning algorithms. To obtain higher HAR performance, adequate data pre-processing is essential [30]; and as input to the model, the segmented data has to be transformed into the appropriate forms. More precisely, since the raw inertial data from wearables changes significantly over time, segmentation processes are needed when executing HAR tasks to utilize the data [32]. Characteristics of data segment or window are influenced by window size, type, and overlapping [8]. Among the techniques implemented in HAR for segmentation are grid search strategy to optimize window size [7], and sliding window [9,16,29] with window size commonly not exceeding 3 s [8]. In this study, we consider clock synchronization and incorrect timestamp in the preprocessing.

15.2.4 Feature Selection

Feature selection is a technique for decreasing the input variable to a model through the use of just pertinent data and the elimination of irrelevant data. With feature selection, pertinent characteristics for a machine learning model are selected according to the kind of issue that is being attempted to be solved. The properties of the data that are used to train machine learning models have a significant impact on the results that may be obtained. The quality and type of features extracted from various sensor data can affect the performance of activity recognition models. Features extracted from sensor data used for HAR are usually statistical features with mean as the most common [4,9,16,23,25,27,28,33]. Other studies utilizing pressure sensor extract additional features such as maximum and minimum of the approximate 1st derivative [25], time gap [23], difference between maximum and minimum values [24], mean crossing rate [27], time domain, frequency domain [11], H-FIS (Hierarchical FIS) [22], and CARIN features [2]. Dealing with overlapping activities and issue on time stamp extension of nursing activities should also be taken into account as these affect the performance of time-series activity recognition [15].

15.2.5 Performance Evaluation

The effectiveness of trained machine learning models is determined using performance evaluation metrics. This helps in determining how a more effective model may perform on the dataset. There are various ways to evaluate a machine learning model's performance, such as confusion matrix, accuracy, precision, recall, specificity, F1 score,precision-recall curve. We must be able to choose a way to evaluate the performance of the model, especially the data imbalance. The issue of the imbalanced dataset has become a concern in recent years [3,10,17,31]. Certain class imbalances in the dataset may make certain prediction approaches less effective for learning[17]. Some studies utilize F1 Score[3,15,17,21,31], Accuracy[3,15,21], or even both [3,15,21] for this issue, although there are obviously many more. While retaining strong overall performance in terms of macro F score, Katrin Tomanek and Udo Hahn [26] can increase classifier performance and lessen class imbalance.

Real-world data of nurse care activities with self-labeling as expected entails problems such as incorrect timestamp, incomplete record or label, missing start or stop time, and data imbalance. In the study of Inoue et al. [15], both F1 score and accuracy were measured for evaluation of user-dependent models considering skew of timestamps, overlapping labels, and data imbalance. In this study, we measured both the accuracy and F1 score of the system. To calculate the overall F1 score for a dataset with more than one class, we use the Macro F1 score because here we assume all classes are equally important and the macro F1 assigns each class the same importance, while the micro F1 gives equal importance to each observation.

15.3 METHOD

In this section, we describe the system architecture, data collection, model data, and integrating nursing care records with activity recognition.

15.3.1 Data Collection

The data was gathered from 4544 activity labels from 15 nurses at Nagoya University Hospital using three devices: a barometric pressure sensor, a Quuppa sensor, and a smartphone. Participants are required to bring a barometric pressure sensor placed in a chest pocket and a personal mobile disinfectant that is equipped with a Quuppa sensor, including IoT, hanging around their waist as shown in Figure 15.1. When nurses went into an SICU room, they used gel to clean their hands and then performed the activity.

Devices are well selected and packaged for the reason that nurses are comfortable when they work, especially in complex activities. We adapt to the nurse's situation. The barometric pressure sensor is packaged in a small size that can fit in a chest pocket. The Quuppa sensor is placed on the disinfectant lid. In this way, nurses do not feel disturbed by the sensor devices used so that they can maintain the quality of their performance.

Because we expected self-labeling, participants were asked to choose the activity from the list in our app (Fonlog) by click or voice using a smartphone before and after doing the activity. The Fonlog user interface navigated by users is shown in Figure 15.2. The objective is to classify activities into one of the 33 activities performed as listed in Table 15.1. The data gathering overview is shown in Figure 15.3.

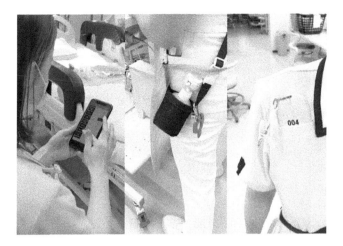

Figure 15.1 Nurse using Fonlog with disinfectant on the waist and the barometric pressure sensor on pocket.

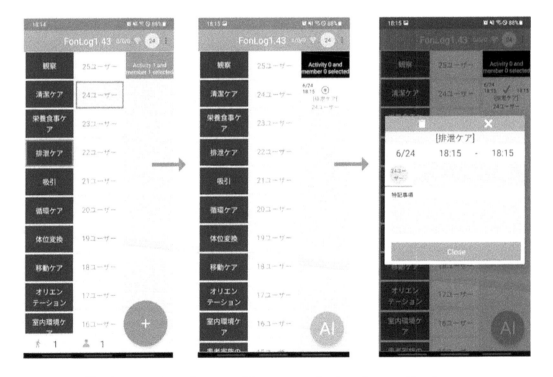

Figure 15.2 Fonlog user interface used by nurses during data gathering.

15.3.2 System Architecture

Quuppa locator was installed on the ceiling of the hospital. It was used to record the address of a barometric pressure and Quuppa sensors for each nurse. When the air pressure changes, the locator in the SICU (Surgical Intensive Care Unit) room can

TABLE 15.1 Activity Classes

Activity Group	Activity Name
Patient care	Observation, clean care (help patients such as with bathing or wiping the body), nutritional dietary care (help patients such as making healthy recipes), excretion assistance (provide excretion assistance according to the condition of the person being treated), suction (perform care such as clearing the airway), circulatory care (perform care such as blood circulation), posture change (changing the position of the patient), movement support (support for patient movement), family support (help for the patient's family), rehabilitation/recreation, care for other patients
Medical assistance	Injection support, dosage (prescribe and administer medicine to patients), treatment support, X-ray support, blood gas measurement, drug management, other medical assistance
Environmental arrangement	Indoor environmental, cleaning the room, other environment maintenance, compatible with medical devices
Documentation/ communication	PC record, handwriting record, conference (a meeting held at a nursing or medical facility), patient information gathering, report to doctor, transfer matter (ongoing work transfer), information sharing, operational coordination, other records, report or contact, committee activities, nursing staff guidance

record location information and send the data to the Quuppa server. The Quuppa server is located in the hospital, so internet connection disruptions have no effect on data gathering. With a strong connection, the data is sent from the local server to the cloud server. In the same way as for data labels, we temporarily store data on the smartphone's internal storage before transferring it to a cloud server when connected to the internet. This system also makes sure that there is not too much data in the internal storage because data that has been successfully sent to the cloud will be deleted automatically. Data processing is done on this cloud server. Although we use a cloud system, the system we propose does not depend entirely on the internet network, which means that our system can still work well even if there are problems with the connection. This is very important in the implementation of IoT because using IoT, an object is embedded with technologies such as sensors and software with the aim of communicating, controlling, connecting, and exchanging data with other devices while still connected to the internet.

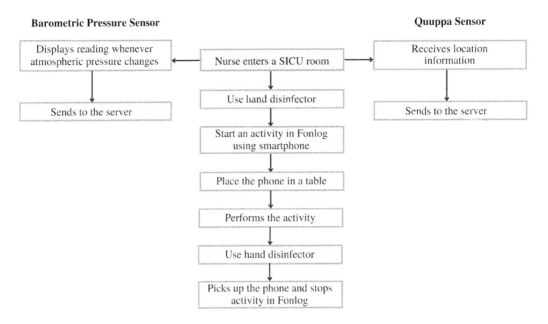

Figure 15.3 Overview of data gathering set-up.

15.3.3 Preprocessing

Preprocessing was performed to address clock synchronization and incorrect timestamps. In our experiment, we used three devices, so synchronization was necessary. Using a barometric pressure sensor, the dimensions of the data set we use are timestamp, device name, and pressure value in Pascal units. The dimensions of the data obtained from the Quuppa sensor are timestamp, device name, position (X and Y), and area. The device name should match the device used by each nurse. The pressure value in Pascal units and positioning on the X and Y axes of the Quuppa sensor are the values assigned to the classification model. Instead of the clocks synchronizing directly from three devices, we chose to split the Quuppa and barometric pressure sensors first, but still based on self-labeling by the user using the smartphone. This approach can avoid the error occurring in one device affecting all the data collected if three devices were synchronized. Furthermore, this allows us to compare the evaluation results with and without the barometric pressure sensor. In our combination, we separate the Quuppa feature synchronization with the labeling time of the smartphone and the pressure feature from the labeling time. We then set the basic variables for activity, start time, end time, and user identity. After that, the results of synchronization between Quuppa features and pressure features are merged based on basic variables. In this way, a missing value at a certain moment in one sensor will not affect the sensor value at the same moment in the other device. Another preprocessing technique done is extending the activity label time, as one of the risks of self-labeling that needs to be considered is incorrect time[15].

Therefore, we alter each activity's label to be wider than the recorded segment with some of the alternative times described in Section 15.3.6. This is applied before the start time or after the end time, or both.

15.3.4 Feature Extraction

From our experiment, we got the pressure value in units of Pascal and the position on the X and Y axes from the Quuppa sensor. To maximize data usage, a sliding window for data segmentation is applied. In this paper, we perform sliding windows with a one-minute duration without overlapping. The features extracted are mean, standard deviation (STD), maximum, minimum, maximum-minimum, summation, variance, skewness, and kurtosis. We also include in the feature vector the spending time of each user when performing activities at a certain hour since change in time due to temperature fluctuation can affect the value of the barometric pressure sensor. For each sample, we use 30 features with the barometric pressure sensor and 21 features without the barometric pressure sensor.

15.3.5 Evaluation Method

Random forest is used for classification. To maintain the imbalance among activity classes in the dataset, we limit the data samples to no more than 3000 (three thousand) for each activity, as well as other activity classes, and then combine them. The model is then evaluated using cross-validation, with activity data on one day used as test data, and the other day used for training. Validation of both training and testing followed. This flow is repeated for all the available days. Both accuracy and F1 score were measured to assess the model. The evaluation results in terms of accuracy and F1 scores are shown in Table 15.2.

The same method is used to test the performance with and without the barometric pressure sensor. If the values for both metrics are greater, they indicate that the model can classify observations into classes. Accuracy is the most intuitive performance measure, which only displays the observed ratio that is as expected. The F1 score, which accounts for both false positives and false negatives, is the weighted average of precision and recall.

15.3.6 Timestamp Extension

In real-life data collection, obtaining accurate labels is a challenging task. In our experiment, we asked nurses to do self-label. Self-labeling refers to the process of gaining confidence in oneself. Therefore, it is unavoidable to rely on nurses to provide labels. With this method, timestamp accuracy becomes a challenge. Nurses need to input an activity label before or after they perform the activity. This can happen too soon or too late so that the inserted timestamp might be erroneous compared to that of the actual activity. Therefore, to overcome this problem, we need to use several methods to extend the timestamp.

TABLE 15.2 Accuracy and F1 Score with and without Barometric Pressure Sensors

Activity	with		without	
	Accuracy	F1 Score	Accuracy	F1 Score
Observation	0.98	0.98	0.95	0.94
Clean care	0.94	0.92	0.91	0.88
Nutritional dietary care	0.88	0.72	0.82	0.48
Excretion assistance	0.93	0.84	0.84	0.58
Suction	0.97	0.92	0.9	0.74
Circulatory care	0.86	0.9	0.96	0.96
Posture change	0.97	0.92	0.82	0.78
Movement support	0.66	0.4	0.75	0.46
Indoor environmental care	0.83	0.7	0.81	0.52
Family support	0.91	0.78	0.87	0.3
Rehabilitation/recreation	0.77	0.52	0.75	0.14
Dosage	0.9	0.76	0.87	0.6
Care for other patients	0.92	0.86	0.88	0.72
Injection support	0.82	0.82	0.83	0.8
Treatment support	0.9	0.86	0.85	0.72
X-ray support	0.83	0.54	0.9	0.64
Blood gas measurement	0.93	0.88	0.89	0.76
Drug management	0.75	0.74	0.91	0.92
Other medical assistance	0.83	0.72	0.74	0.4
Cleaning the room	0.89	0.72	0.82	0.46
Other environment maintenance	0.9	0.86	0.79	0.62
Compatible with medical devices	0.7	0.24	0.78	0.2
PC record	0.95	0.96	0.86	0.86
Handwriting record	0.9	0.58	0.84	0.6
Conference	0.93	0.88	0.92	0.76
Patient information gathering	0.96	0.94	0.91	0.8
Report to doctor	0.88	0.66	0.89	0.7
Transfer matter	0.92	0.9	0.93	0.88
Information sharing	0.92	0.82	0.81	0.58
Operational coordination	0.97	0.98	0.94	0.98
Other records, report or contact	0.7	0.16	0.89	0.74
Committee activities	0.8	0.6	0.8	0.5
Nursing staff guidance	0.95	0.6	0.92	0.64

With, with barometric pressure sensor; without, without barometric pressure sensor.

From our observations, the smallest average duration of activity is four minutes, but many activities are recorded for less than that. The presence of such a short duration motivated us to investigate the extension of the timestamp to improve the accuracy of activity recognition. In this section, we focus on the value with the barometric pressure sensor because the barometric pressure sensor has better accuracy than without the barometric pressure sensor, but the extension with other sensors is also shown in Figure 15.8 and explained in Section 15.4.

For the timestamp extension, we initially added the time sequentially, starting from 5 minutes before, 5 minutes after, and up to 30 minutes before and after. Figure 15.4 shows the accuracy of each activity when the extension is carried out, and Figure 15.5 shows the F1 score for each activity. From Figures 15.4 and 15.5, we can see that there are different peaks for different activity classes, such as movement support activity that has peak accuracy at 20 minutes before and 15 minutes after extension, while circulatory care has accuracy peaks at 5 minutes before. For the F1 score, excretion assistance has a peak of 10 minutes before and after, while nutritional dietary care has a peak of 15 minutes before and 20 minutes after. This indicates that each activity has a different impact at each time, so it is necessary to consider an extension of time based on the type of activity the nurses do. In addition, for each time the extension is added, the overlap also increases (Figure 15.6). Therefore, we use another method to find better results. We make the timestamp extension more flexible, the first approach by taking into account the time each user spends on certain activities, then adding the average time each user spends

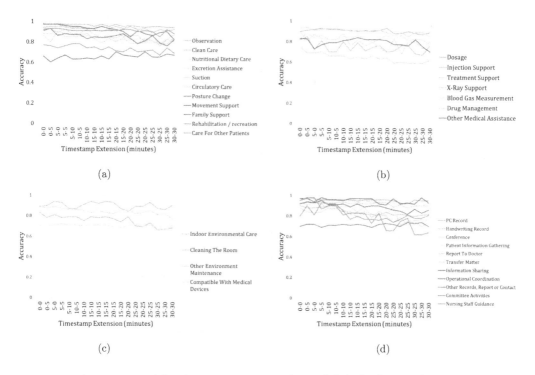

Figure 15.4 Accuracy with timestamp extension of labels for each activity class. (a) Patient care, (b) medical assistance, (c) environmental arrangement, and (d) documentation/communication.

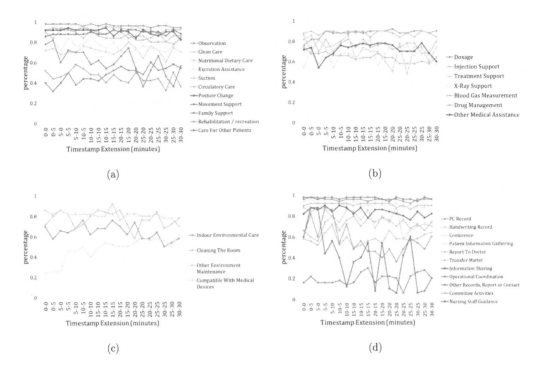

Figure 15.5 F1 score with timestamp extension of labels for each activity class. (a) Patient care, (b) medical assistance, (c) environmental arrangement, and (d) documentation/communication.

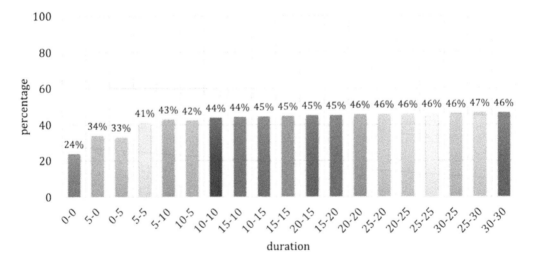

Figure 15.6 Percentage of overlapping.

on the short duration, and the second approach is to change the short time by the average time the user spends. We assume the following conditions for the flexible timestamp extension approach:

$$\text{T1: if } xi < \frac{\sum x}{n} \text{ then } \frac{\left(\frac{\sum x}{n}\right)}{2} \text{ else } xi$$

$$\text{T2: if } xi < \frac{\sum x}{n} \text{ then } \frac{\left(\frac{\sum x}{n}\right) - (xi)}{2} \text{ else } xi$$

Where T1 and T2 are the flexible timestamp extension, x is the duration of each user on a particular activity, xi is the current duration, and n is the number of samples.

Using this method, the impact of feature pressure increases even for all features, and the overlap for the second approximation (T2) can be reduced from the sequential extension of timestamp, but in the first approximation (T1) the overlap is getting bigger, we show it in Figure 15.7.

15.3.7 Relationship between Timestamps Extension and Pressure Features

When using a barometric pressure sensor, not only body movement but also the speed of movement and body high and low states will affect sensor readings. Therefore, investigating the relationship between timestamp extension and pressure features needs to be explored. By calculating scores for each feature, we can determine which features' attributes are most associated with the model's predictions.

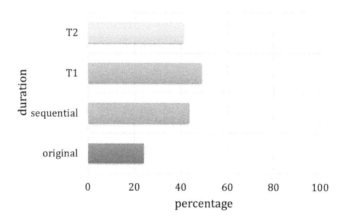

Figure 15.7 Percentage of overlapping for flexible timestamp extensions. Original, original label duration; sequential, the sequential extension of timestamp; T1, the flexible timestamp extension with add the short duration; T2, the flexible timestamp extension with change the short duration.

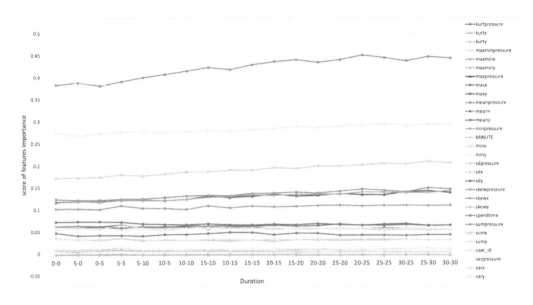

Figure 15.8 Correlation between Timestamp extensions and all features.

A higher score indicates that the specific feature will have a greater impact on the model, which is used to predict a certain variable. To get the scores for each feature, in this paper, we use mean-decrease accuracy. This technique uses the mean decrease in accuracy to calculate the feature importance of permuted out-of-bag samples. Based on the score of the feature importance shown in Figure 15.9, we thoroughly investigated the nursing care record data. We found the pressure feature worked better when we extended the label compared to other sensors (see Figure 15.8), especially in nursing activities.

15.4   RESULT

In this chapter, we identified activity classes that can improve activity recognition for complex nursing care. In Table 15.2, we show the accuracy of activity recognition. We can see with a barometric pressure sensor that the number of activities as much as 73% of 33 activity classes better such as Observation, Clean Care, Nutritional Dietary Care, Excretion Assistance, Suction, Posture Change, Indoor Environmental Care, Family Support, Rehabilitation, Dosage, Care For Other Patients, Treatment Support, Blood Gas Measurement, Other Medical Assistance, Cleaning The Room, Other Environment Maintenance, PC Record, Handwriting Record, Conference, Patient Information Gathering, Information Sharing, Operational Coordination, Nursing Staff Guidance. Even activity of posture change can improve very much by up to 15%, the reason is the barometric pressure sensor not only affects the large movements but also the subtle movements of the human body, which means that when the posture changes, the human or body position does not change, but the speed of movement during the activity will be affected. Meanwhile, activity classes such as circulatory care, movement support, injection support, X-Ray support, drug management, compatible with medical devices, report to doctor, transfer matter, other records, report or contact are better without a barometric pressure sensor. In addition to body motion and speed movement, the height of the body when carrying out activities can impact the sensor readings. This makes the barometric pressure sensor important in recognizing complex activities, especially in nursing care. The average accuracy for nurse activities without a barometric pressure sensor is 85%, while the accuracy of activity recognition by entering the pressure sensor value increases by 3%–88%. In addition, with the barometric pressure sensor, the macro F1 score is 75%, and 66% without the barometric pressure sensor. F1 scores increase for 24 activities, but they decrease for several records.

We take a closer look into the results after changing or adding timestamps that came before and/or after the label timestamp. Overlapping occurs more often when we modify or prolong the timestamp when the start and finish times are increased, the percentage of overlap is shown in Figure 15.6. In order to manage label overlap across activities, activity recognition is carried out as one vs rest to reduce the amount of overlapping data. For each activity class, the accuracy is shown in Figure 15.4 while altering the label timestamp extension sequentially, and the F1 score is shown in Figure 15.5 when conducting the similar approach successively. We grouped the activities into four categories based on the work the nurse did to make it easy to see a comparison. In each category, both accuracy and F1-score reach a peak at different times for each activity. Movement Support in the patient care category has the highest accuracy when adding 20-minutes-before and 15-minutes-after the label timestamp, while Committee Activities for the documentation category have a similar trend when extending the label timestamp by 5-minutes-before and after. However, Drug Management in the medical assistance category and Indoor Environmental Care in the environmental arrangement category perform better without extension. In terms of F1-score, for example, Movement Support achieves the highest value when a 20-minute-before and 25-minute-after label timestamp extension is applied; Compatible With Medical Devices exhibits similar trends with a 30-minute before and after label timestamp extension; and Drug Management performs better without an extension. Accuracy and F1-score for flexible timestamp extension can be seen in Table 15.3. These findings point to the need of taking into account extending the length of the various label times for each activity.

We also investigated the relationship between timestamp extension and pressure features. By computing scores for each feature, we can discover which feature has the most influence on the model's predictions. A feature will have a bigger impact on the model used to predict a certain variable if it receives a higher score. In Figure 15.8 we show the correlation between timestamp extensions and features for all features.

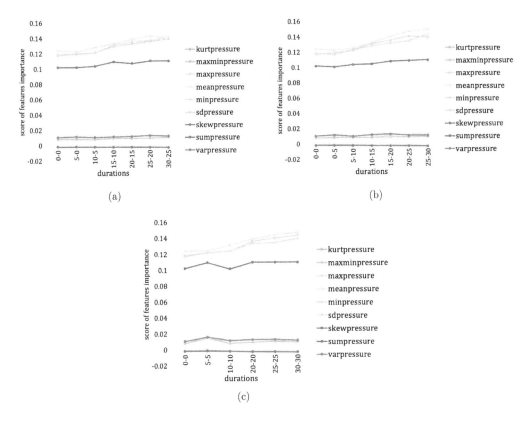

Figure 15.9 Correlation between timestamp extensions and pressure features. (a) Extension before time activity, (b) extension after time activity, and (c) extension before and after time activity.

Specifically for the barometric pressure sensor feature shown in Figure 15.9, when we extended 5 minutes before the activity time, the number of features increased by 66.7%, an extension of 5 minutes after gave an impact of 55.6% the number of features that experienced an increase, and an extension of 10 minutes (5 minutes before and after) had an impact on all features (the accuracy of all features increases), including from the 5-minute extension before or after, which means the 10-minute extension has a larger effect on the model. In addition, after an extension of 10 minutes (5 minutes before and after) to 60 minutes (30 minutes before and after) there are two features that do not show any improvement, namely skewness and kurtosis. Overall, timestamp extension has a greater impact on pressure features with 83.3% features can improve their performance, but the highest values are different for each features and time.

However, certain activities, like Committee Activities, get benefit most from extensions when the more flexible timestamp extension is determined by considering the average duration. Both the accuracy and F1-score of the second approach (T2) are much higher than those of the first approach (T1). This result can be seen

TABLE 15.3 Accuracy and F1 Score of the Pressure Feature with Flexible Timestamp Extension

Activity	Accuracy			F1 Score		
	Ori	T1	T2	Ori	T1	T2
Observation	0.98	0.96	0.96	0.98	0.96	0.96
Clean care	0.94	0.91	0.96	0.92	0.92	0.96
Nutritional dietary care	0.88	0.85	0.86	0.72	0.68	0.7
Excretion assistance	0.93	0.9	0.92	0.84	0.78	0.8
Suction	0.97	0.95	0.96	0.92	0.88	0.9
Circulatory care	0.86	0.69	0.85	0.9	0.76	0.9
Posture change	0.97	0.94	0.96	0.92	0.88	0.9
Movement support	0.66	0.77	0.71	0.4	0.72	0.6
Family support	0.91	0.81	0.93	0.78	0.46	0.74
Rehabilitation/recreation	0.77	0.78	0.78	0.52	0.58	0.4
Care for other patients	0.92	0.91	0.93	0.86	0.86	0.84
Dosage	0.9	0.9	0.9	0.76	0.82	0.8
Injection support	0.82	0.73	0.78	0.82	0.74	0.74
Treatment support	0.9	0.75	0.91	0.86	0.72	0.9
X-ray support	0.83	0.82	0.89	0.54	0.58	0.74
Blood gas measurement	0.93	0.89	0.9	0.88	0.84	0.84
Drug management	0.75	0.7	0.76	0.74	0.74	0.78
Other medical assistance	0.83	0.81	0.87	0.72	0.78	0.8
Indoor environmental care	0.83	0.8	0.88	0.7	0.74	0.84
Cleaning the room	0.89	0.92	0.94	0.72	0.82	0.88
Other environment maintenance	0.9	0.83	0.87	0.86	0.82	0.86
Compatible with medical devices	0.7	0.74	0.75	0.24	0.54	0.54
PC record	0.95	0.94	0.94	0.96	0.94	0.94
Handwriting record	0.9	0.86	0.87	0.58	0.54	0.48
Conference	0.93	0.89	0.91	0.88	0.86	0.86
Patient information gathering	0.96	0.93	0.95	0.94	0.9	0.92
Report to doctor	0.88	0.84	0.95	0.66	0.68	0.86
Transfer matter	0.92	0.91	0.91	0.9	0.88	0.88
Information sharing	0.92	0.92	0.94	0.82	0.86	0.88
Operational coordination	0.97	0.9	0.78	0.98	0.94	0.84
Other records, report or contact	0.7	0.67	0.88	0.16	0.24	0.76
Committee activities	0.8	0.82	0.88	0.6	0.66	0.76
Nursing staff guidance	0.95	0.96	0.97	0.6	0.66	0.7

Ori, original duration; T1, the flexible timestamp extension with add the short duration; T2, the flexible timestamp extension with change the short duration.

in Table 15.3. The impact of flexible timestamp extensions on all features (100% number of features) increased, as reflected in Figure 15.10, which indicates that the extension has a greater influence on the model. These findings demonstrate that the feature is more significantly affected over time when each user's behavior is differentiated at extended timestamps. This occurs because the barometric pressure sensor affects variations in weather, altitude, and movement speed in addition to the user's movement.

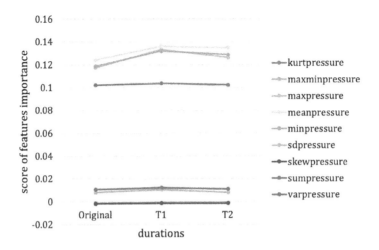

Figure 15.10 Correlation between flexible timestamp extensions and pressure features.

15.5 DISCUSSION AND FUTURE WORK

As a result of the evaluation, we demonstrate the performance of the classification for activity recognition, and our proposed method can improve activity recognition for several activity classes in real life using the pressure sensor that has environmental disturbances to identify user activities. We evaluate complex activities in nurses rather than simple activities. This becomes one of the challenges when we use pressure sensors. Accuracy and F1 score improved well with the pressure sensor. Random forest achieved the highest accuracy of 98%, and the F1 score was also 98%, with a better number of activities as much as 73% of 33 activities compared to that without a barometric pressure sensor. In addition, when we conducted experiments in our lab with fewer activities, there were two activities that had accuracy below 50% while in real life with uncertain conditions, the lowest accuracy was only 66%. This shows that the pressure feature works well in real life for complex nurse care activity recognition.

Our experiment applies self-labeling for label collection, which can reduce the high cost of third-party observers. We provide a timestamp solution to ensure the adequacy of sensor data and if the time participants input the activity label is different from the actual activity. Timestamp extension is another challenge in study using barometric pressure sensors because not only body movements but also outliers impact the reading, such as changes in altitude, temperature, and weather [22,23]. Therefore, various approaches as described in Section 15.3.6 have been shown for modifying the timestamp, performing sequential extensions and paying attention to the time each nurse spends doing activities. Compared to the

Quuppa feature, over time the pressure feature has a bigger impact than the Quuppa feature, which means the pressure feature works better when we extend the label timestamp. This information can be helpful for timestamp solutions when working with barometric pressure sensors.

On the other hand, we also provide the results of an investigation into the relationship between timestamp extension and pressure features so that it can be considered for nursing care activities using barometric pressure sensors. Timestamp extension has a greater impact on pressure features, especially in flexible extensions, which can have an impact over time, but the highest values are different for each feature and time. The pressure feature that works well when we extend the label is meanpressure. Because the identification of body movement using a barometric pressure sensor also affects the altitude and speed of movement, which will be different every day and every time, the meanpressure feature works better than other features.

We realized that in the current work, we did not explore the target patients of the nursing care activities and the objects used, which may also affect the accuracy. For example, the same nursing care activities but with different positions of the patient for example, lying on the mattress or sitting in a chair [23] will affect the barometric pressure sensor because of the different height of the state. This system can also be used in other fields or other activities, but paying attention to building environment is important because the same activity on different floors [12,28] will provide different barometric pressure sensor readings. And it needs to be understood that it will be very difficult if we recognize complex activities performed in outdoor environment [13,23] without a reference sensor.

In the future, analyzing big and small activities to identify activities that are strenuous for nurses using pressure and Quuppa sensors can be taken into the scope. Because to improve the quality of work, nurses must strike a balance between their health and their workload. Big movements can be stressful, especially for nurses who are over 50 years old. Statistical data on nursing services in Japan shows that 26.3% of nurses are aged 50 and over, and 56.3% of assistant nurses are in the same age group.

15.6 CONCLUSIONS

In this chapter, our method integrates the barometric pressure sensor and Quuppa data into the activity classifier and proposed timestamp extension for the inaccurate labels. Using this method, we contributed to the investigation of complex nurse care activity recognition that can exhibit several characteristics of pressure features, such as identifying activity classes that can improve when we use barometric pressure sensors and investigating the relationship of pressure features with the modification of label durations, which is often required in complex and realistic applications. This provides insight into the impact of extended label timestamps on the barometric pressure sensor with multiple time alternatives.

Even with self-labeling, our system is successful in gathering data on nursing activities without sacrificing the quality of the user's work. Although we have used almost the same method in previous experiences using smartphones, employing three devices at once is a challenge in field experiments we try to solve. In this paper, we have compiled the findings from our experience working in hospitals. The findings demonstrate that even though the barometric pressure sensor is influenced by outlier factors, identification accuracy can still be depended upon and may even increase when compared to utilizing merely a Quuppa sensor. Moreover, our study's findings show that flexible time has a beneficial impact on the overall pressure sensor feature.

Future studies will focus on identifying workplace mental health issues that may impact the quantity and quality of nursing care. Staff who are assigned to the appropriate tasks at the appropriate times and who have a good mentality on life will undoubtedly perform better at work, of course, supported by good teamwork as well. We want to study physically demanding activities such as big movements that can cause stress.

BIBLIOGRAPHY

[1] Mira Asmirajanti, Achir Yani S. Hamid, Rr Hariyati, and Tutik Sri. Nursing care activities based on documentation. *BMC Nursing*, 18(1):1–5, 2019.

[2] Yunhao Bai and Xiaorui Wang. Carin: Wireless CSI-based driver activity recognition under the interference of passengers. *Proceedings of the ACM on Interactive, Mobile, Wearable and Ubiquitous Technologies*, 4:1–28, 2020.

[3] Mohamed Bekkar, Hassiba Kheliouane Djemaa, and Taklit Akrouf Alitouche. Evaluation measures for models assessment over imbalanced data sets. *Journal of Information Engineering and Applications*, 3(10):27–38, 2013.

[4] Jesús D. Cerón, Diego M. López, and Bjorn Eskofier. Human activity recognition using binary sensors, BLE beacons, an intelligent floor and acceleration data: A machine learning approach. In *UCAmI*, Punta Cana, Dominican Republic, 2018.

[5] Jingyuan Cheng, Mathias Sundholm, Bo Zhou, Marco Hirsch, and Paul Lukowicz. Smart-surface: Large scale textile pressure sensors arrays for activity recognition. *Pervasive and Mobile Computing*, 30:97–112, 2016.

[6] Florenc Demrozi, Graziano Pravadelli, Azra Bihorac, and Parisa Rashidi. Human activity recognition using inertial, physiological and environmental sensors: A comprehensive survey. *IEEE Access*, 8:210816–210836, 2020.

[7] Luigi D'Arco, Haiying Wang, and Huiru Zheng. Assessing impact of sensors and feature selection in smart-insole-based human activity recognition. *Methods and Protocols*, 5(3):45, 2022.

[8] Anna Ferrari, Daniela Micucci, Marco Mobilio, and Paolo Napoletano. Trends in human activity recognition using smartphones. *Journal of Reliable Intelligent Environments*, 7(3):189–213, 2021.

[9] Zhongzheng Fu, Xinrun He, Enkai Wang, Jun Huo, Jian Huang, and Dongrui Wu. Personalized human activity recognition based on integrated wearable sensor and transfer learning. *Sensors*, 21:885, 2021.

[10] Vaishali Ganganwar. An overview of classification algorithms for imbalanced datasets. *International Journal of Emerging Technology and Advanced Engineering*, 2(4):42–47, 2012.

[11] Iván González, Jesús Fontecha, Ramón Hervás, and José Bravo. An ambulatory system for gait monitoring based on wireless sensorized insoles. *Sensors*, 15:16589–16613, 2015.

[12] Xianping Tao Haibo Ye, Tao Gu and Jian Lu. Scalable floor localization using barometer on smartphone. *Wireless Communications and Mobile Computing*, 16:2557–2571, 2016.

[13] Bo-Jhang Ho, Paul Martin, Prashanth Swaminathan, and Mani Srivastava. From pressure to path: Barometer-based vehicle tracking. In *Proceedings of the 2nd ACM International Conference on Embedded Systems for Energy-Efficient Built Environments*, Seoul, South Korea, pp. 65–74, 2015.

[14] Zawar Hussain, Quan Z. Sheng, and Wei Emma Zhang. A review and categorization of techniques on device-free human activity recognition. *Journal of Network and Computer Applications*, 167:102738, 2020.

[15] Sozo Inoue, Paula Lago, Tahera Hossain, Tittaya Mairittha, and Nattaya Mairittha. Integrating activity recognition and nursing care records: The system, deployment, and a verification study. *Proceedings of the ACM on Interactive, Mobile, Wearable and Ubiquitous Technologies*, 3(3):1–24, 2019.

[16] Asif Iqbal, Farman Ullah, Hafeez Anwar, Ata Rehman, Kiran Shah, Ayesha Baig, Sajid Ali, Sangjo Yoo, and Kyung Kwak. Wearable internet-of-things platform for human activity recognition and health care. *International Journal of Distributed Sensor Networks*, 16:155014772091156, 2020.

[17] Clement Kirui, Li Hong, and Edgar Kirui. Handling class imbalance in mobile telecoms customer churn prediction. *International Journal of Computer Applications*, 72(23):7–13, 2013.

[18] Sotiris B. Kotsiantis, Dimitris Kanellopoulos, and Panagiotis E. Pintelas. Data preprocessing for supervised leaning. *International Journal of Computer Science*, 1(2):111–117, 2006.

[19] Binghao Li, Bruce Harvey, and Thomas Gallagher. Using barometers to determine the height for indoor positioning. *2013 International Conference on Indoor Positioning and Indoor Navigation (IPIN)*, Montbeliard, France, pp. 1–7, 2013.

[20] Ajaykumar Manivannan, Wei Chien Benny Chin, Alain Barrat, and Roland Bouffanais. On the challenges and potential of using barometric sensors to track human activity. *Sensors*, 20(23):6786, 2020.

[21] Axiu Mao, Endai Huang, Haiming Gan, Rebecca S. V. Parkes, Weitao Xu, and Kai Liu. Cross-modality interaction network for equine activity recognition using imbalanced multi-modal data. *Sensors*, 21(17):5818, 2021.

[22] Fabien Massé, Roman R. Gonzenbach, Arash Arami, Anisoara Paraschiv-Ionescu, Andreas R. Luft, and Kamiar Aminian. Improving activity recognition using a wearable barometric pressure sensor in mobility-impaired stroke patients. *Journal of Neuroengineering and Rehabilitation*, 12(1):1–15, 2015.

[23] Fabien Massé, Alan Bourke, Julien Chardonnens, Anisoara Paraschiv-Ionescu, and Kamiar Aminian. Suitability of commercial barometric pressure sensors to distinguish sitting and standing activities for wearable monitoring. *Medical Engineering & Physics*, 36:739–744, 2014.

[24] Hitoshi Matsuyama, Kenta Urano, Kei Hiroi, Katsuhiko Kaji, and Nobuo Kawaguchi. Short segment random forest with post processing using label constraint for SHL recognition challenge. In *Proceedings of the 2018 ACM International Joint Conference and 2018 International Symposium on Pervasive and Ubiquitous Computing and Wearable Computers, UbiComp'18*, pp. 1636–1642, New York, 2018. Association for Computing Machinery.

[25] Mathias Sundholm, Jingyuan Cheng, Bo Zhou, Akash Sethi, and Paul Lukowicz. Smart-mat: Recognizing and counting gym exercises with low-cost resistive pressure sensing matrix. *UbiComp 2014: Proceedings of the 2014 ACM International Joint Conference on Pervasive and Ubiquitous Computing*, Downtown Seattle, Washington, US, pp. 373–382, 2014.

[26] Katrin Tomanek and Udo Hahn. Reducing class imbalance during active learning for named entity annotation. In *Proceedings of the Fifth International Conference on Knowledge Capture*, Redondo Beach, California, USA, pp. 105–112, 2009.

[27] Bing Wang, Jingyuan Cheng, Bo Zhou, Orkhan Amiraslanov, Paul Lukowicz, and Mengfan Zhang. Smart-chairs: Ubiquitous presentation evaluation based on audience's activity recognition. *MobiQuitous 2014: 11th International Conference on Mobile and Ubiquitous Systems: Computing, Networking and Services*, London, Great Britain, pp. 350–351, 2014.

[28] Hao Xia, Xiaogang Wang, Yanyou Qiao, Jun Jian, and Yuanfei Chang. Using multiple barometers to detect the floor location of smart phones with built-in barometric sensors for indoor positioning. *Sensors*, 15(4):7857–7877, 2015.

[29] Daqian Yang, Jian Huang, Xikai Tu, Guangzheng Ding, Tong Shen, and Xiling Xiao. A wearable activity recognition device using air-pressure and IMU sensors. *IEEE Access*, 7:6611–6621, 2019.

[30] Liangpei Zhang, Lefei Zhang, and Bo Du. Deep learning for remote sensing data: A technical tutorial on the state of the art. *IEEE Geoscience and Remote Sensing Magazine*, 4(2):22–40, 2016.

[31] Yong Zhang and Dapeng Wang. A cost-sensitive ensemble method for class-imbalanced datasets. In *Abstract and Applied Analysis*, vol. 2013, Hindawi, 2013.

[32] Xiaochen Zheng, Meiqing Wang, and Joaquín Ordieres-Meré. Comparison of data pre-processing approaches for applying deep learning to human activity recognition in the context of industry 4.0. *Sensors*, 18(7):2146, 2018.

[33] Bo Zhou, Harald Koerger, Markus Wirth, Constantin Zwick, Christine Martindale, Heber Cruz, Bjoern Eskofier, and Paul Lukowicz. Smart soccer shoe: monitoring football interaction with shoe integrated textile pressure sensor matrix. *ISWC '16: Proceedings of the 2016 ACM International Symposium on Wearable Computers*, Heidelberg, Germany, pp. 64–71, 2016.

CHAPTER 16

Analysis of Care Records for Predicting Urination Times

Masato Uchimura, Sozo Inoue, and Haru Kaneko

Kyushu Institute of Technology

16.1 INTRODUCTION

In recent years, incontinence has become a problem in nursing care. In a survey in a medical care facility, some patients needed to have their diapers changed more than five times in a day [3]. Incontinence affects hygiene, mental health of elderly, and workload of caregivers. The main problem of incontinence is that the elderly feel mental stress. The shame caused by incontinence hurts the dignity of the elderly. For those reasons, incontinence should be reduced as much as possible for the elderly and caregivers. To solve this problem, we need to consider some methods to reduce incontinence. In this chapter, we will focus on urinary incontinence. Urinary incontinence is a condition in which urine leaks out regardless of one's will. To prevent urinary incontinence, our goal is to create a predictive model of urination and notify caregivers of patients who are close to urinating through a care record application.

In this paper, we analyze the time interval between urination and the behavior of before and after urination using real care record data. In the first analysis, we visualized a heatmap of the correlation coefficients for each time period in order to examine the time interval pattern of urination. In the second analysis, we compare records for the hour before and after urination to see if there was urination routine. Finally, we predicted urination by random forest based on the analysis results.

As a result of first analysis, we found individual differences among the subjects and the routine of urination intervals. In the second analysis, we were confirmed that the three subjects had in common a high rate of urinating before Change dressing assistance. In predicting urination by Random Forest, we found that the urination interval is different between the elderly and the prediction accuracy was improved by adding the pattern of urination intervals as features.

DOI: 10.1201/9781003371540-19

16.2   RELATED WORK

There were some papers aimed at the same concern as above. Toba et al. [13] developed a thin-film type urinary sensor that can attach to a diaper. It can record urination and the collected data can be used to analyze urination patterns. In addition, there was also a paper by Muto et al. using an ultrasonic sensor to measure urine volume in the bladder [11]. However, the measurement of urine volume using devices and sensors involves financial costs and restrictions on the elderly. Therefore, using sensors or devices in nursing care facilities is difficult.

There were some papers that also predicted excretion time without using sensors. Tsuji et al. proposed a mathematical model to estimate the interval time between urination based on the day's exposure temperature and the individual's body weight from a physiological perspective [14]. We have previously proposed a least-squares model to estimate the amount of urine in the bladder from water intake [15]. Similarly, there was a paper by Saitoh et al. that uses a binary classification to predict the presence or absence of defecation in the elderly using random forests and support vector machines [12]. In this study, the prediction was based on the error between the time on the care record and the actual time. However, the mathematical model of ours and Tsuji et al. has the problem that the only factor that determines individual differences in body weight and that water intake is in the adult model, which is often the case in the elderly. Saitoh et al.'s used care records of the past one to three hours as features for binary classification prediction. However, the care records used in this paper include only a small number of care records 1–3 hours before urination. Therefore, it is insufficient to make predictions using only the features from previous studies.

There were some papers that focus on the analysis of urination routine. A paper by Iseki et al. [5] analyzed the distribution of urinary status in 7 bedridden elderly subjects at 30-minute intervals over a 24-hour period and reported a high degree of regularity in both the population and the individuals. In addition, another study by Koizumi et al. reported that 9 out of 25 patients in four geriatric hospitals and geriatric healthcare facilities had a certain pattern of urination [8]. There have been some systems to collect care record data [1,9]. We have also developed a mobile application for collecting nursing care records called FonLog [4,10]. We have also worked to predict the future value of care records using the collected past care record data. In that study, we got 79% average accuracy, although there were some individual differences [6,7].

In this study, based on the challenges and issues of previous research, we predict urination by random forest using nursing care records in order to prevent incontinence. To increase the number of features, we compared to the conventional method, based on the result analysis, which analyzes the urination intervals and routine before and after urination. In addition, we added new features based on the result of analysis, and the accuracy was compared.

16.3 DATA

In this section, we describe the care record data that used in this chapter. A care record records the care given by the caregiver and the health status of the elderly. This care record also records the type of care activity, the details of care activity, and the time. All of care records data that used in this chapter were collected by FonLog [4,10]. Fonlog is a care record application that can create care records from smartphone. Although caregivers are responsible for entering care records, the timing of entering is different from caregiver to caregiver.

16.3.1 Data Structure

Our dataset is divided into activities and records. Table 16.1 shows the relationship between activities and records. For example, in the case of meal care, "meal and medication" are selected as a activity, and meal assistance, meal amount (main meal), meal (side meal), and mount of water are recorded as a record. The type of record and the response type are used to record the patrols and activities of the person being cared for.

TABLE 16.1   The List of Activities and Records

Activity	Record
Meal/medicine	Meal assistance
	Amount of meal (staple meal)
	Amount of meal (side meal)
	Amount of water medicine
Excretion	Excretion assistance
	Excretion method
	Amount of stool
	Amount of urine
	Stool condition
Nighttime user support	Support type
Daytime user support	Support type
Morning gathering/exercises	Exercises
	Morning gathering
Bathing/bed bathing	Bathing assistance
	Bathing method
Outing support	Type
	Place
Treatment	Treatment type
	Treatment site
Oral care	Oral cleaning
	Denture cleaning
Family/guest support	Purpose
Change dressing assistance	Change dressing assistance

In the table, "activity" refers to the log on the right side of the Table 16.1, and "record" refers to the log on the left side. There are 11 types of activities, and each activity has a total of 26 records.

16.3.2 Data Overview

In this paper, we analyze three elderly. These elderly were selected because they have enough number of data with no missing data. The attribute information of each subject is shown in Table 16.2. All subjects were over 85 years old, and those elderly living in a nursing care facility. Care Level is a Japanese standard for assessing the measure of need for nursing care. Care Level 2 indicates that elderly need for assistance not only with housework chores but also with voiding, bathing, eating, etc. Care Level 4 indicates that the elderly find it difficult to do basic activities such as standing and walking on their own, and they are unable to remain seated.

The care record data used in this chapter are include 61 days from May 1, 2018 to June 30, 2018. Figure 16.1 shows the total amount of samples of all subjects for each record type . As you can see from this figure, there is a bias in the number of data. In particular, "Oral cleaning," "Denture cleaning," and "Treatment site" have very little data. The total number of care records collected for the three subjects is 8069, including 941 records of urination.

16.4 ANALYSIS

This section describes the analysis performed in this study. The analysis is divided into two parts, with a summary and results in each section. The first analysis is to examine the time interval of urination based on whether or not there is a correlation between the times of urination. The study by Iseki et al. focused on the peak of urinary distribution [5]. In the present analysis, we analyzed whether there is a regular pattern in the time interval of urination by the correlation coefficient between times. This analysis allows us to extract the time interval of urination for each individual based on the correlation between the times. While previous studies focused on the peak urination time, we can expect to know the interval time by looking at the correlation. The second analysis examines whether or not the patient has a habit of urinating before and after urination. In the study by Saito et al., the caregiver records of a few hours ago were used as features for the binary classification of whether or not the record was a record of defecation [12]. In the present analysis,

TABLE 16.2   Subjects Information

	Age	Sex	Care Level
A	91	Man	Need care Lv.2
B	89	Woman	Need care Lv.2
C	85	Man	Need care Lv.4

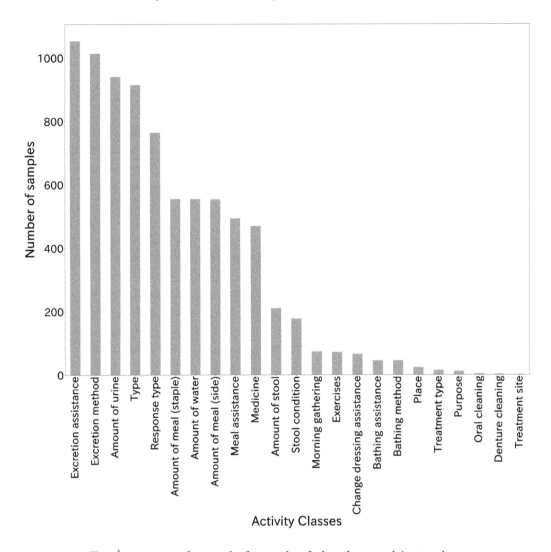

Figure 16.1 Total amount of records for each of the three subjects. As you can see from this figure, there is a bias in the number of data.

we focus on the past and future records of urination and examine whether habits exist before and after urination for each subject. By looking at habits before and after urination, we expect to be able to use care records related to urination as predictive features.

16.4.1   Analysis 1: Interval of Urination Time

First, to see the urination status, the number of times each subject urinated during the 61-day period is shown in a bar graph by time (Figures 16.2–16.4). The vertical axis of the bar chart represents the number of times, and the horizontal axis represents the time period from 0:00 to 23:00. Although the distribution and frequency

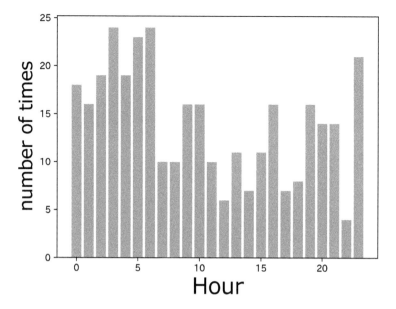

Figure 16.2 Bar graph of urination time for subject A. The total number of urination is 340.

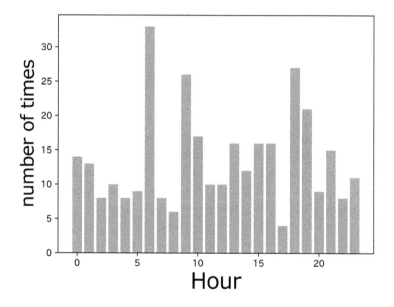

Figure 16.3 Bar graph of urination time for subject B. The total number of urination is 327.

of urination varied, the peak of urination frequency was commonly observed around 6:00 AM.

The data for the 61 days were then divided into 24-hour periods, and the time when urination occurred was set to 1, and the time when it did not occur was set

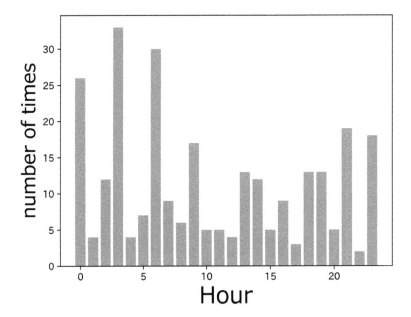

Figure 16.4 Bar graph of urination time for subject C. The total number of urination is 274.

to 0. Then, the correlation coefficients were compared for each time period and summarized on a heat map (Figures 16.5–16.7). The numbers on the vertical and horizontal axes represent time (hour), and the numbers on the heat map represent correlation coefficients. Values with correlation coefficients close to zero are plotted with black tiles, negative correlation coefficients are plotted with blue tiles, and positive correlation coefficients are plotted with red tiles.

The results show that the correlation coefficients are between −0.5 and 0.4. It can be said that the correlation coefficients of adjacent times are negative more than half of the time in common throughout. In other words, it can be seen that all subjects urinate relatively infrequently every hour in the present study. However, there are a few other time periods with positive or negative correlation coefficients in common. Focusing on Subject A, time periods (2, 6), (3, 7), and (4, 8) have high correlation coefficients in common. This indicates that the subject urinates every four hours during the morning hours.

16.4.2 Analysis 2: Routine of before and after Urination

In this analysis, each record for each subject is divided into three groups according to the time of day: one hour before urination, one hour after urination, and the other. Then, by representing the ratio of the records as a heat map, we analyze the presence of habits before and after urination. As shown in Table 16.1, all the meals are recorded as the amount of meal (staple) and the amount of meal (side) in the record of this care record. Therefore, in this analysis, we rewrote the records

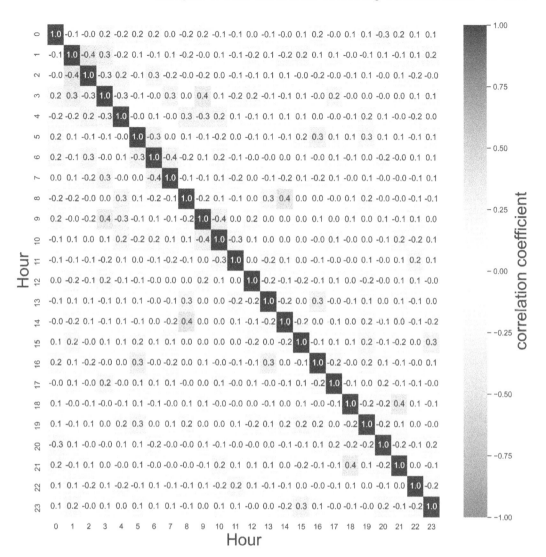

Figure 16.5 Heatmap plotting the correlation coefficient between each time against the urination time of Subject A. The subjects have relatively high correlations at 2, 3, and 4 o'clock and 6, 7, and 8 o'clock, respectively.

of amount of meal(main) as breakfast, lunch, and dinner so that we could identify the time of the day when the meals were eaten. The time period from 5:00 to 10:00 was defined as breakfast, the time period from 11:00 to 16:00 was defined as lunch, and the other time period was defined as dinner. Since the number of records was unevenly distributed, the records used in this analysis are seven records for each time period, i.e., meals, medicine, response type, types, exercises, bathing assistance, and changing dressing assistance. Other records were excluded from this practice because of their small number of inputs.

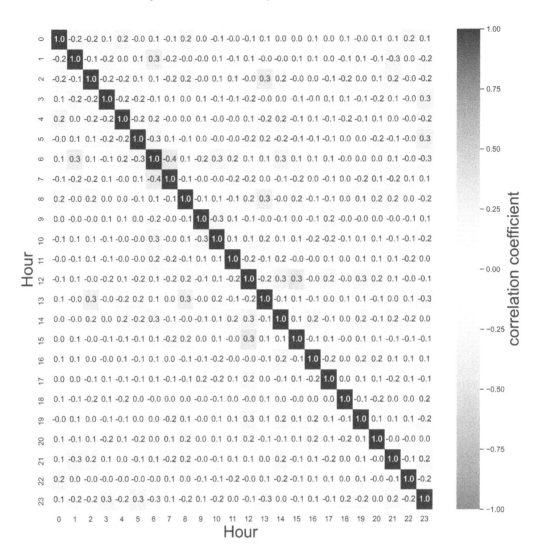

Figure 16.6 Heatmap plotting the correlation coefficient between each time against the urination time of Subject B. This subject has a high percentage of negative correlation coefficients for the two time difference coordinates, indicating that he allows two hours for urination.

The results are shown in Figures 16.8–16.10. The first column in the upper row indicates the percentage (%) of records that corresponded within the past one hour when urination was recorded. Similarly, the second column in the upper row indicates the percentage (%) of records that corresponded within the future one hour when urination was recorded. The third column in the upper row indicates the percentage (%) in which no urination was performed in the hour before or after the care record. The heatmap of the lower panel shows the total number of records for that subject for 62 days.

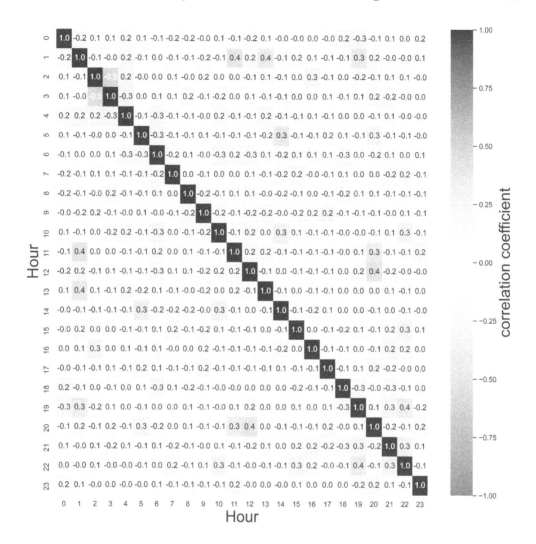

Figure 16.7 Heatmap plotting the correlation coefficient between each time against the urination time of Subject C. Compared to the other subjects, there is no coherent rule, but there are areas where the correlation is positive even at close intervals between 19:00 and 23:00.

Although the number of records is relatively small, the tendency to change clothes after urination is observed in all subjects. Conversely, fewer records of bathing after urination are seen. In subject B, we can see that the rate of urination is higher before and after water intake and before and after lunch and dinner than in the other two subjects. As can be seen, the percentage of records differs from subject to subject in some areas, indicating that there are individual differences in urination habits. Then, the total percentage of records may exceed 100% because one record may exist at an overlapping time with respect to another urination record.

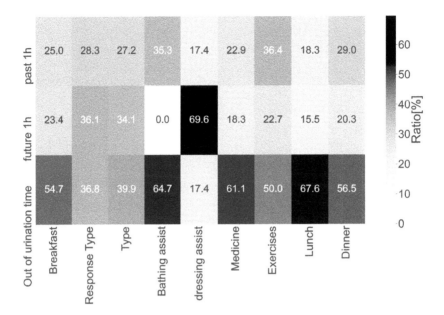

Figure 16.8 Heatmap plotting care records before and after subject A urinated for 1 hour and care records outside of urination. Among the records of changing dressing assistance, we find that a large percentage come one hour after the future of urination. Compared to the other two subjects, bathing came before urination in a higher percentage of cases.

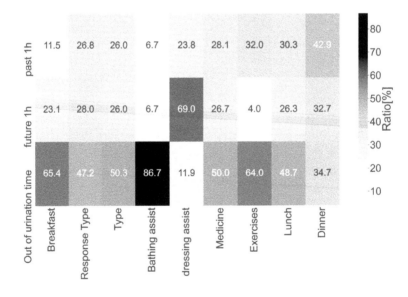

Figure 16.9 Heatmap plotting care records before and after subject B urinated for 1 hour and care records outside of urination. This subject also has a high percentage of changing assistance coming after urination. Compared to the other two subjects, a higher percentage went to urinate before dinner.

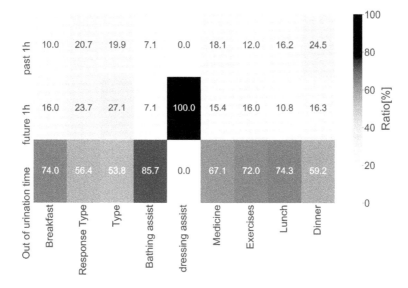

Figure 16.10 Heatmap plotting care records before and after subject C urinated for 1 hour and care records outside of urination. This subject also has a high percentage of changing assistance coming after urination. Compared to the other two subjects, the overall percentage of records that come in the hour before and after urination is lower

16.5 PREDICTION OF URINATION TIME USING RANDOM FOREST

In this chapter, we predict whether or not the elderly urinates after one hour later for each record. In addition to the random forests model [12] with traditional features, we add some features based on the results of analysis in Chapter 4 and compare the prediction accuracy. Random Forest is one of the machine learning methods using multiple weak decision trees [2]. Prediction by Random Forests and SVM was also performed in the previous papers [12], but the results showed that random forests were more accurate. Therefore we use random forests in this paper.

16.5.1 Experiment

In this section, we predict whether there is urination activity in one hour later using nursing care record data. However, to exclude the nursing care at the same time with urination, we excluded the records that include the items of the excretion assistance, the excretion method, and the stool condition from all care records. In this paper, we use Random Forest as a machine learning algorithm. Random forests have the advantage that they are less over fitting even when the number of features is large. The data used in this section is the same with the analysis in Section 16.4. In learning, one subject train and test one model. Care record data were randomly split 75% as a training data, and other 25% as a test data.

16.5.2 Features

There are three types of features that we used in this paper. The first type is a feature of traditional model. The values one hour before each record are used as the following six-dimensional features.

Pattern 1

1. Recorded time [h]
2. Number of bathing activity before 1 hour
3. Number of water intake activity before 1 hour
4. Amount of drinking water [mL].
5. Number of meal activity before 1 hour
6. Number of urination activity before 1 hour

The results of the analysis in Section 16.4.1 show that the interval of urination is different between subjects. Therefore, we consider the following features for the second pattern in addition to the pattern 1.

Pattern 2

7 Number of urination activity before 2 hour
8 Number of urination activity before 3 hour
9 Number of urination activity before 4 hour

From the results of the analysis in Section 16.4.2, it was found that the three patients had in common that they had changing assistant records one hour after urinating. Since we were able to confirm the routine of after urination, the third pattern is based on pattern 1 plus the number of times of bathing, meal, and changing assistance in after 2 hours of each record.

Pattern 3

10 Number of bathing activity after 2 hour
11 Number of meal activity after 2 hour
12 Number of changing cloth activity after 2 hour

16.5.3 Result of Estimation

The results of the three subjects are shown in Table 16.3. The results show that the percentage of accuracy is almost same for all patterns. However, we can see that the recall and F1-score are improved in Pattern 2. The overall low recall and F1-score is due to the difference of the number of records that urinate within an hour and those that do not. The table summarizes the importance of the three subjects' features for each pattern of this random forest (Table 16.4). The numbers in the columns of the table indicated the number of each feature. It can be seen that the recorded time feature accounts for the largest percentage.

TABLE 16.3   Prediction Results of Urination in Each Pattern for 3 Subjects

	Accuracy (%)	Precision	Recall	F1-Score
Pattern1	77	0.45	0.12	0.19
Pattern2	78	0.51	**0.29**	**0.37**
Pattern3	77	0.47	0.16	0.23

Pattern 2 shows an improvement in the accuracy of recall and F1-score. Pattern 2 shows the best score in each evaluation metric as shown in bold.

TABLE 16.4   The Average of the Feature Importance of the Three Subjects for Each Pattern

Features	Pattern 1	Pattern 2	Pattern 3
1	**0.69**	**0.65**	**0.60**
2	0.06	0.03	0.05
3	0.02	0.01	0.01
4	0.07	0.04	0.06
5	0.01	0.01	0.01
6	0.15	0.05	0.11
7		0.05	
8		0.06	
9		0.09	
10			0.02
11			0.07
12			0.06

Record time has the highest importance. Record time (Feature 1) has the highest importance for each pattern as shown in bold.

16.6   DISCUSSION

The present model for predicting whether or not a patient would urinate one hour later was 78% accurate. The same percentage of urination would be predicted if notified by an actual caregiver record application. However, there is room for improvement because the F1-score is low, which indicates a high miss rate predicting that the patient did not urinate even though he or she did in fact urinate. The causes of incontinence include, for example, the following.

- Loosening of pelvic floor muscles
- Abnormal bladder or nerve function
- Dysuria
- Decline in physical and cognitive functions

Of these, urinary incontinence due to cognitive decline could be prevented by notifying patients when it is time to urinate with the care recording app. We then need to consider when incontinence occurs. Urination itself has a peak time, indicating that it occurs at some fixed time (Figures 16.2–16.4). We do not know how much incontinence is included in peak hours, so analysis is needed to produce predictable results for each time period.

As for the analysis, the heat map in the first analysis (Figure 16.5), time periods (2,6), (3,7), and (4,8) were commonly distributed in Subject A with high correlation coefficients. This is because the time interval is the same four hours in each case and the time deviation slides in a staircase-like manner. Thus, if a urination pattern is observed on the heat map, it is likely to be distributed in a staircase-like pattern. In the second analysis, the high rate of urine prior to change dressing assistance may be because the patient urinates while the caregiver is assisting the patient with changing. By combining the first analysis, the interval between urination times, and the second analysis, the routine before and after urination, we believe that it is possible to create a prediction model based on the subject's behavior. Since we were able to binarize the urination status of the same time period in the present verification, we can obtain the probability of urinating at each time of the day. In addition, based on second analysis, we determine the probability of urination in terms of routine. Therefore, we can create a model to predict the time of urination.

In the case of prediction using random forests, the accuracy was improved over the conventional method when Pattern 2 features were used. The prediction of the conventional method, which used nursing care records, used records from one to three hours before defecation as features. The results of conventional methods show a decrease in accuracy as one moves back in time. From the results of the first analysis, some subjects showed a high correlation at an interval of four hours between urination, and the number of urination before four hours was relatively high in terms of the importance of the feature. Therefore, we believe that it is effective to time the characteristic of urination, and that we were able to successfully grasp the subjects' cycles through the present analysis. In addition, the accuracy of pattern 3, which used routine analysis as a feature in predicting urination, was almost the same. This is the reason that there were few records with changing assistance two hours into the future.

16.7 CONCLUSION

The purpose of this study is to develop a model to predict urination time using caregiver records for incontinence prevention. In the previous study, the number of features that could be used was small, so an attempt was made to analyze urination routines in order to increase the number of them.

In this paper, we analyzed three subjects' urination intervals and their routine before and after urination from the correlation coefficients among time periods using nursing care records. Based on these analyses, we predicted urination using random forest. In the first analysis, the correlation between urination times was analyzed to verify the existence of a regular pattern in the time intervals of urination. In the second analysis, we focused on the records before and after urination and examined whether routine existed before and after urination for each subject.

In the first analysis, we found individual differences among the subjects and routine of urination intervals. In the second analysis, it was confirmed that the three subjects had in common a high rate of urinating before changing dressing assistance. The prediction of urination was performed by adding features based on the results of two analyses to the conventional method, and an improvement in accuracy was observed in the first analysis, a pattern in which a feature of the interval between urination times was added.

In the first analysis, the interval of urination time, we manually added features from the results of this analysis. For the future work, we believe that this can be used to determine the optimal urination interval by the autocorrelation function. In addition, although we analyzed only urination in this paper, it would be possible to analyze whether or not there is a pattern in the time of defecation for each subject by examining the time of defecation. The challenge in making predictions is to account for differences in the amount of data. In the present study, the number of records that were applicable to urination after one hour and those that were not were unevenly distributed, resulting in a small recall. One of the problems with nursing care record applications is the possibility of making mistakes in filling out the application. In the present data, there were many defects in the data of urination, and some data could not be included as subjects. In some nursing homes, urination is regularly done by the staff, while in others, urination is done voluntarily. In some cases, a record of urination due to incontinence is also possible. Although we do not know how the patient urinated in this nursing care record, we need to investigate and take into account such differences.

BIBLIOGRAPHY

[1] Bahle, G., Gruenerbl, A., Lukowicz, P., Bignotti, E., Zeni, M., Giunchiglia, F., Recognizing hospital care activities with a coat pocket worn smartphone. In: *6th International Conference on Mobile Computing, Applications and Services*, pp. 175–181 (2014). DOI: 10.4108/icst.mobicase.2014.257777.

[2] Breiman, L., Random forests. *Machine Learning* **45**(1), 5–32 (2001). DOI: 10.1023/A:1010933404324.

[3] Homma, Y., Takai, K., Takahashi, S., Higashihara, E., Aso, Y., Urushibara, A., A survey on urinary incontinence in the institutionalized elderly. *The Japanese Journal of Urology* **83**(8), 1294–1303 (1992). DOI: 10.5980/jpnjurol1989.83.1294.

[4] Inoue, S., Lago, P., Hossain, T., Mairittha, T., Mairittha, N., Integrating activity recognition and nursing care records: The system, deployment, and a verification study. *Proceedings of the ACM on Interactive, Mobile, Wearable and Ubiquitous Technologies (IMWUT)* **3**(3) (2019). DOI: 10.1145/3351244.

[5] Iseki, T., Matsunaga, M., Tauchi, M., Regular urinary drainage pattern and its characteristics in bedridden elderly patients (in Japanese). *Journal of Physiological Anthropology* **14**(3), 97–107 (2009). DOI: 10.20718/jjpa.14.3_97.

[6] Kaneko, H., Hossain, T., Inoue, S., Analysis of feature importances for automatic generation of care records. *UbiComp'21: Adjunct Proceedings of the 2021 ACM International Joint Conference on Pervasive and Ubiquitous Computing and Proceedings of the 2021 ACM International Symposium on Wearable Computers*, pp. 316–321. Association for Computing Machinery, New York (2021). DOI: 10.1145/3460418.3479354.

[7] Kaneko, H., Hossain, T., Inoue, S., Estimation of record contents for automatic generation of care records. In: M. A. R. Ahad, S. Inoue, D. Roggen, K. Fujinami (eds.), *Activity and Behavior Computing*, pp. 289–306. Springer, Singapore (2021). DOI: 10.1007/978-981-15-8944-7-18.

[8] Koizumi, M., Kanda, A., Kawaguchi, T., Regular urinary drainage pattern and its characteristics in bedridden elderly patients (in Japanese). *The Showa University Journal of Medical Sciences* **63**(1), 30–42 (2003).

[9] Lester, J., Choudhury, T., Borriello, G., A practical approach to recognizing physical activities. In: K. P. Fishkin, B. Schiele, P. Nixon, A. Quigley (eds.), *Pervasive Computing*, pp. 1–16. Springer, Berlin, Heidelberg (2006).

[10] LLC, AUTOCARE, Fonlog. https://autocare.ai/2020/11/20/fonlog/.

[11] Muto, M., Kaburaki, T., Kurihara, Y., Development of a model for predicting the amount of animal urine in the bladder and error correction methods for ultrasonic measurements (in Japanese). Technical Report 5, Aoyama Gakuin University (2017).

[12] Saitoh, T., Yamada, I., Yu, Y., Excretion prediction using nursing record system log data. In: *2018 57th Annual Conference of the Society of Instrument and Control Engineers of Japan (SICE)* (2018). DOI: 10.23919/SICE.2018.8492590.

[13] Toba, K., Sudo, N., Nagano, K., Egashira, M., Kanzaki, T., Akishita, M., Hashimoto, M., Ouchi, T., Orimo, H., Yumida, K., Hara, M., Fukushima, Y., An attempt to improve the quality of life of elderly patients with functional urinary incontinence using a thin-film voiding sensor (in Japanese). *Journal of the Japanese Geriatrics Society* **33**(9), 681–685 (1996). DOI: 10.3143/geriatrics.33.681.

[14] Tuji, A., Kuwahara, N., Morimoto, I., Fundamental considerations for the management of body water content in the elderly (in Japanese). *Journal of Human Interface* **16**(2), 97–102 (2014). DOI: 10.11184/his.16.2_97.

[15] Uchimura, M., Kaneko, H., Inoue, S., Toward a predictive model of urination from a physiological perspective using care record data (in Japanese). *Proceedings of the 23rd Annual Conference of the Kyushu Branch of the Japanese Society for Fuzzy Informatics*, pp. 70–72. Online (2021).

CHAPTER 17

Predicting User-Specific Future Activities Using LSTM-Based Multi-Label Classification

Mohammad Sabik Irbaz, Lutfun Nahar Lota
Islamic University of Technology

Fardin Ahsan Sakib
George Mason University

17.1 INTRODUCTION

Activity prediction from sensor data is a relatively untapped field in machine learning. It has many real-life applications in domains like healthcare, transportation, and so on. This topic is mainly studied in computer vision and activities were recognized by visual data from the video feed. But it is computationally expensive and not feasible to implement on a large scale. In ubiquitous computing, however, if we can collect the data from commonly available sensors like accelerometers and use the sensor data from activity recognition, which makes it is eligible for using numerous fields. The first three nurse care activity challenges dealt with human activity recognition from sensor data from the real world. The fourth challenge takes it one step ahead and deals with the next activity prediction from sensor data, which will enable caregivers to provide services efficiently to the patients.

In the healthcare domain, due to the lack of datasets and complex interpretability and explainability of the sensor data, nurse care activity prediction has always been a challenging field. These datasets generally come up with some common challenges: a lot of noisy and unreliable samples, overlapping time frame, irregular sampling rate, inconsistency between lab and field data and so on [9]. That's why, processing these datasets is often very tricky. Furthermore, predicting the future activities of a particular user from the previous activities is even more challenging.

DOI: 10.1201/9781003371540-20

To address these problems, the fourth [13] nurse care activity recognition challenge aims to deal with nurse or caregiver activity prediction from previous activities of a particular user. The goal of this challenge is to make the task scheduling of the nurses or caregivers easier by predicting the probable activities of the next hour based on their activities in previous hours. The challenge provides raw data that contain the records of nurse care activity in a particular hour with a start and end time.

We preprocess the raw data so that it can be used for the multi-label next activity prediction task. We propose a model architecture that leverages LSTM and Bi-LSTM as the backbone. Using our novel two-stage training approach, i.e., user agnostic pre-training and user-specific fine-tuning, we achieve the best performance.

17.2 RELATED WORKS

Activity recognition on health care data has not been studied much due to the complexity and limited availability of the dataset. And the works are mostly focused on patient activities [4,12,18]. This task is unique because it not only depends on the nurse who performs the activity but also on the patient who receives it. The first nurse care activity challenge collected a multi-modal dataset in a controlled environment [9]. Kadir et al. [1] used kNN classifier and achieved 87% accuracy on 10-fold cross-validation and 66% accuracy on leave-one-subject-out cross-validation. Haque et al. [5] used a GRU-based approach with an attention mechanism and achieved 66.43% validation accuracy for person-wise one leaving out cross-validation. Although in the test data, the accuracy was lower.

The second nurse care activity recognition challenge [3] used both lab and real-world data for activity recognition. This partially solved the weakness of the first challenge as it reduced the gap between lab simulation and the real world. Rasul et al. [15] used a basic imputation strategy for preprocessing, used a CNN model, and achieved a validation accuracy of 91.59%. Although in the test data, the accuracy was lower. Irbaz et al. [10] achieved a validation accuracy of 75% and test accuracy of 22.35%. They used both a high pass and a low pass filter to shape the data in the spatial domain during preprocessing and used the kNN classifier. They concluded that traditional machine learning techniques can also be quite useful in activity recognition.

The third care nurse care activity recognition challenge [8] focused on recognizing the activities of a nurse based on the accelerometer data as it is the cheapest and the most feasible way of collecting activity data. Using random forest, Sayem et al [16] achieved a validation accuracy of 72%. But in the test data, the highest accuracy achieved was 12.97%. Although test data became available after the challenge, accuracy rose up to as much as 80% for a few activities.

17.3 DATASETS

Dataset from the third [7] and fourth [13] Nurse Care Activity Recognition Challenge are used for this research. As both of the datasets are part of the same dataset, the structure of the datasets is almost similar. Data collection process for the datasets is same [8]. The datasets contain a total of 28 labels or activity types performed by caregivers or nurses.

17.3.1 Third Nurse Care Activity Recognition Challenge Dataset

There are three tabular datasets. Since our challenge task only focused on the next activity type prediction, we could only utilize the activity data *(label_ train.csv)*. The size of the dataset is 27,448. In this dataset, they have three types of users: nurses, managers, and care managers. We only took the nurse user data which was more relevant to the fourth Nurse Care challenge objective. The size of the nurse user data is 25,874. There are nine nurse users in total: 5, 6, 7, 9, 12, 17, 19, 21, 22. In Figure 17.1, we can see the distribution of this data which is very unbalanced.

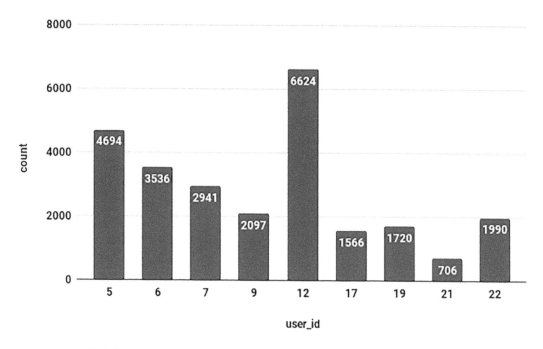

Figure 17.1 Third nurse care data distribution.

17.3.2   Fourth Nurse Care Activity Recognition Challenge Datasets

There are five different sets of data. We are using *Care Record Data.zip* as training set and *Test Data.zip* as validation set. Both of them have five users: 8, 13, 14, 15, and 25. The training set contains 10,985 samples and the validation set contains 6643 samples. In Figure 17.2, the distribution of both the training and validation datasets is shown with respect to the users. We can see that user 25 has the lowest number of both types of samples.

17.3.3   Challenges in Nurse Care Datasets

We faced several challenges when working with the datasets. Two major challenges were pre-processing the raw datasets and working with imbalanced and noisy data.

The raw datasets of both challenges only have user_id, date, hour, and activity type per record. Even though the goal of the fourth Nurse Care challenge is to predict the activities of an hour based on the activities of previous hours, the datasets are not organized for that particular goal. So, they required some manipulation and pre-processing to be used as a sequence prediction dataset.

From Figures 17.1 and 17.2, we can conclude that the datasets are imbalanced. It contains 6,624 training samples for user 12, but only 706 samples for user 21. Moreover, we also found out that the training and validation datasets were inconsistent with each other which results in lower accuracy and F1 score.

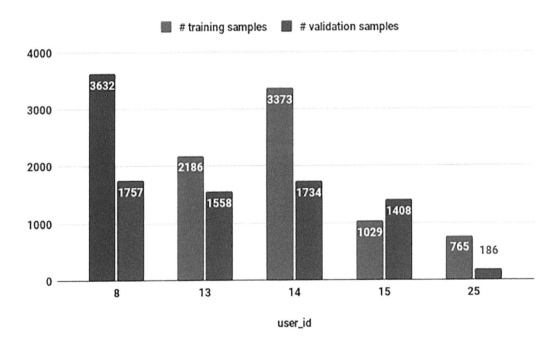

Figure 17.2   Fourth nurse care data distribution.

17.4 PROPOSED METHODOLOGY

Our proposed methodology can be divided into three steps. They are data pre-processing, user-agnostic pre-training, and user-specific fine-tuning. In the case of the user-agnostic pre-training approach, we do not specify or give preference to any users. But, we only provide specific user data during the user-specific fine-tuning stage.

17.4.1 Data Preprocessing

We pre-processed and organized the raw datasets to be used for the multi-label next activity prediction task. All user data from third and fourth Nurse Care challenges have been pre-processed in a similar manner. First of all, for each user and a particular date and hour, all the activities are listed sequentially based on the starting time of those activities. For a specific date and hour, the unique activities are also listed. Second, if there is only one instance of a particular date, we remove that record from the dataset because it does not help us in predicting the activities of the next hour. To build the final dataset, we gather the hourly tasks of a particular date and iterate through them. During the iteration, the pointer indicates the unique tasks for the next hour, and the task in the preceding hours is considered the previous task. Table 17.1 provides some examples of the data after pre-processing.

17.4.2 User-Agnostic Pre-Training

We used LSTM [6] and BiLSTM [17] as backbone of our model architecture to train the model. Both the third and fourth Nurse Care Challenge data for this pre-training were provided without specifying or giving preference to any user. The processed data is reconstructed in a particular format to utilize the sequential long-term and short-term dependencies of LSTM. For each previous hour in the processed data shown in Table 17.1, we took the hour, added a separator, an array of activity type frequencies of that hour, another separator, and, finally, another array of activity type binary which indicates if an activity among the 28 was conducted in that hour. After adding all of the hourly activities in a sequence, we added another separator and concatenated the next hour with it. This input is passed to an LSTM layer. The output of the LSTM is passed to a ReLU and a dropout layer and again passed into a Linear Fully connected layer. The result of the Linear layer goes through the same process again, and finally, the logit values are passed to a

TABLE 17.1 Examples of Pre-processed Data

Previous Hours	Previous Activities	Next Hour	Next Activities
(7, 8)	((10, 23, 6, 6, 6, 6), (6))	8	(10)
(7)	((6, 6, 6, 23, 10, 6))	9	(6)
(7, 8)	((6, 6, 6, 23, 10, 6), (6))	10	(10, 24)

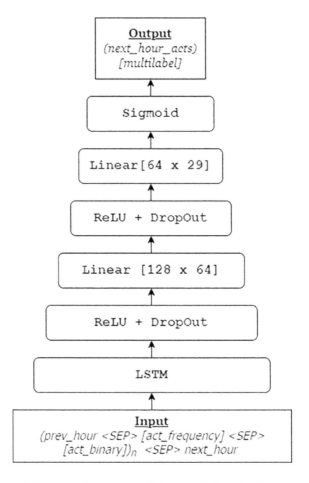

Figure 17.3 Model architecture for pre-training and fine-tuning.

sigmoid layer to generate the output predictions. We get an array as output that specified if a particular type of activity was conducted or not. We also conducted another experiment replacing LSTM with BiLSTM. Figure 17.3 provides a detailed architecture of the modeling approach.

17.4.3 User-Specific Fine-Tuning

The pre-trained model is fine-tuned on the fourth Nurse Care Challenge Data. We conduct user-specific fine-tuning for all five users. All the input processing and modeling approaches are the same.

17.5 EXPERIMENTAL ANALYSIS

To train and evaluate our proposed methodology, we did a couple of experiments in two stages. In the first stage, we trained an LSTM and BiLSTM-based model on fourth Nurse Care Data and later on both third and fourth Nurse care data without specifying users. In the second stage, we used the pre-trained models of the first stage and fine-tuned them using specific user data (user 8, 13, 14, 15, and 25) separately.

To evaluate the performances of each stage and each modeling approach, we considered accuracy (exact match), precision, recall, and F1 score. The accuracy or exact match is the strictest metric for multi-label classification because the result drastically decreases even if there is one mismatch of a particular record during inference. F1-score provides a more balanced result considering the precision and recall and giving some reward for some matches. That's why, in most multi-label classification tasks, F1 score is much higher than the accuracy.

17.5.1 Experiment Setup

We trained all our models using a RAM of 12.68 GB, Intel(R) Xeon(R) CPU @ 2.30 GHz, and Tesla P100-PCIE GPU. The batch size was set to 2, and the maximum sequence length to 1200. We set the dropout rate to 0.1 and the learning rate to 4e-4. The models were trained for 50 epochs. Adam [11,14] was used as the optimizer, and Binary Cross Entropy with logit loss as the loss function. The threshold was set to 0.5 which means if the sigmoid value is greater than or equal to 0.5 after inference, we reset it to 1 or else 0. It takes 400 seconds to train the model and 0.0324 seconds for inference per test sample. We processed and converted the data in *Care Record Data.zip* for training and *Test Data.zip* for validation.

17.5.2 Results and Discussion

We trained the LSTM and BiLSTM models using our proposed model architecture in Figure 17.3. First of all, different experiments were conducted for user-agnostic pre-training. Table 17.2 shows the performance of the conducted experiments.

The BiLSTM model pre-trained on the fourth Nurse Care data shows the best performance in recall which identifies that the number of true positives among the actual positives is high. The LSTM model pre-trained on the same data, shows the best performance in precision and F1 score.

The LSTM model pre-trained on both third and fourth Nurse Care data gives the best performance in accuracy. These pre-trained LSTM and BiLSTM models were used for further user-specific fine-tuning.

During user-specific fine-tuning, we use a specific user's activity data for fine-tuning. Table 17.3, shows the results of all the fine-tuning experiments. Different

TABLE 17.2   User-Agnostic Pre-training Performance

Model	Nurse Care Data	Accuracy	Precision	Recall	F1-Score
BiLSTM	Fourth	0.2414	0.4848	**0.6781**	0.5327
LSTM	Fourth	0.2452	**0.5111**	0.6776	**0.5485**
BiLSTM	Third and fourth	0.2414	0.4848	0.6781	0.5327
LSTM	Third and fourth	**0.2548**	0.4908	0.6862	0.5453

Note: The bold values indicate the best results.

TABLE 17.3 User-Specific Fine-Tuning Performance

Model	User_ID	#Valid_Samples	Accuracy	Precision	Recall	F1-Score
LSTM	**8**	128	0.0703	0.5067	0.6353	0.5313
	13	74	0.3108	0.5532	0.7005	0.5958
	14	119	0.3333	0.6523	0.7582	0.6729
	15	139	0.5286	0.6472	0.7674	0.675
	25	66	0.3182	0.4758	0.5227	0.4786
	Average		**0.3158**	**0.5794**	**0.6931**	**0.6038**
BiLSTM	**8**	128	0.0469	0.4459	0.6505	0.4985
	13	74	0.3108	0.5491	0.7288	0.601
	14	119	0.2583	0.6768	0.7019	0.6683
	15	139	0.5143	0.6865	0.7618	0.6875
	25	66	0.303	0.4192	0.596	0.4658
	Average		**0.2875**	**0.5729**	**0.6957**	**0.5972**

users had different sizes of validation samples. Hence, a weighted average is considered when aggregating the results.

Table 17.3 shows the lowest user-specific performance for user eight even though it contains the highest number of training samples (Figure 17.2). This indicates that the training and validation samples are inconsistent and noisy. Although user 15 contains the second lowest number of training samples, we observed the best user-specific performance for it. From these observations, it can be inferred that the overall dataset is very noisy because we can see the opposite of general deep learning model trends.

After aggregating the results as a weighted average, the table shows that LSTM fine-tuning achieved the best performance in accuracy, precision, and F1-score. These fine-tuned models are employed for final inference in the test dataset. The test results are: accuracy 92% and F1-score 19%.

Comparing Tables 17.2 and 17.3, we can infer the following: (1) Adding third Nurse Care Data with the fourth Nurse Care data gave us better performance in fine-tuning. (2) User-agnostic fine-tuning would have resulted in worse performance than user-specific fine-tuning. (3) If we did not conduct the two-stage training approach, our highest accuracy might have been around 24%–25%. Employing this approach, resulted in 5%–6% more accuracy and F1-score.

17.6 CONCLUSION AND FUTURE WORKS

The fourth Nurse Care activity recognition challenge came up with a very unique and strenuous problem, but, if we consider the real-life implications, this task will facilitate increasing the efficiency of the nurse and caregivers and help them get rid of procrastination. This problem aims to predict the personalized probable activities of the next hour based on their activities in previous hours. We proposed an LSTM-based multi-label sequence prediction model and conducted a two-stage training approach, i.e., user-agnostic pre-training and user-specific fine-tuning, to utilize both third and fourth nurse care activity recognition challenge datasets. Finally, we achieved the validation accuracy of 31.58%, precision 57.94%, recall 68.31%, and F1 score 60.38%.

Even though we achieved good performance with our two-stage training approach, there are still some problems that we would like to pursue further in the future. First of all, the dataset was very imbalanced. We plan to work more on this problem to handle the data imbalance problem for care record data. Second, we would also like to explore how different data processing approaches would correlate with the performance of the task. Finally, we would also like to try some more advanced sequence models, like transformers, to compare the results with LSTM and BiLSTM.

BIBLIOGRAPHY

[1] Kadir, Md Eusha and Akash, Pritom Saha and Sharmin, Sadia and Ali, Amin Ahsan and Shoyaib, Mohammad. Can a simple approach identify complex nurse care activity? In *Adjunct Proceedings of the 2019 ACM International Joint Conference on Pervasive and Ubiquitous Computing and Proceedings of the 2019 ACM International Symposium on Wearable Computers*, London, United Kingdom, pp. 736–740, 2019.

[2] Sayeda Shamma Alia, Kohei Adachi, Tahera Hossain, Nhat Tan Le, Haru Kaneko, Paula Lago, Tsuyoshi Okita, and Sozo Inoue. Summary of the third nurse care activity recognition challenge: Can we do from the field data? In *Adjunct Proceedings of the 2021 ACM International Joint Conference on Pervasive and Ubiquitous Computing and Proceedings of the 2021 ACM International Symposium on Wearable Computers, UbiComp'21*, pp. 428–433, New York, 2021. Association for Computing Machinery.

[3] Sayeda Shamma Alia, Paula Lago, Kohei Adachi, Tahera Hossain, Hiroki Goto, Tsuyoshi Okita, and Sozo Inoue. Summary of the 2nd nurse care activity recognition challenge using lab and field data. In *Adjunct Proceedings of the 2020 ACM International Joint Conference on Pervasive and Ubiquitous Computing and Proceedings of the 2020 ACM International Symposium on Wearable Computers, UbiComp-ISWC'20*, pp. 378–383, New York, 2020. Association for Computing Machinery.

[4] Macarena Espinilla, Javier Medina, and Chris Nugent. UCAmi cup. analyzing the UJA human activity recognition dataset of activities of daily living. *Multidisciplinary Digital Publishing Institute Proceedings*, 2(19):1267, 2018.

[5] Md. Nazmul Haque, Mahir Mahbub, Md. Hasan Tarek, Lutfun Nahar Lota, and Amin Ahsan Ali. Nurse care activity recognition: A gru-based approach with attention mechanism. In *Adjunct Proceedings of the 2019 ACM International Joint Conference on Pervasive and Ubiquitous Computing and Proceedings of the 2019 ACM International Symposium on Wearable Computers, UbiComp/ISWC '19 Adjunct*, pp. 719–723, New York, 2019. Association for Computing Machinery.

[6] Sepp Hochreiter and Jurgen Schmidhuber. Long short-term memory. *Neural Computation*, 9(8):1735–1780, 1997.

[7] Sayeda Shamma Alia, Kohei Adachi, Nhat Tan Le, Haru Kaneko, Paula Lago, and Sozo Inoue. Third nurse care activity recognition challenge, 2021.

[8] Sozo Inoue, Paula Lago, Tahera Hossain, Tittaya Mairittha, and Nattaya Mairittha. Integrating activity recognition and nursing care records: The system, deployment, and a verification study. *The Proceedings of the ACM on Interactive, Mobile, Wearable and Ubiquitous Technologies (IMWUT)*, 3(3):1–24, 2019.

[9] Sozo Inoue, Paula Lago, Shingo Takeda, Alia Shamma, Farina Faiz, Nattaya Mairittha, and Tittaya Mairittha. Nurse care activity recognition challenge. *IEEE Dataport*, 1:4, 2019.

[10] Mohammad Sabik Irbaz, Abir Azad, Tanjila Alam Sathi, and Lutfun Nahar Lota. Nurse care activity recognition based on machine learning techniques using accelerometer data. In *Adjunct Proceedings of the 2020 ACM International Joint Conference on Pervasive and Ubiquitous Computing and Proceedings of the 2020 ACM International Symposium on Wearable Computers*, Virtual Event, Mexico, pp. 402–407, 2020.

[11] Diederik P. Kingma and Jimmy Ba. Adam: A method for stochastic optimization. arXiv preprint arXiv:1412.6980, 2014.

[12] Paula Lago, Fréderic Lang, Claudia Roncancio, Claudia Jiménez-Guarín, Radu Mateescu, and Nicolas Bonnefond. The ContextAct@ A4H real-life dataset of daily-living activities. In *International and Interdisciplinary Conference on Modeling and Using Context*, Trento, Italy, pp. 175–188. Springer, 2017.

[13] Sozo Inoue, Defry Hamdhana, Christina Garcia, Haru Kaneko, Nazmun Nahid, Tahera Hossain, Sayeda Shamma Alia, and Paula Lago. Fourth nurse care activity recognition challenge datasets, 2022.

[14] Ilya Loshchilov and Frank Hutter. Decoupled weight decay regularization. arXiv preprint arXiv:1711.05101, 2017.

[15] Md. Golam Rasul, Mashrur Hossain Khan, and Lutfun Nahar Lota. Nurse care activity recognition based on convolution neural network for accelerometer data. In *Adjunct Proceedings of the 2020 ACM International Joint Conference on Pervasive and Ubiquitous Computing and Proceedings of the 2020 ACM International Symposium on Wearable Computers, UbiComp-ISWC'20*, pp. 425–430, New York, 2020. Association for Computing Machinery.

[16] Faizul Rakib Sayem, M. D. Mamun Sheikh, and Md Atiqur Rahman Ahad. Feature-based method for nurse care complex activity recognition from accelerometer sensor. In *Adjunct Proceedings of the 2021 ACM International Joint Conference on Pervasive and Ubiquitous Computing and Proceedings of the 2021 ACM International Symposium on Wearable Computers, UbiComp'21*, pp. 446–451, New York, 2021. Association for Computing Machinery.

[17] Mike Schuster and Kuldip K. Paliwal. Bidirectional recurrent neural networks. *IEEE Transactions on Signal Processing*, 45(11):2673–2681, 1997.

[18] Maja Stikic, Diane Larlus, Sandra Ebert, and Bernt Schiele. Weakly supervised recognition of daily life activities with wearable sensors. *IEEE Transactions on Pattern Analysis and Machine Intelligence*, 33(12):2521–2537, 2011.

Nurse Activity Recognition Based on Temporal Frequency Features

Md. Sohanur Rahman, Hasib Ryan Rahman, Abrar Zarif, and
Yeasin Arafat Pritom

University of Dhaka

Md Atiqur Rahman Ahad

University of East London

18.1 INTRODUCTION

In recent years, the Human Activity Recognition (HAR) domain has been buzzing with new ideas and inventions. HAR in layman's terms can be said to be a way of understanding the movements and actions of the body from different wearable sensors like accelerometers in our smartphones and smartwatches, gyroscopes, magnetometers, etc. HAR is getting increasingly popular because it can be applied in areas that are directly related to well-beings of humans like healthcare[1], elderly people care [2,3], human-robot interactions [4], etc.

The rising number of patients in hospitals and the inadequate amount of healthcare professionals to tend to their needs is a concern in a lot of countries. A way to solve this type of predicament can be using tools like machine learning and HAR to work alongside professionals. Nurse Care Activity Recognition aims to gather information about the behavior of nurses during their duty time and use that information to improve their efficiency. The few public data sets available are used to train various machine learning models like XGBoost, Random Forest (RF), Support Vector Machines(SVM) [5,6] to achieve that.

Nurse activity recognition is different and more complex than normal activity recognition. Activities like sitting or standing can be easily recognized by Convolutional Neural Networks (CNN) [7]. However, nurse activities are harder to detect as

DOI: 10.1201/9781003371540-21

they help other persons to complete physical tasks. That involves complex movements and body motions. Because of this, deep learning models such as a hybrid of CNN and Recurrent Neural Network (RNN) are being used in order to get a better detection of the activities, and the efforts have proven to be quite fruitful [8]. However, we have not explored any methods of deep learning in this paper. A simple overview of our proposed method is illustrated in Figure 18.2.

18.2 RELATED WORKS

The field of understanding human activity recognition (HAR) has been booming with new inventions and research since the 21st century. There are several methods for determining activities based on video, image, skeleton data, depth maps, mobile apps-based data, and various IoT sensor data, e.g., accelerometer, gyroscope, etc. These methods have been implemented in smartphones, wristwatches, and many more smart devices.

Lester et al. [9] in their paper showed how wearable devices can be used to recognize a range of physical activities. They used a cost-sensitive subset of the sensors and data features. Even though their test subjects were young and healthy individuals, it failed to cover all types of individuals and health conditions.

L. Bao and S. Intille [10] achieved an overall accuracy rate of over 80% on a variety of 20 different activities everyday from 20 different subjects. This also showed that acceleration data can be used to recognize household movements and actions.

Haresamudram et al. [11] explored the role of data representations in HAR using wearables. They have shown that conventional activity recognition chain and feature learning methods together can provide comparable or better performance than deep learning systems. This shows the necessity of suitable feature representations.

Paiva, J. O. V. et al. [12] have studied how mobile applications for elderly healthcare have been addressed in the literature in the past years and how we can use the data to better care for them.

Extracting features from accelerometer and then using feature selection methods has been proven to be very useful in HAR challenges. Class imbalance seems to be the main culprit in conducting proper research on nurse care activities. Reference [13] and Rahman et al. [14] attempted to solve this problem using RF classifier and they have achieved 65.9% average cross-validation accuracy which opens up a new avenue in the field.

B. Su et al. [15] proposed a low-cost HAR method that is based on biology-based hierarchical model and Kinect's skeleton data. The structure is based on anatomy, but the feature extraction method is based on kinematics. Their deep learning method has significantly improved result in comparison to experimental results.

A. Bayat et al. [16] have achieved accuracy up to 91.15% by using a single tri-axial accelerometer. They used different classifiers for evaluating recognition performance. They also showed that recognition activities can detect activities independent of smartphone's position.

L. Xia et al. [17] created a novel approach for HAR where they used histograms. They extracted skeletal joint locations from Kinect depth maps using Shotton et al.'s method [18]. One of the key points of their work is the considerable advantage of using 3D data to recognize human actions. There are lot of methods for using the accelerometer.

Our project work is based on a dataset having accelerometer data as well as care record data for understanding nurse care activity and predicting different activities. Using care record data, there is almost no method we can find. Therefore, this chapter addresses on this dataset for the 4th challenge globally in 2022. Details of the dataset and methodology are provided in the later sections.

18.3 DATASET DESCRIPTION

The challenge dataset accommodates two types of data: care record data and accelerometer data. Care record data mainly contains data of activity labels according to a certain start and finish time. The accelerometer data comprises of three-axial sensory data collected through mobile phone carried by the respective subjects. Provided data are a part of the dataset which was used in organizer's previous work, titled "Integrating Activity Recognition and Nursing Care Records: The System, Deployment, and a Verification Study" [19].

The data accumulation process was done in an experimental and controlled setup in the lab. The data was gathered in the Smart Life Care Unit of the Kyushu Institute of Technology, Japan. The accelerometer data and the care record data are provided for five users (8, 13, 14, 15, and 25). These users' data were accumulated mostly between April and June 2018 and was split into 70:30 ratio for training and testing for the challenge purpose. The users carrying the mobile phone performed 28 different tasks in different timestamps. Though the users performed all these activities, they did not perform those with equal frequency. As a consequence, a class imbalance problem has made its way into the dataset. Activities 24, 25, 26, 27, and 28 were discarded because there was insufficient data. We worked on 23 activities. In Figure 18.1, we can see the class disparity that exists for various users. This is to be noted that the distribution shown here is after preprocessing the dataset mentioned in Section 5.1.

18.4 METHODOLOGY

In our proposed method, we have focused our priority to simplify and make an efficient model in order to minimize any complexities while working with the data

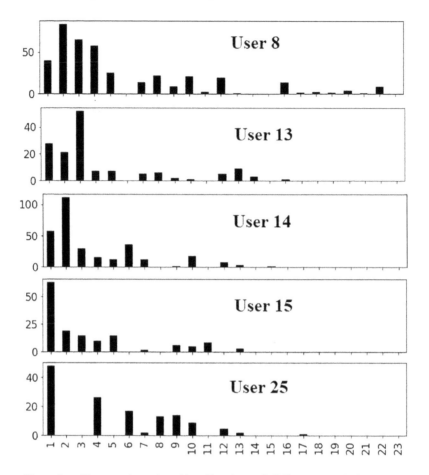

Figure 18.1 Bar plot illustrating the distribution of different activities per user.

above everything else. As a consequence of such focal point, we have built our model using traditional machine learning methods and simple features. Due to the inconsistency and imbalance of accelerometer data, we have been forced to model our project using care data alone. We have extracted and pulled off time-based features from the care data by making use of the embedded timestamps. Prior to engineering those features, the care data have been undergone some fundamental data cleaning and preprocessing techniques. In Figure 18.2, we can comprehend the full workflow methodology laid out.

18.4.1 Data Cleaning and Pre-Processing

Our data of concern was the care data which stores the activity label of the challenge. This care data file holds the activity data of a certain activity in two times-tamps: "start" and "finish". Processing the care data has followed the ensuing methods:

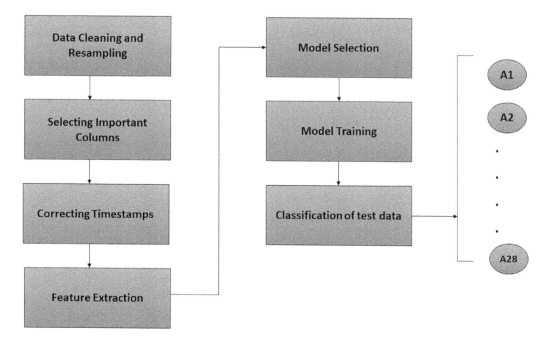

Figure 18.2 Methodology of our proposed work in brief workflow.

Dropping unnecessary columns: Care data holds some irrelevant columns (*user_id*, *activity_type*, *target_id*, *activity2user_id*). They have been dropped to reduce the computational cost.

Fixing timestamps: The care datasets' "start" and "finish" columns were recorded as non-uniform regional data. We changed the time zone for both timestamp columns to "UTC" to create some consistency.

Duplicates: There were some duplicate entries in the datasets. First, the dataset has been sorted by the "start" column and then using the pandas package of python, all duplicated entries have been dropped clean.

Truncation: There were some entries where the "finish" timestamp was greater than the "start" timestamp. In such cases, we have shortened the labels on the dataset.

Sampling: Am upsampling operation has been executed on the data. By doing so, we resampled our timestamp from Date: Hour: Minute: Second to Date: Hour.

Preventing bias: To prevent recognition bias due to class imbalance, we have chosen to follow a selective measure. Therefore, we have only used activities that occurred more than ten times during the given period.

18.4.2 Feature Extraction

For the purpose of extracting valuable information from the dataset, we analyzed the frequency of hourly activities and the repetition of these activities across different timestamps. We have extracted five time-based features: Month, Quarter, Day of Month, Day of Week, Part of day. Our provided care record dataset has distinct similarities with weather prediction data. So, it would follow the same characteristics as the weather prediction data. We can correlate the behavior of the care record data in a cyclic manner, like data of 5 hours entries are provided, we have to model our method as to predict the 6th hours' activities. With our reasoning, our extracted features claim a strong point. The accelerometer data was erratic and lacking in consistency, so we were unable to extract any statistical features from it.

18.4.3 Classification

We have experimented on several types of classifiers and three of them performed splendidly. These are - Random Forest (RF), Extra Trees (ExT) and K-Nearest Neighbors (KNN). KNN and ExT are sensitive to skewed data and require heavy regularization while RF utilizes Bagging (Bootstrap Aggregating) to construct trees, which shrinks some imbalanced behaviours from the dataset. Due to the fact that multiple activities can happen in an hour, we had to be cautious when choosing our target variable since our dataset had multi-label classification. It is observed that the performance of five models trained for five users individually is better than a single model trained for five users. In order to evaluate our models, we used 5-fold cross-validation because the dataset was small. As there was a high imbalance, we used the average of Precision, Recall and F1 score as metrices for model performance. Our average accuracy over five users was 30%.

18.5 RESULTS AND DISCUSSIONS

The provided dataset was quite demanding. So, we have faced an arduous journey working with the data. Despite the fact that the provided data comprised both care record data and accelerometer data, we had to work with the care record data and develop a model to complement its pattern prediction. This is because the accelerometer data were extremely inconsistent. First, we tried to map the accelerometer data with the care record data, but it resulted in a major data loss. We have received only a handful of activity labels in users 13, 14 and 15 out of 28 activities. Users 8 and 25 returned a blank data frame. So, to overcome this predicament, we tried our hand in working with the third nurse care data and merged it with this year's challenge data. Even though we mostly succeeded in receiving the activities while labeling, the data processing made the class imbalance painfully clear. Regardless of the unforeseen outcome, we tried our best to re-sample and handle the imbalance problem. We employed some statistical and frequency-based features on the data and tried to train a model with it, but the model predictions were extremely poor with a predictive bias toward the high-frequency activities. So, we abandoned the idea of working with accelerometer data and focused on the care record data only.

As our work suggests, it is not quite easy to replicate HAR like nurse care activity with weather data. This can be due to nurse care activities being much unpredictable as humans adapt to upcoming needs while weather follows a specific pattern. If we analyze the frequency of activities, only a handful of activities, for example, activity 1 (Vital), 2 (Meal/Medication), 3 (Oral Care) and 4 (Excretion) has high frequency. It is obvious that these are the most important parts of nurse care. Meanwhile activity 7 (Morning gathering/Exercises) and 11 (Night care) has quite low frequency. Some other activities like activity 22 (Doctor visit Correspondence), 23 (Preparation and Checking of Goods), 24 (Organization of Medications), 25 (Family/Doctor Contact), 26 (Break), 27 (Emergency response such as Accident), 28 (Special Remarks/Notes) have insufficient data for a proper comment.

Time-based features extracted in our study are: month, quarter, day of month, day of week, and part of day. We found that part of day and day of week has much weight in predicting data. As our model favors frequent activities more, this is the reason it gives more importance to these two features. Day of month is used only when the activity is mildly frequent. Rarely frequent activities are skewed and not consistent.

The bane of using Bagging algorithm like RF classifier is that it increases variance while reducing bias. This is evident in the set of confusion matrices in Figure 18.3. For instance, CM for act-7, act-11 and act-15 clearly shows that the model is having troubles predicting the activity and it's always predicting "NO". Our response to this study is that regular activity frequency is necessary for temporal-based frequency to be useful in predicting nurse care data. Same method can not be applied to activities with low frequency as we need more information on human movement and their positions to predict the activity.

In our study, we worked with RF classifier, KNN and EXT classifier. Due to high-class imbalance, RF classifier performs the best. Although it is clearly visible that some of the activities are predicted wrong, most frequent activities have good performance. We took average of Precision, Recall and F1 Score and took the best one as our final model. Table 18.1 shows the performance of RF classifier as we got Precision, Recall, F1 score of 52.98%, 50.13%, and 50.21%, respectively. Tables 18.2 and 18.3 show the performance of KNN classifier and EXT classifier as their performance was formidable given that data is highly skewed. Our observation suggests that RF classifier utilizes Bagging algorithm rigorously which is why it has better metrics than the other two classifiers. RF builds separate decision trees which allows it to combat imbalance and predict correctly. In the end, we also kept

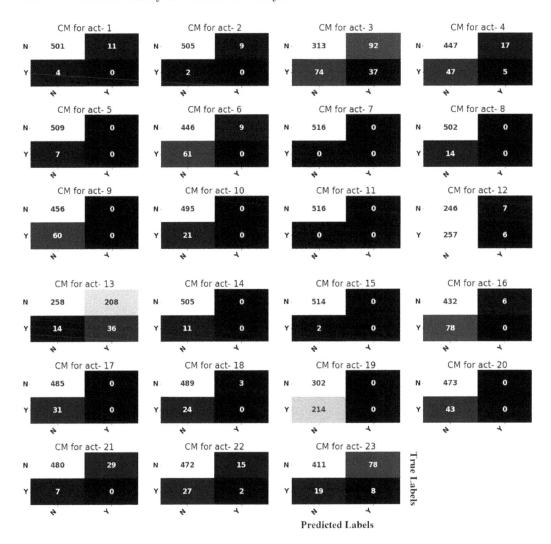

Figure 18.3 Confusion matrices of our RF model shown per activity.

TABLE 18.1 Performance in % of Our Trained
Models Using RF Classifier

User ID	Precision	Recall	F1 Score
25	47.64	37.63	40.43
15	66.55	56.66	60.04
14	58.38	62.56	59.79
13	42.93	49.46	45.94
8	49.39	44.35	44.84
Average	**52.98**	**50.13**	**50.21**

TABLE 18.2   Performance in % of Our Trained Models Using KNN Classifier

User ID	Precision	Recall	F1 Score
25	44.01	36.49	39.72
15	58.35	47.14	59.90
14	51.62	52.94	45.96
13	39.03	35.91	47.53
8	57.21	37.53	42.11
Average	**50.04**	**42.02**	**47.04**

TABLE 18.3   Performance in % of Our Trained Models Using EXT Classifier

User ID	Precision	Recall	F1 Score
25	49.29	33.06	36.75
15	58.44	52.38	54.05
14	58.38	56.86	54.70
13	45.93	42.81	38.08
8	43.54	40.41	41.81
Average	**51.11**	**45.10**	**45.07**

model prediction time in mind as it is important for scaling our project. RF only takes 0.4 seconds to predict on test data while KNN takes 1.1 seconds and EXT takes 1.3 seconds. We omitted accuracy values in our study because they are not valuable in multi-label classification challenge.

18.6   CONCLUSION

We have described our journey in proposing an efficient way to predict the hourly health care data in a nurse care facility in this chapter. The salient feature of this pipeline is to help healthcare centers to smartly plan out their courses of action and make sure the nurses are working in an optimized manner and a healthy workplace. Although it is apparent that it is not entirely possible to make a perfectly assembled model. There are too many unpredictable elements that require consideration. If we attempt that at our present condition, it would be like biting off more than one can chew. So, we narrowed down our focus and set our goal to maximize the accuracy of hourly activity prediction.

A novel aspect of our pipeline is the comparison between healthcare frequency and weather forecasts. In a similar manner to weather forecasts, our model tries to predict the activities that are about to take place within the next few hours. This way we can minimize the unknown variables to a great extent. As we can see from our results, the model is capable of safely predicting high-frequency activities with high precision, but it falls short of predicting low-frequency activities in a given dataset. We were not able to observe the movements of healthcare officials using accelerometer data, which was crucial for predicting any rarely performed activities. In the foreseeable future, we will intensify our efforts to complete our ensemble using semi-supervised learning with accelerometer data and care record data. To further strengthen and advance our work, we would like to include time-lag-based features.

18.A APPENDIX

Features used: time of day, day of week, quarter, month of year, day of month

Programming language: Python 3.9

Libraries: Numpy, scipy, sklearn, matplotlib, pandas

Machine specification: Google colab

Training time: 15.38 seconds

Testing time: 0.4 seconds

BIBLIOGRAPHY

[1] Rodgers, M. M., Pai, V. M., and Conroy, R. S., Recent advances in wearable sensors for health monitoring. *IEEE Sensors Journal*, 15(6):3119–3126, 2015. doi: 10.1109/JSEN.2014.2357257.

[2] Wang, Z., Yang, Z., and Dong, T., A review of wearable technologies for elderly care that can accurately track indoor position, recognize physical activities and monitor vital signs in real time. *Sensors*, 17:341, 2017. doi: 10.3390/s17020341.

[3] Tun, S. Y. Y., Madanian, S., and Mirza, F., Internet of Things (IoT) applications for elderly care: A reflective review. *Aging Clinical and Experimental Research*, 33:855–867, 2021. doi: 10.1007/s40520-020-01545-9.

[4] Keizer, S., Foster, M. E., Wang, Z., and Lemon, O., Machine learning for social multi-party human–robot interaction. *ACM Transactions on Interactive Intelligent Systems*, 4(3):32, 2014. doi: 10.1145/2600021.

[5] Sayem, F. R., Sheikh, M., and Ahad, A. R., Feature-based method for nurse care complex activity recognition from accelerometer sensor. In *Adjunct Proceedings of the 2021 ACM International Joint Conference on Pervasive and Ubiquitous Computing and Proceedings of the 2021 ACM International Symposium on Wearable Computers (UbiComp- ISWC '21 Adjunct)*, ACM, New York, September 21–26, 2021. doi:10.1145/3460418.3479388.

[6] Dewi, C. and Chen, R., Human activity recognition based on evolution of features selection and random forest. *2019 IEEE International Conference on Systems, Man and Cybernetics (SMC)*, pp. 2496–2501, 2019. doi: 10.1109/SMC.2019.8913868.

[7] Ha, S., Yun, J.-M., and Choi, S., Multi-modal convolutional neural networks for activity recognition. In *2015 IEEE International Conference on Systems, Man, and Cybernetics*, IEEE, Kowloon Tong, Hong Kong, pp. 3017–3022, 2015.

[8] Ordez, F. and Roggen, D., Deep convolutional and LSTM recurrent neural networks for multimodal wearable activity recognition. *Sensors*, 16:115, 2016.

[9] Lester, J., Choudhury, T., and Borriello, G., A practical approach to recognizing physical activities. *International Conference on Pervasive Computing*, Springer, Dublin, Ireland, 2006.

[10] Bao, L. and Intille, S., Activity recognition from user-annotated acceleration data. In *International Conference on Pervasive Computing*, Vienna, Austria, pp. 1–17, 2004.

[11] Haresamudram, H., Anderson, D. V., and Plötz, T., On the role of features in human activity recognition. *Proceedings of the 23rd International Symposium on Wearable Computers: ISWC'19*, London, United Kingdom, pp. 78–88, 2019. doi:10.1145/3341163.3347727.

[12] Paiva, J. O. V., Andrade, R. M. C., de Oliveira, P. A. M., Duarte, P., Santos, I. S., Evangelista, A. L., et al., Mobile applications for elderly healthcare: A systematic mapping. *PLoS One*, 15(7):e0236091, 2020. doi: 10.1371/journal.pone.0236091.

[13] Faisal, A. A., Siraj, S., Abdullah, T., Shahid, O., Abir, F. F., and Ahad, M. A. R., A pragmatic signal processing approach for nurse care activity recognition using classical machine learning. In *Adjunct Proceedings of the 2020 ACM International Joint Conference on Pervasive and Ubiquitous Computing and Proceedings of the 2020 ACM International Symposium on Wearable Computers (UbiComp-ISWC '20)*, Association for Computing Machinery, New York, pp. 396–401, 2020. doi: 10.1145/3410530.3414337.

[14] Rahman, A., Nahid, N., Hassan, I., and Ahad, M. A. R., Nurse care activity recognition: Using random forest to handle imbalanced class problem. In *Adjunct Proceedings of the 2020 ACM International Joint Conference on Pervasive and Ubiquitous Computing and Proceedings of the 2020 ACM International Symposium on Wearable Computers (UbiComp-ISWC'20)*, Association for Computing Machinery, New York, pp. 419–424, 2020. doi: 10.1145/3410530.3414334.

[15] Su, B., Wu, H., Sheng, M., and Shen, C., Accurate hierarchical human actions recognition from kinect skeleton data. *IEEE Access*, 7:52532–52541, 2019.

[16] Bayat, A., Pomplun, M., and Tran, D. A., A study on human activity recognition using accelerometer data from smartphones. *Procedia Computer Science*,34:450-457, 2014. doi: 10.1016/j.procs.2014.07.009.

[17] Xia, L., Chen, C.-C., and Aggarwal, J. K., View invariant human action recognition using histograms of 3D joints. *IEEE 2012 IEEE Computer Society Conference on Computer Vision and Pattern Recognition Workshops (CVPR Workshops)*, Providence, RI, pp. 20–27, 2012. doi:10.1109/cvprw.2012.6239233.

[18] Shotton, J., Fitzgibbon, A., Cook, M., Sharp, T., Finocchio, M., Moore, Kipman, R. A., and Blake, A., Real-time human pose recognition in parts from a single depth image. In *CVPR*, IEEE, Colorado Springs, CO, 2011.

[19] Inoue, S., Lago, P., Hossain, T., Mairittha, T., and Mairittha, N., Integrating activity recognition and nursing care records: The system, deployment, and a verification study. *Proceedings of the ACM on Interactive, Mobile, Wearable and Ubiquitous Technologies*, 3(3):24, 2019. doi: 10.1145/3351244.

Ensemble Classifier for Nurse Care Activity Prediction Based on Care Records

Björn Friedrich

Carl von Ossietzky University

Andreas Hein

OFFIS R+D Division Health, Escherweg

19.1 INTRODUCTION

Nurse–patient ratio is an indicator for good quality of care and is associated with survival of patients in intensive care as well [5,6,12]. In Germany, where the level is set by the federal states, and in Japan, where the level is set by the government in the Medical Care Act, the nurse–patient ratios are 10 to 1 and 15 to 1, respectively [13,15]. In the future, demographic change and lack of nurses will likely affect that ratio in a negative way. The more patients one nurse has to take care of, the less time the nurse can spend with each patient. Eventually, this leads to a decrease in quality of care. One way of solving this problem is to increase the nurse–patient ratio; however, this solution needs trained professionals and sufficient funds. Another way would be to relieve the nurses of task or support them to have more time for patient care.

Following the latter idea, *Sozo Lab* organised the *Fourth Nurse Care Activity Recognition Challenge* [1,2]. The task of the challenge was to predict nurse care activities. Nurses spend a lot of their time on documenting their tasks of the whole shift. A system that automatically fills care records would save the nurses time because checking if the records were correctly filled and approving them takes less time than completely filling. In this regard, the organisers developed an information system for recording nurse care activities and Inertial Measurement Unit (IMU) data and deployed it in a care facility [10]. The second and third nurse care activity recognition challenges were only focused on IMU data [3,11]. Besides the IMU data, the care records were provided for this year's challenge.

The real–world data of five nurses/caretakers collected in three months was released. In regard to the real–world character of the data, several challenges arose; the classes were strongly imbalanced, and there were only a few labeled, 36 in total IMU samples. So, we decided to discard the IMU data and use the care records. While there is a lot of research for nurse care activity recognition using IMU data available, there is no previous research only using care records so far. For an overview of the contributions to the previous challenges, please refer to the summary papers [3,11].

For developing our approach, we kept the imbalance in mind and followed the strategy of using highly specialised ensemble classifiers, one ensemble per participant, containing one classifier for each class, instead of a single one–shot classifier. Before training the classifiers, a total of 60 features based on expert knowledge were hand-engineered. After that, time intervals from 1h to 24h hours were used to compute the samples. In the end, our classifiers achieved at least 90% in precision, recall, F1-Score, and accuracy for each participant. Our source code, results, and additional information are available at the https://doi.org/10.57782/976PGQ research data repository of the University of Oldenburg [7]. The summary and results of the *Fourth Nurse Care Activity Recognition Challenge* were published in Ref. [10].

19.2 MATERIALS AND METHODS

In this section, our pipeline is explained. First, we show the main challenges concerning the challenge dataset. Second, the used feature engineering approach is described. After that, the preprocessing is illustrated. Second to last, our classification approach is described in detail. Lastly, an additional metric for evaluating the performance of the classifiers is introduced.

19.2.1 Dataset

The dataset was provided by the challenge organisers. It was comprised of data of three months from five nurses/caretakers and was collected in a healthcare facility. The challenge test data was taken from the following three months. There were 28 different activities, i.e. classes. A first analysis revealed that the data was very imbalanced. In fact, there even were missing activities for the participants. The measures regarding the imbalance were applied on the classifier level and no data augmentation was used. Figure 19.1 presents the class distribution in the raw dataset. Please refer to the challenge website or the publication describing the system for a detailed description of the classes, i.e. activities [1,10].

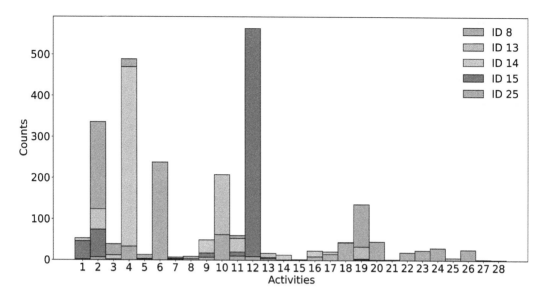

Figure 19.1 The number of samples for each class in the raw records after dropping duplicated entries.

19.2.2 Feature Engineering

Our approach was to use hand–engineered features based on expert knowledge. The features were computed on hourly scale; that means all records in one hour were combined into one sample. The resulting features were nominal, ordinal, and scaled features. Our nominal features were

- caregiver: 1 if we assumed the participant was a caregiver, 0 otherwise; we know that caregivers are not allowed to prepare and apply or give medication in Japan. Every participant without activity 24 was considered as caregiver.

- X: 1 if the activity X was present, 0 otherwise; $X = 1, \ldots, 28$

- Weekend: 1 if the day was on weekend, 0 otherwise

  The ordinale feature was

- ampm: 1 if after noon, 0 otherwise

  The scaled features were

  1. prob_X: the probability that activity X occurs in hour H

  2. activity_duration: the average duration of the activity applied to different patients; sometimes activities were done multiple times to different patients in the same hour.

3. target_count: the number of treated patients in hour H

4. Day of week: 0–6, the day of the week

5. Day: 0–30, the date

6. Hour: 0–23, the hour of the day

7. Week: 0–3, the week of the month

8. Percent of day: how many percent of the day had passed

9. Percent of week: how many percent of the week had passed

10. Percent of month: how many percent of the month had passed

In total, 60 features were engineered.

19.2.3   Preprocessing

Basically, the data was preprocessed in three steps. In the first step, we computed samples covering different time intervals of 24 hours with a step size of 1 hour. For each sample the last 1–24 hours were used to generate a new sample, which contained the past information. So, one sample spawned 24 new samples. Table 19.1 provides an example of the sample computation and Figure 19.2 shows the final label distribution.. The features prob_X, were averaged, and the features X were treated as categorical features; X was set to 1 if activity X occurred in the interval. From here on, we dropped the features which were not of interest for the specific participant. We assumed that participants have a fixed set of activities and we dropped all features belonging to an activity the participant did not perform, e.g. participant X was never doing activity Y; so, we dropped the features prob_Y and Y. In the next step, the data was randomly split into training (75%), validation (15%), and test (10%) sets and we refer to these sets as our internal sets. The ensemble approach turned the multi–class classification problem into a binary classification problem. Therefor, we first chose the positive class, i.e. the class we want to predict, then we computed the total number of samples for each of the internal datasets. To balance the sets, the remaining samples were drawn randomly without replacement from the other classes. If the class was treated as outlier and used with an unsupervised classifier, the positive (i.e. outlier) samples were split, and the remaining samples of the other classes were added to the sets. Still, the datasets remained to be imbalanced. Finally, we had one set of data for each class. Lastly, the metric features (prob_Y, ...) were scaled to the interval

TABLE 19.1   Example of Sample Computation; the Last Line Contains the Sample That Incorporates the Last Hour

Timestamp	Probability	Caregiver	Hour
2018-02-26 13:00:00	0.019	0	1
2018-02-26 14:00:00	0.023	0	2
2018-02-26 14:00:00	0.021	0	2

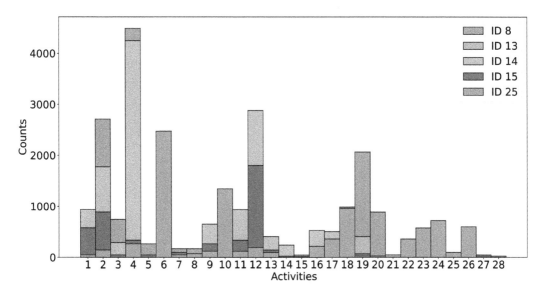

Figure 19.2 The number of samples per class after preprocessing.

between 0 and 1. There was no need for scaling the categorical and ordinal features (Y, caregiver, ampm) since they were 0 or 1.

To predict the classes on the challenge test set, we computed the interval samples and if any of them was labeled with 1, we predicted the activity as present.

19.2.4 Classification

Having analysed the data, we believed that the dataset size was insufficient for approximating the underlying distribution for all participants and activities. Moreover, we saw that some activities had much fewer samples than others. With this in mind and considering Bellman's principle of optimality, we chose an ensemble approach and treating each participant separately [4]. Our ensembles consisted of one classifier for each class, and we used a grid search approach with traditional classifiers to find the best classifier for each class. If the sample count for one class was 100 or smaller, we decided to use an unsupervised learning approach. All remaining classes were classified in a supervised fashion. Using the ensemble approach also gives us the flexibility to react on new or obsolete activities, e.g. if a caregiver passes the nursing board exam and becomes a registered nurse and hence is allowed to do additional activities a new classifier can be added to the ensemble.

19.2.5 Metrics

The challenge required the evaluation of the common metrics precision, recall, F1-Score, and accuracy. In addition, we computed the Wilson score interval for the classification error on the internal test sets [14]. Since the classification error varies with test set size, the choice of the test samples amongst others, the Wilson score interval tells us what error we can expect on unseen data. In contrast to other score intervals (e.g. Hoeffding score interval [9]), the Wilson score interval is asymmetric and does neither suffer from overshooting nor zero–width problems. To compute the Wilson score interval the error is considered as binomial distributed, positive (1) for a false classification and negative (0) for a correct classification. Moreover, the error must be normally distributed. This is usually the case and can be proven by evaluating the model several times on different test sets. The Wilson score interval is defined as follows

$$p = \frac{n_s + \frac{1}{2}z^2}{n + z^2} \pm \frac{n}{n + z^2}\sqrt{\frac{n_s n_f}{n} + \frac{z^2}{4}} \qquad (19.1)$$

where n is the sample size (i.e. experiment count), n_s the number of correct classification (i.e. successful experiments), n_f the number of false classifications (i.e. unsuccessful experiments), and z the quantile of the standard normal distribution corresponding to the confidence (e.g. 2.575 for 99% confidence).

19.3   RESULTS

Overall, the average F_1–Score was 92.63% (accuracy 97.70%) on our internal test sets and 12.4% (accuracy 74.00%) on the challenge test set. The scores, averaged over the classes, for each participant are shown in Table 19.2. All scores for all classes can be found in the folder *metrics* in our source code. Table 19.2 reveals that the ensemble of participant 15 had the highest scores on the internal test sets, except for accuracy, where the highest score can be found for participant 14. The lowest performance had the ensemble of participant 25, except for the lowest recall, which was found at participant 8. In accordance with the scores, participant 15 had the lowest classification error, and participant 25 had the highest; however, the smallest Wilson score interval was computed for participant 14, and the largest for participant 25. Regarding the differences between the internal validation and test scores, the mean differences and standard deviation (SD) for precision, recall, F1-Score, and accuracy were respectively, 1.22% (SD: 0.90%), 2.10% (SD: 0.00%), 1.74% (SD: 1.00%), and 1.75% (SD: 0.46%).

TABLE 19.2   The Results for Each of the Five Participants

ID	Precision (%)	Recall (%)	F_1–Score (%)	Accuracy (%)	Wilson Interval
8	92.54	90.52	91.04	97.39	1.18 [0.96,1.44]
13	94.17	94.60	93.68	97.44	0.79 [0.60,1.06]
14	93.51	93.34	92.69	98.39	0.69 [0.52,0.88]
15	95.42	96.34	95.54	98.38	0.63 [0.41,0.98]
25	91.34	91.52	90.17	96.91	1.51 [1.19,1.90]
Average	93.40	93.26	92.62	97.70	/

The scores are reported for the internal test sets. The Wilson score interval was computed for the classification error on the internal test sets with a confidence of 99%.

TABLE 19.3   The Best Classifier for Each Class and Each Participant

ID	Isolation Forest	Random Forest	Decision Tree
8	13, 14, 21, 23, 27, 28	1, 3, 11, 16, 18, 20	2, 4, 5, 7, 8, 9, 10, 12, 17, 19, 22, 24
13	3, 5, 7, 8, 15, 18, 20, 23, 24, 25, 27	1, 2, 9, 10, 13, 19	4, 11, 12, 14, 16, 17
14	5, 6, 7, 15, 18, 19, 26, 27	3, 10, 17	1, 2, 4, 9, 11, 12, 13, 14, 16
15	3, 5, 7, 10, 14, 15, 19, 28	2	1, 4, 9, 11, 12, 13, 16, 18, 26
25	1, 7, 8, 13, 25, 27, 28	17, 18, 23, 24	2, 4, 6, 9, 10, 11, 12, 16, 22, 26

Looking at Table 19.3, we see that the best set of classifiers contained three different types. The two supervised classifiers were Random Forest (RF) classifiers and Decision Trees (DT). The best performing unsupervised classifier was Isolation Forest (IF).

19.4   DISCUSSION

At a first glance, our results looked promising, but considering our interval approach for computing the samples qualifies the good results. The example in Table 19.1 gives a good impression on how similar the samples, incorporating 1–24 hours, were. Especially, for classes with a small number of samples this approach leads to overoptimistic results. Even though the sets have been drawn randomly the probability that samples which were very similar, e.g. 1, 2, and 3 hours, may have been assigned to the three different sets. Having nearly the same samples in the internal sets –training set, validation set, and test set– causes very good results. Comparing the F_1–Scores of 92.36% and 12.40% supports that.

The final set of classifiers contained three different types of classifiers. Evaluating the other classifier types revealed that many of them perform very similarly. The chosen classifiers were just the first ones found with the best score. A more sophisticated way of choosing the classifiers would be to use Occam's razor principle. The least complex model with the best score is preferred over a more complex model. Transferred to machine learning, the model with fewer trainable parameters should be preferred. This may lead to better results on new data because a model with fewer parameters is less prone to overfitting than a model with more trainable parameters.

When considering the three subsets the overall dataset size comes into play as well. The larger the dataset, the better it can approximate the underlying distribution. The same holds for the training, validation, and test split. Since the dataset was quite small the approximation might be inaccurate. Intuitively, increasing the test set size would lead to a better approximation and hence to a more meaningful classifier result regarding the performance on new unseen data. As a consequence, the training and validation set sizes would be reduced. As a result, the approximation of the underlying distribution becomes inaccurate and the quality of the decision boundaries learned by the classifiers would decrease and the performance would also do accordingly.

Furthermore, our approach was suffering from the curse of dimensionality. We had classes with a very small number of samples and created up to 60 features. Classifiers have a hard time finding good decision boundaries in sparsely filled high-dimensional spaces. Hence, the classifier is not generalising well. Keeping that in mind, the results on the challenge test set are standing to reason.

Naturally, the impact of a prediction system has positive and negative aspects. On the one hand, to relieve nurses from extensive documentation tasks may improve their working conditions and the quality of care, because they could spend more time with each patient and give the appropriate care. On the other hand, the system would enable employers to monitor the nurses and compute accurate key performance indicators and to identify allegedly less productive employees. Consequently, the nurses would be pressured and always be feeling monitored. As a result, the working conditions would become worse.

19.5 CONCLUSION

In this chapter, an ensemble approach, achieving an average F_1–Score of 92.63%, for predicting nurse care activities using care records. In total, 60 features were derived from the care record data of three months of five participants. In regard to the dataset and the feature engineering, the results must be taken with a pinch of salt. Some classes had only a single record entry and the feature engineering process generated very similar samples. In future work, the effect of the curse of dimensionality could be mitigated by using the principal component analysis (PCA) reducing the sample dimensions and finding better decision boundaries. An in-depth analysis of the prob_X features may help to improve the performance as well. The metric features have been averaged over the time intervals. Analysing if the probabilities of different activities are independent may improve the way of combining the probabilities in the time intervals and help engineering new features. If the probability of an activity occurring is independent of the previous occurrence, the probabilities can be multiplied instead of being averaged. The new features could be engineered in a similar way. The new features could be the dependent or independent probability of activity X occurring after activity Y.

ACKNOWLEDGEMENT

The final experiments were performed at the HPC Cluster CARL, located at the University of Oldenburg (Germany) and funded by the DFG through its Major Research Instrumentation Programme (INST 184/157-1 FUGG) and the Ministry of Science and Culture (MWK) of the Lower Saxony State. Moreover, we gratefully acknowledge the support of the NVIDIA Corporation with the donation of the TITAN V GPU used for this research.

BIBLIOGRAPHY

[1] Fourth nurse care activity recognition challenge. https://abc-research.github.io/challenge2022/. Accessed: 2022-08-11.

[2] Sozo lab. https://sozolab.jp/. Accessed: 2022-08-11.

[3] Sayeda Shamma Alia, Kohei Adachi, Tahera Hossain, Nhat Tan Le, Haru Kaneko, Paula Lago, Tsuyoshi Okita, and Sozo Inoue. Summary of the third nurse care activity recognition challenge: Can we do from the field data? In *Adjunct Proceedings of the 2021 ACM International Joint Conference on Pervasive and Ubiquitous Computing and Proceedings of the 2021 ACM International Symposium on Wearable Computers, UbiComp'21*, pp. 428–433, New York, 2021. Association for Computing Machinery.

[4] Richard Bellman. On the theory of dynamic programming. *Proceedings of the National Academy of Sciences*, 38(8):716–719, 1952.

[5] Timothy M. Dall, Yaozhu J. Chen, Rita Furst Seifert, Peggy J. Maddox, and Paul F. Hogan. The economic value of professional nursing. *Medical Care*, 47(1):97–104, 2009.

[6] Andrea Driscoll, Maria J. Grant, Diane Carroll, Sally Dalton, Christi Deaton, Ian Jones, Daniela Lehwaldt, Gabrielle McKee, Theresa Munyombwe, and Felicity Astin. The effect of nurse-to-patient ratios on nurse-sensitive patient outcomes in acute specialist units: A systematic review and meta-analysis. *European Journal of Cardiovascular Nursing*, 17(1):6–22, 2018.

[7] Bjoern Friedrich. 4th Nurse Care Activity Recognition Challenge Software, 2022.

[8] Defry Hamdhana, Christina Garcia, Nazmun Nahid, Haru Kaneko, Shamma Alia Alia, Tahera Hossain, and Sozo Inoue. Summary of the fourth nurse care activity recognition challenge: Predicting future activities. In Md Atiqur Rahman Ahad, Sozo Inoue, Guillaume Lopez, and Tahera Hossain (eds.), *Human Activity and Behavior Analysis: Advances in Computer Vision and Sensors*, pp. 416–432. CRC Press, Boca Raton, FL, 2024.

[9] Wassily Hoeffding. Probability inequalities for sums of bounded random variables. *Journal of the American Statistical Association*, 58(301):13–30, 1963.

[10] Sozo Inoue, Paula Lago, Tahera Hossain, Tittaya Mairittha, and Nattaya Mairittha. Integrating activity recognition and nursing care records: The system, deployment, and a verification study. *The Proceedings of the ACM on Interactive, Mobile, Wearable and Ubiquitous Technologies (IMWUT)*, 3(3):1–24, 2019.

[11] Paula Lago, Sayeda Shamma Alia, Shingo Takeda, Tittaya Mairittha, Nattaya Mairittha, Farina Faiz, Yusuke Nishimura, Kohei Adachi, Tsuyoshi Okita, François Charpillet, and Sozo Inoue. Nurse care activity recognition challenge: Summary and results. In *Adjunct Proceedings of the 2019 ACM International Joint Conference on Pervasive and Ubiquitous Computing and Proceedings of the 2019 ACM International Symposium on Wearable Computers, UbiComp/ISWC'19 Adjunct*, pp. 746–751, New York, 2019. Association for Computing Machinery.

[12] Anna Lee, Yip Sing Leo Cheung, Gavin Matthew Joynt, Czarina Chi Hung Leung, Wai-Tat Wong, and Charles David Gomersall. Are high nurse workload/staffing ratios associated with decreased survival in critically ill patients? A cohort study. *Annals of Intensive Care*, 7(1):46, 2017.

[13] Noriko Morioka, Suguru Okubo, Mutsuko Moriwaki, and Kenshi Hayashida. Evidence of the association between nurse staffing levels and patient and nurses' outcomes in acute care hospitals across japan: A scoping review. *Healthcare*, 10(6), pp. 1-13, 2022.

[14] Edwin B. Wilson. Probable inference, the law of succession, and statistical inference. *Journal of the American Statistical Association*, 22(158):209–212, 1927.

[15] Britta Zander-Jentsch, Franz Wagner, Nargiz Rzayeva. et al. Innovation and intellectual property rights. In Anne Marie Rafferty, Reinhard Busse, Britta Zander-Jentsch, and et al., editors, *Strengthening Health Systems through Nursing: Evidence from 14 European Countries*, Number 52, Chapter 4, pp. 266–290. European Observatory on Health Systems and Policies, Copenhagen (Denmark), 2019.

CHAPTER 20

Addressing the Inconsistent and Missing Time Stamps in Nurse Care Activity Recognition Care Record Dataset

Rashid Kamal, Chris Nugent, Ian Cleland, and Paul McCullagh

Ulster University, Northern Ireland

20.1 INTRODUCTION

Approximately 771 million people will be aged 65 years or older in by the end of 2022, which is three times the number in 1980 [2]. There will be an increase in the burden on hospitals and residential care homes as a result of this trend. A number of data science research areas have emerged to assist the elderly, including monitoring of elderly commotion [19,20], transportation issues [18], context-aware approaches [3,11,13], home security [5], and human-robot interaction [12].

The categorization of care activities has afforded quantification of workload in the healthcare sector.[1] Comparatively, it is easier to recognize simple activities such as walking, sitting, than to recognize nurse care activities. This is because care involves complex activities such as bathing and exercising. Indeed, it is necessary to perform the same activity differently in accordance with each patient's condition. Automated recognition of activity may allow care givers to devote more time and effort to core activities rather than to administrative tasks, such as document preparation. As part of monitoring, it is necessary to ensure that all care activities for each patient have been completed [7].

DOI: 10.1201/9781003371540-23

The fourth Nurse Care Activity Recognition Challenge, organized by Sozolab, provides an opportunity to better identify the daily activities of caregivers and nurses in healthcare facilities. Organizers provided care record data collected from smartphones [1]. A description of activities can be found in Table 20.1. From a data perspective; there are difficulties associated with the dataset due to its high noise, imbalance, and inconsistency. Indeed some data from accelerometers and care records did not match due to a mismatch in timestamps. Furthermore, the

TABLE 20.1   Descriptions of Each Activity Are Further Divided into Categories

Activity Type ID	Activity Type	Categories
activityTypeid1	Vital	
activityTypeid2	Meal/medication	
activityTypeid3	Oral care	
activityTypeid4	Excretion	
activityTypeid5	Bathing/wiping	
activityTypeid6	Treatment	
activityTypeid7	Morning gathering/exercises	
activityTypeid8	Rehabilitation/recreation	
activityTypeid9	Morning care	Activities of direct care
activityTypeid10	Daytime user response	
activityTypeid11	Night care	
activityTypeid12	Nighttime user response	
activityTypeid13	Family/guest response	
activityTypeid14	Outing response	
activityTypeid19	Get up assistance	
activityTypeid20	Change dressing assistance	
activityTypeid21	Washing assistance	
activityTypeid27	Emergency response such as accident	
activityTypeid15	Linen exchange	
activityTypeid16	Cleaning	Activities of residence cleaning
activityTypeid23	Preparation and checking of goods	
activityTypeid24	Organisation of medications	
activityTypeid17	Handwriting recording	
activityTypeid18	Delegating/meeting	Doc/communication activities
activityTypeid22	Doctor visit correspondence	
activityTypeid25	Family/doctor contact	
activityTypeid26	Break	Other activities
activityTypeid28	Special remarks/notes	

Note: As a description of the data, this table was provided by the Sozo lab [1].

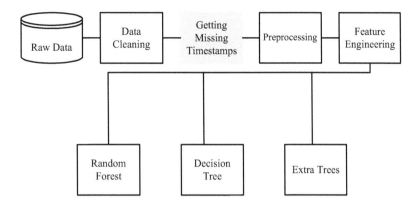

Figure 20.1 An overview of the overall model pipeline. Algorithm20.1 contains the algorithm for obtaining missing time stamps. Preprocessing involves obtaining the day of the week and time of the day from the timestamp.

accelerometer data set was not provided for the testing set. Therefore, we used only the care record datasets in our model.

To improve the classification of complex nurse care activities, we propose a novel algorithmic pipeline that includes preprocessing and feature extraction techniques. The detailed pipeline of this approach can be found in Figure 20.1.

Section 20.2 of the paper discusses related work in the detection of physical activity and nursing care activities. The dataset is described in Section 20.3. Technical aspects of the proposed methodology are discussed in Section 20.4. In Section 20.5, the findings of the study are summarized, and in Section 20.6, we discuss the overall experiment and results, while in Section 20.7, conclusions are presented.

20.2 RELATED WORK

Researchers are exploring new approaches for accurately identifying human activities. A variety of preprocessing and feature extraction approaches have been proposed in previous works for recognizing nurse care activity, based on the types of sensor data characteristics and activities [4,14,15].

Basak et al. [4] extracted various features from lab and field data by filtering noise and applying windowing techniques. After merging lab and field data, the best model was identified through 10-fold cross-validation. As a result of this challenging dataset, a Random Forest classifier achieved 65% accuracy with a 40% F1 score. Using a Random Forest-based resampling method, Arafat et al. [15] addressed the problem of class imbalance in a nurse care activity dataset. The process included resampling, selecting features based on Gini Impurities. The Gini Impurity specifies what the probability is that an observation will be misclassified. Training and validating models used stratified K-Fold cross-validation. With an average cross-validation accuracy of 65.9% they claimed, the Random Forest classifier successfully classified 12 nurse activities conducted in both laboratory and real-life settings.

Using "The Second Nurse Care Activity Recognition Challenge Using Lab and Field Data", Md. Golam Rasul et al. [16] proposed the use of Convolution Neural Network (CNN) models. Their algorithm reported an accuracy of 91.59%, outperforming existing algorithms. The model used by Faizul et al. [17] was a Random Forest model. Their study indicates that their model was capable of classifying several challenging activities with a 72% accuracy rate. In "The Third Nurse Care Activity Recognition Challenge." according to Arafat et al. [14], minority classes are subject to higher misclassification costs because of changes made to the class weights They combined weighted base classifier outputs with different weights using a stacked generalization method. Using this approach, they were able to leverage the skills of a diverse group of high-performing base learners while also balancing their limitations and strengths. This hybrid technique allowed them to achieve an average cross-validation balanced accuracy of 70.8% when classifying 28 activities performed by nurses in real life scenarios.

Based on the results presented in Ref. [9], K-Nearest Neighbor (KNN) and the extraction of necessary features produced better results than deep learning algorithms. Irbaz et al. [8] highlighted the necessity of integrating frequency-domain features into traditional machine learning (ML) algorithms in order to evaluate their performance. When overlapping sliding windows with a hop-size of ten, KNN provided the best results. As a result of their findings, the authors concluded that machine learning classifiers combined with feature extraction could assist in identifying activity at a low computational cost. Various features were extracted from lab and field data independently using windowing techniques according to Basak et al. [4]. A cross-validation technique was used to determine the best performing Random Forest (RF) model. Various methods were employed by Matsuyama et al. [10] to address the overfitting of the model. The best results were achieved by using Random Forest classifier.

The nature of previous challenges was different. During the competition, the accelerometer data was provided to the competitors so that they could classify the activities. However, this time they only provided caregiver records for both training and testing. This makes classification more challenging. To achieve good accuracy scores, researchers have used tree-based algorithms in the past. It is possible that this is due to an imbalance in the classes in the dataset. According to the Sozo lab, the baseline score is very low. There is a F-score of only 0.14 for user 8 because there are missing time stamps and incorrect timestamps. As far as we are aware, there has not been a study that utilizes this dataset in order to determine the correct timestamps of records. To improve accuracy, we believe that imputation of the missing time stamps with modeled timestamps are the key elements.

20.3 DATASET DESCRIPTION

Sozolab provided datasets for five users (8, 13, 14, 15 and 25). A dataset containing care records and accelerometer data was included in the study. However, this time they only provided caregiver records for both training and testing. The time stamp of the accelerometer and the care record were not identical. Care records were dated from February 2018 to July 2018 and accelerometers were dated from May 2018 to June 2018. A further inconsistency was the absence of accelerometer data for testing. For care data recorded between May 2018 and June 2018, the testing data differed from the training data. The care record contains the following information: id, user id, activity type id, activity type, target id, activity2userid, start, finish, and year month date hour. The caregivers performed a total of 28 activities. Not all activities were carried out by each caregiver. There are 28 activities derived from four activity groups. Figure 20.3 presents the frequency of activities performed by each caregiver for each day of the week. From the figure, it can be seen that the intensity of the activities varies according to the caregiver or patient assigned to the task. Figure 20.2 illustrates the frequency of activities performed by each caregiver during the day. The 12–19 takes place between 09 and 20 at specific times. It illustrates a pattern that will be helpful in the development of a machine learning model for caregivers.

Several entries did not have their finish time recorded. A number of activities were completed within too short period of time to be reasonable, which implies some erroneous data. According to a data provider, nurses recorded the data at the end of their shift, which may account for the short total time recorded. In addition, many of the activities are unclear in terms of nature and scope, and they may be indicative of a wide range of activities.

20.4 METHODOLOGY

This Section provides a comprehensive explanation of "Nurse Care Activity Recognition" from Care Record Data. The development of the system involved four significant steps: preprocessing the data, identifying features, selecting features, and selecting a model. Following the extraction of time domain and frequency domain features from the window, some of the features are dropped because they are the same for all entries, such as ID. As well, we dropped the feature start date and end date in order to predict based on the day and time rather than the date and time. A variety of machine learning models were then used to train the classifiers such as Decision Trees, Random Forest, and Extra Trees (Figure 20.3).

20.4.1 Preprocessing

Five caregiver datasets were included. It is pertinent to note that not all activities were performed by each user. In Table 20.1, a list of the Activities and their

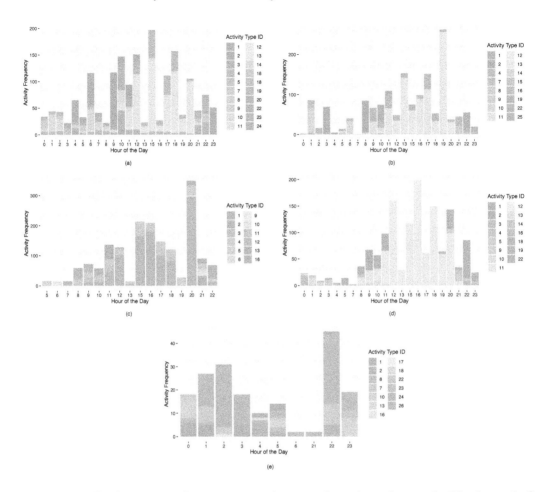

Figure 20.2 The frequency of activities per hour is plotted on the graph. The legend of each activity indicates the color of each activity. In the graph, the X axis represents the hour of the day, while the Y axis represents the frequency distribution of each class/activity. From panel (a)–(e), the figure depicts users 8, 13, 14, 15, and 25.

groups can be viewed. The accuracy of the models could be improved by finding missing time stamps of finish times. A number of missing and duplicate values have been identified in the provided data. To maintain consistency, duplicates have been removed from each user data.

The activities were categorized based on the type of activity using the data description [1]. After calculating the maximum time for each group of activities, we noted that most of the time difference between the start and end time was very small, sometimes only a few seconds, which is erroneous. Possibly, this is because

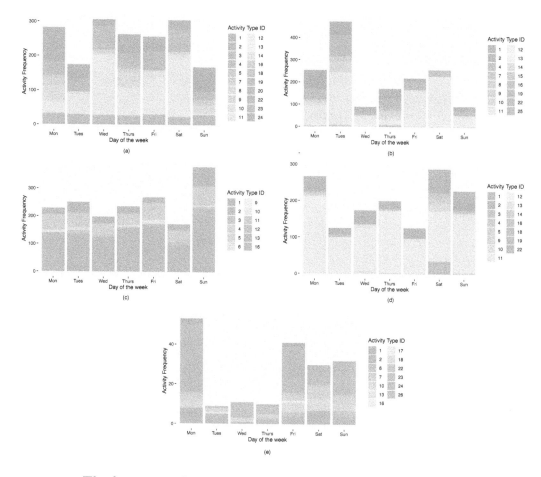

Figure 20.3 The frequency of activities per day is plotted on the graph. The legend of each activity indicates the color of each activity. In the graph, the X axis represents the day of the week, while the Y axis represents the frequency distribution of each class/activity. Users 8, 13, 14, 15, and 25 are depicted in the figure from panel (a)–(e), respectively.

users record the data at the end of their shift and simply enter the start and end times. In other words, it does not accurately reflect the actual time stamps. Our hypothesis was that finish times (actual time stamps) should be accurate in the provided dataset. A new label has been added, *Timetaken*. To calculate *Timetaken* the maximum time for each group and then subtract the standard deviation for each group. In the final step, the finish time was substituted for the start time plus the time taken. Detailed information can be found in the Algorithm 20.1.

Algorithm 20.1 An Algorithm for Getting Missing Finish Timestamps

---

Require: $df = userdata$
Require: $activityGroupNum \leftarrow activityCatogries$
   $activityDirectCare \leftarrow (1, 2, 3, 4, 5, 6, 7, 8, 9, 10, 11, 12, 13, 14, 19, 20, 21, 27)$
   $activityResidenceCleaning \leftarrow (15, 16, 23, 24)$
   $activityDocumentationCommunication \leftarrow (17, 18, 22, 25)$
   $otherActivities \leftarrow (26, 28)$
   $Std \leftarrow 0$
   $Max \leftarrow 0$
   $timeTaken \leftarrow []$
   for $i \leftarrow 1$ to 4 **do**
      $Std = sd(df[activityGroupNum == i, "timetaken"])$
      $Max = max(df[activityGroupNum == i, "timetaken"])$
      $timeTaken[i] = Max - Std$
   end for
      $n \leftarrow len(df)$
      for $i \leftarrow 1$ to 4 **do**
         for $j \leftarrow 1$ to n **do**
            $df[activityGroupNum][j] == i$
            $df[finish][j] = df[start][j] + timeTaken[i]$
         end for
      end for

20.4.2 Feature Extraction and Selection

The second step was the engineering of features following the data processing. Based on the start and revised finish time stamps acquired during data processing, we selected five features: start hour, finish hour, time of day, start day number, and finish day number (number as weekday number, e.g. 1 for Monday). As a result of obtaining the weekday number, the features can be used for future prediction independent of the date. To make the prediction hourly basis, we have to drop some of the features which can add noise to final classification. We removed the start time stamp with date from the data set and only used the time of the day and day number (e.g., Monday as 1 and so on), and also for the finish time stamp, we only used the time of the day and day number (e.g., Monday as 1 and so on). We also drop activity type (activity name) because we are using activity type number (1–28 activities), and user id because we are using each user data set separately (user 5, user 13, etc.).

20.4.3 Classification

Different algorithms are tested on the dataset, among them SVM, KNN, Gaussian, AdaBoostClassifier, and Tree-based classifiers. In our study, we found that tree-based classifiers performed well. For all predictions in this study, Random

Forest (RF), Extra Trees, and Decision Trees algorithms were selected and used. In particular, the RF algorithm is useful for problems involving missing values, high dimensions, or a large number of classes, because it combines the results of multiple classifiers of the same type or of a different type. In decision trees, the data is continuously split according to a specified parameter and the outputs are explained (that is, you provide the inputs and the outputs in the training data). The tree can be explained by two entities, namely decision nodes and leaves. In contrast, Extra Trees is an ensemble machine learning algorithm that combines predictions from a number of decision trees.

20.5 EXPERIMENTAL RESULTS & DISCUSSION

By using a clean and modified dataset (created by feature engineering), we generate results for the Random Forest (RF), Extra Trees, and Decision Tree evaluation metrics. Table 20.2 indicates that Decision Trees and RF classifiers performed better than Extra Trees. From the raw data, the most relevant features which provide the best accuracy were selected. In the case of User 15, we achieved 91%accuracy using Decision Trees, and in the case of User 8, we achieved 79% accuracy using Decision Trees. It is necessary to extract the important features required for analysis in order to be able to correctly and efficiently distinguish between the various activities. In spite of the unbalanced dataset, our proposed approach is also capable of identifying minority classes to a certain extent based on precision, recall, and F-measure. We also note that Activity 4 was relatively high in false positives when compared to the broad category of Activities of Direct Care. To provide a better understanding of the performance of our final model, we present the confusion matrix in Figure 20.6.

TABLE 20.2 Classifiers Score for All Users

User ID	Classifier	Accuracy	F1 Score	Precision	Recall
25	Decision tree classifier	0.836	0.533	0.529	0.537
25	Extra trees classifier	0.816	0.538	0.596	0.490
25	Random forest classifier	0.843	0.556	0.587	0.529
15	Decision tree classifier	0.917	0.461	0.487	0.439
15	Extra trees classifier	0.888	0.443	0.457	0.430
15	Random forest classifier	0.898	0.458	0.500	0.423
14	Decision tree classifier	0.802	0.474	0.461	0.488
14	Extra trees classifier	0.810	0.465	0.475	0.456
14	Random forest classifier	0.816	0.473	0.486	0.461
13	Decision tree classifier	0.865	0.470	0.475	0.464
13	Extra trees classifier	0.856	0.504	0.514	0.494
13	Random forest classifier	0.853	0.464	0.507	0.428
8	Decision tree classifier	0.795	0.655	0.642	0.669
8	Extra trees classifier	0.618	0.579	0.603	0.557
8	Random forest classifier	0.675	0.627	0.653	0.603

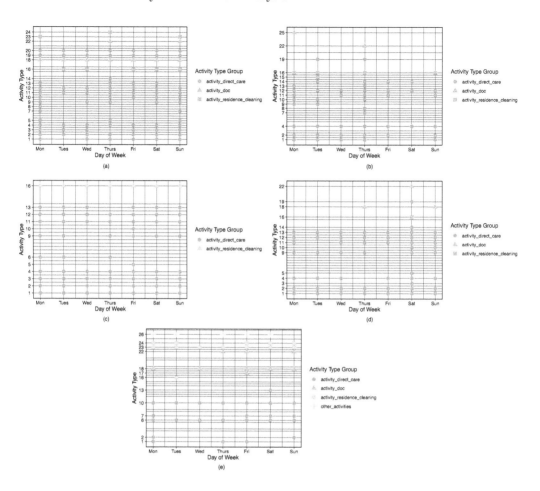

Figure 20.4   The activities per day are plotted on the graph. The legend of each activity indicates the color of each activity group. In the graph, the X axis represents the day of the week, while the Y axis represents the distribution of each class/activity. From panel (a)–(e), the figure depicts users 8, 13, 14, 15, and 25.

The Decision Tree provided the highest accuracy rate in our study. Compared to the base score provided by the organizers, our method has achieved significant improvements in overall accuracy. Compared with baseline scores of 0.14, 0.27, 0.45, 0.34, and 0.42 for users 8–25, we achieve an F-score of 0.61 for user 8, 0.50 for user 13, 0.47 for user 14, and 0.46 for user 15, and 0.55 for user 25. In the validation phase, we received an accuracy of 51% and an F-Score of 0.026 [10].

The first step in analyzing the data is to divide each activity into its respective categories. Our next step is to create a graph based on each activity and the specific hour at which it occurred. Figure 20.4 shows the activity and the time it occurred. According to this graph, the documentation activity follows the direct care activity. This figure also allows for the analysis of the overall distribution of each nurse throughout the day. In Figure 20.5, we use a similar approach to show

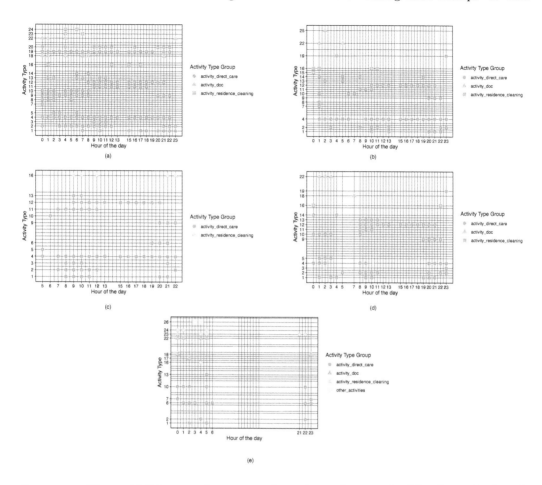

Figure 20.5 The activities per hour are plotted on the graph. The legend of each activity indicates the color of each activity group. In the graph, the X axis represents the hour of the day, while the Y axis represents the distribution of each class/activity. Users 8, 13, 14, 15, and 25 are depicted in the figure from panels (a)–(e), respectively.

the distribution of activities and activity groups over the course of a full week. Data analysis indicates that not all activities were performed by each individual user. This is due to the fact that different caregivers performed different activities in accordance with their regular routines or those requested by the patient.

To understand the distribution of activities performed by each individual user, it is also very important to classify each user. For each individual user, we calculated the frequency of classes and generated two sets of graphs that display the frequency of classes over the course of the day, as shown in Figure 20.2. We also showed the distribution of classes throughout the week in Figure 20.3.

As a result of our analysis, we have found an accuracy rate of over 91%. However, there was a relatively high number of false positives for activity 4. There is a possibility that the classifiers were unable to distinguish between the activities since they were so similar. Table 20.2 shows the overall classification score of all five users. The table also demonstrates that calculating the time taken and determining the inferred time of completion was a good approach, since our score is much better than the base score provided by the Sozolab [1].

20.6 CONCLUSION

In this paper using data from the care record, nurse care activities were identified using a data science approach. It was necessary to preprocess the data in order to remove noisy instances, e.g., to determine the inferred time of finish. The method described in Section 20.4 can be used to determine the inferred time of completion. Classification algorithms were evaluated using accuracy, precision, recall, and F-score. Our results for the RF, Extra Trees, and Decision Tree evaluation metrics are derived by using a clean and modified dataset (created by feature engineering). Based on the results of Table 20.2, Decision Trees outperformed both RF and Extra Trees classifiers.

We eliminate duplicate labels and select only relevant features by dropping some features such as start date and end data and instead using start hour, finish hour, start day, and end day (e.g., number of week days) and extracting relevant information. According to our results, User 15 achieved 91% accuracy using Decision Trees, while User 8 achieved 79% accuracy using Decision Trees. There are a number of factors that contribute to this high percentage. To be able to distinguish between various activities correctly and efficiently, it is necessary to extract the relevant features for analysis. Although the dataset is unbalanced, our proposed approach is also capable of identifying minority classes to a certain extent based on precision, recall, and F-measure. Figure 20.6 provides a better understanding of the performance of our final model. When using the Decision Tree classifier, the proposed method performed the best among all the classifiers used in our study. We were able to improve our classification performance by correcting the missing finish timestamps.

Activity 4 was relatively high in false positives when compared to the broad category of Activities of Direct Care. Due to the similarities between the activities, the classifiers may have had difficulty distinguishing them. Using automated tracking and documentation, caregivers can spend that extra time providing services to patients. It is difficult to predict the hourly basis on an hourly basis. However, multiple activities may take place in a single hour. It is possible to achieve more accurate results if the prediction is made on a quarterly basis rather than an hourly basis.

To achieve increased accuracy and automate the caregiving record system, more data must be collected and combined with accelerometer data. As a result, caregivers will be able to utilize their time more efficiently.

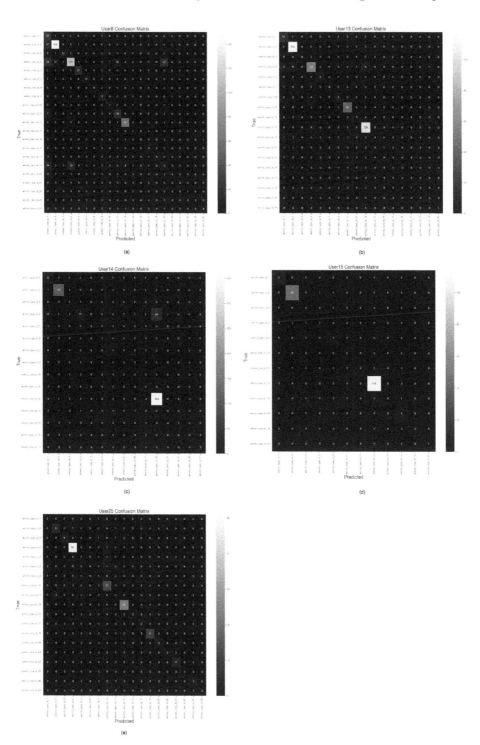

Figure 20.6 Plots of confusion matrix for all users. In the graph, the X axis represents the predicated class/activity, while the Y axis represents the true class/activity. From panel (a)–(e), the figure depicts users 8, 13, 14, 15, and 25.

ACKNOWLEDGMENT

This project was supported by Invest Northern Ireland under Competence Centre Programs Grant RD0513853 - CHIC (Connected Health Innovation Centre).

Note

1. https://abc-research.github.io/challenge2022/.

BIBLIOGRAPHY

[1] Fourth Nurse Care Activity Challange. https://abc-research.github.io/challenge2022/data/. Accessed: 2022-08-08.

[2] UNO World Population Prospects, United Nations Department of Economic and Social Affairs, Population Division (2022). World Population Prospects 2022: Summary of Results. UN DESA/POP/2022/TR/NO. 3, 2022.

[3] Christoph Anderson, Isabel Hübener, Ann-Kathrin Seipp, Sandra Ohly, Klaus David, and Veljko Pejovic. A survey of attention management systems in ubiquitous computing environments. *Proceedings of the ACM on Interactive, Mobile, Wearable and Ubiquitous Technologies*, 2(2):1–27, 2018.

[4] Promit Basak, Shahamat Mustavi Tasin, Malisha Islam Tapotee, Md Mamun Sheikh, A. H. M. Nazmus Sakib, Sriman Bidhan Baray, and Md Atiqur Rahman Ahad. Complex nurse care activity recognition using statistical features. In *Adjunct Proceedings of the 2020 ACM International Joint Conference on Pervasive and Ubiquitous Computing and Proceedings of the 2020 ACM International Symposium on Wearable Computers*, Virtual Event Mexico, pp. 384–389, 2020.

[5] Bowei Dong, Qiongfeng Shi, Yanqin Yang, Feng Wen, Zixuan Zhang, and Chengkuo Lee. Technology evolution from self-powered sensors to AIoT enabled smart homes. *Nano Energy*, 79:105414, 2021.

[6] Defry Hamdhana, Christina Garcia, Nazmun Nahid, Haru Kaneko, Shamma Alia Alia, Tahera Hossain, and Sozo Inoue. Summary of the fourth nurse care activity recognition challenge: Predicting future activities. In Md Atiqur Rahman Ahad, Sozo Inoue, Guillaume Lopez, and Tahera Hossain (eds.), *Human Activity and Behavior Analysis: Advances in Computer Vision and Sensors*, 416–432, CRC Press, Boca Raton, 2024.

[7] Sozo Inoue, Paula Lago, Shingo Takeda, Alia Shamma, Farina Faiz, Nattaya Mairittha, and Tittaya Mairittha. Nurse care activity recognition challenge. *IEEE Dataport*, 1:4, 2019.

[8] Mohammad Sabik Irbaz, Abir Azad, Tanjila Alam Sathi, and Lutfun Nahar Lota. Nurse care activity recognition based on machine learning techniques using accelerometer data. In *Adjunct Proceedings of the 2020 ACM International Joint Conference on Pervasive and Ubiquitous Computing and Proceedings of the 2020 ACM International Symposium on Wearable Computers*, Virtual Event Mexico, pp. 402–407, 2020.

[9] Md Eusha Kadir, Pritom Saha Akash, Sadia Sharmin, Amin Ahsan Ali, and Mohammad Shoyaib. Can a simple approach identify complex nurse care activity? In *Adjunct Proceedings of the 2019 ACM International Joint Conference on Pervasive and Ubiquitous Computing and Proceedings of the 2019 ACM International Symposium on Wearable Computers*, London, United Kingdom, pp. 736–740, 2019.

[10] Hitoshi Matsuyama, Takuto Yoshida, Nozomi Hayashida, Yuto Fukushima, Takuro Yonezawa, and Nobuo Kawaguchi. Nurse care activity recognition challenge: A comparative verification of multiple preprocessing approaches. In *Adjunct Proceedings of the 2020 ACM International Joint Conference on Pervasive and Ubiquitous Computing and Proceedings of the 2020 ACM International Symposium on Wearable Computers*, Virtual Event Mexico, pp. 414–418, 2020.

[11] Abhinav Mehrotra and Mirco Musolesi. Intelligent notification systems. *Synthesis Lectures on Mobile and Pervasive Computing*, 11(1):1–75, 2020.

[12] Christina Moro, Shayne Lin, Goldie Nejat, and Alex Mihailidis. Social robots and seniors: A comparative study on the influence of dynamic social features on human–robot interaction. *International Journal of Social Robotics*, 11(1):5–24, 2019.

[13] Martin Pielot, Tilman Dingler, Jose San Pedro, and Nuria Oliver. When attention is not scarce-detecting boredom from mobile phone usage. In *Proceedings of the 2015 ACM International Joint Conference on Pervasive and Ubiquitous Computing*, Osaka, Japan, pp. 825–836, 2015.

[14] Arafat Rahman, Iqbal Hassan, and Md Atiqur Rahman Ahad. Nurse care activity recognition: A cost-sensitive ensemble approach to handle imbalanced class problem in the wild. In *Adjunct Proceedings of the 2021 ACM International Joint Conference on Pervasive and Ubiquitous Computing and Proceedings of the 2021 ACM International Symposium on Wearable Computers*, Virtual Event USA, pp. 440–445, 2021.

[15] Arafat Rahman, Nazmun Nahid, Iqbal Hassan, and Md Atiqur Rahman Ahad. Nurse care activity recognition: Using random forest to handle imbalanced class problem. In *Adjunct Proceedings of the 2020 ACM International Joint Conference on Pervasive and Ubiquitous Computing and Proceedings of the 2020 ACM International Symposium on Wearable Computers*, Virtual Event Mexico, pp. 419–424, 2020.

[16] Md Golam Rasul, Mashrur Hossain Khan, and Lutfun Nahar Lota. Nurse care activity recognition based on convolution neural network for accelerometer data. In *Adjunct Proceedings of the 2020 ACM International Joint Conference on Pervasive and Ubiquitous Computing and Proceedings of the 2020 ACM International Symposium on Wearable Computers*, Virtual Event Mexico, pp. 425–430, 2020.

[17] Faizul Rakib Sayem, Md Mamun Sheikh, and Md Atiqur Rahman Ahad. Feature-based method for nurse care complex activity recognition from accelerometer sensor. In *Adjunct Proceedings of the 2021 ACM International Joint Conference on Pervasive and Ubiquitous Computing and Proceedings of the 2021 ACM International Symposium on Wearable Computers*, Virtual Event USA, pp. 446–451, 2021.

[18] Md Sadman Siraj, Md Ahasan Atick Faisal, Omar Shahid, Farhan Fuad Abir, Tahera Hossain, Sozo Inoue, and Md Atiqur Rahman Ahad. UPIC: User and position independent classical approach for locomotion and transportation modes recognition. In *Adjunct Proceedings of the 2020 ACM International Joint Conference on Pervasive and Ubiquitous Computing and Proceedings of the 2020 ACM International Symposium on Wearable Computers*, Virtual Event Mexico, pp. 340–345, 2020.

[19] Soe Ye Yint Tun, Samaneh Madanian, and Farhaan Mirza. Internet of Things (IoT) applications for elderly care: A reflective review. *Aging Clinical and Experimental Research*, 33(4):855–867, 2021.

[20] Zhihua Wang, Zhaochu Yang, and Tao Dong. A review of wearable technologies for elderly care that can accurately track indoor position, recognize physical activities and monitor vital signs in real time. *Sensors*, 17(2):341, 2017.

CHAPTER 21

A Sequential-Based Analytical Approach for Nurse Care Activity Forecasting

Md. Mamun Sheikh

University of Dhaka

Shahera Hossain

University of Asia Pacific

Md Atiqur Rahman Ahad

University of East London

21.1 INTRODUCTION

Due to the dramatic evolution of technologies and sophisticated machine learning algorithms, the number of care facilities is expanding continually. Because of the need for caregiver human resources, enhancing the efficiency of care services is essential. The assessment of caregivers' behaviors is vital in enhancing service standards. It also provides trustworthy care services and minimizes hospitalization time [1,2].

Activity classification and forecasting utilizing mobile sensors are feasible owing to their low cost, easy maintenance, and reduced processing capabilities. There are many more challenges to forecasting caregivers' behaviors; for instance, nurses have to do a vast range of tasks and there is intra-class variability across the same classes. In addition, complex activity sequences, discontinuous activities, and other complications associated with the data acquisition protocol make the task more challenging.

DOI: 10.1201/9781003371540-24

In this research, we have developed a complete, sequential-based technique for forecasting nurse care activities. The objective of our work is to automate and enhance care facilities. The primary contributions of our methodology are:

- A comprehensive problem formulation strategy and solution employing a sequential-based approach.

- Numerous pre-processing and post-processing techniques capable of finding optimum performance.

Activity classification utilizing embedded mobile sensors is ubiquitous owing to its advantages over conventional sensors [3,4]. However, activity forecasting using sensor data is novel in this domain. The fourth Nurse Care Activity Recognition Challenge accommodates the challenge of predicting future activity employing prior information [5]. Many scholars in this area have published numerous accomplishments utilizing machine learning and deep learning approaches. Sozo Lab organized competitions in healthcare activity recognition to enhance the service quality of care facilities. In 2021, the winner of the competition [6] proposed a features-based approach to identify complicated nurses' actions using the Random Forest Classifier (RFC) utilizing raw accelerometer data [7]. They adjusted the hyper-parameters of their models and experimented with various window settings while segmenting the raw data. The author of Ref. [8] offered different feature extraction approaches, a feature selection methodology, and a Light Gradient Boosting Classifier to attain outstanding results. In Ref. [9] paper, the author proposed several signal processing techniques and overlapping windowing approaches to identify the nurses' activities using RFC. Arafat Rahman [11] presented a cost-sensitive hybrid ensemble classifier to handle the imbalanced class issue in the nursing care domain. They also integrated several base classifier outputs using a stacked generalized technique.

For classification issues employing the RFC in the competition of 2020, the authors of Ref. [10] used a feature-based conventional machine learning model. They attained a reasonable accuracy of 65% using a stratified 10-fold cross-validation method. They used an RFC from another algorithmic pipeline provided by Ref. [11] for their re-sampling, feature selection, and validation, and they achieved a cross-validation accuracy of 65.9%.

In the 2019 competition, the authors of Ref. [12] used a collection of K-Nearest Neighbors (KNN) classifiers on various hand-created features extracted from raw data. Xin Cao et al. [13] provided another 3D motion capture pipeline based on the Spatial-Temporal Graph Convolutional Network (ST-GCN) to classify activities. For recognizing nurse action [14], presented a two-layer stacked Gated Recurrent Unit (GRU) module with a context attention mechanism.

When processing sensor data, deep learning-based models perform well compared to conventional machine learning models. Several deep learning models, including Convolutional Neural Networks (CNN) and Recurrent Neural Networks (RNN), have successfully recognized human behaviors in a recent study. Inoue et al. proposed that combining CNN and RNN architecture may perform with better precision [15]. Zia Uddin and Hassan [16] extracted the Gaussian kernel-based PCA features, fed them into the CNN architecture, and found promising results. With the ability to extract and categorize features, the author of Ref. [17] introduced a novel CNN architecture for multi-channel time series. They searched for a hidden pattern of human behavior across the model.

21.2 DATASET DESCRIPTION

The fourth Nurse Care Activity Recognition Challenge dataset comprises tri-axial accelerometer mobile sensors carried by caregivers. The positioning of the sensors (mobile) was at an arbitrary position, like a pocket. A total of 28 activities performed by the caregivers are further divided into the four major categories listed in Table 21.1.

TABLE 21.1   List of Activities Performed by Caregivers

Activity Name	Number of Activities	Label	Activity Description
Activity of direct care	18	1	Vital
		2	Meal/medication
		3	Oral care
		4	Excretion
		5	Bathing/wiping
		6	Treatment
		7	Morning gathering/exercises
		8	Rehabilitation/recreation
		9	Morning care
		10	Daytime user response
		11	Night care
		12	Nighttime user response
		13	Family/guest response
		14	Outing response
		19	Get up assistance
		20	Change dressing assistance
		21	Washing assistance
		27	Emergency response such as accident
Activities of residence cleaning	4	15	Linen exchange
		16	Cleaning
		23	Preparation and checking of goods
		24	Organization of medications
Documentation/ communication activities	4	17	Handwriting recording
		18	Delegating/meeting
		22	Doctor visit correspondence
		25	Family/doctor contact
Other activities	2	26	Handwriting recording
		28	Delegating/meeting

Five people participated in the 2022 challenge, and the data were acquired in May and June 2018. The training and test files are split such that the identical subject exists in both the training and test files. The training files provided us with both the accelerometer data (x, y, z) and label files in different folders. Both data and label files include the timestamp but are distinct in the format as well as different time-zone settings. The caregiver file comprises the activities list and their start and finish timings. Labels and data are combined to yield the (X, y) pair.

The test file comprises several hours of data for each day and we are required to forecast the following hour's data utilizing these prior sequences. In the submission file, they offer us the list of activities that we have to forecast using the test data. Each hour prediction output may contain the multiple activities performed within that particular hour which transforms our challenge into a multi-label classification/forecasting problem.

21.3 METHODOLOGY

The methodology lies at the core of each real-world problem-solving effort. A superior technique may boost productivity in any circumstance. In this part, we discussed our procedure for accurately classifying and predicting future activities in the nursing care area utilizing prior actions. Our paradigm is structured into numerous sections, including:

- Data pre-processing

- Problem formulation

- Sequences generation and features extraction

- Model development

- Training and evaluation

- Post-processing

Using the aforementioned techniques, we may forecast the caregiver's future behaviors within a certain hour by analyzing previous and current actions. Figure 21.1 depicts the process diagram of our proposed methodology.

21.3.1 Data Pre-Processing

Any methodology's novelty largely depends on how we pre-process the raw data. The better the pre-processing method, the better the models' performance. The dataset we have used consists of the training, test sets, and submission files. For the training and test dataset, they provide us with tri-axial accelerometer sensor data (x, y, z) as well as activity labels. The list of activities we must predict from the test data is included in the submission files.

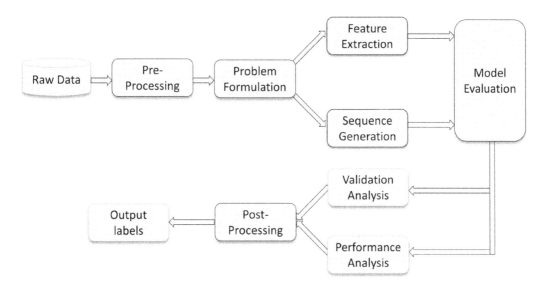

Figure 21.1 The workflow diagram of our proposed methodology.

The main challenges in this section deal with time-series data. The timestamp they have provided in the training as well as the test set have different timezone and different formatting. We at first converted all timezone into standard timezones like UTC. After that, we converted the all timestamp into same-time formatting. The treatment of the missing values is the second major challenge (i.e., missing timestamps or accelerometer data). Discarding the missing row is the simple solution to this issue. However, doing so will result in a reduction in the amount of the training data, which is unsatisfactory for a generalized machine learning model. We have filled in the start and finish times to ensure that the missing row has the same statistics as the activity performed by the same subject. Another good estimator can be the median of the period for that activity. The raw data must be filled in by the mean value of the particular activity performed by a specific subject.

After the data has been sorted, the raw data and labels have been combined. Numerous accelerometer data points without labels are also removed. In this circumstance, having many columns with identical start and end times is redundant. Additionally, the duplicated rows yield redundant features, which might cause the model to overfit, making the duplicated rows drop-outs.

21.3.2 Problem Formulation

Properly addressing and resolving problems in a real-world environment is the ultimate purpose of every challenge. The main objective of this challenge is to forecast future activities using knowledge from the present. Therefore, one such strategy is utilizing the accelerometer data to predict future actions. However, only one of the five users has 19 data segments that match the label files, which is insufficient to train a machine learning model.

That is why we merely made a future prediction using the label files. The start and finish times are the only information available for each activity, which is crucial for training the models. Therefore, the difficult but feasible approach is re-generating the underlying pattern using just the start and finish timings.

We are requested to forecast the activities of a certain hour in the submission file using data from previous actions. So, based on an hourly activity prediction, we may make a decision. To determine the hourly basis of activity forecasting, we have enumerated the activities performed within a certain hour. But the concern is, can the problem be generalized using the only available activity sequence? For this reason, we have generated the data and extracted a few statistical timestamps that could assist us in forecasting future action.

We first produce the period for an activity from the list of activities, together with their start and finish timestamps. Then, from the period, we retrieved several statistical features (such as mean, variance, median, and percentile). The Appendix contains a list of all generated timestamps and features.

In between the start and finish times, we have generated the hourly basis data (i.e., a list of the actions that occurred during that time). It produces several data samples that are used to train the model. Even if there may be no data on a given day, it is clear that the caregiver data is not continuous. The hourly basis activities will result in a large number of samples with no activity, which will cause our model to under-fit.

Therefore, we made the decision to incorporate the hours' data from the label files. We will get the n samples for the n hours of data by using this procedure. We will get a total of $(n-1)$ samples from n hours of data if we use the present activity to forecast the activity for the next hour. There is insufficient data in these $(n-1)$ samples. Because of this, we permit multiple prior sequences rather than simply one (the present sequence).

We will be able to more effectively generalize our issue and extend the sample size with the aid of the history of multiple sequences. However, how long will it take to include the prior sequences? Because the activities carried out on the previous day do not convey enough knowledge to forecast the actions on the next day, our approach is to permit the sequences to be constrained within that single day. How are the data samples (X, y pair) produced? A detailed explanation is provided below with illustrations.

For instance, from the 1st to $(n-1)^{th}$ sequence, we may predict the nth sequence (y) if we have total n sequences (n hours of data) (X). Sequences 2 through $(n-1)$ are then used to forecast the nth sequence, and so on. For the following prediction, the sequences 1 through $(n-2)$ must be used, and so on. This method enables us to combine n sequences into a total of $\frac{n \cdot (n-1)}{2}$ samples. Figure 21.2 visually represents this technique. These sequences are then used to extract the feature and input it into the machine learning models.

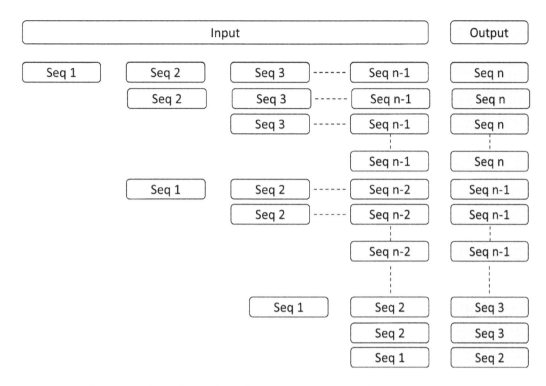

Figure 21.2 Sequence-based problem formulation approach.

21.3.3 Features Extraction

Dealing with time-series data is quite challenging. There are two sorts of methods for resolving this problem. The first is the training using raw data, while the second is the training utilizing the extracted features. Training with raw data is challenging since we must understand the models better. The models can automatically suppress the noise, conduct data standardization, and predict the hidden patterns, which need the model to be novel and scaleable. The second one is the manual feature extraction from the raw data, enabling the model to circumvent the various processes indicated above. On the other hand, feature extraction-based models require less computation power than deep-learning models.

The hourly basis sequences enable us to generate a list of actions encompassing that particular hour and transform the problem into multi-class multi-label classification problems. We extract features from the timestamps from the hourly-based activity forecasts, which helps us generate the final sequences (X) to train the models. Several temporal statistical features are retrieved from the timestamps data, which are the time-period data. Finally, from each period, we estimated the features such as an hour, minute, and second. On the other hand, we have extracted some additional features from the date-time-related timestamp, including a week-day, days-in-a-month, and week. All the specifications of the features list are provided in the Appendix.

In addition, we have also incorporated the activity information into the features list. This activity information also helps to predict future activity or activity forecasting. As the activities are different for various users, the features' duration will also differ for different users. On the other hand, the activities list of each hour data has a different number of activities, resulting in dynamic length features for each data. The next part will present a novel way to alleviate this challenge.

21.3.4 Sequences Generation

Sequence classification has various real-world applications, including language translation, speech recognition, and numerous others. This problem's main challenge is dealing with the variable length input size. Similar to the language translation, each word is turned into an embedding vector similar to the feature space in our situation. Nevertheless, the feature vector has a variable input size in our instance.

We restrict the maximum number of segments to extract the features to handle the variable length input size. If an hour contains segments greater than the predefined MAX_SEG, the remaining segments are disregarded for feature extraction. On the contrary, if hourly data includes a segment more diminutive than the MAX_SEG, then the remaining segments are padded with the zero value to preserve the fixed input length.

However, we have designed our challenge to retrieve numerous historical data rather than a single-hour history (current hour). We have taken the maximum number of prior sequences to a specified value, which is often less than or equal to the MAX_SEQ value. To forecast a future value, if we have the length of the sequence less than the MAX_SEQ, the remaining sequences are padded to retain the constant input form, which is a precondition to training a machine learning model. The visual representation of the generation of sequences is depicted in Figure 21.3.

21.3.5 Model Development

Divide and conquer is one of the most fundamental issue-solving strategies for dealing with a sizeable, challenging task. The problem is separated into multiple sections and recombined to obtain the appropriate objective. In our challenge formulation phase, we formulated our challenge to have many actions in an hour. This issue is a multi-class classification/forecasting problem if there is a single action each hour. However, the problem has turned into a multi-class, multi-label problem to have many activities. We have addressed this challenge by utilizing machine learning approaches. In our dataset, we have trained three distinct models: Binary-Relevance, Classifier-Chain, and Label-Power-Set. The in-depth concepts of each paradigm are given below.

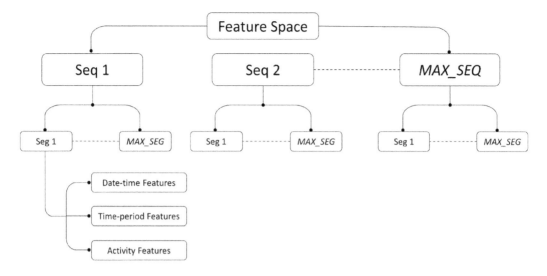

Figure 21.3   Generation of feature space utilizing sequences.

21.3.5.1   Binary Relevance

The Binary Relevance model works based on the divide and conqueror strategy. It turns the multi-label classification issue into a binary classification problem. A multi-label classification issue is converted into L different labels. It converts the problem into L independent binary classification problems. It utilized the same underlying classifier for all classification tasks. After that, all the forecasts are combined to get the final output. It takes the union of all classifier outputs.

21.3.5.2   Classifier Chain

The classifier chain model employs the chaining technique to generate the final result. For improved performance, the multiple classifiers are connected into a chain. The very first classifier is trained using the training data. The next classifier is generated using the combined input and the preceding classifier. In this sequential procedure, one classifier output is utilized as an input for the next classifier in the classifier chain. This model can preserve the correlation between labels.

21.3.5.3   Label Power Set

The Label Power Set concept translates multi-label classification into a multi-class problem. It regenerates the labels using a unique combination of labels retrieved from the dataset. The principal purpose of this model is to assign a new value to each unique label combination and fit the newly formed labels for categorization. Thus, the classifier has allocated the new value for categorization. This strategy tends to offer us more reliability.

21.3.6 Post-Processing

Post-processing techniques are necessary to improve the performance and robustness of any methodology. In general, both the computing cost and model complexity are improved. We used two post-processing techniques: feature selection and model ensemble. In this part, we thoroughly study how these methods assist us in achieving promising results.

21.3.6.1 Features Selection

The feature selection approach is quite efficient with large-scale features in the dataset. It assists us in identifying the crucial features within the feature space. This method lowers both the over-fitting issue and the cost of computing. In our instance, we chose the feature importance method for feature selection.

The Random Forest Classifier (RFC) uses a tree-based strategy to find the most important features. It naturally learns how to improve the purity of the node by decreasing the Gini Impurity over the nodes. The greatest impurity drop occurs at the beginning of the nodes, whilst the slightest impurity decrease occurs at the end. We obtain the subset of the most important features by pruning the trees below a particular node. The importance of features is shown in the result section.

21.3.6.2 Model Ensemble

An ensemble of models is a robust machine-learning technique that combines the output from different models to generate the final prediction. The ensemble members who contribute to the ensemble process are the same in our scenario. The ensemble process is done using statistical or more sophisticated methods that teach how much to trust each ensemble member.

Many methods, like averaging, max voting, and bagging, ensemble the members. We have used the max voting technique to generate the final prediction. In the problem statement, we have formulated that if there is total n hour data and we have to predict n^{th} hour activities, the prediction can be made using the total $(n-1)$ samples. Each $(n-1)$ samples can predict the nth sequence. After that, the predictions from these $(n-1)$ ensemble members are ensembled to generate the final prediction using the majority voting technique. The visual illustration of how the ensemble method is performed is shown in Figure 21.4.

21.4 RESULTS AND ANALYSIS

Analytical approaches aid in the identification of the problem and its solution. This section discusses the general performance of the various models, the rationale for their use, and numerous performance metrics.

Dealing with missing data is crucial in the pre-processing processes, as it enhances the overall performance of the models. Rather than discarding the missing values, we filled them with statistics such as the mean value. As a result, it increases

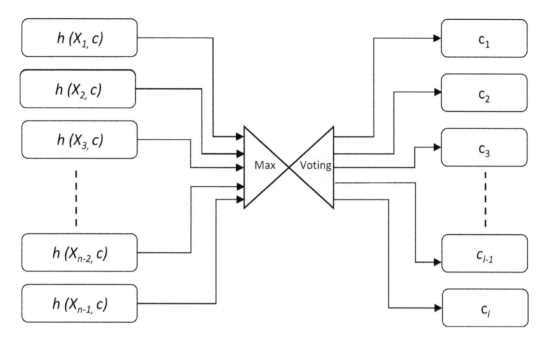

Figure 21.4 Ensemble of different output to generate final prediction.

the number of data samples and classification accuracy as well. The baseline model dramatically increases classification accuracy by exploiting missing variables (Binary Relevance using RFC as the base estimator without hyper-parameter tuning).

Due to insufficient samples of the raw accelerometer data, we have just utilized the care record data from the training and test files. At first, we trained our baseline model on Ref. [5] dataset as well as [6] dataset. We have obtained significant accuracy from both datasets. To test the robustness of our models, we have used different validation methods, as discussed in the methodology section. For the first time, we used a 20% random validation split to validate the models. The baseline model's accuracy (random split) for both datasets (including test data of Ref. [5]) are shown in Tables 21.2 and 21.3, respectively. We trained the model separately for each user since the submission files had a varying amount of actions for each user.

On both datasets, our baseline model performed well. Nevertheless, the question arises, "Can this model actually handle our classification tasks?" When we just changed our validation schema from random to date-wise (using 80% of the data for training and the remaining 20% for validation), the validation accuracy of baseline models deteriorated drastically. The date-wise validation accuracy for both datasets is provided in Tables 21.4 and 21.5.

However, how can we argue if our model is generalized or robust? The basic answer is yes, and our model is generalized and robust, as demonstrated in Tables 21.2 and 21.3. However, the low accuracy of the baseline model displayed in Tables 21.4 and 21.5 is due to a modest correlation between the activities performed on one

TABLE 21.2 Accuracy and Hamming Loss for Baseline Model Using 20% Random Validation Split on Dataset [5]

Dataset	Schema	Accuracy (%)					Hamming Loss				
		s8	s13	s14	s15	s25	s8	s13	s14	s15	s25
Dataset [5]	Train	81.51	84	82.91	92.30	82.2	0.184	0.201	0.164	0.077	0.178
	Test	82.32	79.89	83.51	87.43	81.50	0.176	0.164	0.164	0.125	0.185

TABLE 21.3 Accuracy and Hamming Loss for Baseline Model Using 20% Random Validation Split on Dataset [6]

Dataset	Schema	Accuracy (%)					Hamming Loss				
		s3	s6	s12	s19	s22	s3	s6	s12	s19	s22
Dataset [6]	Train	92.31	94.15	85.31	90.63	83.25	0.076	0.058	0.146	0.093	0.167

TABLE 21.4 Accuracy and Hamming Loss for Baseline Model Using 20% Date–Wise Validation Split on Dataset [5]

Dataset	Schema	Accuracy (%)					Hamming Loss				
		s8	s13	s14	s15	s25	s8	s13	s14	s15	s25
Dataset [5]	Train	7.23	11.11	32.41	24.24	8.25	0.927	0.888	0.675	0.757	0.917
	Test	4.20	10.40	34.17	42.3	10.42	0.958	0.896	0.658	0.577	0.895

TABLE 21.5 Accuracy and Hamming Loss for Baseline Model Using 20% Date–Wise Validation Split on Dataset [6]

Dataset	Schema	Accuracy (%)					Hamming Loss				
		s3	s6	s12	s19	s22	s3	s6	s12	s19	s22
Dataset [6]	Train	15.15	4.20	1.11	20.05	10.45	0.848	0.958	0.988	0.799	0.895

day and those conducted on another. The models (or even humans) will not be able to anticipate future actions in subsequent days by using the activities being conducted now.

Therefore, it is evident that the activities predicted for a time coincide with the activities carried out by the users on that day. Because of this, we solely used the test data to create the submission files. The test data, however, only contains a small number of samples, making it impossible to train the models. To address this issue, we developed a unique sequence-generating approach covered in the problem formulation section. This method allows us to create the $\frac{n \cdot (n-1)}{2}$ from n sequences. After that, we trained the various multi-label classifiers mentioned in the methods section. We also adjusted the hyper-parameter for the RFC and Adaptive Boost Classifier baseline estimators. There is a list of hyper-parameters in Appendix. The models are first trained using a 20% random validation split to identify the effectiveness before being trained using the whole dataset. In Table 21.6, the validation accuracy of several models for various subjects is shown.

Additionally, we evaluated the various performance metrics given in Appendix. Binary Relevance outperforms the other two models. The Binary Relevance model with an Ada-Boost Classifier outperforms the two baseline estimators. Table 21.7 illustrates several performance metrics for the Binary Relevance Classifier utilizing Ada-Boost as the baseline estimator.

We used our post-processing technique in the last stage to yield the final predictions. The total $(n-1)$ sub-sequences mentioned in the problem formulation section can be used to forecast the n_{th} sequence. The final predictions are then created by combining the predictions from all $(n-1)$ samples. The merging is done using the majority voting technique. The prediction using a sub-sequence t is denoted as $h(X_t, c_i)$ where $t = 1, 2, \ldots (n-1)$ and c_i is the prediction of ith class. The final predicted classes are the highest average scores calculated on all $h(X_t, c_i)$ sub-sequences predictions using the following equation:

$$c_i = \operatorname{argmax}_i \left(\frac{1}{(n-1)} \cdot \sum_{t=1}^{n-1} h(X_t, c_i) \right) \tag{21.1}$$

The performance metrics of Binary Relevance Classifier using Ada-Boost as the baseline estimator after performing the post-processing are shown in Table 21.8.

21.5 CONCLUSION

This research illustrates the capabilities of a machine learning model to predict a complicated caregiver's activities using a unique problem-solving strategy. We have acknowledged that the present activities substantially correlate with the actions conducted in the previous hours. The forecasting algorithms utilized the data on an hourly basis in our instance. However, there might be another technique other

TABLE 21.6 Performance Metrics of Different Classifiers without Hyper-Parameter Tuning Using Ada-Boost as the Baseline Estimator

Dataset	Schema	Model	Estimator	Sub	Performance Metrics	
					Accuracy (%)	Hamming Loss
Dataset [5]	Test: validation	Binary relevance	Random forest	s8	67.04	0.329
				s13	72.72	0.272
				s14	69.01	0.309
				s15	78.94	0.210
				s25	35.89	0.641
			Ada-Boost	s8	80.68	0.192
				s13	88.63	0.113
				s14	85.91	0.140
				s15	88.42	0.115
				s25	58.97	0.410
		Classifier chain	Random forest	s8	67.04	0.329
				s13	75.00	0.250
				s14	66.19	0.338
				s15	77.89	0.221
				s25	33.33	0.670
			Ada-Boost	s8	84.09	0.157
				s13	88.63	0.113
				s14	8169	0.183
				s15	87.36	0.126
				s25	53.84	0.461
		Label power set	Random forest	s8	81.82	0.182
				s13	84.09	0.159
				s14	80.28	0.197
				s15	81.05	0.189
				s25	53.85	0.462
			Ada-Boost	s8	15.91	0.841
				s13	36.36	0.636
				s14	14.08	0.859
				s15	54.74	0.453
				s25	20.51	0.795

TABLE 21.7 Performance Metrics of Binary Relevance Classifier Using Ada-Boost as the Baseline Estimator after Tuning Hyper-Parameters

Dataset	Schema	Sub	Performance Metrics					
			Accuracy	Sensitivity	Specificity	Precision	F1-Score	Hamming Loss
Dataset [5]	Test: valid	s8	99.91	90.93	99.76	97.65	94.17	0.001
		s13	98.88	86.84	99.72	95.65	91.03	0.011
		s14	98.20	90.86	99.28	94.84	92.81	0.017
		s15	99.05	93.75	99.71	97.56	95.61	0.009
		s25	98.99	88.47	99.65	94.07	91.18	0.010
	Test: train	All	100.0	100.0	100.0	100.0	100.0	0.000

TABLE 21.8 Performance Metrics of Binary Relevance Classifier Using Ada-Boost as the Baseline Estimator Using Post-Processing Technique (Max Voting)

Dataset	Schema	Sub	Performance Metrics					
			Accuracy	Sensitivity	Specificity	Precision	F1-Score	Hamming Loss
Dataset [5]	Test: valid	s8	100.0	100.0	100.0	100.0	100.0	0.000
		s13	99.32	89.45	99.86	96.42	92.11	0.006
		s14	98.27	90.92	99.32	94.96	93.02	0.017
		s15	99.18	94.05	99.78	96.82	96.57	0.008
		s25	99.12	88.75	99.77	94.82	92.07	0.009
	Test: train	All	100.0	100.0	100.0	100.0	100.0	0.000

than hourly, such as a quarter of the day or a minute basis. In this context, we have used the caregiver's data solely. Nevertheless, the accelerometer data is better associated with the activities performed by the subject if we can adequately preprocess it. We have employed a sequential-based method to mine data for our machine-learning models. Another data augmentation approach, such as Generative Adversarial Network (GAN), may provide more sophisticated and correlated data, a method of choice. We merely trained the typical machine learning model to predict future actions. Other sequential-based deep learning models may handle such scenarios, such as Gated Recurrent Unit (GRU) or Long Short-Term Memory (LSTM). We have just implemented the Gini impurity-based feature selection. However, additional feature selection approaches like variance thresholds, dispersion ratio, and recursive feature elimination may greatly assist us.

An interactive process between caregivers and patients is nurse care activity forecasting. For improved healthcare services, it establishes service standards. Identifying and defining the requirements for activity forecasting is made easier with the use of nursing activity forecasting. By adjusting certain variables (such as MAX_SEQ and MAX_SEG) to estimate future events, forecasting horizons for both the long-term and short-term may be established. Our proposed methodology, on the other hand, places a strong emphasis on creating healthcare activity forecasting by employing a straightforward sequential technique.

To generate the feature space, we have confined the maximum number of segments inside a specific hour to 15 and the number of sequences (history in an hour) to 10. We selected these numbers as the 75 percentile value for each situation. Any combination of MAX_SEG and MAX_SEQ may be selected to decide how our model performs. In the post-processing step, we employed ensemble techniques to give the final prediction. The ensemble is accomplished using the majority vote mechanism. However, ensemble approaches like weighted average or cost-sensitive learning are more robust.

The criteria described above may be implemented to increase the model performance. Addressing all the challenges is rather tough to integrate into our solution. In the future, we will address the issue of constructing a robust and generic activity forecasting model.

21.A APPENDIX

TABLE 21.A.1   List of Extracted Timestamps and Features

Serial	Scenario	Name	Total Features
1	Timestamp	start, finish, difference, mean, standard deviation maximum, minimum, median, range, percentile, z_score	
2	Features	year, month, day, quarter, day of week, day of the year, week of the year, days in the month, is month end, is month start is the quarter end, is the quarter start, week hour, minute, seconds periods of (hour, minute, second, total seconds)	637 / sequence
3	Feature Space		637*MAX_SEQ

TABLE 21.A.2   List of Hyper-Parameters

Serial	Scenario	Name	Values
1	Hyper-parameters	estimators	[RFC, Ada-Boost]
		max_depth	[500,1000,2000,5000, no. of features]
		max_features	[auto,500,1000,2000,5000, no. of features]
		n_estimators	[20, 50, 100, 200, 250, 500]
2	Best parameters	estimators	Ada-Boost
		max_depth	5000
		max_features	5000
		n_estimators	200

TABLE 21.A.3   Confusion Matrix

		Predicted	
		Positive	Negative
Actual	Positive	TP	FN
	Negative	FP	TN

Formulas for different performance metrics are given below

$$Accuracy = \frac{TP + TN}{TP + TN + FP + FN} \tag{21.2}$$

$$Sensitivity = \frac{TP}{TP + FN} \tag{21.3}$$

$$Specificity = \frac{TN}{TN + FP} \tag{21.4}$$

$$Precision = \frac{TP}{TP + FP} \tag{21.5}$$

$$F1 - score = \frac{2 \cdot Precision \cdot Sensitivity}{Precision + Sensitivity} \qquad (21.6)$$

$$HammingLoss = \frac{FP + FN}{TP + TN + FP + FN} \qquad (21.7)$$

TABLE 21.A.4   Miscellaneous Information

Name	Description
Dataset Used	Dataset [?,?]
Data Used	Only Caregivers' data
Model Types	Feature-based Machine Learning Model
Classification Model	Binary Relevance with Ada-Boost Classifier
Total Features	6370+ / sample
Post-processing	Yes
Performance Metrics	Accuracy, Sensitivity, Specificity, Precision, F1-Score, Hamming Loss
Device Specification	Google Colab
Programming Languages	Python and MATLAB
Library Used	Numpy, Pandas, Matplotlib, Scipy, sklearn, skmultilearn

BIBLIOGRAPHY

[1] Sozo Inoue, Paula Lago, Tahera Hossain, Tittaya Mairittha, and Nattaya Mairittha. 2019. "Integrating activity recognition and nursing care records: The system, deployment, and a verification study. *The Proceedings of the ACM on Interactive, Mobile, Wearable and Ubiquitous Technologies (IMWUT)* 3(3), 1–24, doi: 10.1145/3351244.

[2] Md Mamun Sheikh, Faizul Rakib Sayem, and Md Atiqur Rahman Ahad. 2021. "A residual network with focal loss to handle class-imbalance problem on nurse care activity recognition." In *2021 Joint 10th International Conference on Informatics, Electronics & Vision (ICIEV) and 2021 5th International Conference on Imaging, Vision & Pattern Recognition (icIVPR)*, Kitakyushu, Japan, pp. 1–8, IEEE.

[3] Martin Berchtold, Matthias Budde, Dawud Gordon, Hedda Rahel Schmidtke, and Michael Beigl. 2010. "ActiServ: Activity recognition service for mobile phones." *International Symposium on Wearable Computers (ISWC) 2010*, pp. 1–8, doi: 10.1109/ISWC.2010.5665868.

[4] Zhenyu He and Lianwen Jin. 2009. "Activity recognition from acceleration data based on discrete consine transform and SVM." *2009 IEEE International Conference on Systems, Man and Cybernetics*, pp. 5041-5044, doi: 10.1109/ICSMC.2009.5346042.

[5] Sozo Inoue, Defry Hamdhana, Christina Garcia, Haru Kaneko, Nazmun Nahid, Tahera Hossain, Sayeda Shamma Alia, and Paula Lago. May 22, 2022. "Fourth nurse care activity recognition challenge datasets." *IEEE Dataport*, doi: 10.21227/vchd-s336.s.

[6] Sayeda Shamma Alia, Kohei Adachi, Nhat Tan Le, Haru Kaneko, Paula Lago, and Sozo Inoue. April 29, 2021. "Third nurse care activity recognition challenge." *IEEE Dataport*, doi: 10.21227/hj46-zs46.s.

[7] Faizul Rakib Sayem, Md Mamun Sheikh, and Md Atiqur Rahman Ahad. 2021. "Feature-based method for nurse care complex activity recognition from accelerometer sensor." In *Adjunct Proceedings of the 2021 ACM International Joint Conference on Pervasive and Ubiquitous Computing and Proceedings of the 2021 ACM International Symposium on Wearable Computers*, New York NY, USA, pp. 446–451.

[8] M. Ashikuzzaman Kowshik, Yeasin Arafat Pritom, Md. Sohanur Rahman, Ali Akbar, and Md. Atiqur Rahman Ahad. 2021. "Nurse care activity recognition from accelerometer sensor data using Fourier- and wavelet-based features." In *Adjunct Proceedings of the 2021 ACM International Joint Conference on Pervasive and Ubiquitous Computing and Proceedings of the 2021 ACM International Symposium on Wearable Computers (UbiComp'21)*, Association for Computing Machinery, New York, pp. 434–439, doi: 10.1145/3460418.3479387.

[9] Zubair Rahman Tusar, Maksuda Islam, and Sadia Sharmin. 2021. "Accelerometer based complex nurse care activity recognition using machine learning approach." In *Adjunct Proceedings of the 2021 ACM International Joint Conference on Pervasive and Ubiquitous Computing and Proceedings of the 2021 ACM International Symposium on Wearable Computers (UbiComp'21)*, Association for Computing Machinery, New York, pp. 452–457, doi: 10.1145/3460418.3479390.

[10] Promit Basak, Shahamat Mustavi Tasin, Malisha Islam Tapotee, Md. Mamun Sheikh, A. H. M. Nazmus Sakib, Sriman Bidhan Baray, and M. A. R. Ahad. 2020. "Complex nurse care activity recognition using statistical features." In *Adjunct Proceedings of the 2020 ACM International Joint Conference on Pervasive and Ubiquitous Computing and Proceedings of the 2020 ACM International Symposium on Wearable Computers (UbiComp-ISWC'20)*, pp. 384–389, doi: 10.1145/3410530.3414338.

[11] Arafat Rahman, Nazmun Nahid, Iqbal Hassan, and Md Atiqur Rahman Ahad. 2020. "Nurse care activity recognition: Using random forest to handle imbalanced class problem." In *Adjunct Proceedings of the 2020 ACM International Joint Conference on Pervasive and Ubiquitous Computing and Proceedings of the 2020 ACM International Symposium on Wearable Computers (UbiComp-ISWC'20)*, pp. 419–424, doi: 10.1145/3410530.3414334.

[12] Md. Eusha Kadir, Pritom Saha Akash, Sadia Sharmin, Amin Ahsan Ali, and Mohammad Shoyaib. 2019. "Can a simple approach identify complex nurse care activity?" In *Adjunct Proceedings of the 2019 ACM International Joint Conference on Pervasive and Ubiquitous Computing and Proceedings of the 2019 ACM International Symposium on Wearable Computers (UbiComp/ISWC'19 Adjunct)*, pp. 736–740, doi: 10.1145/3341162.3344859.

[13] Xin Cao, Wataru Kudo, Chihiro Ito, Masaki Shuzo, and Eisaku Maeda. 2019. "Activity recognition using ST-GCN with 3D motion data." In *Adjunct Proceedings of the 2019 ACM International Joint Conference on Pervasive and Ubiquitous Computing and Proceedings of the 2019 ACM International Symposium on Wearable Computers (UbiComp/ISWC'19 Adjunct)*, pp. 689–692, doi: 10.1145/3341162.3345581.

[14] Md. Nazmul Haque, Mahir Mahbub, Md. Hasan Tarek, Lutfun Nahar Lota, and Amin Ahsan Ali. 2019. "Nurse care activity recognition: A GRU-based approach with attention mechanism." In *Adjunct Proceedings of the 2019 ACM International Joint Conference on Pervasive and Ubiquitous Computing and Proceedings of the 2019 ACM International Symposium on Wearable Computers (UbiComp/ISWC'19 Adjunct)*, pp. 719–723, doi: 10.1145/3341162.3344848.

[15] Masaya Inoue, Sozo Inoue, and Takeshi Nishida. 2018. "Deep recur-rent neural network for mobile human activity recognition with highthroughput." *Artificial Life and Robotics*, 23(2), 173–185.

[16] Md Zia Uddin and Mohammad Mehedi Hassan. 2019. "Activity recognition for cognitive assistance using body sensors data and deep convolutional neural network." *IEEE Sensors Journal*, 19, 8413–8419, doi: 10.1109/JSEN.2018.2871203.

[17] Charissa Ann Ronao and Sung-Bae Cho. 2016. "Human activity recognition with smartphone sensors using deep learning neural networks." *Expert Systems with Applications*, 59, 235–244, doi: 10.1016/j.eswa.2016.04.032.

CHAPTER 22

Predicting Nursing Care with K-Nearest Neighbors and Random Forest Algorithms

Jonathan Sturdivant, John Hendricks, and Gulustan Dogan

University of North Carolina

22.1 INTRODUCTION

Activity recognition, like other applications of machine learning, involves first training and then testing a model. The data is typically time-series data that is segmented into windows for feature extraction. Human activity recognition (HAR) applies this methodology to human behavior. It attempts to classify the activity performed by the subject based on input data, typically from video footage but also from accelerometer data and data from other kinds of sensors [1]. HAR remains a challenging field due to the complexity and variety of human behavior [2]. It has important applications in sports, video surveillance, and robotics, to name a few [3].

This field is especially relevant as it has the potential to improve healthcare services and reduce the workload of healthcare providers [4]. As people live longer, the elderly population in many countries is increasing. As a result, there is a demand for increased healthcare services for the elderly. Although research into HAR began in the 1990s, research into the application of HAR to healthcare is still novel [5]. One of the unique challenges to nursing care data is that there is a significant class imbalance, as well as large intra-class variability [6].

Various kinds of sensors have been applied to improve HAR [7]. In the Second Nurse Care Activity Recognition Challenge (2019), motion sensors such as mocap were used. Researchers have tested other types of sensors, such as ECG [8] and temperature [9], among others. However, the challenge last year and this year used only accelerometer data from a smartphone as the sensor. The rest of the data for this year's challenge is comprised of other types of information, such as the beginning and end of the activity, and with which patient the activity was performed.

DOI: 10.1201/9781003371540-25

Despite progress in HAR, challenges remain. Chen and Xue note that a common problem is feature extraction, especially since many human behaviors share similar movements and patterns. There is also a lack of data in HAR since collecting data is expensive and takes a long time [10]. Moreover, data collection can prove burdensome for both the nurses and the participants since this can involve frequent logging of their activities [5]. Therefore few publicly available datasets exist [6]. This is especially problematic for CNN, which requires large datasets to accurately perform. HAR has mainly been achieved under very simple tasks, e.g. sitting, walking, etc [10]. More complex activities remain a challenge as they require more context, such as an understanding of the relationship between the subject and the environment. There is also a need to reduce inherent noise in the signal, especially when working with accelerometer data [10].

The challenge this year tackles some of these problems. For example, predicting all activities performed hourly deals with the issue of multiple activities occurring at the same time. By using a smartphone to track data, nurses can work quickly while tracking their activity with a device they are familiar with. Our solution to this challenge was to create a traditional machine learning model that can predict which activities occur each hour based on date and time features. Our Random Forest Classifier (RFC) model achieved an average F1 score of 59.2% across all users on the training set.

22.2 DATASET

The data was acquired by the Kyushu Institute of Technology in May and June 2018, and was part of their study, "Integrating Activity Recognition and Nursing Care Records: The System, Deployment, and a Verification Study", on which the challenge is based upon. A single smartphone was carried by nurses during their daily work routine at a healthcare facility. It consists of accelerometer data and nurse care information, such as the type of activity performed, by who, and at what time.

The accelerometer data consists of a subject ID (the nurse providing care), the timestamp, and the triaxial acceleration. The nurse care date consists of the nurse's ID, the ID of the activity performed, as well as the start and end times of the activities. The timestamps of the accelerometer data do not align well with the timestamps of the activities performed. As a result, the data for analyzing accelerometer data is very limited, with only around ten or so matching timestamps for each nurse.

There were a total of 28 activities, which were categorized into four groups. This data is more limited than the previous challenge because twelve nurses were monitored the year before whereas there were five nurses (8, 13, 14, 15, 25) monitored this year. Some activities were performed frequently while many were rarely performed. The training and test files were separated by the date recorded, as well as the user ID.

22.3 RELATED WORK

Previous research in HAR has focused on predicting activities based on video sequences from visible-light cameras [11]. Researchers have also studied methods that require no video footage. Ignatov and Strijov used tri-axial accelerometer data to predict the activity of the user using a smartphone. The activities were either walking, jogging, stair climbing, sitting, or standing. They extracted the fundamental period from the time-series data in order to effectively segment the data. Next, they used an algorithm based on KNN to predict the activity performed, which achieved over 96% accuracy. Due to the small length of the segmentations, it is possible to use this algorithm for real-time activity recognition [12].

Friedrich et al. trained KNN classifiers on MoCap data to classify various activities as part of the *Bento Packaging Activity Recognition Challenge*. They used principal component analysis to reduce feature dimensions. They then trained a classifier for each feature and analyzed each possible combination of classifiers. The best performing feature was decided based on the results of this assessment. The best feature was 42% accurate on test data. The authors believe the next steps include building one-versus-all classifier to determine the best feature for each activity [13].

Adachi et al. used data augmentation to improve the accuracy of 3D pose estimation using single-camera video. They used video data from Berkeley Multimodal Human Action Database (HMAD) and used video from a single camera to determine the pose at each frame. Random Forest with Gini criterion was used for 2D poses, 3D poses, and 3D poses with data augmentation. The training data was augmented by rotating the pose around the z-axis. Accuracy improved by up to 55.7% using data augmentation [14].

Adachi et al. applied learning using privileged information (LUPI) to activity recognition of complex activities. LUPI approaches machine learning problems by adding additional (privileged) information to exclusively the training data, and only the original information to the test data. The privileged information in this case was additional sensor positions. The original and privileged data were trained using SVM+, a LUPI classifier. The authors then built an ensemble classifier that combined SVM+ with a baseline model, SVM. First, they trained SVM using (x, y). Then they trained SVM+ using $(x, x*, y)$, then combined the two with ensemble averaging. Four different data sets were used, comprised of both simple and complex activities. SVM+ showed less accuracy than SVM, which suggests no benefit to using LUPI. The performance of the ensemble was slightly higher than SVM, but this result could be due to the use of the ensemble rather than the use of LUPI. Therefore, the authors do not yet recommend LUPI for classifying complex activities like nursing behavior [15].

Deep architecture has also been used, but requires a large dataset. Chen and Xue 2015 used a CNN model on tri-axial acceleration signals and achieved 93% accuracy. The dataset consists of 31,688 samples from eight activities [16]. This sharply contrasts the dataset from this challenge, which consists of a few usable samples from 28 activities, some of which were not performed at all.

Accelerometer data has been paired with data from sensors to optimize activity recognition of nurse activity. In "Multimodal transformer for Nurse Activity Recognition", a multi-modal transformer network was used to fuse accelerometer data and spatio-temporal skeletal features to perform activity recognition. This approach outperformed the single-modality approach. Their model performed better than current GRUs, ST-GCNs, and KNNs [17]. Sensors were not applied in the challenges from last year or this year, which limits the amount of data accessible for training models.

Faiz et al. performed multilabel classification on nursing data using position sensors and absolute pressure sensors, including temperature measurement. Activities were split into 60s time windows. They approached the problem as multiclass and multilabel. Random Forest and Binary Relevance performed poorly, whereas Random Forest SRC performed well. The authors attribute the success to Random Forest SRC to the use of the Gini index. Random Forest SRC had above 70% accuracy on average for each nurse. These results suggest that multilabel classification can adequately classify nurse care data [18].

The dataset this year is similar to that of the year before. The summary paper for last year noted several challenges their dataset had in terms of activity recognition. Dataset had several null values, the duration of activities varied and the frequency of activities varied as well, and some samples were unlabeled.

Team Horizon tested Random Forest Classifier (RFC), XGBoost classifier (XGB), K-Nearest Neighbors (KNN), and Support Vector Classifier (SVC), with RFC performing the best. Linear interpolation was used to find the best fit for data points. After segmentation, the sliding window approach was performed with different window sizes and step sizes. They found that a 10-second window with a 2-second step size performed best. Fast Fourier Transform was used on the time domain signals. Over 100 features were extracted, including kurtosis, mean, and standard deviation. The data were resampled using linear interpolation. A second-order Butterworth low-pass filter with a cut-off frequency of 3 Hz was implemented to remove noise from re-sampled data [6].

The data this year was taken from a previous work, titled "Integrating Activity Recognition and Nursing Care Records: The System, Deployment, and a Verification Study". The authors suggest extending the start and end times of the activities because they noticed that nurses would mark the start of an activity before beginning and mark an activity as having ended after the activity was completed. However, one risk of this strategy is overlapping activities [19], which was a challenge faced during this year's challenge.

22.4 METHODS

This section describes our proposed method for "The Fourth Nurse Activity Recognition Challenge" [20]. Due to difficulty matching enough of the accelerometer data to the provided timestamps we opted against using the accelerometer data in our implementation. Our process is as follows first we loaded in the training data from a single user. Then we converted the start and finish times of each activity to date time variables. Next, we created features from the start time of each activity. The created variables include year-month-date, hour, year-month-date-hour, and weekday. Next, we created a categorical variable for the time of day. We encoded any activity performed between 6 AM and 10 AM as morning, an activity performed between 10 AM and 4 PM as Midday, an activity Performed between 4 PM and 8 PM as Evening, and any activity performed between 10 PM and 6 AM as Night. A result data frame was then created by counting the number of times each activity occurred each hour and reducing any value greater than one to one. Duplicates were then dropped from the validation set. we created the two models and using 75% of the training data used as the experimental training set, we trained two models an RF classifier and a KNN classifier, and then tested the model on the remaining 25% of the data using fivefold cross-validation. We trained using a shared node of the Pittsburgh Supercomputing Center Bridges-2 system. The node contained eight NVIDIA Tesla V100-32GB SXM2 GPUs, 512GB of RAM, and Two Intel Xeon Gold 6248 CPUs. Training and Testing each took less than a second.

22.5 RESULTS

In this section, we discuss our experimentation using two different models: K-Nearest Neighbor classifier (KNN) and Random Forest Classifier (RFC).

Table 22.1 shows the results of our models during our validation, the RFC outperformed the KNN classifier. User 8 was the most difficult user to classify and had significantly worse results than the other users. We achieved a 0.47 F1 score on user 8. User eight had a higher variety of actions performed and more activities per hour when compared to the other users, which helps explain the lower results. The rest of the users had similar results to one another. We achieved an F1 score of 0.56 for user 25, user 15 had an F1 score of 0.62, user 13 had an F1 score of 0.64, and user 14 had an F1 score of 0.67. Our recall scores were lower than the precision, which suggests that our model was not making enough predictions. The results of our model on the testing data were an accuracy of 0.90 and an F1 score of 0.19. The high accuracy can likely be attributed to a high number of true negatives in the test set. The lower F1 score on testing can either be caused by low precision,

TABLE 22.1   Results for Random Forest Model

User	Precision	Recall	F1
8	0.62	0.42	0.47
13	0.64	0.63	0.64
14	0.82	0.60	0.67
15	0.71	0.61	0.62
25	0.64	0.57	0.56

low recall, or both. Based on the high accuracy results I believe the cause was low recall, which would reinforce that our model was not making enough predictions on the less represented categories.

22.6 DISCUSSIONS

The nurse care activity dataset was challenging. There were two challenges that we faced while creating this model. The first of the challenges was that nurses could report their actions at the end of their shift. Allowing a delay in reporting created inconsistencies in the timing of the activity and the related accelerometer readings. To solve this, we intended to increase the duration of activities. We could not find a window that would align the two data sources. After that, we decided to ignore the accelerometer data and see how far the activity data could get us on its own. The second challenge we faced was class imbalance. There was a class imbalance across all users. Most hours had at least one of activities 2, 4, or 12 occurring, while many other activities were hardly represented. As expected our model was much more effective at classifying the Activities with more support. After analyzing the previous Nurse Activity Recognition challenges, we noticed traditional machine learning generally performed better than deep learning and decided to use machine learning methods. To improve our methodology in the future we could utilize some resampling methods or change the class weights to favor the less frequent activities to reduce the effects of the class imbalance.

22.7 CONCLUSION AND FUTURE TASK

In this chapter, we used time-based features to create predictions of nurse activities using Random Forest. Of the two models, the Random Forest classifier performed the best. Some important observations have been noted that should be addressed to get better outcomes. A better result might be obtained if we had applied and used accelerometer data or resampled training data. In the future, we want to work on those issues and extract other important features. Furthermore, we want to implement other types of models. The recognition result for the testing dataset will be presented in the summary paper of the challenge [20].

ACKNOWLEDGMENT

Our heartfelt appreciation goes to the members of Mitsui Fudosan Co., Ltd., Kashiwano-Ha Farm Inc., Kashiwa-shi, National Agriculture and Food Research Organization (NARO, Tsukuba-shi, Japan), and The University of Tokyo who provided considered support, feedback, and comments. This work used the Extreme Science and Engineering Discovery Environment (XSEDE), which is supported by the National Science Foundation grant number ACI-1548562. Specifically, it used the Bridges-2 system, which is supported by NSF award number ACI-1928147, at the Pittsburgh Supercomputing Center (PSC).

BIBLIOGRAPHY

[1] M. Vrigkas, C. Nikou, and I. A. Kakadiaris, "A review of human activity recognition methods," *Frontiers in Robotics and AI*, vol. 2, pp. 1–28, 2015.

[2] E. Kim, S. Helal, and D. Cook, "Human activity recognition and pattern dis- covery," *IEEE Pervasive Computing*, vol. 9, no. 1, pp. 48–53, 2010.

[3] S. K. Yadav, K. Tiwari, H. M. Pandey, and S. A. Akbar, "A review of multimodal human activity recognition with special emphasis on classification, applications, challenges and future directions," *Knowledge- Based Systems*, vol. 223, p. 106970, 2021.

[4] S. Inoue, N. Ueda, Y. Nohara, and N. Nakashima, "Mobile activity recognition for a whole day: Recognizing real nursing activities with big dataset," in *Proceedings of the 2015 ACM International Joint Conference on Pervasive and Ubiquitous Computing, UbiComp'15*, New York: Association for Computing Machinery, 2015, pp. 1269–1280.

[5] S. S. Alia, K. Adachi, T. Hossain, N. T. Le, H. Kaneko, P. Lago, T. Okita, and S. Inoue, *Summary of the Third Nurse Care Activity Recognition Challenge: Can We Do from the Field Data?* New York: Association for Computing Machinery, 2021, pp. 428–433

[6] F. Sayem, M. M. Sheikh, and M. A. R. Ahad, "Feature-based method for nurse care complex activity recognition from accelerometer sensor," *UbiComp '21: Adjunct Proceedings of the 2021 ACM International Joint Conference on Pervasive and Ubiquitous Computing and Proceedings of the 2021 ACM International Symposium on Wearable Computers*, New York: Association for Computing Machinery, September 2021, pp. 446–451.

[7] M. M. Hassan, M. G. R. Alam, M. Z. Uddin, S. Huda, A. Almogren, and G. Fortino, "Human emotion recognition using deep belief network architecture," *Information Fusion*, vol. 51, pp. 10–18, 2019

[8] R. Jia and B. Liu, "Human daily activity recognition by fusing accelerometer and multi-lead ecg data," in *2013 IEEE International Conference on Signal Processing, Communication and Computing (ICSPCC 2013)*, KunMing, China, 2013, pp. 1–4.

[9] A. Barna, A. K. M. Masum, M. E. Hossain, E. H. Bahadur, and M. S. Alam, "A study on human activity recognition using gyroscope, accelerometer, temperature and humidity data," in *2019 International Conference on Electrical, Computer and Communication Engineering (ECCE)*, Cox'sBazar, Bangladesh, 2019, pp. 1–6

[10] K. Chen, D. Zhang, L. Yao, B. Guo, Z. Yu, and Y. Liu, "Deep learning for sensor-based human activity recognition: Overview, challenges, and opportunities," *ACM Computing Surveys*, vol. 54, no. 4, pp. 1–40, 2021.

[11] K. Aggarwal and L. Xia, "Human activity recognition from 3D data: A review," *Pattern Recognition Letters*, vol. 48, pp. 70–80, 2014.

[12] A. D. Ignatov and V. V. Strijov, "Human activity recognition using quasiperiodic time series collected from a single tri-axial accelerometer," *Multimedia Tools and Applications*, vol. 75, no. 12, pp. 7257–7270, 2016.

[13] B. Friedrich, T. Orsot, and A. Hein, Using K-nearest neighbours feature selection for activity recognition, in M. A. R. Ahad, S. Inoue, D. Roggen, and K. Fujinami (eds), *Sensor- and Video-Based Activity and Behavior Computing*. Singapore: Springer Nature, 2022, pp. 217–225.

[14] K. Adachi, P. Lago, T. Okita, and S. Inoue, *Improvement of Human Action Recognition Using 3D Pose Estimation*. Singapore: Springer, 2021, pp. 21–37.

[15] K. Adachi, P. Lago, Y. Hattori, and S. Inoue, Using LUPI to improve complex activity recognition, 2022, pp. 39–55.

[16] Y. Chen and Y. Xue, "A deep learning approach to human activity recognition based on single accelerometer," in *2015 IEEE International Conference on Systems, Man, and Cybernetics*, Hong Kong, China, 2015, pp. 1488–1492.

[17] M. Ijaz, R. Diaz, and C. Chen, "Multimodal transformer for nursing activity recognition," in *2022 IEEE/CVF Conference on Computer Vision and Pattern Recognition Workshops (CVPRW)*, New Orleans, LA, 2022.

[18] F. Faiz, Y. Ideno, H. Iwasaki, Y. Muroi, and S. Inoue, Multilabel classification of nursing activities in a realistic scenario, 2021, pp. 269–288.

[19] S. Inoue, P. Lago, T. Hossain, T. Mairittha, and N. Mairittha, "Integrating activity recognition and nursing care records: The system, deployment, and a verification study," *The Proceedings of the ACM on Interactive, Mobile, Wearable and Ubiquitous Technologies (IMWUT)*, vol. 3, no. 3, pp. 1–24, 2019.

[20] D. Hamdhana, C. Garcia, N. Nahid, H. Kaneko, S. A. Alia, T. Hossain, and S. Inoue, "Summary of the fourth nurse care activity recognition challenge - predicting future activities," in M. A. R. Ahad, S. Inoue, G. Lopez, and T. Hossain (eds.), *Human Activity and Behavior Analysis: Advances in Computer Vision and Sensors*, pp. 416–432, Boca Raton, FL: CRC Press, 2024.

CHAPTER 23

Future Prediction for Nurse Care Activities Using Deep Learning Based Multi-Label Classification

Md. Golam Rasul

Universitat Potsdam

Wasim Akram and Sayeda Fatema Tuj Zohura

East West University

Tanjila Alam Sathi and Lutfun Nahar Lota

Islamic University of Technology

23.1 INTRODUCTION

The Human Activity Recognition (HAR) system has become a prominent field in the pervasive computing area [1]. HAR techniques can be used in health care, elderly care, human behavior analysis, robotics, arts and entertainment, security, and surveillance domain. HAR brings patients and physicians close for real-time monitoring in healthcare management [2]. Prediction of future occurrence of the activities is an addition of activity recognition that can forecast persons' behaviors in advance and it is beneficial to detect human intention as it can be applied to criminal detection, driver behavior prediction, and smart services [3]. Future activity prediction in health care monitoring and management will help patients to conduct their lifestyle and give the power to their nurses or care givers to accurately monitor and understand them.

The growth made in the human activity recognition system during the last few years motivates researchers to make progress in recognition performance. Traditionally, the human activity recognition problem is often seen as one of the certain applications of time series data analysis [4]. Some research studies on predicting future values of time series data used recurrent neural networks (RNNs), EM algorithm, ARIMA algorithm, and convolutional neural networks(CNN) [5–7]. Probability-based algorithms such as dynamic Bayesian network (DBN), independent predictor (IP), and recurrent activity predictor (RAP)[8,9] are the most common techniques used in HAR Systems.

Predicting the future occurrence of nurse care activities is very complex due to the nature of the data, which is very noisy. Another challenge that makes HAR systems complex is different patterns of performing the same activity by different nurses. Moreover, traditional HAR systems are multi-class classification, whereas future activity prediction is a multi-level classification problem. Multilevel classification in time series data is another challenging task. Four Nurse Care Activity Recognition Challenge [10] aims to mitigate the challenges, by predicting next activities, using the given dataset consisting of care record data and accelerometer data, collected from smartphones.

Considering the aforementioned challenges this chapter focuses on future activity prediction using deep learning model for Multi-label Classification (MLC). Inputs for the model are segmented time series data of previous hours and outputs are predefined future activities for next hour, for a particular patient, performed by a nurse. One major contribution of the paper is converting the given dataset into a binary dataset for fitting into a MLC model. The second contribution is using the MLC model for future activity prediction outperforming the given baseline score for the Fourth Nurse Care Activity recognition Challenge [10].

23.2 RELATED WORK

Human Activity Recognition (HAR) is a very challenging task due to the nature of the data. Most of datasets are highly imbalanced, noisy and time frames are overlapped. To solve the HAR problem traditional machine learning models with necessary feature extraction and several deep learning models, transfer learning models and multi-level classifier are used. Mohamed et al.[1] applied a multi-label classification approach to recognize various physical human activities with different sensor placements using accelerometer sensor data. They used a Label Combination (LC) approach and incorporated with several well-known base classifiers such as rotation forest (RF), support vector machine (SVM), decision tree (J48), and multilayer perceptron (MLP). To implement LC approach they converted the features into a multilevel vector and outputs the most probable class, which is actually a set of labels.

In Ref. [2] authors discussed data mining techniques such as artificial neural networks (ANN), K-Nearest-neighbors(KNN), support vector machine (SVM), C4.5 (J48) decision tree, classification and regression tree (CART), random forests (RF), rotation forest (RoF), etc. They applied the methods in MHEALTH dataset containing 12 physical activities. Random Forrest and Support Vector machine outperformed the other techniques in their study.

There has not been much work found for future activity prediction. Very few methods and techniques are discussed here on future activity recognition. Vito Magnanimo et al. [9] used Dynamic Belief Networks(DBN) for estimating the current task and predicting the most probable future pairs of action-object they validated their study on three typical tasks of a kitchen scenario. In Ref. [11] also used DBN for identifying nursing care activity recognition. In Ref. [12] used deep learning models for idetifying future terrorist activities.

The use of several deep learning methods like LSTM, BiLSTM, CNN, and RNN is becoming famous in Human Activity recognition domain. In Ref. [13] authors propose a Gated Recurrent Unit (GRU) model with an attention mechanism to recognize the nurse's activities. In Ref. [14] used CNN after necessary pre-processing like noise reduction, duplication removal, segmentation, standardization, etc., and achieved 91% accuracy using second nurse care activity recognition challenge data.

23.3 METHODOLOGY

In this section, the proposed method for future activity prediction for the fourth nurse care activity recognition using Multi-Label Classification (MLC) is explained comprehensively.

23.3.1 Data Preprocessing

The dataset provided for the fourth nurse care activity recognition challenge [10] consists of accelerometer data and care record data of five users (8, 13, 14, 15, 25). We only worked with care record data. Since the given timestamp of accelerometer data is not matched with the timestamp of care record data, we could not use accelerometer data.

The data is preprocessed and converted the data into binary format to fit into our MLC model. Each column is divided into multiple columns and then set the binary TRUE (1) in the necessary position. For example, "year-month-date-hour" column is divided into four separate columns "year", "month", "date", and "hour". After that, each of the column is divided into multiple columns like dividing month into 12 columns. As the whole dataset provided for 2018 year's data, we only kept single column for year. The date is divided into 31 columns, in the same way the hour is divided into 24 columns. In this way, a total of 68 binary input columns are obtained. The binary preprocessed data is represented in Table 23.1.

One of the major problems in the dataset was overlapping time frame which means in a single hour various activities can occur. To solve this issue, we squeezed

TABLE 23.1   Preprocessed Dataset

	Act	y	m1.	m12	d1.	d31	h0.	h23	act1.	act28
2018-1-1-5	1, 5, 9	1	1	0	1	0	0	0	1	0
2018-3-8-0	5, 2 , 28	1	0	0	0	0	1	0	0	1

the rows of year-month-date-hour which represents same hour, into one row and listed all the activities that happened in that particular time frame. The model is trained using this preprocessed care record data.

23.3.2 Proposed Method

In this research, a multi-label classification with deep learning model is proposed to predict the future nurse care activities. Traditional neural network model is configured to fit in a MLC problem.

23.3.2.1 Multi-Label Classification (MLC)

Formally, multi-label classification can be described as a problem to identify a model that sets zero or one for each label, in the output of binary vector Y for particular inputs X. In normal classification techniques, class labels are mutually exclusive but when it is multi-label classification it demands specialized ML algorithms that confirm the prediction of multiple mutually non-exclusive classes. The MLC approach efficiently reduces efforts and time and also handles the complexity of big dataset. Conventionally defining MLC, binary vector Y and input X mentioned above, there is a pattern of class labels $Y_1 : J = Y_1, Y_2, Y_3 \ldots, Y_J$ where $Y_1, K = 1, 2, 3 \ldots, J$ are multi-label vectors and it explains the pattern. When every node has one or more class labels, it enables MLC to learn properly from some set of input signals. Binary cross-entropy loss function, ReLU activation function, and Sigmoid activation function have been used in the proposed MLC method with deep learning model. These functions are discussed in the next sub-sections.

23.3.2.2 Binary Cross-Entropy Loss Function

Binary cross entropy measures every predicted probability from the actual class output that can be either 0 or 1. It calculates the score of probabilities that how much far or close it is from the actual value. The score is calculated with the Equation 23.1

$$\text{Loss Function} = \text{Binary CrossEntropy}/\text{Log Loss} \qquad (23.1)$$

If Equation 23.1 returns lower score then it refers to good prediction. On the other hand, high score refers to bad prediction.

23.3.2.3 Activation Function (ReLU)

Rectified Linear Unit, also known as ReLU is the most widely used activation function in the Neural Network Model. The Equation 23.2 acts as a non-linear activation function for negative values and linear function for positive values.

$$\text{Relu}(z) = \max(0, z) \qquad (23.2)$$

23.3.2.4 Activation Function (Sigmoid)

The sigmoid neuron is the building chunk of deep neural networks and they are similar to perceptrons. However, they are a little bit modified because the output from the sigmoid neuron is more balanced than the perceptrons. The Equation 23.3 represents the Sigmoid function.

$$\sigma(z) = \frac{1}{1 + e^{-z}} \tag{23.3}$$

Our proposed model will help to reduce the complexity of multi-label human activity recognition problem. The structure of the model is discussed in the System Architecture subsection.

23.3.2.5 System Architecture

Our proposed system architecture of Multi-Label Classification with neural networks is demonstrated in Figure 23.1.

From the preprocessed squeezed datasets, 68 columns will be fed into the model as input. Two hidden layers are used in the model. In the first hidden layer, we use Dense Layer which consists of 68 neurons and later Relu Activation function is applied. For second hidden layer, another Dense Layer has been used which consists of 28 neurons and Sigmoid Activation function is incorporated later. Binary_Cross entropy loss function is used and for optimizing the loss and Adam optimizer is used with the learning rate 0.01. Figure 23.2 describes the summary of the model.

23.4 EXPERIMENT AND RESULTS

To evaluate our MLC model, experiments were performed on the dataset, provided for the fourth nurse care activity recognition challenge. In this section, we will mainly focus on the datasets and look over the interesting patterns and observations of the experiment results.

23.4.1 Dataset Description

Accelerometer data were collected using smartphones, with the help of nurses and caregivers while they were on their regular duty. The device was placed at some random position of the body. Total 28 types of activities happened during the data collection process which can be categorized into 4 groups. Activities 1–14, 19–21, 27 were grouped into category "Activities of Direct Care"; 15, 16, 23, 24 into category "Activities of Residence Cleaning"; 17, 18, 22, 25 into "Documentation/ Communication Activities"; 26, 28 into "Other Activities".

The dataset contains both care record data and Accelerometer data. Only care record data was utilized for the experiment. The data consists of five different users/nurses (8,13,14,15,25). These data were gathered and piled up on the time frame between May and June 2018. We preprocessed all the datasets and converted

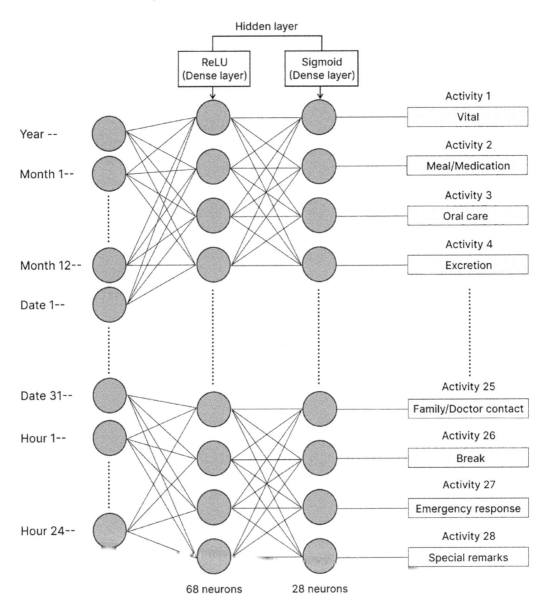

Figure 23.1 MLC with deep learning model.

all the values into Binary format to feed the data into our model. The preprocessed part is already described in detail in Section 23.3.1. After pre-processing, we got five other new datasets for each user. We squeezed the rows representing the same time frame (hour basis), resulting lower number of rows compared to the original care record data. As a result, the complexity of the datasets was reduced, producing more readable data for our experiment. After squeezing all the activities listed on that particular time frame helped our model to predict future activities. Table 23.2 describes the comparison of the original datasets with the preprocessed datasets.

TABLE 23.2   Preprocessed Datasets Comparison with the Original Care Datasets

	User 8	User 13	User 14	User 15	User 25
Original	3632	2186	3373	1029	765
Preprocessed	153	91	146	167	82
Squeezed (%)	4.2	4.1	4.3	16.2	10.7

23.4.2 Experimental Setup

To train the model, we used Google Colab and it's system specification is 2vCPU@2.2 GHz, Ram: 13 GB, Disk: 100 GB. We split the dataset into 70%–30%, which means 70% was kept for training and the rest of the data were used for validation. A binary cross-entropy loss function has been used in our model. We used Adam optimizer with 0.01 learning rate in our experiment and batch size was 30 with 100 epoch. Average computational time for all users is 11.8 seconds while training.

23.4.3 Result Analysis

Squeezed preprocessed datasets were used for the experimentation. The following metrics are used to analyze our model robustness towards the result: Accuracy, Precison, Recall, F1-Score, and AUC-Score. We calculated each of the metrics for all five users. The following five users accuracy result: 46% (user8), 65% (user13), 59% (user14), 76% (user15) and 67% (user25). After averaging all of the user metrics, we got the following result: 63% Accuracy, 72% Precision, 61% Recall, 65% F1 Score, 78.8% AUC score. Our result actually turned out very good compared to the given user wise challenge baseline scores. Figure 23.3 demonstrates the comparison between the user-wise metrics produced by our model with the baseline score.

To get an overall idea of the efficiency of our model, we averaged all user metrics and compared with the baseline scores. From Figure 23.3, it is clearly shown that our proposed model performed better than baseline scores.

```
Model: "sequential"

_____
 Layer (type)              Output Shape              Param #
=================================================================
 dense (Dense)             (None, 68)                4624

 dense_1 (Dense)           (None, 28)                1932

=================================================================
Total params: 6,556
Trainable params: 6,556
Non-trainable params: 0
```

Figure 23.2   Model summary.

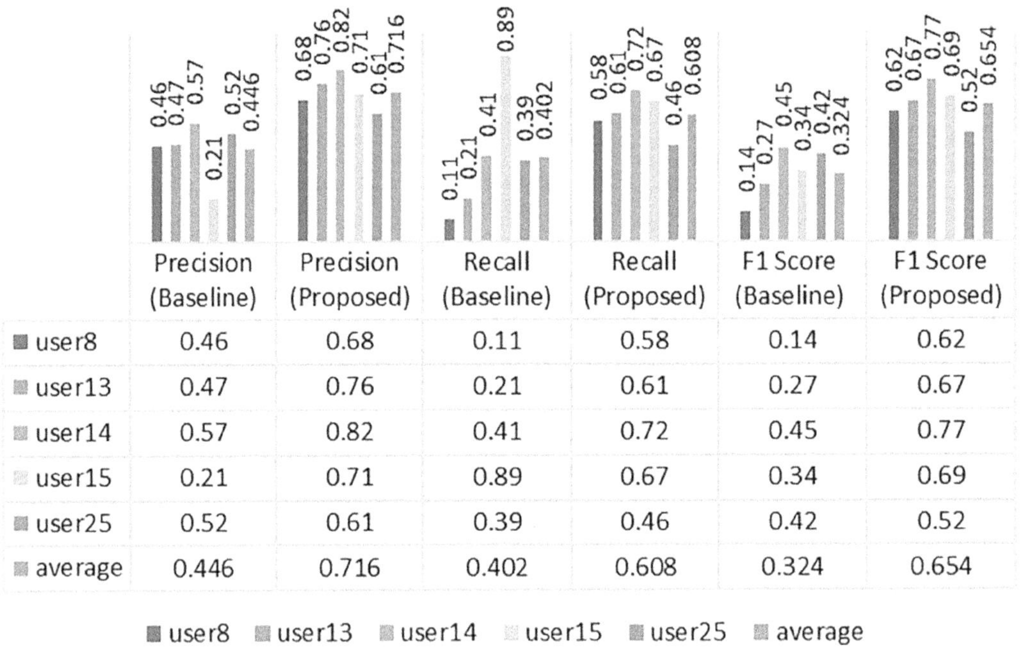

	Precision (Baseline)	Precision (Proposed)	Recall (Baseline)	Recall (Proposed)	F1 Score (Baseline)	F1 Score (Proposed)
user8	0.46	0.68	0.11	0.58	0.14	0.62
user13	0.47	0.76	0.21	0.61	0.27	0.67
user14	0.57	0.82	0.41	0.72	0.45	0.77
user15	0.21	0.71	0.89	0.67	0.34	0.69
user25	0.52	0.61	0.39	0.46	0.42	0.52
average	0.446	0.716	0.402	0.608	0.324	0.654

■ user8 ■ user13 ■ user14 ■ user15 ■ user25 ■ average

Figure 23.3 Metrics comparison between baseline scores and proposed scores.

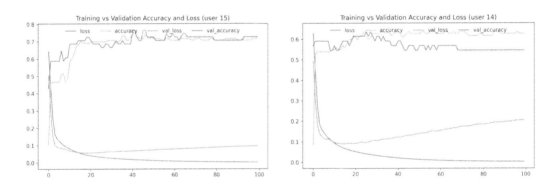

Figure 23.4 Training vs validation accuracy and loss.

We have also inspected our model performance by generating the accuracy and loss graph for each user but due to the space limitation, we only demonstrated graphs for only users 14 and 15. We used 100 epochs to investigate our model. From the Figure 23.4, for user 14, training accuracy is higher than the validation accuracy. This scenario happens when the model is over-fitted. Users 8, 13, and 25 also followed the same pattern. On the other hand, user 15 followed opposite direction. From Section 23.4.1, we also know that user 15 has the highest squeezed preprocessed data. It concludes that our model performed best for user 15 compared to the other users. Our model is struggling when the dataset has less data which also explains that if we have enough data our model can perform on unseen data and predict future activities on a specific time frame.

For further analysis, we conducted experiment by generating the confusion matrix activity wise for each user. Our model produced 28×28 confusion matrix. Diagonally elements of the confusion matrix represent the model performance. Figure 23.5 represents the confusion matrix of user 15. Out of total (167) pre-processed data , 30% data (51) were used for validation.

Our model was able to predict 39 data correctly out of 51 with the 76% accuracy. Activities 1, 2, and 12 were predicted correctly most of the time, whereas activity 1 is recognized as activity 11 for 3 times. The reason behind the perfect prediction for Activity 12 was the availability of sufficient data. The model was struggling to predict other activities correctly because of the imbalanced dataset.

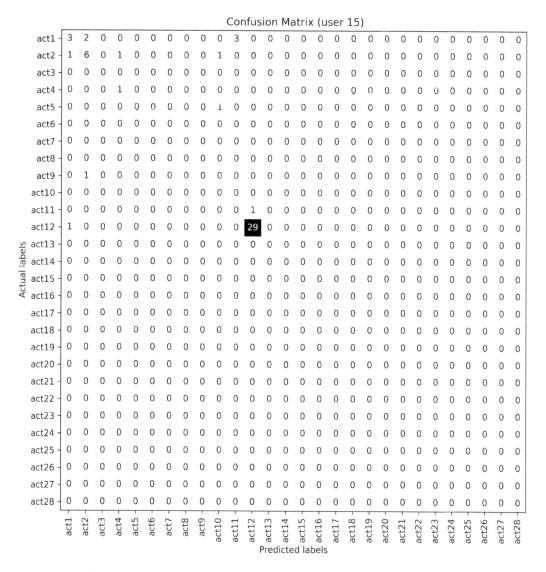

Figure 23.5 Confusion matrix gained by the MLC deep learning method.

23.5 CONCLUSION AND FUTURE WORK

In this research, a multi-label classification approach with deep neural network model is used for predicting future activities for Fourth Nurse Care Activity Recognition Challenge. The given dataset was converted to binary format to fit into our model. Sixty-three percent accuracy was achieved from our model in spite of having highly imbalance and noisy data. Later, our model was evaluated with the test results of 87% accuracy and 11% F1-score [10]. Improvement can be achieved by implementing data balancing techniques. However, our model was robust enough to produce good metric scores compared to the baseline scores, which can be effective for both future human activity recognition and multi-label classification.

BIBLIOGRAPHY

[1] Mohamed, R., Zainudin, M.N.S., Sulaiman, M.N., Perumal, T. and Mustapha, N., 2018. Multi-label classification for physical activity recognition from various accelerometer sensor positions. *Journal of Information and Communication Technology*, 17(2), pp. 209–231.

[2] Subasi, A., Radhwan, M., Kurdi, R. and Khateeb, K., 2018, February. IoT based mobile healthcare system for human activity recognition. In *2018 15th Learning and Technology Conference (L&T)*, Jeddah, Saudi Arabia (pp. 29–34). IEEE.

[3] Chen, K., Zhang, D., Yao, L., Guo, B., Yu, Z. and Liu, Y., 2021. Deep learning for sensor-based human activity recognition: Overview, challenges, and opportunities. *ACM Computing Surveys (CSUR)*, 54(4), pp. 1–40.

[4] Yang, J., Nguyen, M.N., San, P.P., Li, X.L. and Krishnaswamy, S., 2015, June. Deep convolutional neural networks on multichannel time series for human activity recognition. In *Twenty-Fourth International Joint Conference on Artificial Intelligence*, Argentina, pp. 3995–4001.

[5] Assaad, M., Boné, R. and Cardot, H., 2008. A new boosting algorithm for improved time-series forecasting with recurrent neural networks. *Information Fusion*, 9(1), pp. 41–55.

[6] Shumway, R.H. and Stoffer, D.S., 1982. An approach to time series smoothing and forecasting using the EM algorithm. *Journal of Time Series Analysis*, 3(4), pp. 253–264.

[7] Pavlyshenko, B.M., 2016, August. Linear, machine learning and probabilistic approaches for time series analysis. In *2016 IEEE First International Conference on Data Stream Mining and Processing (DSMP)*, Lviv, Ukrain (pp. 377–381). IEEE.

[8] Minor, B., Doppa, J.R. and Cook, D.J., 2015, August. Data-driven activity prediction: Algorithms, evaluation methodology, and applications. In *Proceedings of the 21th ACM SIGKDD International Conference on Knowledge Discovery and Data Mining*, Sydney (pp. 805–814).

[9] Magnanimo, V., Saveriano, M., Rossi, S. and Lee, D., 2014, August. A Bayesian approach for task recognition and future human activity prediction. In *The 23rd IEEE International Symposium on Robot and Human Interactive Communication*, Edinburgh (pp. 726–731). IEEE.

[10] Inoue, S., Lago, P., Hossain, T., Mairittha, T. and Mairittha, N., 2019. Integrating activity recognition and nursing care records: The system, deployment, and a verification study. *Proceedings of the ACM on Interactive, Mobile, Wearable and Ubiquitous Technologies*, 3(3), pp. 1–24.

[11] Inomata, T., Naya, F., Kuwahara, N., Hattori, F. and Kogure, K., 2009, May. Activity recognition from interactions with objects using dynamic bayesian network. In *Proceedings of the 3rd ACM International Workshop on Context-Awareness for Self-Managing Systems*, Nara, Japan, (pp. 39–42).

[12] Saidi, F. and Trabelsi, Z., 2022. A hybrid deep learning-based framework for future terrorist activities modeling and prediction. *Egyptian Informatics Journal*, 23(3), pp. 437–446.

[13] Haque, M.N., Mahbub, M., Tarek, M.H., Lota, L.N. and Ali, A.A., 2019, September. Nurse care activity recognition: A GRU-based approach with attention mechanism. In *Adjunct Proceedings of the 2019 ACM International Joint Conference on Pervasive and Ubiquitous Computing and Proceedings of the 2019 ACM International Symposium on Wearable Computers*, London, UK, (pp. 719–723).

[14] Rasul, M.G., Khan, M.H. and Lota, L.N., 2020, September. Nurse care activity recognition based on convolution neural network for accelerometer data. In *Adjunct Proceedings of the 2020 ACM International Joint Conference on Pervasive and Ubiquitous Computing and Proceedings of the 2020 ACM International Symposium on Wearable Computers*, Mexico, (pp. 425–430).

[15] Hamdhana, D., Garcia, C., Nahid, N., Kaneko, H., Alia, S.S., Hossain, T. and Inoue, S., 2024. Summary of the fourth nurse care activity recognition challenge: Predicting future activities. In Ahad, M.A.R., Inoue, S., Lopez, G. and Hossain, T. (eds.), *Human Activity and Behavior Analysis: Advances in Computer Vision and Sensors*. CRC Press, Boca Raton, FL, (pp. 416–432).

CHAPTER 24

A Classification Technique Based on Exploratory Data Analysis for Activity Recognition

**Riku Shinohara, Huakun Liu, Monica Perusquía-Hernández,
Naoya Isoyama, Hideaki Uchiyama, and Kiyoshi Kiyokawa**

Nara Institute of Science and Technology

24.1 INTRODUCTION

Activity recognition is a task to recognize predefined actions using sensors that collect time-series data, such as accelerometers and gyroscopes [2]. Their processing speed and miniaturization have improved in recent years, making them simpler to install than those that use images or LiDAR. Also, the hardware requirements have decreased. This advancement has made it a research field that has been attracting more and more attention in recent years. Human activity recognition is referred to as HAR (Human Activity Recognition). The HAR system is especially applied in hospitals and other institutions, where it is used for the care of elderly people and health care [6].

The HAR for practical scenarios has become very challenging in recent years. Competitions targeting the prediction of nurses' behavior have been held in 2019 [5], 2020 [4], and 2021 [2]. The datasets in these competitions were obtained from actual nurses in the hospitals [11]. The results of the teams participating in this competition were used to improve nurses' daily behavioral awareness. "The Fourth Nurse Care Activity Recognition Challenge" [10] is a competition to create predictive models in the HAR field, specifically for predicting nurse behaviors. In general, nurse behaviors are more complex than daily behaviors. This is due to the large number of actions that they need to perform per unit of time. These include taking vitals and responding to outpatient visits. Therefore, creating a predictive model

DOI: 10.1201/9781003371540-27

of nurses' behaviors is challenging. This competition aims to infer from 28 different activities nurses perform in an hour.

In "The Third Nurse Care Activity Recognition Challenge" last year, several teams made inferences using a random forest based machine learning model. Another team used the Light Gradient Boosting Machine classifier [17]. Further back in "The Second Nurse Care Activity Recognition Challenge", CNN [15] based models and Deep Learning [8] were used. The winning team of the year also used a CNN-based model. In addition, kNN was the most accurate model for that year's winning team [12]. It is not easy to interpret the prediction results in solving problems using these machine learning models. This is so-called black boxing. In recent years, research in explainable AI (XAI) has been active [16]. In this chapter, we create a predictive model based on exploratory data analysis (EDA) [7] that does not rely on machine learning methods.

24.2 EXPLORATORY DATA ANALYSIS

Exploratory Data Analysis (EDA) is one of the most important methods for creating a predictive model. In the dataset for the competition, nurse behavioral data were used in their unprocessed form. Therefore, careful data analysis is required. In this section, we analyzed the care record data for all users and for each user, including basic data analysis of missing values, duplicate data, and frequency analysis of activity labels. We also investigated the characteristics of acceleration data by clarifying the relation.

24.2.1 Dataset Description

The provided dataset consists of two types of data: a three-axis acceleration measured on a smartphone in a nurse's pocket of choice and a record of the nurse's activities in the hospital facility and elsewhere. The acceleration data consists of acceleration data along x, y, and z axes, the acquired date (datetime), and a user id (`subject_id`). The care record data consists of `id`, `user_id`, `activity_type_id`, `activity_type`, `target_id`, `start`, `finish`, and `year-month-date-hour` columns. For convenience, we refer to the acceleration data as "acceleration data" and the data including the activity label information as "care record data".

Those data were collected from nurses with user id (8, 13, 14, 15, 25) from February to July 2018. The data were also split into train and test data from February to May and May to July, respectively. The care record datasets are further divided into the following four categories.

- Activity of Direct Care (1–14, 19–21, 27)

- Activities of Residence Cleaning (15, 16, 23, 24)

- Documentation Communication Activities (17, 18, 22, 25)

- Other Activities (26, 28)

24.2.2 Care-Record Data

The analysis was first performed on the care record data. There are 10,985 cases of care record data available in the train data. Among them, 402 contain missing values. Similarly, the test data has 44 missing values out of 6643 cases. All missing values are present only in the "finish" column.

Next, the distribution of the frequency of each activity label is examined because this task is a multi–class classification. Many datasets offered in competitions like kaggle [1] are uniformly distributed in terms of class distribution because those datasets are pre-formatted beforehand. However, the dataset in the series of the challenges is obtained at the actual hospital [11] and nothing is altered. Therefore, the class frequency distribution might not be uniform. To create a prediction model with high generalization performance, it is essential to investigate these class frequency distributions in advance. The activity frequencies for train and test data are shown in Figure 24.1. The visualized graphs show a bias in the activity distributions in the training and test data.

We also visualized the activity frequencies for each user. The care record data contains the pairs of the user id and the performed activity labels. Therefore, the activity frequencies for each user can be obtained by summing up the number of activity labels for each user. In Figure 24.2, user 8 and user 13, user 14 and user 15 have similar activity frequency distributions. This distribution is similar not only for the training data but also for the test data. This result indicates that the nurse can be divided into several groups in terms of their activities. In many cases, two or more nurses are likely to take care of each patient. For example, when a nurse has to attend to each patient or when a nurse has to attend to the elimination of urine. Figure 24.2 suggests that several clusters exist among users and that users in the same cluster inevitably have a similar distribution of activity frequencies.

24.2.3 Acceleration Data

Similar data analysis was performed for the acceleration data, which consisted of four columns: datetime, accelerations in x, y, and z axes. The acceleration data were obtained from a smartphone acceleration in the nurse's pocket. These data contain many duplicates due to signal problems during acquisition. Of the total 54,182,553 duplicate data, 45,800,259 are duplicates. This indicates that only a small amount of data is available among the data provided.

Next, we analyzed the relationship between the acceleration data and the care record data. Not all of the duplicate data can be linked to all of the care record data provided. Therefore, we investigated how much acceleration data is available for each user and compared the start and finish datetime of the care record data with the datetime of the acceleration data. As a result, we found that the available acceleration data for each user was limited. The results are shown in Table 24.1. The total means the amount of acceleration data in each train and the test data period. The "kind" means how many different activity labels the acceleration data can be used. For instance, user_id 8 has no available acceleration data in the

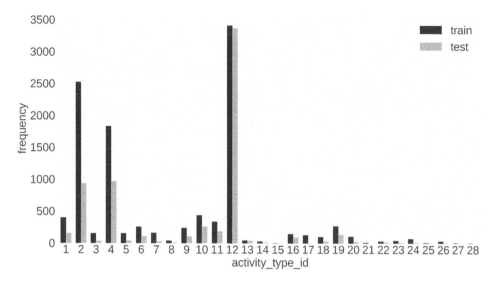

Figure 24.1　Activity frequency.

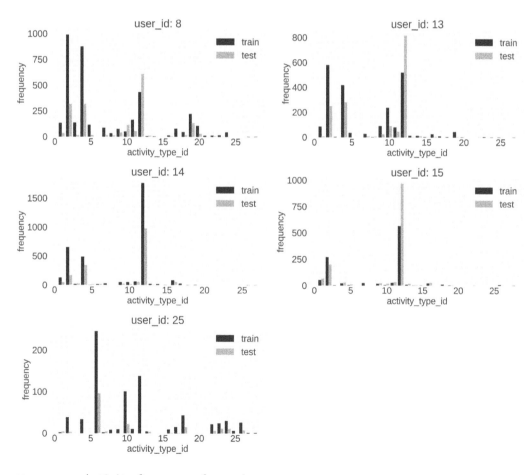

Figure 24.2　Activity frequency for each user.

TABLE 24.1 Available Acceleration Data in Each User

User_ID		Train	Test
8	Total	0	54
	Kind		1, 2, 4, 7, 8, 9, 10, 12, 13, 19, 20
13	Total	17	146
	Kind	2, 10	1, 2, 4, 9, 10, 11, 12, 14, 16
14	Total	13	464
	Kind	2	1, 2, 3, 4, 9, 11, 12, 13, 16
15	Total	29	0
	Kind	12, 16, 26	
25	Total	0	8
	Kind		6, 10, 18, 24

training period. Additionally, there are 54 available acceleration data and 11 types of activity labels that have the acceleration data in the test period.

24.2.4 Time Scale

We analyzed the activity duration. The activity duration is defined as the value obtained by subtracting the start column from the finish column of the care record data. We tried understanding the trend of the data based on the activity duration in Figure 24.3.

First, we look at the distribution of activity duration. The activity duration of nurses is considered to be the time required for each activity. For example, in many cases, break time is determined for breaks, and the activity duration distribution is expected to be constant. In the case of activities such as eating and taking medication, where one label includes two or more different activities, the distribution of activity duration is expected to have two or more peaks. This is because the time

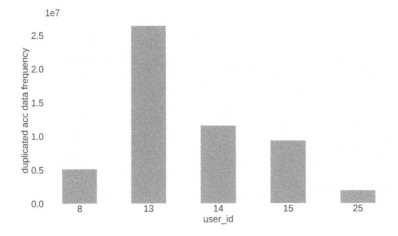

Figure 24.3 Acceleration duplicated data.

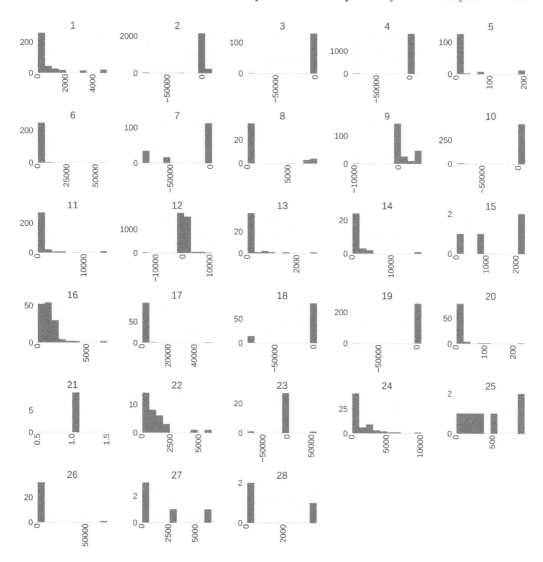

Figure 24.4 Time length of each activity.

required for each activity is different. The actual activity duration for each activity is shown in Figure 24.4. The activity duration is distributed differently for each activity. In addition, some of the data have negative or extremely long activity duration. This may be due to a manipulation error by the nurse. The nurses recorded the activity labels through their smartphones. Therefore, it is possible that some data may not be consistent due to human errors, such as nurses pressing the wrong button or forgetting to press a button.

The activity duration of the train data for the care record data was binned by an arbitrary range, as shown in Figure 24.5. The data in the 0–2, 100–1000, and 1000–10,000 second intervals had the most significant number of data. In general, the activity labels given in this study are all actions that require several to several

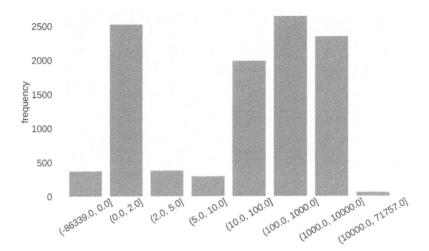

Figure 24.5 Time length bins.

tens of minutes. Among them, the data in the 0–2 second interval is primarily due to human error on the part of the nurses. It is thought that the existence of extremely short data labels was due to nurses being unfamiliar with the measurement system or not being adequately briefed.

Next, we analyzed the actual number of days recorded for each user. The care record data were obtained from approximately the beginning of February to the end of May. However, not all users have daily care record data for that period. Therefore, the number of days of measurement differs among users. User 8 has label data for almost all dates, while user 13 and user 15 do not have label data for all dates. Therefore, the model is generalized to user 8 if we create a prediction model for each user. To prevent this, clustering is used to divide users into several groups. We believe that clustering allows us to create a moderately high generalization performance model.

Finally, we analyzed the average activity duration for each activity. As mentioned above, there is variation in the activity duration. This may be because users are not thoroughly familiar with the measurement system, and the time required for each activity is short. Therefore, we were able to get a rough idea of each user's skill level with the system and activity trends by calculating the total activity duration for each user. In calculating the duration, we excluded negative values and data larger than 10,000 seconds. The graph shows that user 8 has an extremely low total activity duration. On the contrary, user 13 and user 14 have high total activity duration. However, the total activity duration is less than user13's one. This may be because user 8 is unfamiliar with the measurement system or does not fully understand the experiment's rules and has made a mistake in annotating the labels. Therefore, the total activity duration is smaller than user 13 even though user 8 has more labels than the other users and a similar activity distribution to that of user 13.

24.3 METHOD

In this section, we explain the methodology to solve this problem. The proposed methodology consists of two steps. Through the detailed data analysis, we noticed that human activity pattern depends on the user_id and hour. Thus, the first step is to create heatmaps of activity hours for each user to predict the activity per hour. The analysis of the activity frequency of each user shows that behavioral similarities are observed among some users, as we mentioned in Section 24.2.2. Therefore, the second step is to cluster users into three groups using k-means based on their heatmaps.

24.3.1 Heatmap of Activity-Hour

We represent the user behavior prediction model by using heatmaps. We create heatmaps by focusing on the frequency of activity per hour in the care record data. The creation of the heatmap is done as the following steps.

1. A 28×24 heatmap with zero-filled labels is prepared to create a unique heatmap with no differences in activity labels among users because some activity labels do not exist for some users.

2. We summarize the care record data for each of the user_id(8, 13, 14, 15, 25). The care record data is obtained for each user_id.

3. The care record data for each user_id is further aggregated by the hour. The hour is created from the year-month-date-hour column. The care record data for each user and each hour (0–23) are obtained here.

4. We count up the care record data for each activity_type_id. Then, we get the total number of activity frequency for each user.

5. We create heatmaps with an hour on the horizontal axis and activity type on the vertical axis from summarized care record data.

In this way, we can obtain the frequency of activity for each time and activity type for each user.

24.3.2 Clustering

Clustering is performed on all users from the heatmap created by aggregating the care record data. We can classify users into several clusters and create a predictive model by clustering.

From the care record data, we can see several frequency distribution activity trends among users. Therefore, we created a heatmap of time vs. activity frequency and performed clustering using the k-means method.

To perform k-means, we created a time-activity frequency heatmap. The care record data was summarized by time and activity type for each user, and the hourly activity frequency was counted. The above heatmaps were transformed into 28×24 dimensional vectors for clustering.

In clustering, we did not use the activity frequency as it is but normalized it by the total activity time for each user. As a result, we could classify the users into three classes: user 8 and user 13, user 25 and user 14, and user 15. Based on the clustering results, we divided the users into three groups and created a behavior prediction model using the averaged heatmaps belonging to each group.

24.4 RESULTS

For model evaluation, we split the provided data into training and test data. For the training data, we used the entire period from February to July, and for the test data, we used the period from May to July.

Heatmaps were used to make predictions using the training and test data in the following two steps.

1. The user_id and hour data were used as input data.

2. The user_id was used as an index to specify the cluster.

We could get the prediction using two input data, one is user_id, the other is hour. The prediction is binary data of 28 activity labels according to the input hour data. In the evaluation, we used two data. One was the prediction data, the other was the test data used as validation. We choose the F1, precision, recall, micro average, and macro average as evaluation metrics.

Tables 24.2–24.6 show that the predictive model has high precision while recall is low. The overall accuracy and F1 were 0.73, 0.346. These results can be attributed to the small number of data for each user and the bias in the activity labels. This can also be seen from previous models [9,14,15]. Many of the previous models showed large discrepancies in accuracy when evaluated on the validation and test data sets. This can be attributed to the fact that most of the past teams overfitting as a result of employing machine learning or deep learning models despite the small number of data provided. In particular, for user 25, the number of data was very small and some activity labels were seen that were not seen by other users. Even if we trained under such circumstances, it is not always possible to create a good model.

The first step in creating a better predictive model is to improve the dataset. As mentioned in Inoue et al. [11], the provided dataset has a lot of problems; missing values, bias of activity labels, the amount of data etc. In particular, we recommend providing angular acceleration data and explaining to nurses how to use the system. IMU angular acceleration data is very useful for estimating nurse posture [13]. In addition, there is a lot of noise-like data in this dataset due to nurses' unfamiliarity with the system. Also, nurses are busy and might forget to log in information. A capturing system that provides reminders would improve data collection. Solving these issues and improving the quality of the dataset will contribute to the development of the competition and the creation of better models.

TABLE 24.2   Result User 8

Labels	Precision	Recall	F1-Score	Support
Label_1	0.94	0.28	0.43	157
Label_2	1.00	0.46	0.63	239
Label_3	0.96	0.20	0.33	119
Label_4	1.00	0.77	0.87	266
Label_5	1.00	0.16	0.28	61
Label_6	0.00	0.00	0.00	0
Label_7	1.00	0.23	0.37	31
Label_8	1.00	0.08	0.15	86
Label_9	1.00	0.25	0.40	120
Label_10	1.00	0.39	0.56	98
Label_11	1.00	0.36	0.53	163
Label_12	1.00	0.63	0.78	177
Label_13	0.94	0.15	0.26	101
Label_14	1.00	0.04	0.07	53
Label_15	0.00	0.00	0.00	0
Label_16	0.88	0.13	0.22	109
Label_17	0.00	0.00	0.00	0
Label_18	1.00	0.24	0.39	152
Label_19	1.00	0.45	0.62	266
Label_20	1.00	0.21	0.35	206
Label_21	0.00	0.00	0.00	0
Label_22	1.00	0.19	0.32	53
Label_23	0.75	0.11	0.19	28
Label_24	0.75	0.09	0.16	66
Label_25	0.00	0.00	0.00	0
Label_26	0.00	0.00	0.00	0
Label_27	0.00	0.00	0.00	0
Label_28	0.00	0.00	0.00	0
Micro average	0.97	0.35	0.52	2551
Macro average	0.69	0.19	0.28	2551
Weighted average	0.98	0.35	0.49	2551
Samples average	0.97	0.37	0.50	2551

TABLE 24.3   Result User 13

Labels	Precision	Recall	F1-Score	Support
Label_1	0.81	0.16	0.27	79
Label_2	0.98	0.52	0.68	82
Label_3	0.00	0.00	0.00	0
Label_4	0.97	0.65	0.78	146
Label_5	0.00	0.00	0.00	0
Label_6	0.00	0.00	0.00	0
Label_7	1.00	0.08	0.15	12
Label_8	1.00	0.05	0.09	21
Label_9	0.93	0.46	0.62	28
Label_10	1.00	0.32	0.48	75
Label_11	0.82	0.44	0.57	32
Label_12	0.98	0.60	0.74	70
Label_13	0.64	0.14	0.23	49
Label_14	0.87	0.32	0.46	41
Label_15	0.00	0.00	0.00	0
Label_16	0.69	0.22	0.33	51
Label_17	0.00	0.00	0.00	0
Label_18	0.00	0.00	0.00	0
Label_19	0.80	0.24	0.38	49
Label_20	0.00	0.00	0.00	0
Label_21	0.00	0.00	0.00	0
Label_22	0.67	0.05	0.10	37
Label_23	0.00	0.00	0.00	0
Label_24	0.00	0.00	0.00	0
Label_25	0.00	0.00	0.00	16
Label_26	0.00	0.00	0.00	0
Label_27	0.00	0.00	0.00	0
Label_28	0.00	0.00	0.00	0
Micro average	0.80	0.37	0.51	788
Macro average	0.43	0.15	0.21	788
Weighted average	0.86	0.37	0.49	788
Samples average	0.84	0.43	0.53	788

TABLE 24.4 Result User 14

Labels	Precision	Recall	F1-Score	Support
Label_1	0.88	0.28	0.42	163
Label_2	0.93	0.50	0.65	159
Label_3	0.96	0.19	0.32	118
Label_4	1.00	0.79	0.88	316
Label_5	0.00	0.00	0.00	2
Label_6	0.55	0.13	0.21	46
Label_7	1.00	0.13	0.22	8
Label_8	0.00	0.00	0.00	0
Label_9	0.97	0.45	0.61	67
Label_10	0.88	0.16	0.27	43
Label_11	0.95	0.52	0.67	115
Label_12	1.00	0.52	0.69	288
Label_13	0.90	0.20	0.32	96
Label_14	0.00	0.00	0.00	1
Label_15	0.00	0.00	0.00	0
Label_16	1.00	0.22	0.36	128
Label_17	0.00	0.00	0.00	0
Label_18	0.00	0.00	0.00	0
Label_19	0.06	0.09	0.07	11
Label_20	0.00	0.00	0.00	0
Label_21	0.00	0.00	0.00	0
Label_22	0.00	0.00	0.00	0
Label_23	0.00	0.00	0.00	0
Label_24	0.00	0.00	0.00	0
Label_25	0.00	0.00	0.00	0
Label_26	0.00	0.00	0.00	0
Label_27	0.00	0.00	0.00	0
Label_28	0.00	0.00	0.00	0
Micro average	0.90	0.45	0.60	1561
Macro average	0.40	0.15	0.20	1561
Weighted average	0.94	0.45	0.58	1561
Samples average	0.92	0.55	0.64	1561

TABLE 24.5   Result User 15

Labels	Precision	Recall	F1-Score	Support
Label_1	0.90	0.30	0.46	125
Label_2	0.98	0.45	0.61	139
Label_3	1.00	0.04	0.08	93
Label_4	1.00	0.19	0.32	253
Label_5	0.50	0.50	0.50	2
Label_6	0.00	0.00	0.00	0
Label_7	0.00	0.00	0.00	0
Label_8	0.00	0.00	0.00	0
Label_9	1.00	0.50	0.67	48
Label_10	0.86	0.15	0.25	41
Label_11	1.00	0.30	0.46	101
Label_12	1.00	0.75	0.86	220
Label_13	1.00	0.23	0.37	80
Label_14	1.00	1.00	1.00	1
Label_15	0.00	0.00	0.00	0
Label_16	0.88	0.06	0.12	109
Label_17	0.00	0.00	0.00	0
Label_18	0.70	1.00	0.82	7
Label_19	0.20	0.07	0.11	14
Label_20	0.00	0.00	0.00	0
Label_21	0.00	0.00	0.00	0
Label_22	0.50	1.00	0.67	1
Label_23	0.00	0.00	0.00	0
Label_24	0.00	0.00	0.00	0
Label_25	0.00	0.00	0.00	0
Label_26	0.00	0.00	0.00	0
Label_27	0.00	0.00	0.00	0
Label_28	0.00	0.00	0.00	0
Micro average	0.93	0.34	0.49	1234
Macro average	0.45	0.23	0.26	1234
Weighted average	0.96	0.34	0.46	1234
Samples average	0.96	0.40	0.53	1234

TABLE 24.6   Result User 25

Labels	Precision	Recall	F1-Score	Support
Label_1	1.00	0.05	0.10	185
Label_2	0.94	0.11	0.20	141
Label_3	0.00	0.00	0.00	0
Label_4	1.00	0.09	0.17	240
Label_5	0.00	0.00	0.00	0
Label_6	0.99	0.53	0.69	229
Label_7	0.83	0.08	0.15	61
Label_8	0.60	0.05	0.09	59
Label_9	0.00	0.00	0.00	0
Label_10	0.98	0.27	0.42	210
Label_11	0.00	0.00	0.00	0
Label_12	0.00	0.00	0.00	0
Label_13	0.89	0.06	0.11	141
Label_14	0.50	0.02	0.04	86
Label_15	0.00	0.00	0.00	0
Label_16	0.90	0.07	0.13	132
Label_17	0.82	0.09	0.17	95
Label_18	0.90	0.30	0.44	88
Label_19	0.00	0.00	0.00	0
Label_20	0.00	0.00	0.00	0
Label_21	0.00	0.00	0.00	0
Label_22	0.89	0.16	0.27	105
Label_23	0.96	0.37	0.54	70
Label_24	0.89	0.17	0.29	143
Label_25	1.00	0.05	0.09	62
Label_26	1.00	0.63	0.77	48
Label_27	0.00	0.00	0.00	0
Label_28	0.00	0.00	0.00	0
Micro average	0.91	0.19	0.31	2095
Macro average	0.54	0.11	0.17	2095
Weighted average	0.92	0.19	0.28	2095
Samples average	0.94	0.21	0.31	2095

24.5 CONCLUSION

In this chapter, we performed an EDA to capture the characteristics of our data. Considering that analysis, we created a predictive model without machine learning for complex nursing behavior. Based on the trends in the dataset, we clustered the data into three classes for all users. A heatmap was created for each of the three classes of users, and the predictive model was created using the averaged heatmaps. We succeeded in creating a prediction model that was not limited by machine learning methods. In the future, we would like to create a prediction model that fully considers acceleration data.

24.A APPENDIX

Used Sensor modalities	Care record data
Features used	Columns: user_id, activity_type_id, year-month-date-hour, time_length(finish-start)
Preprocessing	Removed of data from February to the end of March Remove negative time_length
Train and Test split	Train: February-July Test: May-July
Programming language and libraries used	Languages: Python Libraries: numpy, pandas, matplotlib
Machine specification (RAM, CPU)	RAM: 32GB CPU: Intel(R) Xeon(R) W-2255 CPU @ 3.70GHz

Figure 24.A.1 Information.

BIBLIOGRAPHY

[1] Kaggle. https://www.kaggle.com

[2] Md Atiqur Rahman Ahad, Anindya Das Antar, and Masud Ahmed. *IoT Sensor-Based Activity Recognition*. Springer Nature, Berlin, 2020.

[3] Sayeda Shamma Alia, Kohei Adachi, Tahera Hossain, Nhat Tan Le, Haru Kaneko, Paula Lago, Tsuyoshi Okita, and Sozo Inoue. Summary of the third nurse care activity recognition challenge-can we do from the field data? In *Adjunct Proceedings of the 2021 ACM International Joint Conference on Pervasive and Ubiquitous Computing and Proceedings of the 2021 ACM International Symposium on Wearable Computers*, pp. 428–433, USA, 2021. Association for Computing Machinery.

[4] Sayeda Shamma Alia, Paula Lago, Kohei Adachi, Tahera Hossain, Hiroki Goto, Tsuyoshi Okita, and Sozo Inoue. Summary of the 2nd nurse care activity recognition challenge using lab and field data. In *Adjunct Proceedings of the 2020 ACM International Joint Conference on Pervasive and Ubiquitous Computing and Proceedings of the 2020 ACM International Symposium on Wearable Computers, UbiComp-ISWC'20*, New York, USA, pp. 378–383, 2020. Association for Computing Machinery.

[5] Anindya Das Antar, Masud Ahmed, and Md Atiqur Rahman Ahad. Challenges in sensor-based human activity recognition and a comparative analysis of benchmark datasets: A review. In *2019 Joint 8th International Conference on Informatics, Electronics & Vision (ICIEV) and 2019 3rd International Conference on Imaging, Vision & Pattern Recognition (icIVPR)*, Spokane WA, USA, pp. 134–139, 2019. IEEE.

[6] Akin Avci, Stephan Bosch, Mihai Marin-Perianu, Raluca Marin-Perianu, and Paul Havinga. Activity recognition using inertial sensing for healthcare, wellbeing and sports applications: A survey. In *23th International Conference on Architecture of Computing Systems 2010*, Hannover, Germany, pp. 1–10, 2010. VDE.

[7] John T. Behrens. Principles and procedures of exploratory data analysis. *Psychological Methods*, 2(2):131, 1997.

[8] Yiwen Dong, Jingxiao Liu, Yitao Gao, Sulagna Sarkar, Zhizhang Hu, Jonathon Fagert, Shijia Pan, Pei Zhang, Hae Young Noh, and Mostafa Mirshekari. A window-based sequence-to-one approach with dynamic voting for nurse care activity recognition using acceleration-based wearable sensor. In *Adjunct Proceedings of the 2020 ACM International Joint Conference on Pervasive and Ubiquitous Computing and Proceedings of the 2020 ACM International Symposium on Wearable Computers*, Mexico, pp. 390–395, 2020.

[9] Yiwen Dong, Jingxiao Liu, Yitao Gao, Sulagna Sarkar, Zhizhang Hu, Jonathon Fagert, Shijia Pan, Pei Zhang, Hae Young Noh, and Mostafa Mirshekari. A hierarchical sequence-to-one approach for nurse care activity recognition using vibration-based wearable sensor. *Proceedings of HASCA 2020*, Mexico, 2020.

[10] Defry Hamdhana, Christina Garcia, Haru Kaneko, Nazmun Nahid, Sayeda Shamma Alia, Tahera Hossain, and Sozo Inoue. Summary of the fourth nurse care activity recognition challenge: Predicting future activities. *Activity and Behavior Computing*, 2022.

[11] Sozo Inoue, Paula Lago, Tahera Hossain, Tittaya Mairittha, and Nattaya Mairittha. Integrating activity recognition and nursing care records: The system, deployment, and a verification study. *Proceedings of the ACM on Interactive, Mobile, Wearable and Ubiquitous Technologies*, 3(3):1–24, 2019.

[12] Mohammad Sabik Irbaz, Abir Azad, Tanjila Alam Sathi, and Lutfun Nahar Lota. Nurse care activity recognition based on machine learning techniques using accelerometer data. In *Adjunct Proceedings of the 2020 ACM International Joint Conference on Pervasive and Ubiquitous Computing and Proceedings of the 2020 ACM International Symposium on Wearable Computers, UbiComp-ISWC'20*, New York, pp. 402–407, 2020. Association for Computing Machinery.

[13] Manon Kok, Jeroen D. Hol, and Thomas B. Schon. Using inertial sensors for position and orientation estimation. *Foundations and Trends® in Signal Processing*, 11(1–2):1–153, 2017.

[14] Carolin Lubbe, Bjorn Friedrich, Sebastian Fudickar, Sandra Hellmers, and Andreas Hein. Feature based random forest nurse care activity recognition using accelerometer data. In *Adjunct Proceedings of the 2020 ACM International Joint Conference on Pervasive and Ubiquitous Computing and Proceedings of the 2020 ACM International Symposium on Wearable Computers*, Mexico, pp. 408–413, 2020.

[15] Md Golam Rasul, Mashrur Hossain Khan, and Lutfun Nahar Lota. Nurse care activity recognition based on convolution neural network for accelerometer data. In *Adjunct Proceedings of the 2020 ACM International Joint Conference on Pervasive and Ubiquitous Computing and Proceedings of the 2020 ACM International Symposium on Wearable Computers*, Mexico, pp. 425–430, 2020.

[16] Gabriele Tolomei, Fabrizio Silvestri, Andrew Haines, and Mounia Lalmas. Interpretable predictions of tree-based ensembles via actionable feature tweaking. In *Proceedings of the 23rd ACM SIGKDD International Conference on Knowledge Discovery and Data Mining*, Halifax NS, Canada, pp. 465–474, 2017.

[17] Dehua Wang, Yang Zhang, and Yi Zhao. LightGBM: An effective mirna classification method in breast cancer patients. In *Proceedings of the 2017 International Conference on Computational Biology and Bioinformatics*, Newark nj, USA, pp. 7–11, 2017.

CHAPTER 25

Time Series Analysis of Care Records Data for Nurse Activity Recognition in the Wild

Md. Kabiruzzaman

American International University-Bangladesh

Mohammad Shidujaman

Independent University

Shadril Hassan Shifat and Pritom Debnath

American International University-Bangladesh

Shahera Hossain

University of Asia Pacific

25.1 INTRODUCTION

Human activity recognition is one of the much research topics due to its importance in various sectors of the society. This is due to its application in the human-robot interaction, artificial intelligence, and so on. The main purpose of inclusion of the robots in different purposes e.g., aged people caring, autistic children caring is to minimize the human error [1]. Moreover, it is argent to train the robots because the necessity of caring the aged old people and autistic children is increasing day by day. It is estimated that by 2050 the number of old people (over 80 years old) will be raised to 19% of total people in the world [2]. Hence, the nursing of these people in home or hospitals for the medication timely, helping in different daily activities and so on, needs engaging the human or robots. Moreover, the nursing of the autistic children including playing with them, helping them to develop their brains also necessitates some associates either human or machines. In these cases, even though it is better to care them by the humans, however, sometimes it is difficult to manage them or unavailability of them.

As a procedure of recording the human activities especially the nurse care activities, nowadays the data are collected using different sensors e.g., accelerometer, gyroscope, image sensors, and so on. These sensors are available in the smartphones, wearable sensors, and IoT. Taking of the data using these sensors have many noises, unwanted data, missing data and so on. To make them more reliable, we need to preprocess them. Preprocessing of these type of data are challenging task. In this aim, "Fourth nurse activity recognition challenge" has been planned.

In this challenge, the time series analysis of care records data for the nurse activity recognition in the open space has been proposed.

In this chapter, the contribution is as follows: Section 25.2 will discuss literature review associated with the nursing care recognition. The description of the dataset [3] given in this challenge is discussed in Section 25.3. Section 25.4 will provide the preprocessing of the data. The results of our method along with discussion are given in Section 25.5 followed by conclusion in Section 25.6.

25.2 LITERATURE REVIEW

Reducing the human workload and improving the efficiency in the healthcare system are done in many ways by many research groups. Machine learning (ML) is considered one of the promising ways in this regard [4,5]. In the specific healthcare system, e.g., nurse care recording system in hospital or controlled environment lab [6], elderly aged care facilities [7] already ML is used to recognize the nursing activities and helping in different management systems of the nurses or caregivers. Recognizing these nursing activities is done by collecting the data through the accelerometer and mobile sensors.

Recent advances in artificial intelligence (AI) have increased human curiosity about new research topics by helping us to recognize objects, comprehend the world, analyze time series, and forecast future sequences. AI researchers are becoming increasingly interested in recurrent neural networks (RNN), which have important applications in speech recognition, language modeling, video processing, and time series analysis. One of the challenging questions in this fascinating subject of AI that seeks solutions is the recognition of human behavior, often known as the Human Activity Recognition (HAR). It can primarily be utilized for eldercare and childcare as an assistive technology when combined with advancements like the Internet of Things (IoT). HAR also covers a wide range of real-world applications, including healthcare, gaming, and personal fitness [8]. The multi-input CNN-GRU model for HAR that is suggested in Ref. [9] makes use of the robustness of CNNs in feature extraction as well as the benefits that GRUs provide for classifying time series data. The proposed multi-input CNN-GRU model outperformed some of the existing DL models used for the human activity recognition challenge because it is both temporally and spatially deep. In study [10], created distance-based reward rule, an intelligent auto-labeling scheme was created using the DQN technique that may more effectively address the issue of improperly classified motion data in daily life. The on-body sensor data, context sensor data, and personal profile data were seamlessly integrated using a multi-sensor-based data fusion technique. Wi-Sense HAR system is introduced in Ref. [11], a system that uses RF sensing and deep learning methods to identify human behaviors, including falls. To gather the CSI data, the sensing module of Wi-Sense employs two laptops, one of which serves as a transmitter and the other as a receiver. Nine subjects engaged in four tasks while collecting CSI data: walking, falling on the mattress, sitting in a chair, and picking something up off the floor. In study [12] found 108 articles that discussed the various methods used for data acquisition, data preprocessing, feature extraction, and activity classification while highlighting the most popular techniques and their alternatives and come to the conclusion that cellphones are ideal for HAR studies in the health sciences. In study [13], a generic HAR framework based on Long Short-Term Memory (LSTM) networks for time-series domains is provided for smartphone sensor data. To examine the effects of using various types of smartphone sensor data, four baseline LSTM networks are compared. Additionally, a four-layer CNN-LSTM hybrid LSTM network is suggested to enhance recognition performance. On a public smartphone-based dataset of UCI-HAR, the HAR technique is assessed using several configurations of sample generation methods (OW and NOW) and validation protocols (10-fold and LOSO cross-validation). In addition, Bayesian optimization methods are used in this study since they are useful for fine-tuning each LSTM network's hyperparameters. In comparison to earlier state-of-the-art methods, the experimental results show that the proposed four-layer CNN-LSTM network performs well in activity recognition, increasing the average accuracy by up to 2.24%.

The second challenge to recognize nursing care activities The crucial topic of care and the requirement for support systems in the nursing industry, such as automatic documentation systems, are addressed in Using Lab and Field Data. An accelerometer that was affixed to the nurses' right arm was used to record information about 12 distinct care actions. Data from the field and from the lab were both considered. Based on the accelerometer data, each action has been categorized. On internal test set, trained a Random Forest classifier and attained an accuracy of 61.11% [14]. In study [15], used the Random Forest-based resampling approach to address the issue of class imbalance in the nurse care activity dataset from Heiseikai data. Resampling, feature selection based on Gini impurity, model training and validation with Stratified KFold cross-validation are all components of this approach. Using the Random Forest classifier, classified 12 actions carried out by nurses in both lab and real-world contexts with an average cross-validation accuracy of 65.9%. Using sensor-based accelerometer data, a second research in the "Second Nurse Care Activity Recognition Challenge Using Lab and Field Data" predicts 12 actions carried out by nurses in both lab and field environments. Due to a significant class imbalance, processing the raw data from this dataset is the major challenge. Additionally, not all subjects have participated in all activities. Data has been handled by "Team Apophis" using noise filtering and windowing techniques in the time and frequency domain to clearly identify different characteristics from lab and field data. The 10-fold cross-validation approach has been used to identify the model with the greatest performance following the merging of lab and field data [16]. In study [17], Light Gradient Boosting Machine Classifier was used and obtained accuracy 87.00%. Using hybrid approach in study [18], classified 28 actions carried out by nurses in actual situations with an average cross-validation balanced accuracy of 70.8%.

25.3 DATASET

The dataset provided in this challenge is the integration of activity recognition and nursing care records. In this dataset, there are four groups of activities namely, activities of direct care, activities of residence cleaning, documentation/communication activities, and other activities. These four groups again subdivided into 28 types of activities. The details of these categories are given in Ref. [7] which is shown in Table of Figure 25.1. The data were collected for 4 months in

Principal activity type (A): Activities of Direct Care			
AC1	Vital	AC10	Daytime user response
AC2	Meal/medication	AC11	Night care
AC3	Oral Care	AC12	Night time user response
AC4	Excretion	AC13	Family/ guest response
AC5	Bathing/wiping	AC14	Outing response
AC6	Treatment	AC19	Get up assistance
AC7	Morning gathering/ exercises	AC20	Change dressing assistance
AC8	Rehabilitation/recreation	AC21	Washing assistance
AC9	Morning Care	AC27	Emergency response such as accident
Principal activity type (B): Activities of Residence Cleaning			
AC15	Linen exchange	AC23	Preparation and checking of goods
AC16	Cleaning	AC24	Organization of medications
Principal activity type (C): Documentation/ Communication Activities			
AC17	Handwriting recording	AC22	Doctor visit correspondence
AC18	Delegating/ meeting	AC25	Family/doctor contract
Principal activity type (D): Other Activities			
AC26	Break	AC28	Special remarks/notes

Figure 25.1   All different activities in the dataset.

nursing care facilities and through sensors integrated with the mobile phones. The dataset included 38,076 activity labels, 2834 hours of sensor data, and 46,803 care details. The speciality of the dataset is to propose a theory of including the start time and end time to enhance the accuracy of the prediction rate. Moreover, the next day's activities can be also predicted based on the previous days activities which would be helpful for proactive care management [3,7].

In this challenge, the data of 5 (8, 13, 14, 15, 25) users separated by accelerometer and care record data have been provided. Among these, care record data has been considered for the analysis. The accelerometer data was considered since a large number of imbalances inside the data were found.

The activity distribution in these five users is shown in Figure 25.2. The figure depicts a large difference in the activities of all users. In case of user 8, activity type 2 (meal/medication) is obtained maximum. Moreover, the second and third largest data, activity type 4 (Excretion) and activity type 12 (nighttime user response), respectively are obtained which are 8% lower and 10% lower than the maximum amount of activity type AC2. The amount of other activities are below the 40% of the AC2. It is interesting to note that, AC12 type activity was done maximally by users 13, 14, and 15. This type of activity was obtained as second largest for user 25 and third largest for user 8.

25.4 METHODOLOGY

The following section thoroughly outlined the procedure for the collection of data based on five different users. The experiment can be divided into three parts: Data preprocessing, Feature Extraction, Classification, and Model Selection. In Figure 25.3 the method has been shown by flow diagram. Afterward all steps have been explained in detail.

25.4.1 Data Pre-Processing

In the first step, during pre-processing and before analyzing of Care Record data, missing values of finished time were found. Since it was not possible to replace missing value of time, those missing values were dropped in raw-wise. Moreover, the amount of missing value was less than the total amount of data. After that, the timestamp data was reorganized according to year, month, week, day, hour, minute, and second in column wise. In the training data, we found few activity types ID was missing in test submission file. Hence, we dropped that activity from the train data. In the same way, test submission file has few activity types ID, that was not found in train data. In that case that activity type ID was added in the train data and replaced that columns co-responding value with zero. We have done this process because if there is any activity in test submission file and when the data was trained without that activity type ID then model would predict wrongly. Therefore we merged our activity type ID in train data and test submission file to ensure that there is no mismatch between train data and test submission file. In this challenge,

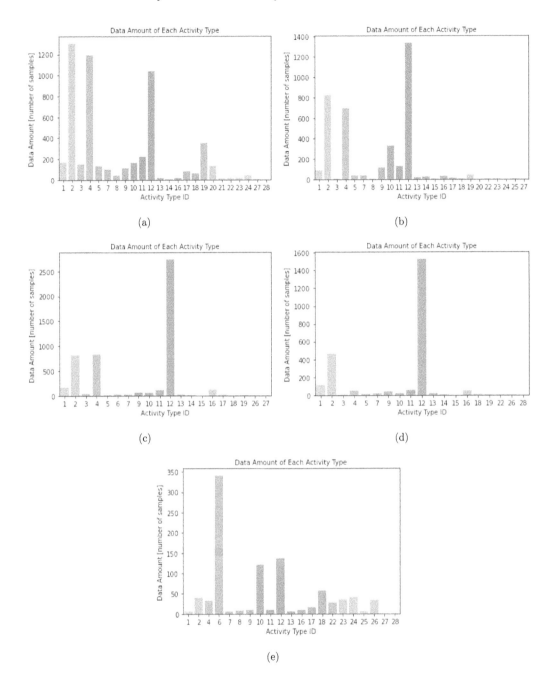

Figure 25.2 Amount of activities in the five users (a) user 8 (b) user 13 (c) user 14 (d) user 15 (e) user 25.

organizer provided us train data, test data, and test submission file. There have been no deference between train data and test data file. That is the reason we merged our train data and test data and after that we split this data for train and test.

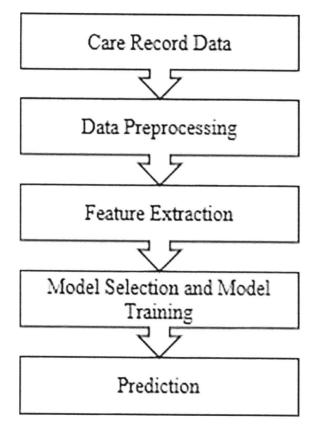

Figure 25.3 Flow diagram of our method.

25.4.2 Feature Extraction

Initially, we examined the frequency of hourly actions and the repeat of these activities across various timestamps in order to extract useful information from the dataset. The time based features: Year, Month, Day of Month, Day of Week, Part of day were extracted. We were unable to extract any statistical features from the accelerometer data due to its unpredictable and inconsistent nature.

25.4.3 Classification and Model Selection

After time series features extraction, these features were used for classification. Figure 25.2 indicate, five difference user activity for sample data. It shows most significant variation among various activities that means it contains class imbalance. For that reason, the considered model for classification provided poor accuracy. Four different models were trained to train the data. In Table 25.1, the classification model is summarized to evaluate Users performance. Researcher already have been experienced to use different classification models for activity recognition. They do not proposed any fixed classification model for this particular reason. To collate and contrast the performance between classifiers, here, Random Forest classifier,

TABLE 25.1   User Accuracy Based on Different Classifiers

Classifiers	Five Different Users				
Name	User 8 (%)	User 13 (%)	User 14 (%)	User 15 (%)	User 25 (%)
Random forest	11.92	25.96	29.32	31.23	25.35
Decision tree	10.26	15.66	2.03	66.89	20.18
MLP	4.10	1.93	6.01	62.47	14.55
KNN	5.96	23.39	31.87	60.10	16.90

Decision Tree classifier, Multi-layer Perceptron classifier and k-nearest neighbors classifier were explored. Here, the dataset has been split into 70% for train data and 30% for test data.

25.5   RESULT AND ANALYSIS

To evaluate the results, here accuracy was used as main performance matrice. From Table 25.1, it can be observed that, less than average accuracy was obtained using Random Forest, Decision Tree and KNN. On the other hand, using multilayer perceptron, we get very lower accuracy specially for users 8, 13 and 14. The maximum accuracy for user 15 was obtained for every classification and we obtain the least for user 8. The first reason behind this can be data imbalance. User 8 has huge data imbalance compared to other users. User 15 has less amount of sample data compared to users 8, 13, 14, and 25. One of the reasons for this imbalance is the data mismatch that can be understood in our training period. The selected model's classification accuracy according to the Random Forest classifier is shown in the BAR-chart in Figure 25.4. We determined the model with the best performance

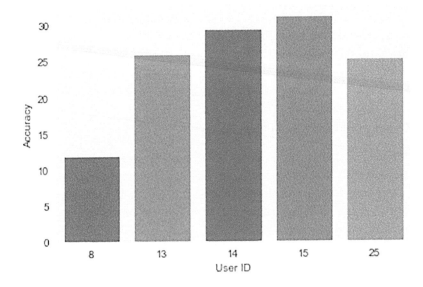

Figure 25.4   Accuracy result based on our model for different users.

based on the evaluation findings by comparing classification accuracy's.The dataset has been observed to work most efficiently for Random Forest classifier. It was obtained highest accuracy in Random Forest classier for users 8, 13, and 25 compared to other classifier. The result itself and its analysis with respect to different classifiers given here for the five users will give you a great insight for discussion with other users and their activities.

25.6 CONCLUSION AND FUTURE TASK

In this work, the care record data was analyzed for five users given for the challenge. Initially, we could conclude from the data visualization that the data has a large imbalance including missing data, overlapping of the data. The reason for this type of imbalance can be considered as the forgetting of recording of the activities, inserting the data in different timestamps and unavailability of internet sometimes and so on. This also verified the previous statement, i.e., analyzing the real field data is not an easy task. Hence, more robust algorithm, different classifier e.g., hybrid mode needs to analyze the field data.

In this work, we also observed that, among the classifiers we used on the dataset, Random Forest classifier is more efficient because it has given the maximum accuracy's for three users. Moreover, it can be concluded that, still there is room to analyze the field data. In future, we will consider the hybrid mode classifier to utilize their corresponding strengths by compensating the weakness of each other. Besides, deep learning also can be a good option to analyze the real field data having a large amount of imbalances.

BIBLIOGRAPHY

[1] Michalis Vrigkas, Christophoros Nikou, and Ioannis Kakadiaris. A review of human activity recognition methods. *Frontiers in Robotics and Artificial Intelligence*, 2:28, 2015.

[2] Norma Bulamu, Billingsley Kaambwa, and Julie Ratcliffe. A systematic review of instruments for measuring outcomes in economic evaluation within aged care. *Health and Quality of Life Outcomes*, 13:179, 2015.

[3] Sozo Inoue, Defry Hamdhana, Christina Garcia, Haru Kaneko, Nazmun Nahid, Tahera Hossain, Sayeda Shamma Alia, and Paula Lago. Fourth nurse care activity recognition challenge datasets, 2022.

[4] Atsushi Miyaji, Yuta Kimata, Tomokazu Matsui, Manato Fujimoto, and Keiichi Yasumoto. Analysis and visualization of relationship between stress and care activities toward reduction in caregiver workload. *Sensors and Materials*, 34(8):2929–2954, 2022.

[5] İpek Deveci Kocakoç. *The Role of Artificial Intelligence in Health Care*, pp. 189–206. Springer Nature Singapore, Singapore, 2022.

[6] Sayeda Shamma Alia, Paula Lago, Kohei Adachi, Tahera Hossain, Hiroki Goto, Tsuyoshi Okita, and Sozo Inoue. Summary of the 2nd nurse care activity recognition challenge using lab and field data. In *Adjunct Proceedings of the 2020 ACM International Joint Conference on Pervasive and Ubiquitous Computing and Proceedings of the 2020 ACM International Symposium on Wearable Computers*, Mexico, pp. 378–383, 2020.

[7] Sozo Inoue, Paula Lago, Tahera Hossain, Tittaya Mairittha, and Nattaya Mairittha. Integrating activity recognition and nursing care records: The system, deployment, and a verification study. *The Proceedings of the ACM on Interactive, Mobile, Wearable and Ubiquitous Technologies (IMWUT)*, 3(3):1–24, 2019.

[8] Chamani Shiranthika, Nilantha Premakumara, Huei-Ling Chiu, Hooman Samani, Chathurangi Shyalika, and Chan-Yun Yang. Human activity recognition using CNN & LSTM. In *2020 5th International Conference on Information Technology Research (ICITR)*, Moratuwa, Sri Lanka, pp. 1–6, 2020, IEEE.

[9] Nidhi Dua, Shiva Nand Singh, and Vijay Bhaskar Semwal. Multi-input CNN-GRU based human activity recognition using wearable sensors. *Computing*, 103(7):1461–1478, 2021.

[10] Xiaokang Zhou, Wei Liang, Kevin I-Kai Wang, Hao Wang, Laurence T. Yang, and Qun Jin. Deep-learning-enhanced human activity recognition for internet of healthcare things. *IEEE Internet of Things Journal*, 7(7):6429–6438, 2020.

[11] Muhammad Muaaz, Ali Chelli, Martin Wulf Gerdes, and Matthias Patzold. Wi-sense: A passive human activity recognition system using wi-fi and convolutional neural network and its integration in health information systems. *Annals of Telecommunications*, 77(3):163–175, 2022.

[12] Marcin Straczkiewicz, Peter James, and Jukka-Pekka Onnela. A systematic review of smartphone-based human activity recognition methods for health research. *NPJ Digital Medicine*, 4(1):1–15, 2021.

[13] Sakorn Mekruksavanich and Anuchit Jitpattanakul. LSTM networks using smartphone data for sensor-based human activity recognition in smart homes. *Sensors*, 21(5):1636, 2021.

[14] Carolin Lübbe, Björn Friedrich, Sebastian Fudickar, Sandra Hellmers, and Andreas Hein. Feature based random forest nurse care activity recognition using accelerometer data. In *Adjunct Proceedings of the 2020 ACM International Joint Conference on Pervasive and Ubiquitous Computing and Proceedings of the 2020 ACM International Symposium on Wearable Computers*, Mexico, pp. 408–413, 2020.

[15] Arafat Rahman, Nazmun Nahid, Iqbal Hassan, and Md Atiqur Rahman Ahad. Nurse care activity recognition: Using random forest to handle imbalanced class problem. In *Adjunct Proceedings of the 2020 ACM International Joint Conference on Pervasive and Ubiquitous Computing and Proceedings of the 2020 ACM International Symposium on Wearable Computers*, Mexico, pp. 419–424, 2020.

[16] Promit Basak, Shahamat Mustavi Tasin, Malisha Islam Tapotee, Md. Mamun Sheikh, Ahsanul Hoque M. Sakib, Sriman Bidhan Baray, and Md Atiqur Rahman Ahad. Complex nurse care activity recognition using statistical features. In *Adjunct Proceedings of the 2020 ACM International Joint Conference on Pervasive and Ubiquitous Computing and Proceedings of the 2020 ACM International Symposium on Wearable Computers, UbiComp-ISWC '20*, New York, pp. 384–389, 2020. Association for Computing Machinery.

[17] Muhammad Ashikuzzaman Kowshik, Yeasin Arafat Pritom, Md Sohanur Rahman, Ali Akbar, and Md Atiqur Rahman Ahad. Nurse care activity recognition from accelerometer sensor data using Fourier-and Wavelet-based features. In *Adjunct Proceedings of the 2021 ACM International Joint Conference on Pervasive and Ubiquitous Computing and Proceedings of the 2021 ACM International Symposium on Wearable Computers*, USA, pp. 434–439, 2021.

[18] Arafat Rahman, Iqbal Hassan, and Md Atiqur Rahman Ahad. Nurse care activity recognition: A cost-sensitive ensemble approach to handle imbalanced class problem in the wild. In *Adjunct Proceedings of the 2021 ACM International Joint Conference on Pervasive and Ubiquitous Computing and Proceedings of the 2021 ACM International Symposium on Wearable Computers*, USA, pp. 440–445, 2021.

Summary of the Fourth Nurse Care Activity Recognition Challenge - Predicting Future Activities

Defry Hamdhana, Christina Garcia, Nazmun Nahid, Haru Kaneko, and Sayeda Shamma Alia

Kyushu Institute of Technology

Tahera Hossain

Aoyama Gakuin University

Sozo Inoue

Kyushu Institute of Technology

26.1   INTRODUCTION

Human Activity Recognition (HAR) has become one of the most highly discussed topics in ubiquitous computing in recent years [4]. The main purpose of HAR is to understand the daily activities carried out by analyzing data collected through various sensors or videos [17,20]. In addition, microelectronics has enabled sensors including accelerometers [5] and gyroscopes to be integrated into mobile devices with a multitude of benefits, for instance, low cost and small size. People adapt to using sensors and mobile devices as part of their daily lives. There is an increasing interest in HAR research including medical applications specifically for health care monitoring and diagnosis, elderly care, and rehabilitation. In addition, we can recognize nurses' activities by automatically creating corresponding records to reduce documentation time, check routine care schedules for certain patients, and identify risky activities that require special attention [14]. Therefore, nurses can be assisted in managing and improving the quality of their work by recognizing nursing activity.

In previous years, we have introduced FonLog as a mobile app used as a data collection tool in human activity recognition for nursing services. By using Fon-

DOI: 10.1201/9781003371540-29

Log, nurses can identify and record a person's activities using a mobile phone with a series of key features that are required for activity recognition and recording systems: recording target persons, an easy-to-use interface, a recognition feedback interface, detailed records that are customizable, instant activities, and offline accessibility [16]. The nurse care activity challenge has been conducted since 2019 using data collected by FonLog and is continually being refined. The first Nurse Care Activity Challenge had the goal to prove the feasibility of recognizing complex nurse care activities based on movement [14] using dataset collected in a controlled environment with clearly segmented activities. The Second Nurse Care Activity Challenge used both lab and field data [3]. The challenge utilized public data from six users in the field and two users from the lab, while the test data has three users from the field. And The Third Nurse Care Activity Recognition Challenge focused on recognizing the activities of a nurse based on the accelerometer data [2].

As part of the ABC Conference, the Fourth Nurse Care Activity Recognition Challenge is organized this year for predicting [8] the hourly activities performed by nurses in healthcare facilities using care records and accelerometer data [10]. In real-life situations, accelerometer sensors and care record data are noisy, unbalanced, and complex [15]. It is a big challenge to create a machine learning model that can classify unusual activities including simple activities carried out in the lab. Machine learning models designed to classify imbalanced data are biased towards more common classifications [1]. Such a learning bias occurs naturally because the model is better at learning the classes that contain more records. In the healthcare field, it is advantageous to be able to predict human activities. Among which is anticipating certain activities that may pose a threat to a patient, such as falling movements [6] or giving the nurse the right schedule to perform certain tasks. This year, the challenge attempts to predict future activities performed by nurses using care records and accelerometer data. Predicting what nurses have to do at a certain time will help them prepare the right schedule, and better care can be provided to the patients with distributed nurse care workload.

26.2 DATASET

The application of HAR in the real world, especially in the health sector, can greatly help monitor the activities of the elderly or recognize the activities of caregivers remotely to reduce manual work in healthcare facilities. For this challenge, we use a dataset designed to introduce the daily activities of caregivers using the FonLog app. The following sections provide details on the data collection process and the environment.

26.2.1 Data Collection and Details of Activities

The dataset [9] was collected at a healthcare facility in Japan from March to June 2018. The data provided this time is part of the dataset which was used in the previous work on integrating activity recognition and nurse care records [9] where authors proposed that extending of start and end times of the activities can in-

TABLE 26.1   Nurse Care Activities in Categories

Category	Activity Type with Activity ID
Direct care	1:Vital, 2:meal/medication, 3:oral care, 4:excretion, 5:bathing/wiping, 6:treatment, 7:morning gathering/exercise, 8:rehabilitation/recreation, 9:morning care, 10:daytime user response, 11:night care, 12:nighttime user response, 13:family/guest response, 14:outing response, 19:get up assistance, 20:change dressing assistance, 21:washing assistance, 27:emergency response such as accident
Residence cleaning	15:Linen exchange, 16:cleaning, 23:preparation and checking of goods, 24:organization of medication
Documentation/communication	17:Handwriting recording, 18:delegating/meeting, 22:doctor visit correspondence, 25:family/doctor contact
Other activities	26:Break, 28:special remarks/notes

crease the prediction rate. The reason behind the theory is that many of the nurses provided the labels before or after completing an activity. In the paper, they verified and proved this theory.

The data has been collected using one smartphone carried by subjects, which are caregivers and nurses when they were conducting daily work in the healthcare facility. The smartphone was carried in an arbitrary position such as in a pocket. There are a total of 28 recorded activities divided into four categories listed in Table 26.1. A part of this dataset has also been used in last year's third nurse care challenge [2].

26.2.2   Data Format

This time for the challenge, we are providing data from five users (8, 13, 14, 15, 25). The separation dates for training and testing of care record data are listed in Table 26.2. Inside the training data folder shown in Figure 26.1, we provided both care records and accelerometer data. The participants are notified that in accelerometer data folder, the data is not split. In order to use it, the participants can match it with the train and test care record files, as shown in the tutorial on the website.

TABLE 26.2   Train and Test Data Split

User ID	Train File		Test File	
25	2018-02-02	2018-05-07	2018-05-18	2018-07-01
15	2018-02-07	2018-05-20	2018-05-21	2018-07-02
14	2018-02-02	2018-05-16	2018-05-18	2018-07-01
13	2018-02-08	2018-05-18	2018-05-18	2018-07-01
8	2018-02-23	2018-05-23	2018-05-24	2018-07-01

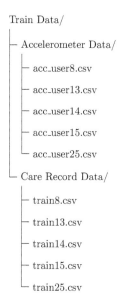

Figure 26.1 Training data folder contains care records and accelerometer data.

In the test folder, the data provided was from everyday recordings during the study on each user in the nursing facility. The following is a brief description of the contents of the test data file: id (label id), user_id(nurse/caregiver), activity_type_id(unique id for each activity type), activity_type (activity name), target_id (patients), activity2user_id, start and finish timestamp of the activity, and year-month-date-hour timestamp. Participants can use this data to match it with the accelerometer data provided. However, it should be noted that the start and end times of the care record data may differ in datetime from the accelerometer file due to different time zone settings.

26.3 DETAILS OF THE CHALLENGE

The challenge started on June 1, 2022, and training data was released on the same date. The test data was released after a month on July 1, 2022. Submission of results was closed on August 7, 2022.

26.3.1 Goal of the Challenge

The goal of this year's Nurse Care Activity Recognition Challenge is to predict the hourly activities of a caregiver/nurse in a healthcare facility based on care record files and accelerometer data collected from smartphones. Along with the time data from the care records, the participants are free to utilize the accelerometer data as an added option to predict the future occurrence of the activities. The activity labels can be found in the care record files. Participants should suggest ways for extracting features from these data, using alternative windowing approaches if possible and simulate through suitable algorithms. Finally, each team needs to use their respective models to predict the activities following the timestamp in the test data.

Time mismatch is part of the challenge. The participants need to think of ways to utilize as much data as possible. Our main focus is the care record data, and the accelerometer data is given as auxiliary information. Data can be used both ways or either way, depending on the participant's preference.

The highly imbalanced accelerometer data is shown in Figure 26.2a and impact of missing values on the classification in this dataset can be observed in the baseline scores shown in the same Figure 26.2b.

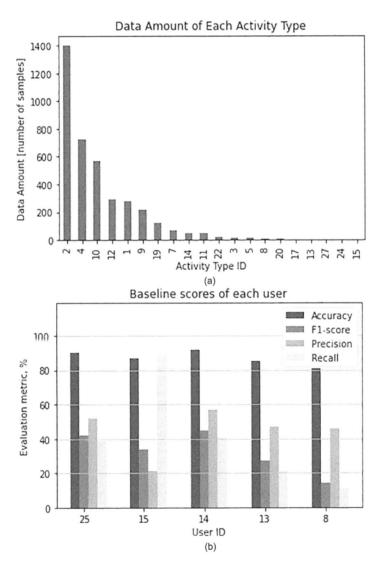

Figure 26.2 Overview of data (a) quantity of each activity type in accelerometer data, (b) baseline score.

TABLE 26.3   Submission File Format

Year-Month-Date-Hour	A1	A2	A3	A4
2018-02-07-17	0	1	0	0
2018-02-07-18	0	0	0	0
2018-02-07-19	1	0	1	1

26.3.2   Evaluation Metrics

As illustrated in the challenge tutorial, participants are required to propose pipelines, predict, and submit activity labels for the testing dataset. The organizers have provided files containing test timestamps for each user as shown in Table 26.3 in which participants need to predict. Each user file specifically contains timestamps and activity_type_ids with columns filled with zeros. The participants are required to replace zeroes with ones in cells in which the activity is supposed to happen and regenerate the files. Participants should maintain the shape of the provided files for evaluation.

Based on Table 26.3, the participants are expected to generate five similar files corresponding to each user on their submission. As the occurrence of activities differs per user, the label files of each user are to be matched during evaluation for checking the number of activities accurately predicted by the participants.

To evaluate the submissions, performance including accuracy, F1-score, precision, and recall were measured and obtained respectively using the following equations [18]:

$$\text{Accuracy} = \frac{TP + TN}{TP + FP + FN + TN} \tag{26.1}$$

$$F1 - \text{score} = \frac{TP}{TP + 0.5(FP + FN)} \tag{26.2}$$

$$\text{Precision} = \frac{TP}{TP + FP)} \tag{26.3}$$

$$\text{Recall} = \frac{TP}{TP + FN)} \tag{26.4}$$

In the equation, the meanings of TP, TN, FP and FN are stated below.

$$TP = \text{True Positive, } TN = \text{True Negative,}$$
$$FP = \text{False Positive, } FN = \text{False Negative}$$

26.4   RESULT OF THE CHALLENGE

Compared to the previous nurse care challenges [2,3,14], this year's event has recorded more participants in terms of registrants and final submission count.

26.4.1 Participating Teams

Originally, a total of 22 different teams registered for the challenge from various countries. During the submission phase, eleven teams submitted their predictions with only nine teams accepted. Two teams were disqualified due to improper submission format. Listed below are the final teams accepted in the challenge.

- T1: *2A&B Core* [7]

- T2: *Alpha* [24]

- T3: *carelab* [23]

- T4: *DataDrivers_ BD* [21]

- T5: *Hippocrates* [19]

- T6: *Horizon* [22]

- T7: *Not a Fan of Local Minima* [11]

- T8: *The Innovators* [12]

- T9: *Ulster Team* [13]

26.4.2 Result of Submissions

The steps of pre-processing, feature extraction, and model recognition to predict nurse activity have their challenges. These include data imbalances between maintenance records and accelerometer data, as well as discrepancies in timing between the two. It is recommended that participants use alternative windowing approaches for their models. All participants have utilized care record data only in their models after assessing the accelerometer data has extremely minimal matching datetime. Six teams [7,12,13,19,22,24] have used machine learning pipelines, three teams used deep learning [11,21,22] while one team maximized heatmap for clustering [23]. Shown in Figure 26.3 is the summary of ML and DL used by the participating teams.

Among the teams who opted for the ML pipeline, Random Forest is the most common algorithm followed by Decision Tree and K-Nearest Neighbors. For DL pipelines, team *Horizon* [22] utilized the Binary Relevance algorithm, *Not a Fan of Local Minima* [11] implemented Long Short Term Memory Network (LSTM), and *DataDrivers_ BD* [21] used Artificial Neural Network (ANN). Meanwhile, *carelab* [23] is the only team that opted for K-Means Clustering algorithm with heatmap.

To implement the activity recognition model, all the teams have used Python as the primary programming language. *Ulster Team* [13] has used R as a secondary language while team *Horizon* [11], also used Matlab in their method. All nine teams have used Pandas library followed by Numpy, Matplotlib, and Scikit-learn. Shown

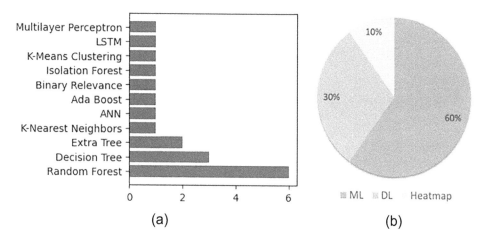

Figure 26.3 (a) Algorithms used by teams and (b) ML and DL pipelines used by teams.

in Figure 26.4 is the summary of the programming languages and libraries used by each team in this challenge.

Table 26.4 displays the average test result for all five users. After evaluating all the submitted predictions, the team *Not a fan of local minima* [11] achieved the highest accuracy of 92%, followed by the *Alpha* team [24] at 90% with a slight difference of 2%. As for the F1 score, only the team *carelab* [23] has exceeded the baseline score achieving 34.6%. In contrast, team *Horizon* and team *2A_B Core* scored 93% on their train results.

For the results of training, both teams *2A_B core* and *Horizon* achieved an average accuracy of 99% for five users. Similarly, both teams achieved the highest

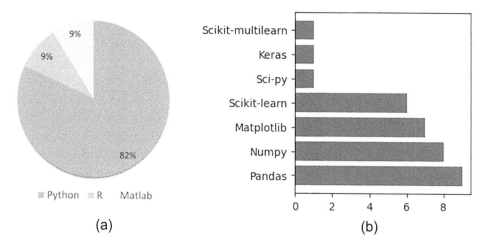

Figure 26.4 (a) Programming languages used by teams and (b) libraries used by teams.

TABLE 26.4 Test Results Average for All Five Users

Team	Precision	Recall	F1 Score	Accuracy
Baseline scores	0.446	0.402	0.324	0.87
T1: *2A_ B Core* [7]	0.11	0.198	0.124	0.74
T2: *Alpha* [24]	0.214	0.182	0.19	0.9
T3: *carelab* [23]	0.242	0.542	0.346	0.73
T4: *Data Drivers_ BD* [21]	0.102	0.148	0.11	0.87
T5: *Hippocrates* [19]	0.056	0.04	0.042	0.85
T6: *Horizon* [22]	0.138	0.132	0.124	0.85
T7: *Not a fan of local minima* [11]	0.21	0.198	0.19	0.92
T8: *The Innovators* [12]	0.18	0.16	0.156	0.88
T9: *Ulster Team* [13]	0.044	0.2	0.026	0.52

average F1-score during training which is 93%. The comparison of average accuracy and F1-score from training and testing is summarized in Figure 26.5. The difficulties encountered in this challenge affecting activity recognition accuracy and prediction performance are attributed to the nature of highly imbalanced real-life data mentioned in Section 3.1 and other issues including mislabeled timestamps and activities, and varied activity duration.

26.5 ANALYSIS AND DISCUSSION

In this chapter, we will present some interesting points from the challenge and participants' results for analysis and discussion.

26.5.1 Evaluation Metrics

The generalization ability of a model can be measured with the help of an evaluation metrics. A performance evaluation can improve the overall predictive power of a model before it is rolled out for production on unseen data. A good choice of metrics is also important when evaluating machine learning models.

However, in this challenge, we have also tried to find out which evaluation metrics is better to measure the accuracy of predictions on nurse activities with the model used by participants. From some of the existing literature reviews, although F-Measure has improved in accuracy, they are still ineffective for answering more general classification evaluation questions. In particular, we still have no way of comparing the performance of different classifiers over a range of sample distributions. Moreover, our data is unbalanced, so we cannot use AUC. In contrast, ROC does not perform well when there is a large change in false positives. The previous explanations illustrate that obtaining an appropriate evaluation metric remains challenging when data is unbalanced. Therefore, we used the F1-score and accuracy as a measure of how good the participants' models were at predicting nurse activities.

26.5.2   Analysis of Algorithms

Based on Accuracy and F1-score, we can see the advantages of each algorithm. K-Mean Clustering with the heatmap approach proved to have the highest score on the F1-score approach, exceeding the baseline score. However, K-Mean Clustering is not better than LSTM, Random Forest, Ada Boost, and ANN in determining the accuracy score to predict nurse activity. We conclude in this challenge that LSTM has outperformed all other algorithms in terms of accuracy scores. Although it doesn't perform better than K-Mean Clustering in F1-score. On the other hand, Decision Trees are not effective for predicting nurse challenge activities. Due to the Accuracy and F1 values, the Decision Tree shows poor results.

26.5.3   Care Record with Accelerometer Data vs Care Record Data

To overcome this challenge, all teams used care record data. As a result, several teams outperformed the existing baseline, both in terms of accuracy and F1 scores. However, we could not directly compare whether teams would have better predictive success if they used care records and accelerometer data because none of the teams did so. Our simulation in the 4th Nurse Care Activity Recognition Challenge tutorial might be able to help us figure out which is better. Using care records and accelerometer data performed better for F1-Score with 32.4% than only care records with 28.6%. However, using care records data outperformed accelerometer data and care records in terms of accuracy. Using only care record data, the accuracy is 89.2% while using both care record and accelerometer data, the accuracy is 87%.

26.6   CONCLUSION

Collected data from real-life settings poses many challenges including incorrect timestamps, lacking and mislabeled activities, imbalance datasets, and varied activity duration. Uncontrolled factors including unstable Wi-Fi connection for proper storage of data in the server, and device issues also affect data frequency. Highly imbalanced and very minimal datasets such as the accelerometer data provided make prediction nearly impossible. Considering the methods of the participating teams, it is definite that correct timestamps of care record data are a contributing factor to higher prediction rate as the majority of the features extracted are time-dependent.

Based on the summary of the submission results, all teams have achieved relatively good classification and prediction performance using a variety of ML and DL pipelines taking into account the data set provided even if only using care record data. Accuracy ranges from 52% to 92% and F1-scores vary from 2.6% to 34.6%. Further investigation is needed to determine how nurse/caregiver activities are predicted using care records and accelerometer measurements. An evaluation metric should be chosen and used in accordance with a good scenario. Due to the fact that the evaluation metric chosen in this challenge depends on the overall challenge, it may not always reflect the best system. In summary, each evaluation metric offers a unique perspective on performance.

26.A APPENDIX

TABLE 26.A.1 Details of Each Team

	T1 [7]	T2 [24]	T3 [23]	T4 [21]	T5 [19]
Team Name	2A&B Core	Alpha	carelab	DataDrivers_BD	Hippocrates
Data used	Care record	Care record	Care record	Care record	Care record
Programming	Python	Python	Python	Python	Python
Libraries	Numpy, Pandas, Matplotlib, Scikit-learn	Numpy, Pandas, Scikit-learn	Numpy, Pandas, Matplotlib	Numpy, Pandas, Matplotlib, Scikit-learn	Numpy, Pandas, Matplotlib, Scikit-learn
Features	probability of activity X happen in hour Y, activity X happen or not, caregiver or not, percent of the day, percent of the week, week of the week, week of month, average activity duration, patient count, hour, day, week, weekend, before or after noon	The hour, the day of the week, a categorical variable for each time of day (6 am to 10 am is morning, 10 am to 4 pm is day, 4 pm to 8 pm is evening, 8 pm to 6 am is morning)	Heatmap created by hour and user	NA	Part of day, day of week, day of month, month, quarter
Classifier	Random forest, decision tree, isolation forest	Random forest	K-means clustering	ANN	Random forest, extra trees, K-nearest neighbors

(Continued)

TABLE 26.A.1 (*Continued*) Details of Each Team

	T1 [7]	T2 [24]	T3 [23]	T4 [21]	T5 [19]
Training time	5 minutes	0.17 seconds	NA	NA	15.38 seconds
Testing time	¡1 seconds	0.03 seconds	NA	NA	0.4 seconds
RAM	256 GB	512 GB	125 GB	8 GB	NA
CPU	2x Intel Xeon CPU E5-2650 v4 12C, 158x Nodes	Two Intel Xeon Gold 6248 _ascade Lake CPUs: 20 cores, 2.503.90GHz, 27.5MB LLC, 6 memory channels	Intel(R), 3.70GHz, Xeon(R) W-2255	Intel Core i5 1135G7	Google Colab
GPU	NA	NA	NA	Google Colab	Google Colab
Average testing accuracy	0.74	0.9	0.73	0.87	0.85
Average testing F1-score	0.124	0.19	0.346	0.11	0.042

TABLE 26.A.1 (*Continued*) Details of Each Team

	T6 [22] *Horizon*	T7 [11] *Not a Fan of Local Minima*	T8 [12] *The Innovators*	T9 [13] *Ulster Team*
Team Name				
Data Used	Care record	Care record	Care record	Care record
Programming Libraries	Python, Matlab Numpy, Pandas, Matplotlib, Scikit-learn, Sci-py, Keras, Scikit-multilearn	Python Numpy, Pandas	Python Numpy, Pandas, Matplotlib	Python, R Numpy, Pandas, Matplotlib, Scikit-learn
Features	mean, std, max, min, median, range, quartile, iqr, z_score	hour, activity_type_id	Year, Month, Day of Month, Day of Week, Part of day	Finish Day number, Target ID, Activity Group, Time of the Day, Start day number, Finish Hour, Start Hour
Classifier	Random Forest, Binary Relevance, Ada Boost	DL	Random Forest, Decision Tree, K-Nearest Neighbors, Multilayer Perceptron	
Training time	2-6 minutes	400 sec	0.58 sec	20 minutes
Testing time	10 sec	0.0324 sec	0.059 sec	2 minutes
RAM	NA	128 GB	8 GB	32 GB
CPU	NA	Intel(R) Xeon(R) CPU @ 2.30GHz	2.2 GHz Dual-Core Intel Core i7	CPU AMD Ryzen 5 3600
GPU	Google Colab	Tesla P100-PCIE	NA	GPU NVIDIA GeForce RTX2080 Super
Avg. Testing Accuracy	0.85	0.92	0.88	0.52
Avg. Testing F1-Score	0.124	0.19	0.156	0.026

BIBLIOGRAPHY

[1] Ali A. Alani, Georgina Cosma, and Aboozar Taherkhani. Classifying imbalanced multi-modal sensor data for human activity recognition in a smart home using deep learning. In *2020 International Joint Conference on Neural Networks (IJCNN)*, pp. 1–8. IEEE, 2020.

[2] Sayeda Shamma Alia, Kohei Adachi, Tahera Hossain, Nhat Tan Le, Haru Kaneko, Paula Lago, Tsuyoshi Okita, and Sozo Inoue. Summary of the third nurse care activity recognition challenge-can we do from the field data? In *Adjunct Proceedings of the 2021 ACM International Joint Conference on Pervasive and Ubiquitous Computing and Proceedings of the 2021 ACM International Symposium on Wearable Computers*, pp. 428–433, 2021.

[3] Sayeda Shamma Alia, Paula Lago, Kohei Adachi, Tahera Hossain, Hiroki Goto, Tsuyoshi Okita, and Sozo Inoue. Summary of the 2nd nurse care activity recognition challenge using lab and field data. In *UbiComp/ISWC'20 Adjunct: ACM International Joint Conference on Pervasive and Ubiquitous Computing and ACM International Symposium on Wearable Computers*. ACM, 2020.

[4] Sayeda Shamma Alia, Paula Lago, Shingo Takeda, Kohei Adachi, Brahim Benaissa, Md Atiqur Rahman Ahad, and Sozo Inoue. *Summary of the Cooking Activity Recognition Challenge*, pp. 1–13. Springer Singapore, Singapore, 2021.

[5] Umran Alrazzak and Bassem Alhalabi. A survey on human activity recognition using accelerometer sensor. In *2019 Joint 8th International Conference on Informatics, Electronics & Vision (ICIEV) and 2019 3rd International Conference on Imaging, Vision & Pattern Recognition (icIVPR)*, pp. 152–159, Los Alamitos, CA. IEEE Computer Society, 2019.

[6] Glenn Forbes, Stewart Massie, and Susan Craw. Fall prediction using behavioural modelling from sensor data in smart homes. *Artificial Intelligence Review*, 53(2):1071–1091, 2020.

[7] Bjorn Friedrich and Andreas Hein. Ensemble classifier for nurse care activity prediction based on care records. In Md Atiqur Rahman Ahad, Sozo Inoue, Guillaume Lopez, and Tahera Hossain (eds.), *Human Activity and Behavior Analysis: Advances in Computer Vision and Sensors*. CRC Press, pp. 323–332, Boca Raton, FL, 2024.

[8] Sozo Inoue. Activity recognition and future prediction in hospitals. In *Adjunct Proceedings of the 13th International Conference on Mobile and Ubiquitous Systems: Computing Networking and Services*, pp. 59–65, 2016.

[9] Sozo Inoue, Paula Lago, Tahera Hossain, Tittaya Mairittha, and Nattaya Mairittha. Integrating activity recognition and nursing care records: The system, deployment, and a verification study. *The Proceedings of the ACM on Interactive, Mobile, Wearable and Ubiquitous Technologies (IMWUT)*, 3(3):1–24, 2019.

[10] Sozo Inoue, Tittaya Mairittha, Nattaya Mairittha, and Tahera Hossain. Integrating activity recognition and nursing care records: the system, experiment, and the dataset. In *2019 Joint 8th International Conference on Informatics, Electronics & Vision (ICIEV) and 2019 3rd International Conference on Imaging, Vision & Pattern Recognition (icIVPR)*, pp. 73–78, Los Alamitos, CA. IEEE Computer Society, 2019.

[11] Mohammad Sabik Irbaz, Lutfun Nahar Lota, and Fardin Ahsan Sakib. Predicting user-specific future activities using lstm-based multi-label classification. In Md Atiqur Rahman Ahad, Sozo Inoue, Guillaume Lopez, and Tahera Hossain (eds.), *Human Activity and Behavior Analysis: Advances in Computer Vision and Sensors.* pp. 301–310, CRC Press, Boca Raton, FL, 2024.

[12] Md Kabiruzzaman, Mohammad Shidujaman, Shadril Hassan Shifat, Pritom Debnath, and Shahera Hossain. Time series analysis of care records data for nurse activity recognition in the wild. In Md Atiqur Rahman Ahad, Sozo Inoue, Guillaume Lopez, and Tahera Hossain (eds.), *Human Activity and Behavior Analysis: Advances in Computer Vision and Sensors.* CRC Press, pp. 405–415, Boca Raton, FL, 2024.

[13] Rashid Kamal, Chris Nugent, Ian Cleland, and Paul McCullagh. Addressing the inconsistent and missing time stamps in nurse care activity recognition care record dataset. In Md Atiqur Rahman Ahad, Sozo Inoue, Guillaume Lopez, and Tahera Hossain (eds.), *Human Activity and Behavior Analysis: Advances in Computer Vision and Sensors*, pp. 333–348, CRC Press, Boca Raton, FL, 2024.

[14] Paula Lago, Sayeda Shamma Alia, Shingo Takeda, Tittaya Mairittha, Nattaya Mairittha, Farina Faiz, Yusuke Nishimura, Kohei Adachi, Tsuyoshi Okita, François Charpillet, et al. Nurse care activity recognition challenge: Summary and results. In *Adjunct Proceedings of the 2019 ACM International Joint Conference on Pervasive and Ubiquitous Computing and Proceedings of the 2019 ACM International Symposium on Wearable Computers*, pp. 746–751, 2019.

[15] Nattaya Mairittha and Sozo Inoue. Crowdsourcing system management for activity data with mobile sensors. In *2019 Joint 8th International Conference on Informatics, Electronics & Vision (ICIEV) and 2019 3rd International Conference on Imaging, Vision & Pattern Recognition (icIVPR)*, pp. 85–90, Los Alamitos, CA. IEEE Computer Society, 2019.

[16] Nattaya Mairittha, Tittaya Mairittha, and Sozo Inoue. A mobile app for nursing activity recognition. In *Proceedings of the 2018 ACM International Joint Conference and 2018 International Symposium on Pervasive and Ubiquitous Computing and Wearable Computers*, pp. 400–403, 2018.

[17] Hitoshi Matsuyama, Kei Hiroi, Katsuhiko Kaji, Takuro Yonezawa, and Nobuo Kawaguchi. Hybrid activity recognition for ballroom dance exercise using video and wearable sensor. In *2019 Joint 8th International Conference on Informatics, Electronics & Vision (ICIEV) and 2019 3rd International Conference on Imaging, Vision & Pattern Recognition (icIVPR)*, pp. 112–117, Los Alamitos, CA. IEEE Computer Society, 2019.

[18] David Powers. Evaluation: From precision, recall and F-factor to ROC, informedness, markedness & correlation. *Machine Learning: Science and Technology*, 2:37–63, 2008.

[19] Md. Sohanur Rahman, Hasib Ryan Rahman, Abrar Zarif, Yeasin Arafat Pritom, and Md Atiqur Rahman Ahad. Nurse activity recognition based on temporal frequency features. In Md Atiqur Rahman Ahad, Sozo Inoue, Guillaume Lopez, and Tahera Hossain (eds.), *Human Activity and Behavior Analysis: Advances in Computer Vision and Sensors*, pp. 311–322, CRC Press, Boca Raton, FL, 2024.

[20] Suneth Ranasinghe, Fadi Al Machot, and Heinrich C. Mayr. A review on applications of activity recognition systems with regard to performance and evaluation. *International Journal of Distributed Sensor Networks*, 12(8):1550147716665520, 2016.

[21] Md. Golam Rasul, Wasim Akram, Sayeda Fatema Tuj Zohura, Tanjila Alam Sathi, and Lutfun Nahar Lota. Future prediction for nurse care activities using deep learning based multi-label classification. In Md Atiqur Rahman Ahad, Sozo Inoue, Guillaume Lopez, and Tahera Hossain (eds.), *Human Activity and Behavior Analysis: Advances in Computer Vision and Sensors*, pp. 377–387, CRC Press, Boca Raton, FL, 2024.

[22] Md. Mamun Sheikh, Shahera Hossain, and Md Atiqur Rahman Ahad. A sequential-based analytical approach for nurse care activity forecasting. In Md Atiqur Rahman Ahad, Sozo Inoue, Guillaume Lopez, and Tahera Hossain (eds.), *Human Activity and Behavior Analysis: Advances in Computer Vision and Sensors*, pp. 349–368, CRC Press, Boca Raton, FL, 2024.

[23] Riku Shinohara, Huakun Liu, Monica Perusquía-Hernández, Naoya Isoyama, Hideaki Uchiyama, and Kiyoshi Kiyokawa. A classification technique based on exploratory data analysis for activity recognition. In Md Atiqur Rahman Ahad, Sozo Inoue, Guillaume Lopez, and Tahera Hossain (eds.), *Human Activity and Behavior Analysis: Advances in Computer Vision and Sensors*, pp. 388–404, CRC Press, Boca Raton, FL, 2024.

[24] Jonathan Sturdivant, John Hendricks, and Gulustan Dogan. Predicting Nursing Care with K-Nearest Neighbors and Random Forest Algorithms. In Md Atiqur Rahman Ahad, Sozo Inoue, Guillaume Lopez, and Tahera Hossain (eds.), *Human Activity and Behavior Analysis: Advances in Computer Vision and Sensors*, pp. 369–376, CRC Press, Boca Raton, FL, 2024.

Index

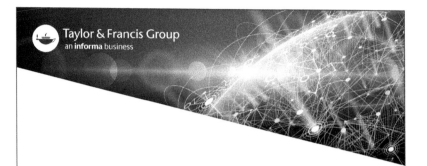

For Product Safety Concerns and Information please contact our EU
representative GPSR@taylorandfrancis.com
Taylor & Francis Verlag GmbH, Kaufingerstraße 24, 80331 München, Germany

www.ingramcontent.com/pod-product-compliance
Ingram Content Group UK Ltd.
Pitfield, Milton Keynes, MK11 3LW, UK
UKHW051828180425
457613UK00007B/255

9 781032 443119